W9-AWM-164

CONSOLIDATION OF BANKING

or How Five Banks Bought 50% of America's Biggest Business

CONSOLIDATION OF BANKING

or How Five Banks Bought 50% of America's Biggest Business

Arnold G. Danielson

To my mother, who taught me the importance
of the written word and an education
that was not available to her

CONTENTS

PREFACE

It was in December 1971 when I drove my Dodge Dart across New York and Pennsylvania on my way to Baltimore where with trepidation I had accepted a job at Maryland National Bank. A part of me was excited about returning to a part of the country I loved, but another part of me felt that getting involved with banking was about as unexciting a career move as one could have imagined. I had justified the change as a temporary safe haven— and a better place from which to seek future employment. After five years at the Federal Trade Commission and five more at an industrial conglomerate, a position as head of planning at Maryland's biggest bank seemed like a good place to ride out a poor economy and avoid any more Rochester winters.

At the time of this career move, I never expected banking would be a lifetime vocation. Yet, 36 years later, six with Maryland National and thirty as a consultant and financial advisor to banks and thrifts, I was still totally immersed in the industry. Why did I stay? Partly because finding a job outside of banking was not easy during the economic doldrums of the mid-1970s, but also because what was once a relatively dull industry was on the threshold of dramatic change.

It may be unfair to have called banking dull, even back then, as banks had long played a central, and sometimes controversial, role in the country's development. A two-party political system was partly a result of Alexander Hamilton forcing a central bank on the country in the late 18th century, and Andrew Jackson used opposition to a central bank and a rural population's dislike for banks of any type to become one of our most famous presidents.

By the early 20th century, bankers like J.P. Morgan and Andrew Mellon were household names, albeit not always viewed positively. The banking they represented, though, was primarily an industry that financed nations and large corporations. It was not banking on Main Street, which is where I was headed, and as my banking career began in the early 1970s, banking outside of New York City was clearly not at the forefront of corporate America. This is certainly not the case today.

The backwardness of banking in 1971 was, of course, in the eyes of the beholder. Many preferred the familiarity of an industry that was tightly constrained by regulations, and nearly everywhere, except in California and New York City, the industry was almost universally local banks run by local people. This feeling was buttressed by lingering, not-so-favorable memories of banking in the Great Depression when banks and thrifts had failed in great numbers and a newly-elected president was forced to call a bank holiday to avoid a national disaster. An industry of local firms, though, normally does not have the money or zeal for industry-changing innovation.

Leaving a *Fortune* 500 industrial firm in 1971 to join a bank also was a cultural shock. For starters, I was hired to install a companywide planning program, but soon learned that I was to do this without directly criticizing departmental plans. Then there were stock options spread among all bank officers instead of providing meaningful amounts to those who really made the decisions and a president who paid himself $65,000 a year. The latter may seem a refreshing change from today, but it put a ceiling on everyone else's remuneration. It also was a far cry from how things were done at the industrial firm I had just left.

From that beginning, it is hard to believe that over a period not much longer than a single generation, banking could undergo such a complete transformation. When I joined Maryland National in 1971, the biggest bank in the country, Bank of America, had assets of about $30 billion, and the next largest outside of New York City, Chicago's Continental, had about $9 billion assets *and* only a single office. Maryland National had $1.4 billion assets, and that was enough to make it the largest bank between Philadelphia and the Carolinas. Today, three American banks have assets over a trillion dollars, one of which has more than 5,000 banking offices. Two of those three banks perennially rank in the top five among all firms worldwide, banks and otherwise, in annual earnings.

Yet, changes in the banking industry were far more than a matter of size. In 1971, the first ATM had been installed only two years earlier; the certificate of deposit, or CD, was just eight years old and still resisted by many bankers; and credit cards represented a small fraction of personal loans. Research on banks was limited as there was no publicly-available data on branch deposits, and call report information—a bank's quarterly income statement and balance sheet—was not available just by a touch of the buttons on a computer. Instead, a written request had to be filed with the proper regulatory authority followed by what was often a lengthy wait for the boxes of photocopies to arrive.

Changes in banking also did not come smoothly. The viability of banks was threatened by a massive outflow of funds in the late 1970s when interest rates and the return on funds rose to levels that banks constrained by federal regulations could not begin to match. The industry then experienced a disastrous thrift crisis in the 1980s; and in the late 1980s and early 1990s, more than 2,000 banks and thrifts failed. The source of these disruptions is arguable, but there is no arguing about the results. The number of banks and thrifts fell from about 19,000 in 1971 to less than 9,000 today, with five of them accounting for almost half of all bank assets.

Having lived through this period of change, I felt the urge to put my views in writing on what had happened during this era of consolidation and innovation that has seen banking evolve from a "mom and pop" business in most parts of the country into a world class model of corporate strength. In particular, this book focuses on the various stages of the consolidation, and how five banks came to control almost 50% of the nation's banking assets.

This book cannot begin to tell the whole story of the consolidation, nor can it include all of the banks and people that made it happen, but it tries to put in one place the many parts that made up the whole. It is a story of statewide bank consolidation from the 1950s through the 1970s; thrift, farm and "oil patch" crises that shared the spotlight with interstate banking in the 1980s; an industry that limped into the 1990s seemingly damaged for years to come; and the megamergers that occurred from 1995 to 2006, but mostly in just three years—1995, 1998 and 2004.

It is a story that I witnessed first from inside of a bank, Maryland National, and since 1977, as an advisor to faltering thrifts, aggressive bank holding companies and community banks attempting to adjust to a changing environment. The consolidation of banking also was something I have been writing about since 1985 in the *Danielson Reports* that have a regional and national perspective.

It was a story for which I also was frequently provided a front row seat, albeit the view was not always pleasant. On the positive side, there was advising Northeast Bankshares in Maine when it was sold to Norstar in 1983. This was the first interstate bank acquisition since the 1930s, and it led to advising Norstar in a rare, successful hostile takeover in Upstate New York. Less pleasant was having only mixed success helping troubled banks and thrifts from California to New Hampshire survive the real estate-driven recession of the late 1980s and early 1990s. Yet for every Pacific Heritage, Bank of Commerce, Amoskeag and Central Bank that did not make it, there were the successful endings for Ramapo, Rockland Trust, Ameribank and First Pacific.

In 1990, my firm, Danielson Associates, was part of a consortium that worked with the Resolution Trust Corporation ("RTC") to study the after-effects and likely costs of one-fourth of the 1988 and 1989 savings and loan ("S&L") bailouts. These were referred to as the "Danny Wall deals" after the head of the RTC at the time, and most of the S&Ls we analyzed were in the Southwest.

As this book should make clear, I am not one who yearns for the past, at least as far as banking is concerned. In the "good old days" banks loaned out less than one-third of their deposits and were limited in the services they offered. Many may not like the big banks we have today, but these banks have been the primary source of innovation. The original Bank of America gave us the credit card; Citibank the CD; and the large banks usually offer the most efficient and convenient remote access services with their ATMs and on-line banking.

Consolidation also helped America's big banks regain their leadership internationally. It is comforting, at least for me, to know that Citigroup and Bank of America are the world's largest banks measured by what counts, earnings, rather than banks in London, Paris, Frankfurt or Tokyo. This almost was not the case. In 1990, the United States did not have a single bank among the top twenty in assets, and it is best to not even think about bank earnings in that recession-plagued year.

Much has changed in banking since I took that trek south from Rochester in the winter of 1971. Most of the change was necessary and positive, but there was a lot of discomfort along the way. It, however, was a fascinating period in the evolution of American banking, not the least of which was the rise of five banks to positions of dominance—and how much they owe this status to the economic fortunes in the markets they served.

Without the stunning collapse of Texas banking during the oil patch crisis of 1986 and 1987 and the devastation of banking in New England, the Middle Atlantic States, Florida and California in the early 1990s, we might have had a very different banking elite. Instead of a banking industry led by Citigroup, JPMorgan, two banks in Charlotte, North Carolina—Bank of America and Wachovia—and a Wells Fargo with its Minneapolis roots, it might have been Citigroup plus the likes of the original Bank of America, Security Pacific, a couple of the big Texas banks, Bank of New England, Sovran and First Fidelity. Most of these are names that have long since been forgotten, but in the late 1980s and early 1990s, they were as big as, or even bigger than, the banks that are today's Bank of America, Wachovia and Wells Fargo.

While chance played a major role in who won and who lost in the race for national banking supremacy, the winners would not have risen to the top without leadership that knew how take advantage of opportunity. Thus, while what follows is primarily a story of banks and economic changes that shifted the balance of power, it also is the story of leaders like Hugh McColl of NCNB/NationsBank, Eddie Crutchfield at First Union, Walter Wriston and Sandy Weill at Citigroup, Richard Kovacevich of Norwest, Terry Murray of Fleet and Royal Bank of Scotland's man in America, Larry Fish, who were ready to step forward when others faltered and were able to turn a deaf ear to the criticism of the investment analysts on Wall Street who always love the sellers, and not the buyers.

What Happened?

T he numbers were eye-catching. Bank of America paid $49 billion to buy Fleet in late 2003, and a few months later JPMorgan announced it would pay about $60 billion to acquire Bank One. These were not the highest prices ever paid for banks—Bank of America, itself, had been part of a more than $70 billion merger in 1998—but these two acquisitions took the bank consolidation process to levels that were once unimaginable. The elimination of the sixth and eighth largest banks—Bank One and Fleet left five banks Citigroup, Bank of America, JPMorgan, Wachovia and Wells Fargo—with almost 50% of all domestic bank assets, and they had left all other American banks far behind.*

It does not seem that long ago that I prepared a report on banking in the Southeast for my good friend Carter Golembe in which I had projected that NCNB and First Union would have assets of $20 billion by 1990. This was 1984, and he shook his head and said how hard it was to believe that two banks in Charlotte, North Carolina could begin to approach such size. If that was hard to believe, try the same two banks—albeit with different names—having assets of $1.5 trillion and $700 billion just 16 years later. The larger of the two, which had since assumed the name Bank of America, would also have 5,500 offices stretching from Portland, Maine to Portland, Oregon.

That was then and this is now, and these five banks being so large in banking and in a broader financial services business also meant much more than what being big meant in most industries. Banks are the intermediaries that make transactions of all types possible, and banks and other financial services companies constitute more than 35% of the market capital of all corporations listed on the national stock exchanges.

Thus, it is hardly surprising that depending on the price of oil in most recent years either Citigroup, the name chosen for the combined Travelers and Citicorp, or Exxon-Mobil was number one in earnings worldwide. In 2005, Citigroup earned more money than Microsoft and Wal-Mart combined, yet a year later, it was barely holding off Bank of America for first place among banks.

* The term "bank" is used for both commercial bank and bank holding company throughout the book.

If it was hard to believe in 1984 that a North Carolina bank could have assets of $20 billion in 1990, let alone assets of $1.5 trillion and bank sale prices reaching $60 billion, such numbers were totally unimaginable four years earlier before the initial steps toward interstate banking had been taken. In 1980, someone working in Washington did not have a downtown bank with an office convenient to his or her suburban home, or even that bank's ATM. This was the case for much of the workforce in New York, Philadelphia, Chicago, St. Louis or any other city that was close to a state line as well. In those days, banking was a local business, and interstate banking was always "two years away."

In 1980, it was double-digit interest rates paid on CDs that were the big story in banking, not the possibility of interstate banking. The high rates on CDs were popular with customers and the recently-received ability to pay these high rates by banks and thrifts had stopped the flow of money out of the banking system—something that had become a real problem in the late 1970s.

Without interstate banking, banks could not branch across state lines, and in many states, they were not even allowed to put offices throughout their home states. In most Midwest and Southwest states, branching within a state was not allowed, and even on the East Coast, such large states as Florida, Pennsylvania and Virginia had county restrictions on branching.

Fast-forward ten years, and even after a decade of interstate mergers that had created large multi-state banking organizations, a headline in the *American Banker* was "Citicorp Drops Out of the World's Top Twenty Banking Companies."[1] In 1980, it had been the largest bank in the world, even without interstate banking. By 1990, not only was Citicorp out of the top twenty internationally, but BankAmerica, the holding company for Bank of America, which had been number three in the world in assets ten years earlier, did not even make the top twenty-five. These were rankings based on assets, which may not be the best measurement of a bank's true status, but earnings or market capital would not have done much for Citicorp or BankAmerica since they were struggling to survive in 1990.

How banking moved from where it was in 1990 to where it is today, or, even more dramatically, away from the totally local nature of the business in 1980, was beyond anyone's thinking at the time. Banks were bigger in 1990 than a decade earlier, and they had finally been allowed to cross state lines, but a real estate-based recession had resulted in large losses for banks and thrifts that had crippled much of the banking industry as the 1990s began. Speculation at the time was not about trillion dollar banks ten years hence, but whether a large New York City bank might fail.

Fortunately, banking did get from where it was in 1980 and 1990 to where it is in 2007, but banking today is a very different industry than a generation earlier. By the end of 2006, the more than 14,000 banks of 1980 had been reduced to a little over 7,000 and there were fewer than 2,000 thrifts. In 2006, states as big as New Jersey, North Carolina, Washington and Maryland had fewer than 80 banks each.

Also, by 2006, the five leading banks—Citigroup, Bank of America, JPMorgan, Wachovia and Wells Fargo—were dominant in every corner of the nation. JPMorgan, Bank of America and Citigroup had the largest deposit shares in the Northeast; Wachovia and Bank of America were one-two in the South; and Bank of America and Wells Fargo were part of a very dominant big three with Washington Mutual in the Far West. Only in the Midwest was there a semblance of local control, and even there, Wells Fargo and JPMorgan had the largest deposit shares.

As for the local leaders in the 1980's, they are mostly memories. This was true nationwide as what is described below for five states was typical of all states.

- In Virginia, the 15 largest banks in 1980 are gone, and the biggest bank with headquarters and offices in Virginia today, TowneBank, opened in 1999.
- In Pennsylvania, out of the 30 largest banks in the state 25 years ago, only PNC remains.
- In Florida, the 15 largest banks or bank holding companies from 1980 are long gone.
- Two of the most storied bank names in California—Bank of America and Wells Fargo—live on, but only because their acquirers out of Charlotte and Minneapolis chose to keep their names. Of the other California banking leaders 25 years ago, only City National is left.
- Even in Illinois, which resisted interstate banking, branching and any other attempt to join the modern banking world, the results were no different. Because of its prohibition on branching, the state's only large banks in 1980 were in Chicago, and all that is left of those banks is Northern Trust, a trust and asset management specialist.

How did this happen so fast? A simple answer is that the time had come for interstate and inter-industry consolidation, and the barriers that had kept banking from going the way of all other large industries could only hold the tide back for so long. In 1980, banks could conduct full-service banking only in the states in which they were domiciled, and generally they were not allowed to offer investment products other than deposits.

This is a simple and correct answer, but it was not a simple process. To get from where it was in 1980 to where it was in 2007, banking had to endure thrift, farm and "oil patch" crises in the 1980s; survive more than 1,400 bank and 1,100 thrift failures between 1984 and 1993; and experience about 10,000 commercial bank acquisitions since 1980.[2]

This book traces the evolution of the bank consolidation process from its antecedents in the 1970s and before through the economic crises and legislation in the 1980s that made state line barriers obsolete and finally the post-1990 megamergers that put so much of banking in the hands of five banks. It is a fascinating story and one whose importance goes far beyond the banking industry.

The consolidation of banking also is a story of people. This includes expansion-minded CEOs, often overwhelmed regulators and the always available lawyers and investment bankers. Occasionally, some stepped over-the-line, and almost all had their critics, but they got the job done; albeit not without a lot of pain.

To fully understand how it all occurred, it is necessary to go back to events preceding 1980. The 1970s were of particular importance as banks positioned themselves to expand when interstate and broader inter-industry banking would be permitted and thrifts were getting caught in a box from which there would be no easy escape.

The Big Five

The story of banking consolidation also is complicated by the many name changes of the leading players. The original Citigroup, Bank of America, JPMorgan, Wachovia and Wells Fargo are not the same banks that today carry those names. In 1980, the legal predecessors to these banks were known as NCNB, Chemical, First Union, Norwest and Commercial Credit or Travelers Insurance, depending how Citigroup's succession is determined. Even then, two of those names, NCNB and Norwest, were fairly recent creations.

This consolidation is a story of far more than these five banks, but this small core played such an important role in the process that an overview of each is helpful in following the process and limiting the confusion of the numerous name changes and acquisitions. Even for those who lived through the consolidation, it is hard to recall that JPMorgan is really the successor to Chemical Bank and the bank that carries the name of Bank of America today is not a California bank, but a bank in Charlotte that most can remember as NationsBank, and NCNB prior to that, but that in 1960 was called American Commercial.

The size disparity between the five biggest banks and other large banks today is striking. Combined, the five largest banks had 47% of all domestic bank assets at the end of 2006 compared to only 8% for a second tier of banks that ranked sixth through tenth. Citigroup had more than twice the total assets of the entire second tier, and the much smaller Wachovia was almost as large as these five second-tier banks combined. Citigroup, Bank of America and JPMorgan each had more earnings and assets in 2006 than the combined second tier.

Largest Domestic Banks, 2006

Bank	Market Capital*	Net Income	Assets	Share of Assets** 2006	1990
	(in billions)				
Citigroup	$273	$21.5	$1,883	11%	6%
Bank of America	238	21.1	1,460	14	–
JPMorgan	167	14.4	1,352	13	–
Wells Fargo	120	8.5	482	4	–
Wachovia	108	7.8	707	5	–
Total	$906	$73.3	$5,894	47%	16%
Banks 6–10***	$171	$13.0	$834	8%	9%
HSBC****	$218	$17.6	$1,277	–	–

* December 31, 2006.
** Domestic bank assets.
*** U.S. Bancorp, SunTrust, Capital One, Regions and National City.
**** Largest foreign bank.
Source: SNL Financial, Charlottesville, Virginia.

This 47% share assets held by just five banks in 2006 was almost three times the 16% held by the five biggest banks in 1990, and at that earlier date, the disparity between the fi ve largest and the next five also was not nearly as large. The second tier in 1990 held 9% of all bank assets, which was less than a two-to-one ratio of five largest to the next five. In 2006, this ratio was almost six-to-one. Also, in 1990, only Citigroup of today's dominant banks ranked among the top five.

Measured by earnings or market capital in 2006, Citigroup and Bank of America also were the two largest banks in the world, and JPMorgan was number four. Only the London-based HSBC kept the American banks from ranking one-two-three. A Japanese bank, Mitsubishi UFJ, was second in assets at the end on 2006, but it not only earned less than Citigroup, Bank of America and JPMorgan, but less than either Wells Fargo or Wachovia as well.

With the completion of Bank of America's announced acquisition of the LaSalle National subsidary of ABN AMRO, the large bank asset share will be further increased by the end of 2007. Assuming there are no other major changes, this acquisition alone would lift the bank asset share of the five banks to about 48%.

Citigroup[3]

If there is any consistency in the evolution of America's leading banks, it is Citigroup. Its name has changed over time, but always with City, or Citi, as part of it, and its acquisition by Travelers in 1997 was more of a management than a corporate change. Even after the takeover changed the name of the holding company from Citicorp to Citigroup, the bank remained Citibank. As to the consistencies, as far back as bank rankings go, it was either the nation's first, second or third largest bank. It also was one of only two large New York City banks, Chemical being the other, to adapt to the tremendous changes in the industry over the last few decades and maintain a national leadership position.

Citigroup's roots go back to 1812 when it opened its doors as the City Bank of New York, but it rose to national prominence as National City Bank, a name it adopted in 1865. By 1894, National City was the largest bank in the country, and in the early 1900s, it also was thought of as the "Rockefeller bank" when National City and J.P. Morgan and Company were the main bankers for the cartels of the "robber baron" era. Its leader, James Stillman, was among the most powerful bankers of his time. By 1929, it was the largest bank in the world. After the Great Depression, National City kept a low profile, but in many of those years, it was still the nation's biggest bank.

In 1955, in one of many mergers among the big New York banks in that decade, National City bought another of the big names of New York banking, First National Bank of New York. By 1955, First National was much smaller than National City, but it was still a high prestige operation. This also was the impetus for another name change as National City became First National City.

The "low profile" disappeared when the first of the three Citigroup CEOs to play a major role in the consolidation process, Walter Wriston, assumed leadership in 1967. In 1974, the holding company name was changed to Citicorp, and two years later the bank name was changed to Citibank.

During Wriston's 17 years at the helm, Citibank and Citicorp were at the leading edge of virtually everything that was going on in banking, and when he retired, Citibank was not only the country's biggest bank, but it also was the only American bank with a true international presence. He led the way in the 1970s in using holding companies to move across state lines, albeit without full-service banking. In 1982, Citicorp was finally able to breach those state lines with full-service banking by using the thrift crisis and the regulators' desperate need to find buyers big enough to rescue large, deeply-troubled thrifts. Its purchase of a failed San Francisco thrift was a major step toward making interstate banking a reality. During his tenure, Wriston also left his chief New York rival, Chase Manhattan, far behind.

Along the way, though, there were some difficult times with foreign loans, and Wriston was forever at odds with the regulators, but he was one of the three bankers that did the most to change the face of American banking during the consolidation process—Hugh McColl and Sandy Weill being the others. This was despite being a CEO for only three of the years after 1980 when the consolidation process moved into high gear.

Wriston's successor, John Reed, never received the "lionization" of Wriston, or even that of Sandy Weill who was to follow Reed as CEO, but his contributions were significant. His legacy, however, also included being in charge in the early 1990s when Citicorp was widely-considered to be close to failure and during its takeover by Travelers Insurance in 1997. Without a $643 million investment by Prince Alwaleed bin Talal of Saudi Arabia in 1990, which at the time constituted about 15% of Citicorp's stock, there might not be a Citigroup today.[4]

Reed's major achievement was shifting much of the emphasis to retail activities and not becoming like most New York money center banks, anachronisms as the environment changed. His primary interest in this shift was the credit card and ATMs, not branches, and Reed made the Citibank card number one in the world.

In 1998, the banking world was stunned to learn that Travelers Insurance, a far less prominent financial corporation, had acquired Citicorp. The biggest shock was not that Citicorp had been bought by a lesser firm, or that the price was $83 billion and represented the return of Weill to the upper echelons of financial services, but rather that merging an insurance company with a commercial bank was not permitted under current banking regulations. Like with its thrift acquisition in 1982 under Wriston, Citicorp again was involved in a merger that pushed beyond existing legal barriers, and this time around, there was no emergency to justify the action. Nevertheless, after the 1970s, it seemed that "whatever Citicorp wanted, Citicorp got," and the merger was approved.

The Travelers' acquisition of Citicorp was a friendly deal and less of a corporate takeover than a change of direction. It also was viewed as an equal merger despite Travelers technically being the acquirer, and Weill and Reed were named co-CEOs. Weill, though, was clearly in charge, and in 2001, Reed resigned. This was sweet revenge for a man who had been pushed out as CEO of American Express in the 1980s.

Weill was not the only top banker to succeed after being dismissed or passed over earlier in his career, but his comeback went beyond that of most others. After leaving American Express, Weill took the helm of a failing Baltimore finance company, Commercial Credit. Then, in a series of transactions over the next decade, he built a financial conglomerate that included one of the country's biggest securities brokerages, Smith Barney; one of the largest investment banks, Salomon Brothers; and a top tier property and casualty insurance company, Travelers.[5]

Weill was a master at buying quality when it was "down," and that also applied to Citicorp, which in 1998 was still recovering from its near failure in the early 1990s. In building his nonbank empire, Weill used the Commercial Credit charter and eventually the Travelers' name.

The Federal Reserve, having blessed this merger, removed the barrier between banking and insurance and, in effect, banking and anything else that resembled financial services. It also blessed the creation of what may be the most powerful corporation in the world whose "next" move is always eagerly awaited by industry observers. Citigroup remained more a bank than an insurance company and, in fact, spun-off its insurance businesses in 2005 with minimal impact on earnings.

All these corporate maneuvers raised the usual complaints about big mergers not doing much for Citicorp shareholders. The Saudi Prince who invested so boldly in 1990 was not among them, though, as his $643 million investment was worth about $7.6 billion by 1998.[6] Even with the sale of a significant portion of these shares since then, the value was up to almost $12 billion in 2005.

Sandy Weill's retirement as CEO in 2004 raised questions about the future direction of Citigroup, and even Prince Alwaleed was expressing some concerns. As stated at the beginning of this biographical sketch, though, if there is one constant in banking, it is Citigroup, and no one really expects it to relinquish its place in the sun.

Bank of America[7]

The origins of the post-1999 Bank of America are as different from Citigroup as could be imagined. Its roots go back to American Trust, a small bank in Charlotte, North Carolina that was founded in 1908 and in the 1950s had assets of less than $200 million. At that time, American Trust brought in a CEO, Addison Reese, from an even smaller bank in central Maryland, who had big ideas, at least on a statewide basis. Thereafter, the climb to the top never ceased.

Under Reese, American Trust took its first big step in 1957 when it bought another Charlotte bank, Commercial National. This purchase made American Trust Charlotte's biggest bank, and it also began a history of name changes. The names of the two banks were combined, and the surviving entity was called American Commercial.

In the early 1960s, Reese's next step was to merge American Commercial with a Greensboro bank, Security National. This created a $500 million asset bank, which may not sound like much today, but at the time, this put it among the largest banks in the South. In North Carolina, only Wachovia was bigger. This merger also was the impetus for changing the name to North Carolina National Bank, and then NCNB. When its holding company was formed in 1968, it used the initials, NCNB, that became synonymous with aggressive bank growth.

In the 1970s, Tom Storrs replaced Reese as CEO, and he continued to expand the banking franchise in North Carolina; but he also made NCNB one of the most successful holding companies in expanding across state lines with nonbank businesses. Nonbank businesses were then legally defined as closely-related to banking, but *not* including the offering of checking accounts. One such move was the acquisition of a trust company in Florida that in 1982 was used by NCNB as a "backdoor" approach to interstate banking a couple of years before other out-of-state banks were able to enter that large and rapidly-growing state. Under Storrs, we also were fortunate enough not to have another name change.

Following Storrs to the helm in 1983 was Hugh McColl. He would continue Storrs' expansion program and, in so doing, McColl also would be replacing Citicorp's retiring CEO, Walter Wriston, as the industry's most innovative and aggressive wielder of change. When NCNB moved into the interstate banking era, McColl made his big move when he struck a deal with the FDIC in 1988 to purchase the good assets and assume the liabilities of the banks that were controlled by First RepublicBank. Prior to its failure, First RepublicBank was the largest bank holding company in

Texas and the 13th largest in the country. This acquisition was done with a $210 million outlay and tax credits that minimized NCNB's shareholder exposure.

The Texas coup was followed in 1990 by a successful, but hostile, takeover of C&S/Sovran, a bank almost as large as NCNB, and in 1993, by the acquisition of a troubled MNC. These banks ranked first or second in deposit share in Georgia, Maryland, Virginia and the District of Columbia.

The numbers tell the story of what these acquisitions did for NCNB. When McColl became CEO, NCNB's assets were about $13 billion. By 1987, after a series of relatively modest acquisitions, he had lifted assets to $29 billion, and that was just the beginning of his efforts. With the "trifecta" of First RepublicBank, C&S/Sovran and MNC in hand, NCNB's assets at the end of 1993 were almost $160 billion, and it had become the nation's third largest bank; except by then it was no longer NCNB. A year earlier, it had become NationsBank, a name much more fitting for coverage that stretched from Baltimore to El Paso, Texas.

NationsBank took a bit of a breather between 1993 and 1997 before it reached for the stars. A breather for McColl, though, still meant acquiring Boatmen's, the largest bank in Missouri, in 1996.

In 1997 and 1998, McColl firmly established NationsBank as Florida's leading bank, and then created the first national retail bank. NationsBank acquired Barnett, Florida's biggest bank, late in 1997 and followed that in early 1998 with the acquisition of the California-based BankAmerica. NationsBank was then second in size to only Citigroup, and it was time for still another name change. The headquarters of the NationsBank-BankAmerica entity stayed in Charlotte, but the acquirer chose to go with the name of the acquiree's bank subsidiary, Bank of America, and after six action-packed years, the NationsBank name was retired.

Bank of America, the original, also had its own lengthy and interesting history. It began in 1904 as the Bank of Italy in San Francisco, and its role in the evolution of the banking industry was at least equally as important as that of its acquirer and is discussed in the next chapter. The original Bank of America, though, limited the confusion factor by sticking with one name, or at least a close variation of that name—its holding company formed in 1968 was called BankAmerica—from 1930 until it was acquired in 1998.

For the new Bank of America, the name changes were over, but even with McColl stepping down in 2001, the acquisitions were not. In 2003, his successor and long-time second-in-command, Ken Lewis, announced the acquisition of the eighth largest bank in the country, Fleet, which had the largest retail deposit share in the Northeast. This took Bank of America into the country's biggest banking market. In 2005, it bought the largest independent credit card company, MBNA. Then in 2007, Bank of America announced the acquisition of ABN AMRO's LaSalle National subsidiary that would make it a market leader in the Midwest, the one remaining part of the country in which it had minimal coverage.

The acquisition binge by McColl and his successor also had its critics who claimed it was harmful to shareholders in that it created size at the expense of earnings per share. Depending on the day the NCNB stock was bought, there is something to the argument, but an investor who had put $1 million into NCNB stock in 1987, which would be just prior to the Texas acquisitions, and held it, would have had an investment worth about $12 million by the end of 2006.

JPMorgan[8]

The nation's third trillion dollar bank, JPMorgan, or JPMorgan Chase, as it is formally known, is less a story of success than survival, and its name changes are, perhaps, the most confusing. This is partly because the major changes are all quite recent and reflect brand imaging rather than the actual surviving entity. Chemical, the predecessor of today's JPMorgan, dates back to 1824 when a newly-formed New York Chemical Manufacturing established a Chemical Bank division. Unlike most of the other New York banks, its name was unchanged until it acquired Chase Manhattan in 1996.

As recently as 1980, five of the seven largest banks in the country—Citicorp, Chase Manhattan, Manufacturers Hanover, J.P. Morgan and Chemical—were in New York City, and they were commonly referred to as money center banks since their primary function was to lend to large corporations and governments. Because of their size, they were feared by other banks as likely to dominate the industry when interstate banking was finally allowed. None of these banks, though, were ready for the changes that were coming, and even the two survivors, Citigroup and Chemical, were fortunate to have made it past those dark days.

The largest of the other three was Chase Manhattan that throughout most of the 1960s and 1970s was second in size only to BankAmerica. It was one of the best-known banks at the time, but under the leadership of David Rockefeller, it slipped from number one in New York to a distant second behind Citicorp by 1980, and its fortunes did not improve after that. By 1990, it was less than half the size of Citicorp.

The fortunes of two of the others, Manufacturers Hanover and Chemical, were not much better. By the late 1980s, there were not only concerns relative to the survival of Citicorp, but Chase Manhattan, Manufacturers Hanover and Chemical were also in dire straits.

In 1991, Chemical, which had recovered better than the others, began the "roll-up" of the last big New York banks, other than Citicorp. In that year, it acquired Manufacturers Hanover, and in 1996, it acquired Chase Manhattan, but in deference to the acquiree's better known name, the new entity was called Chase Manhattan. In 2000, in a more equal merger, Chase Manhattan bought J.P. Morgan, and to get the deal done, it agreed to keep the J.P. Morgan name on the holding company, but with "Chase" stuck at the end. The retail bank, however, kept the Chase name. In all of these changes, Chemical's chief executive—Walter Shipley in the Manufacturers Hanover and Chase Manhattan takeovers and William Harrison in the J.P. Morgan merger—was the CEO of the surviving bank.

There were a lot of questions as to whether the whole would be stronger than the parts, but after some trying moments the verdict appears to be yes. In 2004, a revitalized JPMorgan reduced its overdependence on New York and corporate lending by acquiring the nation's sixth largest bank, Bank One. Not only did this give it a large branch network in the mid-section of the country, but Bank One also had one of the three largest credit card operations in the world. This deal fit nicely with two of Chemical's earlier moves, the purchases of a deeply troubled Texas Commerce and the failed First City Bank, two of the largest banks in Texas.

The Bank One acquisition kept JPMorgan in the top three of American banking and the top four worldwide, and came without a name change. Part of the agreement was that after two years Bank One's CEO, Jamie Dimon, would replace Harrison as the JPMorgan's CEO. This brought Dimon, who had been number two at Citigroup and a prodigy of Sandy Weill, back to New York in charge of Citigroup's main rival.

The benefits of these mergers for shareholders also were questioned since in each case a large premium was forsaken in order to supposedly form a stronger bank, and Shipley and Harrison are not spoken of with the same reverence as a Wriston, Weill or McColl. Yet their feat of taking four struggling banks with similar, outdated money center cultures, and turning them into what JPMorgan is today, was among the major achievements in the consolidation process.

Wells Fargo[9]

Wells Fargo's name can be traced back to the stage coach company, but the true roots of the San Francisco bank bearing that name today are less romantic, albeit not without historic relevance. We can thank some

Minnesota bankers for keeping such a historic and fascinating name in the forefront of American banking.

The origins of today's Wells Fargo go back to the 1920's in the Upper Midwest. In those days, the family farm was not doing well, and this caused many small bank failures in Iowa, Minnesota, Nebraska and the Dakotas. In order to limit the overall damage, bank holding companies were formed as "protectors" for the area's troubled banks and their customers. One of the biggest was Northwest Bancorp in Minneapolis, which by the end of the Great Depression was operating multiple banks in five Upper Midwest states.

The states Northwest covered were among the slowest growing, and some of them were losing population. Thus, after 1933, Northwest grew slowly, but the growth was sufficient to keep it among the thirty largest banks or bank holding companies. By 1970, it was 21st in size with assets of more than $4 billion and had 88 bank subsidiaries in five states. In 1973, the name would be shortened to Norwest.

Norwest's experience in operating banks in multiple states would serve it well when interstate banking was allowed, and in the 1980s, it became one of the most active acquirers of banks and thrifts in the Upper Midwest and Rocky Mountain states. By 1990, Norwest had assets of $31 billion and operated in ten states, but it still was not one of the twenty largest banks. It also was much smaller than the original Wells Fargo, which was the nation's tenth largest bank in 1990 with $56 billion assets.

Assets, however, understated Norwest's true status as it was in the forefront of bank expansion into the sale of nontraditional bank products. This expansion included a nationwide mortgage operation, and today its end result, Wells Fargo Mortgage, is one of the largest originators and servicers of home mortgages.

Like the other national leaders, Norwest's success was dependent on leadership. In 1985, it brought in Richard Kovacevich, who was passed over in the succession to Walter Wriston as Citibank and Citicorp CEO, and Citicorp's loss was Norwest's gain. Kovacevich came out of the retail arm of Citibank, and he made Norwest a leader in retail services, albeit credit cards were not part of the plan. Since his arrival, Norwest has not had a major misstep.

By 1998, Norwest had not caught the original Wells Fargo in asset size, primarily because of the latter's 1996 acquisition of First Interstate with its $58 billion assets, but Norwest was performing far better than the larger West Coast bank. This put it in a favorable bargaining position, and in 1998, the two banks agreed to a merger in which Norwest was the acquirer and Kovacevich would be the CEO, but the Wells Fargo name was retained and the headquarters was in San Francisco.

Unlike the other members of the big five, Wells Fargo was fairly quiet between 1998 and 2006. It concentrated on building its mortgage and other fee businesses and earning the respect of investors. The latter was reflected by market capital of more than $100 billion.

Wachovia[10]

Until 2001, the present day Wachovia was known as First Union, a name that dated back to the 1958 merger of Union National Bank with the First National Bank in Asheville. Union National, the predecessor bank, commenced operations in Charlotte in 1908. The First Union name was changed to Wachovia in 2001 when First Union acquired the original Wachovia, a long-time North Carolina rival.

For at least the last fifty years, First Union has been the "other" bank in North Carolina. First, it was the original Wachovia that outshone First Union, and then it was, and still is, its crosstown rival Bank of America a.k.a. NCNB and NationsBank—that took the spotlight. Being the other bank in North Carolina, though, was tempered somewhat by its having become one of the twelve largest banks in the world.

The emergence of First Union as one of the five banks that dominate American banking owes more to one man than any of the others. In 1973, Ed Crutchfield was named president of First Union at the age of 31. At that time, First Union had assets of only $2.2 billion. He became chairman and CEO in 1985, and when he retired in 1999, First Union's assets were $253 billion.

The other key ingredient in First Union's improbable rise from near obscurity to national prominence was interstate banking. It did not initially make the headline grabbing interstate deals of its North Carolina rivals, but First Union quickly established itself as a banking leader in Florida and Georgia. It also kept its eyes on North Carolina, and First Union's 1985 acquisition of Northwestern Bank in North Wilkesboro made it the biggest bank in its home state.

In the 1990s, First Union accelerated its interstate expansion pace, and along the way, Crutchfield became an industry legend. He picked up the nickname "Fast Eddy" early in his career because he always seemed in a rush to get things done, but it could just as easily have reflected his approach to acquisitions. In the eleven years after becoming chairman, he made almost 70 acquisitions or "by his count, one every 55 days."[11] He also was always there for a good quote of which, perhaps, the most famous was what he said after buying Virginia-based Signet for $3.3 billion "I had a stack of $1 billion bills and just laid them out until he (Signet's CEO, Malcolm McDonald) said yes."[12]

Crutchfield's 1990s' buying spree began in Florida in 1991, and then spread up and down the East Coast. By the time the decade ended, First Union had bought the biggest bank in New Jersey, First Fidelity; the number one bank in the Philadelphia area, CoreStates; the second largest in Florida, Southeast Banking; four substantial banks in the Maryland-DC-Virginia area—Signet, First American, Dominion and Baltimore Bancorp; and to add some interesting geographic "stretch," it acquired a mid-sized bank holding company in Connecticut, Northeast Bancorp, to push its coverage north of New York City.

The only problem was that these were not the best-performing banks, and First Union was not as skilled at consolidating acquisitions as some of the other large banks. The consolidation difficulty was complicated by the one real gem in the mix, CoreStates, having just completed the acquisition of another Philadelphia area bank, Meridian, which had turned into a political fiasco. In 1998, First Union's stock fell from $72 to $26 per share, and its dividend was cut in half. Shortly thereafter, Crutchfield retired in favor of his long-time number two, Ken Thompson.

While the obituaries were still being written for a struggling First Union, it seemingly added to its problems in 2001 by getting into a bidding war with SunTrust for a Wachovia Bank that had suddenly lost its glitter. The stakes were high since the winner would be a co-leader in deposit share in the Southeast with Bank of America, and First Union prevailed by taking the Wachovia name and sharing the holding company board seats equally despite its much greater size, something SunTrust was not willing to do. The victory also reflected a little bit of North Carolina solidarity.

The investor reception to this "win" was not favorable, but First Union learned a lot from its previous difficult mergers, and the Wachovia deal worked so well that in 2004, the new Wachovia was able to offer $14 billion to acquire SouthTrust, and two years later $25 billion for country's second largest remaining thrift, Golden West. The first acquisition improved its position in Florida; made it a leader in Alabama; provided entry into Texas; and left little doubt that the new Wachovia was a big time player. The second gave it almost 300 branches in California. Much of the credit goes to Thompson, but without Crutchfield's earlier "wheeling and dealing," the original Wachovia might have been part of SunTrust and First Union a seller rather than a buyer.

U.S. Bancorp[13]

U.S. Bancorp is not one of the big five, and when Fleet and Bank One were acquired, the gap between it and the other national leaders became more pronounced. In 2006, it was about half the size of Wells Fargo and Wachovia, but it was much larger than the next tier of banks. It also was a solid performer, which is reflected in market capital that put it among the top 20 banks in the world.

It added to the confusion factor as well in that U.S. Bancorp was known as First Bank System throughout most of the years since it was formed in Minneapolis as another "protective association" umbrella for troubled banks in the Upper Midwest. Until the 1980s, it was larger than its crosstown rival, Norwest.

Like Norwest, First Bank System looked westward to expand, and in 1997, it bought the biggest bank in Oregon, U.S. Bancorp. It chose to take the name of the acquired, but it kept its headquarters in Minneapolis. It has continued to buy banks on the West Coast, and it now has the largest bank deposit share in Oregon, third largest in Washington and ninth largest in California. The move west was a natural for First Bank System as its CEO, John Grundhofer, was from California and a top executive with Wells Fargo before leaving to take charge at First Bank System in 1990.

Despite the western expansion, U.S. Bancorp's emphasis has remained on the Midwest. In 1998, U.S. Bancorp merged with Firstar, a combination of the biggest bank in Wisconsin, First Wisconsin, Ohio-based Star Bank and one of the two biggest banks in Missouri, Mercantile. Firstar also happened to be run by Grundhofer's older brother, Jerry. This family get-together resulted in U.S. Bancorp being third behind only Bank One, and then its acquirer, JPMorgan, and Wells Fargo in Midwest deposits.

Crisis Impact on the "Sorting Process"

These brief biographies of the national banking leaders raise a couple of interesting questions—How did two banks from Charlotte and two from Minneapolis come to share the upper echelons of banking leadership with the same number of banks, two, from the financial capital of the world, New York? and, Why did Chicago, Los Angeles, Dallas, Houston, Philadelphia and Boston lose out as banking centers? The outcomes would not have been 1980, or even 1990, expectations.

The reasons for New York City's diminished status were touched on in the Citigroup and JPMorgan stories. The big New York City banks were focused on lending to large companies and governments and were slow to adjust to an environment that favored retail banking domestically and "super banks" internationally.

The other reasons for this unusual geographic outcome will become apparent as the story of bank consolidation is told, but there were two basic underlying reasons. One was the branching laws that continued to constrain intrastate banking long after interstate banking was a reality. This doomed Chicago to second-tier bank status. Another was recessions that hit only parts of the country. The "oil patch" crisis precipitated by a steep decline in oil prices in the mid-1980s, for example, wiped out Texas banking and added Dallas and Houston to the "no chance" list.

The major economic determinant of which cities won and which cities lost as banking centers was the real estate-driven recession that began in 1989 and ran through the early 1990s. It devastated banks in the Northeast, Middle Atlantic states, Florida and on the West Coast. East Coast banks from Miami to Boston and in California were either taken out of contention for national banking supremacy or forced to the acquisition sidelines at a vital time in the consolidation process. Some banks like Fleet and Barnett did an admirable job in overcoming the odds, but the numbers were stacked against their hometowns. This economic downturn also began the consolidation process in earnest.

Thus, it was asset quality problems of banks in Texas, the Northeast and on the West Coast and the inability of most of the big New York City banks to adjust that shifted the balance of power to banks in North Carolina, Minnesota and Ohio. Even the second-tier of large banks was composed almost entirely of banks in the Midwest and Southeast. Strength of balance sheets and geography were clearly decisive factors as to who moved forward and who did not in the bank consolidation process—and with it came the rapid consolidation of the 1990s.

These results are not etched in stone as headquarters do move. If there is any geographic reversal, though, it will likely favor New York, and not the other cities that lost their large banks.

CHAPTER 2

The Early Years

B anking in the United States did not start in 1980 anymore than it can be considered to have ended in 2007, and to understand just how banking got from 1980 to where it was in 2007, it is necessary to understand what happened earlier, particularly, why consolidation went on "hold" from the 1930s to 1980. Since the first domestic banks were chartered in the late 18th century, this covers a lengthy period of time, but it is not a complicated story.

The story is simplified by the fact that for at least the first hundred years of American banking, size and expansion into new states was not an issue. The lack of modern transportation and communications meant that all banks were local, whether it was mandated or not, and as late as 1870, there were less than 2,000 banks in the country.

By 1870, regulations had arrived and banks already were dealing with a dual regulatory system in which some banks were regulated by a federal agency, the Office of the Comptroller of the Currency, and others by state banking agencies. This resulted in different rules for different banks, and at the time, federal rules were far more important since federally-chartered banks outnumbered those in the state system by a five-to-one ratio.

Between 1870 and 1910, the number of banks in the country rose rapidly, and the balance between federal and state-chartered banks was greatly altered. In 1870, there were 1,963 banks.[1] Forty years later, there were almost 25,000, and the vast majority of these, more than 17,000, were state-chartered. With the improvements in communications and growth of a much more industrialized society, there was an obvious need for increased coordination among banks.

An early response to this need was the Federal Reserve Act of 1913 that created the Federal Reserve System and its Board of Governors. This was to be an important step in time, but its initial impact on the regulation of banks was limited as it required only national banks to become members.

The establishment of the Federal Reserve also did nothing to slow the growth of the banking system. There was a net addition of about 6,000 banks between 1910 and 1921 when the total reached 31,076, which would be the historic year-end peak for the number of banks.[2]

With so many banks operating under different types of supervision, the need for some degree of unification of bank supervision was even more necessary. A major step in this direction was the McFadden Act of 1927.

That Act had many provisions, but its most important impact on the future of banking was limiting the expansion of the federally-regulated, or national, banks, to what was allowed for state banks. This meant that if state banks could not expand beyond city, county or state boundaries, then the national banks in the same market could not do so either. This put a hold on almost all interstate banking until the 1980s.

An even more important event in determining the future structure of the banking industry was the stock market crash of 1929 and the ensuing Great Depression. The number of banks, which had been declining steadily since 1921, fell by over 12,000 between year-ends 1928 and 1933.[3] To make matters worse, most of the decline came from failed institutions as more than 9,000 banks went under in the four years after 1929.[4]

The problems of the banking industry caused by the poor economic conditions during this period led to two pieces of legislation in 1933 that, along with the McFadden Act, were major reasons why bank expansion was put on hold. These were the Federal Deposit Insurance Act and the Glass-Steagall Act.

The Federal Deposit Insurance Act would create the Federal Deposit Insurance Corporation ("FDIC") that would provide insurance coverage for bank depositors. The benefits of federally-insured deposits were so obvious that almost all banks became FDIC members. Thus, although most banks remained state-chartered, they now also had a *de facto* federal regulator as well that had a strong interest in the safety and soundness of the institutions whose deposits it was insuring.

The Glass-Steagall Act was a response to a belief held by many at the time that the destabilization of the banking system was at least partly the result of the conflict of interest caused by big banks being both the primary issuer of corporate securities and the primary lenders to corporations. The Act was intended to separate banking from the power to issue most types of securities, and it was the primary reason banks could thereafter do little more than gather deposits, make loans and invest surplus funds in securities until the Glass-Steagall Act was, in effect, repealed by the Gramm-Leach-Bliley Act of 1999.

Early Consolidation by Subtraction

Since there was a dramatic drop in the number of banks during the 1920s and 1930s, it also could be argued that this was the first wave of banking consolidation in America. The early 1920s were the high point in numbers of banks, and at that time, not only were there more than 30,000 banks with about 1,300 branches, but the ten biggest banks held less than 10% of all deposits. In 1940, there were less than half that number of banks, 13,442 at year-end, and the ten largest held a little over 26% of the deposits. Even with the opening of more than 1,000 branches during these years, the number of banking offices, both main offices and branches, declined by more than 14,000 in twenty years.

Banks, Branches and Large Bank Deposit Share, 1920 to 1970

Year	Number of		All Offices		Deposit Share of Ten Largest*
	Banks	Branches	Number	Change	
1970	13,511	21,839	35,350	11,668	18.8%
1960	13,126	10,556	23,682	5,404**	19.9
1950	13,446	4,832	18,278	1,347	18.9
1940	13,442	3,489	16,931	(10,252)	26.4
1930	23,679	3,522	27,201	(4,371)	16.4
1920	30,291	1,281	31,572	–	9.7

* Approximate year in 1930, 1950 and 1960.
** 4,013 since Dec. 31, 1954.
Source: FDIC, Historical Statistics on Banking and Federal Regulation of Banking 1981, Golembe Associates, Inc., Washington, D.C.

Much of this twenty-year decline took place in the first five years of the Great Depression. Between year-ends 1928 and 1933, the number of banks fell by about 10,500, a decline of 44%. There was an increase of about 1,000 banks in 1934 as failed banks were reconstituted. Thereafter, there were modest annual declines until almost the end of World War II.

This is not the commonly-held perception of the impact of the Great Depression on banking. It might be expected that bad times and a national distrust of the banking system would reduce the number of places where banking transactions could be made, but not that the large banks that had supposedly caused the problems in 1929 would almost triple their deposit share during this time of distress.

This sharp drop in the number of banks, though, was not a wave of consolidation like what would occur after 1990, but rather passive deposit share growth by a few large banks that flowed from the disappearance of so many small banks across the country. The result could be described as a "last man standing" outcome, but it also was a reminder that in down times, large firms usually benefit at the expense of the smaller firms. This would be a result replayed over and over in banking in the 1980s and 1990s.

That this early consolidation was the by-product of an economic depression, and not the beginning of a long-term industry trend, was made evident over the next twenty years. The number of banks in the country fell by about 300 between 1940 and 1960, but there was no further gain in the share of deposits held by the ten largest banks. In fact, their share dropped from a little more than 26% in 1940 to less than 20% by 1950.

A.P. Giannini

Bank consolidation not continuing into the 1940s and 1950s was in spite of the efforts of Amadeo Peter Giannini, more commonly known as A.P. Giannini, the founder of Bank of America. In 1904, Giannini opened Bank of America's predecessor, Bank of Italy, in San Francisco and then took full advantage of California removing its restrictions on statewide branching in 1909. He built a pre-1930s retail banking franchise that would remain unmatched until the late 1950s. By 1918, Bank of Italy had 24 branches in 18 California communities. Eight years later, the number of branches had risen to 300, and Bank of Italy's assets were $750 million.[5]

The growth of Giannini's banking empire was aided by California's rapid growth, but like the builders of large branch networks fifty years later, Giannini did not want to be confined by state lines. When he bought Bank of America of New York in 1928, Giannini formed a holding company, Transamerica Corporation, to hold the shares of Bank of America of New York, Bank of Italy and his other California banks that had not been folded into Bank of Italy. After 1928, Transamerica began buying banks in other western states, and in 1930, the name of Bank of Italy was changed to Bank of America.

Transamerica and Giannini did not get a "pass" from the regulators when anti-big bank feelings were running so high. In 1940, Transamerica, which also had a large insurance business, was forced to spin-off Bank of America. It was not until 1958, however, that it was forced to divest its remaining 23 banks in eleven western states into a second holding company, First America Corporation, that later took the name Western Bancorporation and eventually became First Interstate.

With this divestiture, the impact of A.P. Giannina on banking moved beyond Bank of America and Transamerica. First Interstate was acquired by Wells Fargo in 1996. Thus, parts of today's Well Fargo also can be traced back to the early efforts of Giannini.

After being divested in 1940, Bank of America continued to grow. By 1945, Bank of America was the nation's largest bank, and as the 1950s began, it had 525 branches and assets of $6.3 billion. This was far more branches than any other bank had. Its closest competitor was Security First, another California bank that had about 130 branches.

1940s and 1950s

As economic conditions improved, the animosity toward large banks that had curtailed the expansion of Bank of America began to fade and was replaced by a gradual renewal of trust in the banking system. This was reflected in the growth of local banks, not so much in the number of banks, but in the number of banking offices and amount of deposits they held. Between 1940 and 1960, the number of bank branches grew from about 3,500 to more than 10,000, and deposits, other than those held by the ten largest banks, almost quadrupled from $47 billion to almost $185 billion. The deposits of the ten largest banks grew rapidly as well, but not as fast as those of the smaller banks. The big bank deposits only a little more than doubled during this period.[6]

It was this more rapid growth by the local banks that was to sow the seeds of future consolidation as large branch networks emerged outside of California. As long as banks were single market operations, the urge to get larger was constrained by the size of the market. Banks in markets like New York, Chicago and Boston could think on a larger scale and even consider lending beyond their home areas. For most banks, though, its customer potential was narrowly defined by how far a customer was willing to drive, be driven or, in many cases, walk. This willingness frequently coincided with where customers had to go for other shopping needs.

Thus, it was not only the regulatory constraints that made large branch networks a relatively recent phenomenon. The number of branches grew nationally from about 3,500 at the beginning of 1940 to more than 10,000 in 1960. However, most of the increase took place in the 1950s when shopping patterns underwent major changes. In the 1940s, there was a net gain of only about 1,300 branches. In the 1950s, the increase was more than 5,000, and most of that occurred in the latter half of the decade.

The primary reason branching had become an important element of banking in the 1950s *and* the primary *modus operandi* of so many banks in the 1960s was a demographic shift, particularly as related to the afore-mentioned changing shopping patterns. The coming of suburban shopping centers; the growth of suburbs at the expense of the central cities; and a greater use of cars for shopping activities, created a revolution in retailing that went far beyond banking.

As anyone over sixty years old can recall, until the 1950s, retail activity had been almost entirely a Main Street event. A common urban experience while growing up in the 1940s was the weekly trip downtown on a bus or trolley with one of the stops being at a bank. By the 1950s, the trip to the bank was likely to be in combination with a car ride to a grocery store in the suburbs.

With the movement of retail activity away from downtowns and into the suburbs, it was only natural that bankers would want to follow their customers. If they did not, they would lose them to banks that would open in or near the new suburban shopping centers. Since in most states, California and North Carolina being major exceptions, there were state laws keeping the banks from putting branches near these shopping centers, the inevitable reaction was political pressure by banks to have these restrictions removed. This was no easy task given the lingering memories of the Great Depression and the problems it brought to banking and the natural reaction of small banks to resist any moves toward bigness. This resistance was usually supported by a majority of a population that seldom likes change.

The outcome of efforts to remove branching restrictions varied from state to state with major ramifications on how banking developed and responded to consolidation within those states. The efforts typically met with the most success on the two coasts where change was not viewed quite as negatively. It is partly because of the early elimination of branching restrictions that two of the world's biggest banks are now headquartered in North Carolina and because of the continuing prohibition of branching in Illinois that no large retail bank calls Chicago home.

With interstate banking being effectively eliminated by the Great Depression, it was not surprising that only a few banks had interstate banking operations. Western Bancorporation was by far the largest of these banks operating in eleven western states. Other "grandfathered" banks that had branches beyond their home state were the Minneapolis-based bank holding companies, First Bank System and Northwest Bancorp, and a District of Columbia bank holding company, Financial General. The latter was later to take the name First American and would get its fifteen minutes of fame as the centerpiece of the BCCI scandal of the late 1980s. Even these multi-state banks, though, had to abide by the laws of the states in which they operated.

In 1950, the branching laws came in four basic variations:

- *Unrestricted statewide branching* only applied to North Carolina, California and a few other states, most of which were quite small.

- *Unrestricted countywide branching* was common along the East Coast, and most of the larger coastal states had at least this much branching freedom.

- *County or statewide branching with home office protection* allowed banks to branch within their own community and in any other community in the county or state that did not have its own bank. This was New England's approach that did not leave much room for branching beyond the home city, but if the city was as big as Boston, or even Hartford, it allowed a bank to become much larger than other banks in the state.

- *Unit banking* prohibited branching, and it was the reality in almost every state in the country's mid-section in 1950. Even by 1980, Colorado, Illinois, Missouri, Texas and some small Midwest states still had unit banking, but by then, many of them permitted holding company ownership of multiple banks within a state.

As the 1950s progressed, there was a continual movement toward relaxed branching restrictions, but despite the obvious market needs for more flexibility, the pace of change was slow. Maryland, Washington and a few others had joined California and North Carolina in having virtually unfettered statewide branching, but they were the exceptions.

Legislative relaxation of branching restrictions, however, took many intermediate forms that eventually paved the way for more branching flexibility. Pennsylvania went from allowing branching countywide to permitting it in contiguous counties, which, in effect, meant branching was allowed throughout the Philadelphia area west of the Delaware River and in metropolitan Pittsburgh. New Jersey and New York, in gradual moves toward statewide banking, set up regions within which banks could buy other banks and open branches. These regions were scheduled to be phased out in favor of statewide branching in a relatively short time.

As a result of market needs and more relaxed in-state branching regulations, a number of fairly large branch networks had been developed by 1960. The largest, by far, were in California where there were no statewide branching constraints, and in New York City, which was large enough to support many branches without a bank going beyond single or contiguous counties.

The growth of branch networks outside New York and California, though, had done little to change the dominance of money center and California banks. In 1960, eight of the country's fifteen largest banks were in New York—Chase Manhattan, First National City, Chemical, Morgan Guaranty, Manufacturers Trust, Bankers Trust, Hanover Bank and Irving Trust—and four were in California—Bank of America, Security First, Western Bancorporation and Wells Fargo. The only interlopers were two large single office banks in Chicago, First National Bank of Chicago and Continental*, and Pittsburgh-based Mellon.[7]

There were large banks at that time in other big cities as well, but only four other cities—Philadelphia, Detroit, Boston and Cleveland—were represented in the top twenty. The banks were First Pennsylvania in Philadelphia, National Bank of Detroit, First National Bank of Boston and Cleveland Trust.

The Thrift Factor

The banking consolidation saga of the late 20th century, though, was more than just a story about banks. Thrifts, both S&Ls and mutual savings banks, were relatively small factors outside of the Northeast and California until the 1950s, but the pent-up demand for housing after the war and the movement of people from the cities to the suburbs created a much-increased demand for home mortgages, which is the *raison d'etre* for S&Ls and the primary lending orientation of the mutual savings banks.

With the post-war housing boom, S&Ls joined the branching boom and lifted their share of national depository institution assets from a little over 8% to almost 19% during the 1950s. This reduced the commercial bank deposit share from about 81% to less than 70%. It also meant that while the deposit share held by the ten largest banks may have stabilized in the 1950s relative to other banks after a sharp decline in the 1940s, it continued to slide relative to all depository institutions.

The S&L growth was a counter-consolidation movement. S&Ls had a federally-guaranteed interest rate advantage on savings accounts of .25% over banks that were not allowed to pay more than 3% interest on these accounts—i.e., S&Ls could pay as high as 3.25% on savings accounts—and

*Continental Illinois until after 1984.

the expectation was that S&Ls, and, to a lesser extent, mutual savings banks, would grow in perpetuity with the housing industry. In so doing, they would increase deposits at the expense of banks.

Asset Share by Type of Institution, 1950 to 1970

Year	Percent of Assets			
	Banks	Savings & Loans	Savings Banks	Credit Unions
1970	68%	21%	9%	2%
1960	69	19	11	1
1950	81	8	11	–*

* Share was about .5%.
Source: United States League of Savings Institutions, '77 Savings and Loan Fact Book.

In the 1960s and early 1970s, the rapid thrift growth became a major concern for state and national bank associations. They responded by urging members to write their congressman about what they considered the unfair rate advantages of the thrifts, much as they were later urged to do regarding credit union membership rules and tax free status.

Unfortunately for thrifts, their perpetual growth and the continued diminishing of bank dominance was not to be. The erratic interest rate movements of the 1970s and the early 1980s, and a near total reliance on long-term fixed-rate home mortgages for revenues, combined to not only reverse the thrift growth pattern, but resulted in a massive shift of thrift deposits and loans to banks through thrift acquisitions and failures. This, though, is a story for another chapter.

Credit unions were relatively inconsequential during the 1940s and 1950s, but already were showing strong growth. In 1950, they held less than 1% of the nation's deposits. They approximately tripled their share in the 1950s, but that was still well below 2% of all deposits.

Branching in the 1960s

It was in the 1960s when branching really began to move forward and toward its leading role as a key motivator in the coming consolidation. There were more than 11,000 bank branches added in the 1960s, lifting the number of branches nationwide to over 21,000. This was more than twice what had existed a decade earlier. Add in a net gain of 385 banks, and the total increase in banking offices was about 11,700.

The immediate effect of these new branches on concentration was muted nationally by historic prohibitions against banks crossing state lines and the persistence of unit banking in most of the Midwest and Southwest. None of the 11,000 plus new branches were in Illinois, and the few that were in Texas were drive-up facilities within a few hundred yards of the bank's main office. Thus, any consolidation in the 1960s was limited to individual states and generally focused on the two coasts.

The extent of intrastate consolidation also was constrained by what was soon to be the most populous state in the country, California, having already reached a high level of concentration. Statewide branching had been permissible in California since 1909, and by 1960, the state's five largest banks—Bank of America, Security First, Wells Fargo, United California and Crocker-Citizens—had a combined 78% of California's bank deposits. This share actually fell by a percentage point in the 1960s as the state experienced many new bank openings that reflected its rapid population growth. The number of banks in the state grew from 155 to 290 between 1960 and 1970.

Banking Concentration by State, 1960 and 1970

State	Deposit Share			
	Five Largest Banks		Three Largest Banks	
	1970	1960	1970	1960
California	77%	78%	61%	66%
North Carolina	67	57	50	47
Massachusetts	64	59	48	47
Maryland	61	58	42	43
New York	56	55	41	40
Virginia	50	28	35	20
Illinois	39	42	33	36
Pennsylvania	37	39	26	28
Ohio	33	33	23	24
Florida	28	23	20	18
Texas	23	28	16	21

Source: Federal Reserve Bulletin, February 1982.

Also in the 1960s, some unit banking states already had low levels of deposit concentration that went even lower. In Illinois, deposit share of the five largest banks fell from 42% to 39% as the deposit growth of small banks, mostly outside of Chicago, grew faster than the large Chicago banks. Texas shared California's rapid population growth, and with unit banking laws keeping the downtown banks from following the population to the suburbs, the number of banks in Texas rose from 1,195 to 1,470 during the 1960s. Not surprisingly, the share of deposits of its five largest banks fell from 28% to 23%.

In the East Coast states where statewide banking was allowed, the degree to which intrastate banking concentration increased reflected the timing of the relaxation of in-state branching and acquisition prohibitions. North Carolina, Massachusetts and Maryland, three states that moved to statewide banking before 1960, had the five largest banks' share of deposits rise from the 57% to 59% range to above 60%. In North Carolina, the increase was from 57% to 67%.

The gains were not as large in Maryland and Massachusetts as in North Carolina because their biggest banks were based in Boston and Baltimore. Thus, the potential for deposit share gains going beyond their home markets was much less than in North Carolina that had no single, dominant population center. Statewide banking in Massachusetts also was hindered by continuing home rule restrictions, which meant that its banks were not allowed to branch into communities that already had a bank headquartered in that community.

The biggest deposit share gains in the 1960s came in states like Virginia and Florida where the constraints on statewide expansion, if not branching, had been recently removed. These states continued to confine branching to the county where a bank was headquartered, but bank holding companies were allowed to buy banks statewide and then expand the branch networks of the acquired banks within the county in which the acquired bank was based. In Virginia, this resulted in the deposit share of the five largest banks rising from 28% in 1960 to 50% in 1970. The increase in Florida was a more modest 23% to 28%, but that was just the beginning.

New York, Pennsylvania and Ohio participated in the branching explosion of the 1960s, but not in the deposit share growth of the banking leaders. Part of the reason for this was regional expansion restrictions within the state. In Pennsylvania, for example, banks could not branch or acquire banks beyond counties that were contiguous to their home county. The main reason for the lack of deposit share growth by the banking leaders, though, was the slower deposit growth of money center banks, including Pittsburgh-based Mellon, than for the smaller retail banks. This held the deposit share of the five largest banks in these states in 1970 to roughly the same percentages they had in 1960.

Tale of Two Cities

The consolidation process that had started in the 1950s and 1960s and reached a crescendo by the mid-1980s is more than just changes in banking regulations and increases in number of branches. As expansion constraints loosened, market pressures favored larger banks. Hence consolidation was inevitable, but its direction was shaped by a handful of banks in relatively small cities with dynamic leaders. Fifty years ago, it would have been hard to believe that decisions made in Charlotte and Minneapolis would have a far greater impact on the future structure of American banking than those made in Chicago, Philadelphia or Los Angeles.

In the 1960s, Charlotte's NCNB and First Union were among the few banks that aggressively took advantage of the growing importance of bank branches and favorable state rules to move beyond their hometowns and begin their march toward national prominence. NCNB increased its assets from $526 million in 1960 to $1.5 billion in 1970, and its number of banking offices rose from 12 to 162. First Union was slightly smaller with assets of $1.1 billion in 1970, but this was up from $204 million in 1960. Its 180 offices were more than NCNB had, and a big increase from just 20 offices ten years earlier.

As far and as fast as NCNB and First Union had risen by 1970, they were still the second and third largest banks in North Carolina. Wachovia with $1.8 billion in assets and 185 branches was not only the biggest bank in North Carolina, but also the largest in the Southeast and one of the most respected banks in the country. This respect endured, and it is why the Wachovia name lives on—albeit under First Union management and based in Charlotte instead of Winston-Salem.

A good case could be made that the long-term success of NCNB and First Union was fueled by inter-city rivalry, and this "success by twos" can be extended to Minneapolis. That city's two large bank holding companies, First Bank System and Northwest Bancorp, did not have the benefit of the unfettered statewide branching of North Carolina, but having been formed in the late 1920s as "protectors" of their region's troubled banks, they early-on had many subsidiary banks in multiple states operating under their banners. Thus, when the prohibition on interstate banking became nearly iron-clad after

1933, they were already operating in multiple states and became expert in running multi-bank operations. This was a skill they would put to good use.

Other Regional Leaders

NCNB, First Union, First Bank System and Northwest may have had the most lasting success of regional banks that grew to prominence in the 1950s and 1960s, but they were not the only major players in the statewide consolidation process occurring at the time. Among the banks that operated more than 100 banking offices in 1970 were Marine Midland in New York, which would become the core of HSBC's American banking network; BancOhio that was later acquired by National City of Cleveland; Virginia National that would change its name to Sovran; and Maryland National.

Even when county or contiguous county branching limitations or the small size of a state kept a bank from reaching 100 branches, the 1960s saw the dramatic growth by some of the other future leaders in the consolidation process. Prominent among these were Pittsburgh National that was dwarfed by its Mellon neighbor, but under the shortened name of PNC, eventually surpassed Mellon in size; First Pennsylvania, a Philadelphia "shooting star" of the 1970s; a bank in little Rhode Island, whose name, Industrial National, did little to suggest its dynamic future as Fleet; and two Albany banks, State National and National Commerce, that would also show what inter-city competition could do. The latter duo, like Industrial National, opted for more marketable names by becoming Norstar and KeyCorp, respectfully, in the 1980s.

The growth of numerous regional branching networks in the 1960s had not yet altered the national banking leadership picture. The biggest banks looked nearly the same as they had a decade earlier with New York and California banks in most of the top spots. Bank of America was still the nation's largest bank with assets a little over $29 billion. The other banks with assets over $20 billion were Chase Manhattan and First National City. Six other New York banks—Manufacturers Hanover, Morgan Guaranty, Chemical, Bankers Trust, Marine Midland and Charter—and four from California—Security Pacific, Wells Fargo, Western Bancorporation and Crocker-Citizens—ranked among the fifteen largest. As was the case ten years earlier, two Chicago banks—Continental and First National Bank of Chicago—also were in the top fifteen.

The nation's largest banks may have remained the same, but the recognition of the benefits of branching had spread well beyond California and New York. Nevertheless, in 1970, Bank of America with 955 branches and Western Bancorporation with 654, still had far more branches than any other banks, and five of the six banks with more than 200 branches were in California. In New York, four of its six biggest banks were supporting their money center operations with more than 100 retail banking offices, and a fifth had more than ninety. Only Morgan Guaranty had stayed out of the branching game. Most of the big New York City banks' branches were in the metropolitan area, but these banks also had used holding companies to buy a banking presence in the largest upstate cities—Buffalo, Rochester, Syracuse and Albany.

New York also was in the forefront of the development of retail banking operations in which the branches were more important than the main office with its money center type activities. Buffalo-based Marine Midland had banking offices throughout Upstate New York, as well as in the New York City area, and it was the only bank outside of California with more than 200 branches. The ill-fated Franklin National Bank—it was to fail in 1972—went a step further by making it into the top twenty with 96 offices *and* without having a big city base. Its headquarters was in Mineola, a small Long Island town.

The largest thrifts were much smaller than the biggest banks in 1970, but the influence of the liberal branching laws of California was readily apparent with them as well. There were only five savings and loans with assets above $1 billion, and all five were in California.

It was not, however, the California or New York banks or thrifts that would lead the consolidation charge. This leadership came from banks in places like Charlotte, Minneapolis, Columbus, Albany and Providence.

Product Impact

The branching boom of the 1960s and the growth of large branch networks were the key contribution of the 1950s and the 1960s to the future consolidation of banking, but changes in product mix also would play a role. This was most evident in the deposit mix where the introduction of the CD in 1962 by First National City, as Citibank was called then, was almost revolutionary in its impact. The credit card was a slightly earlier Bank of America creation—a card that was to begin as BankAmericard and eventually carry the Visa name. It had a big impact on consumer lending, but that impact was slower to develop than the CD on deposits and affected only one segment of a bank's loan portfolio.

Up through the 1960s, bank deposits were almost totally checking and passbook savings accounts, and deposits funded about 90% of bank assets.

31

By the early 1960s, however, checking accounts had fallen from more than 75% of deposits twenty years earlier to about two-thirds, but this was still a long way from 2006's 9%. In 1961, deposits that could not be classified as either checking or savings accounts were about 7% of total deposits.

Bank Deposit Mix by Type, 1940 to 1970

Year	Percent of Deposits			Deposits/ Assets
	Demand	Savings	CDs	
2006*	9%	56%	35%	66%
1970	51	21	28	85
1961	67	33	–	89
1950	76	24	–	92
1940	75	25	4	90

* For comparison purposes.
Source: FDIC, Historical Statistics on Banking.

The CD with its ability to reflect market rates, at least upon issuance, represented a major industry transformation. It circumvented the guaranteed rate advantage held by thrifts on savings deposits and provided considerable flexibility in the cost of funds whether interest rates went up or down. By 1970, about 28% of all bank deposits were CDs.

During this period, there also was a modest movement away from bank dependence on deposits for funding. Between 1961 and 1970, deposits as a percent of total liabilities and equity fell from 89% to 85%.

The introduction of the CD and the reduced dependence on deposits were initially a competitive advantage, or as some might argue, a leveling of the "playing field" for banks vis-á-vis thrifts, and a tool to manage earnings in times of interest rate change, but they also proved to be consolidation stimulants. The most aggressive banks, the ones building state-wide branching networks, were quick to introduce CDs and promote them vigorously. The big banks went even further by finding alternatives to deposits to fund their lending and investments. Many local banks, on the other hand, felt that CDs and the use of borrowed funds, instead of deposits, introduced risks reminiscent of the 1930s, and as a result, were slow to respond. Not surprisingly, many of them experienced a substantial loss of customers.

Bank Loan Mix by Type, 1940 to 1970

Year	Percent of Loans				Loans/ Assets
	1–4 Family	Other Real Estate	Commer- cial*	Consumer	
2006**	32%	26%	19%	14%	59%
1970	14	10	38	22	52
1960	17	7	36	22	47
1950	20	6	42	19	31
1942	17	7	41	12	26

*Not secured by real estate.
**For comparison purposes.
Source: FDIC, Historical Statistics on Banking.

As noted earlier, the introduction of the bank credit card in 1958 by Bank of America did not have the immediate impact of the CD. At the end of 1969, bank credit card loans were less than $4 billion, or about 6% of all personal loans. The credit card was expanding rapidly, but it also had to struggle with state regulatory constraints, specifically ceilings on the rate that customers could be charged.

The big lending change in the 1950s and 1960s was that banks began to make loans. As late as the early 1950s, bank loans represented only about 30% of all assets and a little over 35% of deposits.

Assets committed to loans increased steadily in the 1950s and 1960s, reaching 52% by 1970, but businesses remained the primary borrowers. Commercial banks lived up to their name as 35% to 40% of bank loans were commercial loans not secured by real estate. Personal loans, usually around 20% of the total, were a distant second.

In the 1960s, real estate lending, both residential and commercial, was a secondary source of revenues for banks, partly because it was the domain of the thrifts. By 1970, real estate loans accounted for about 24% of all bank loans, which was unchanged since 1940, but far less than the 58% they accounted for in 2006.

CHAPTER 3

Uncharted Waters

A s banks entered the 1970s, their interest in geographic and product expansion continued unabated, and because extensive branching in the 1960s had taken many of them fully across their own states, banks were increasingly finding state line barriers confining. This sent them looking in new directions for growth, and there were only two real options—expand into other countries or circumvent interstate banking restraints by using the holding company concept to acquire bank-related businesses, but not banks, in other states. The international route was only feasible for the big banks. Using holding companies to acquire nonbank businesses beyond state lines, however, was possible for banks of all sizes.

The latter, interstate acquisitions via bank holding companies, was a phenomenon that began in the late 1960s, and it became so widely utilized that it raised regulatory concerns. This led to new legislation and a decade long battle with the Federal Reserve over what interstate acquisitions were allowable. The basis for these interstate acquisitions was that the state line restrictions of the 1927 McFadden Act did not apply if the business that was acquired by a bank holding company was a nonbank, which meant that it did not offer checking accounts. This was most of the bank deposits at the time. The subsequent legislation did not put an end to out-of-state nonbank acquisitions, but it established the rules under which they could be made.

During the early 1970s, Citicorp and other large banks shifted their expansion emphasis away from branching toward interstate nonbank acquisitions, and they were joined in doing so by many mid-sized banks. This nontraditional expansion beyond state lines coincided with, and was reinforced by, an expanded use of credit cards. The credit card did not require the proximity of a branch, and it was another way to move across state lines, albeit more a 1980s than 1970s story.

This use of the holding company for expansion and new sources of income also had a strong real estate content. As a result, entering new businesses, some of which were far from the home market, potentially may have been a good source of additional revenues and profits, but in times of economic turbulence, they brought with them considerable risk. As it turned out, risk and the 1970s were closely intertwined.

A sign of this increased risk was that prior to 1970, the FDIC, which began operating in 1934, had never dealt with a troubled bank with deposits in excess of $100 million. In the six years from 1973 through 1978, no less than twelve banks with deposits in excess of $100 million would require regulatory assistance. The combined deposits of these banks were over $6 billion and included one of the nation's twenty largest banks.[1]

Turbulence of the 1970s

It is easy today to forget just how bad the 1970s were for business, in general, and banking, in particular, and it is impossible to understand much of what happened in banking in the 1970s without putting it in the context of the economic conditions of the time. For those who lived through these years, two of the most vivid memories are Watergate and the long lines at the gas pumps, but not far behind were inflation-driven record high interest rates and a dismal stock market performance. For bankers, the outflow of deposits resulting from the high interest rates also would be high on the list of bad memories.

The high rate of inflation in the 1970s was the result of deficits that grew rapidly during the Vietnam War as successive administrations insisted on supplying both "guns and butter," and then enhanced by an oil shortage that drove oil prices to record heights. This inflation also contributed to the poor stock performance and caused the high interest rates.

The average rate of inflation for the decade was 7.1%, and in 1974, and again in 1979, the annual rate reached 11%. Inflation also spilled over into 1980 when the annual rate reached 13.5% before starting down. This was in stark contrast to the previous decade when the average inflation rate was 2.4% and did not exceed 2% until 1966 when the costs of fighting a war in Vietnam began the upward spiral.[2]

Interest rates followed a similar upward pattern forcing the Federal Reserve to raise the discount rates to 8% in 1974, 12% in 1979 and 14% in 1981, respectively. This was translated into corresponding banking industry prime rates—the rate banks charged their best customers for commercial loans—of 10.25%, 15.25% and 20.50%. Since there were restrictions, or "caps," on how high banks could raise the interest paid on savings accounts, the high loan rates helped margins and, as a result, profits. This, though, was a short-term plus as money began to flow out of banks into other investment products that did not have interest rate caps and provided better investment returns, particularly brokerage-run money market funds.

Adding to the turbulence of the 1970s was the negative response of stock prices to Watergate, inflation and a recession that made using stock as acquisition currency difficult, stock options meaningless and some of the new businesses banks had entered treacherous. In the 1970s, the Dow Jones Industrial Index ended about where it started, but after reaching a peak of 1,052 on January 11, 1973 over a two-year period, it fell to 578, a 45% decline in value. The Index did not surpass the January 1972 high until 1982, or stay above that level until 1984.

Unlike the inflation rate, stock performance did not differ much from the 1960s when the annual Dow Jones Industrial Index increase was 1.7%, but the "swings" in the previous decade were far less violent. Two decades of annual stock price gains of about 1% also were quite different from the post-1980 era when so much was expected out of stock prices in terms of attracting investors, increasing market capital and motivating management through stock options.

Bank Holding Company Act Amendments of 1970

In 1970, bankers did not know the problems that lay ahead as they made expansion plans that often were based on circumventing interstate banking restrictions through holding company acquisitions. The Bank Holding Company Act of 1956 was intended to extend the McFadden Act constraints to holding companies, particularly relative to branching across state lines, but this prohibition was eventually interpreted as not applying to one-bank holding companies—i.e., holding companies formed to include only a single bank.

Although many banks in those days wanted to expand beyond state lines, the support for them doing so was not universal even within the banking industry. Small banks, historically, saw any move by big banks across state lines as a threat, and the small banks by the weight of their numbers often controlled state banking associations, and, as a result, had considerable political clout. Regulators and some legislators, whatever their views, pro or con, also saw the circumvention of the interstate banking prohibitions by holding companies as something that should be within their purview if it was to happen.

The result was the passage of new legislation that would bring the one-bank holding company under the regulatory authority of the Federal Reserve. This legislation, the Bank Holding Company Act Amendments of 1970, was signed into law on the last day of that year, and the amendments to the Bank Holding Company Act of 1956 extended the coverage of that earlier legislation to one-bank holding companies.

These "amendments" specifically, gave the Federal Reserve the power to permit bank holding companies, multi-bank and one-bank, to engage in those nonbanking activities that were "determined to be so closely related to banking.....as to be a proper incident thereto" and that "can reasonably be expected to produce benefits to the public, such as greater convenience, increased competition, or gains in efficiency, that outweigh possible adverse effects, such as undue concentration of resources, decreased or unfair competition, conflicts of interest or unsound banking practices."[3] This is a lot of legal terminology, but it clearly made the Federal Reserve the deciding factor as to what could and could not be done relative to banks crossing state lines via holding companies.

Since there had been many nonbank acquisitions by bank holding companies preceding this legislation, the 1970 legislation also established rules relative to these acquisitions. If the acquisition was made after June 30, 1968, and most were made after that date, then it was retroactively subject to the provisions of the Amendments and needed Federal Reserve approval. If this approval was not forthcoming, then the acquisition had to be divested prior to the end of 1980. Acquisitions before June 30, 1968, as long as they were not dormant at any time subsequent to that date, were allowable and, in effect, "grandfathered."

This legislation also directed the Federal Reserve to determine which financial services that banks were not presently allowed to perform would be allowable as separate subsidiaries of a holding company. These services, though, had to be "closely related" to financial services that were already permissible to banks.

The major impact of the legislation was not so much that it added to what banks could do, but rather that it reflected a legislative and regulatory acceptance of an expansion of banking services, including offering them beyond state lines, as long as they conformed to the guidelines of the new Act as interpreted by the Federal Reserve. The McFadden Act, however, still applied, so that even if approved, the new subsidiary could not offer checking accounts at a facility in another state.

Banks had always made loans across state lines, particularly when the state lines divided metropolitan areas—New York, Chicago, Philadelphia and Washington were prime examples—but prior to the late 1960s, there had been little effort to lend across state lines through subsidiaries located in other states. Many banks had loan production offices in other states, but this format did not seem to work well except for big banks lending to large borrowers.

The introduction of regulatory oversight with the Amendments to the Bank Holding Company Act in 1970 did not lessen the interest of banks in using holding companies to go beyond their traditional business. As would be expected, though, the oversight set up some legal battles as banks tried to push beyond the limits of these guidelines.

In the early 1970s, though, most banks were prepared to live within the guidelines as they provided ample room for expansion. Banks of all sizes wanted to have holding company subsidiaries that specialized in such traditional bank lending areas as mortgage, personal and commercial loans and be able to operate them across state lines. Many of them also jumped at the opportunity to get into financial advisory and consulting services, data processing for other financial services companies and other businesses that were deemed as "closely related" to banking by the Federal Reserve.

This eventually led to banks advising, and assuming responsibility for, Real Estate Investment Trusts ("REITs"), which made construction loans primarily for commercial properties. REITs, like other real estate-related activities, were susceptible to economic swings, particularly since the rationale behind them was that real estate values always go up. Since this was not true, REITs became an additional problem for banks during the difficult economic conditions that prevailed throughout most of the 1970s.

This movement by banks to diversify into new businesses and take traditional bank lending activities across state lines affected the bank consolidation process in two ways. It was a trend that was far more likely to be used by large banks, and, when successful, it added to their overall size and marketing power. Perhaps, more importantly, it took banks across state lines and made them even more eager to cross those borders with traditional full-service banking offices that accepted all types of deposits.

The most aggressive large bank in pursuing these new businesses was initially Citicorp, and its efforts raised concern among banks outside of New York. Its purchase of Nationwide Financial with its personal loan offices in multiple states raised the specter of it having an overwhelming advantage when interstate banking was allowed. This proved to be a false alarm, but in the 1970s and 1980s, banks were highly concerned about Citicorp coming into their states.

Two of the most aggressive mid-sized banks using holding companies for interstate expansion in the 1970s were NCNB and First Pennsylvania, but they were far from alone. First Union, Wachovia, Citizens & Southern, Virginia National, Maryland National, Pittsburgh National, National Bank of Detroit, Security Pacific, Northwest, Wells Fargo and many others made significant moves in this direction.

The plans for many of these banks were to have "one of each" of the most important, allowable financial services businesses operating as a subsidiary of their holding company with freedom to go beyond their home state. The starting points were mortgage banking, consumer finance and leasing, as they were businesses with large volume potential. For some, interstate expansion also extended to REITs, but with all-to-frequently disappointing results.

Citicorp—The Initiator

Citicorp was in the forefront of interstate expansion. In 1970, it acquired one of the nation's largest mortgage bankers, Advance Mortgage in the Detroit area, with the intent of making it the focal point of a national mortgage business. "Largest" in mortgage banking in 1970, however, was not quite what it sounded like since mortgage banking was a fragmented business. It was unlikely the biggest mortgage banking firm had as much as 2% of the business nationally, but Advance Mortgage was still a good start toward a national mortgage banking operation for an owner with "deep pockets," a description that certainly fit Citicorp.

Citicorp also was in negotiations to acquire an insurance company in 1970. This would have gone well beyond what was later to be defined as "closely related" to banking, but this transaction was never finalized.[4]

In 1973, Citicorp took a big step with its nonbank geographic expansion when it acquired Acceptance Finance Corporation in St. Louis that operated under the Nationwide Financial Services name. It was a small personal loan company with assets of little over $30 million, but it had 85 loan offices in 14 states. This acquisition was approved by the Federal Reserve in 1973, and in the next two years, Nationwide Financial opened 87 additional offices in seven new states. By the end of 1975, it had assets of $304 million and 172 offices in 21 states.

In Phillip Zweig's excellent biography of Citicorp chairman, Walter Wriston, he quoted Wriston as saying that the strategy behind this purchase was "blanketing the country with store-front 'person-to-person' offices that would sell all sorts of consumer financial services and establish *de facto* interstate banking." Wriston went on to say that this "moves us closer toward the long-range goal of becoming a truly national financial service corporation."[5] In effect, by simply changing the signs above the doors, the finance offices could be converted overnight to branches of Citibank.

The intent also was to use Nationwide Financial to acquire consumer finance companies throughout the country and become truly national. This did not happen as concerns about the size and geographic reach of Citicorp were widespread and the relationship between Citicorp and the Federal Reserve had become adversarial.

The latter became apparent when after approving the purchase of Nationwide Financial in 1973, the Federal Reserve then rejected Citicorp's request for approval of its 1970 acquisition of Advance Mortgage. The rationale was the anticompetitive effect of the nation's largest commercial bank buying the second largest mortgage banking company. Citicorp did not divest Advance Mortgage until 1980, but its disapproval by the Federal Reserve in 1973 put an end to additional nonbank acquisitions for many years to come.

Citicorp had many other options and concerns, and its temporarily losing interest in domestic geographic expansion was based on more than just Federal Reserve opposition. In the 1970s, it was expanding around the world, and, as a result, it experienced one of the major big bank problems of this era—loans to developing countries. This would become a bigger problem in the 1980s, but it was already a concern.

Even though it suspended its interstate nonbank expansion after 1973, to other banks, Citicorp still presented an ominous picture of the future. The fear of smaller banks may have been unduly exaggerated, but if interstate banking had become a reality in the 1970s, Citicorp might have been able to use Nationwide Financial to instantaneously provide a national banking branch network. As it turned out, the thrift crisis provided Citicorp with an even better geographic expansion vehicle in 1982.

NCNB—The Survivor

When the 1970s began, NCNB was far from being a Citicorp. It was not even the biggest bank in North Carolina, but it along with Citicorp, was one of two banks at the forefront of change throughout the consolidation process. Its formation of a holding company in 1968 was the start of its nonbank expansion.

Immediately after forming a holding company, NCNB established an insurance subsidiary and two real estate subsidiaries, the most prominent of which was NCNB Mortgage. It followed these moves in 1969 with the purchase of Stephenson Finance Company, which had 65 consumer finance offices throughout the Carolinas and Georgia. It also bought a factoring company that year, which was an accounts receivable financing business servicing the textile industry. In 1972 and 1973, NCNB stepped up its real estate commitment by acquiring two mortgage banking firms, C. Douglas Wilson in South Carolina and Blanchard & Calhoun in Georgia. Also during this period, it joined forces with banks in Georgia and Virginia to establish an Atlanta-based REIT.

With its expansion in both traditional and nontraditional banking, by 1974, NCNB had become the 26th largest bank holding company in the country with $3.6 billion in assets. This included nonbank businesses that had 250 offices in six states and two foreign countries.

By the end of 1974, though, NCNB was no longer celebrating this seeming success as its rapid expansion in the real estate business ran into high interest rates, a recession and declining values. Unfortunately for NCNB, the greatest negative impact of the down economy of the mid-1970s was felt in the Southeast, particularly Atlanta and the Carolinas, which were the focus of its activities. Losses from the REIT and mortgage banking, and a growing amount of non performing assets (NPAs), temporarily removed the glitter surrounding NCNB; caused some anxious moments; and prompted it to curtail its nonbank expansion and temporarily reduce its commercial real estate exposure.

The strength of its traditional banking business carried the day for NCNB, and despite reduced earnings in the mid-1970s, it did not spend much time looking back. It had become a regional rather than a state bank, and a minor acquisition in 1974 of a nondepository trust company in Florida would be one of the most important steps in opening the door to interstate banking. The notoriety and high stock price that it enjoyed in the early 1970's also was a major plus in its in-state bank acquisition spree during that period. Most important of all, though, its management team had seen the world outside of North Carolina, and for them, there was no going back to the quiet life of small town bankers.

First Pennsylvania—The Overambitious

In retrospect, NCNB may be the most remembered of the regional banks for its aggressive use of nonbank acquisitions in the early 1970s to further its cause because of what it became, but at the start of that decade, much of the attention went to First Pennsylvania. When the decade began, it was the 20th largest bank in the country compared to a 46th place ranking for NCNB; it was in the Northeast and, thus, nearer the centers of the national media; and its new president, John Bunting, seemed to revel in publicity.

In 1968, Bunting became president of this staid old Philadelphia bank that opened in 1812 and immediately began the nonbank expansion. In that year, First Pennsylvania joined the parade of banks forming one-bank holding companies, and a year later, it made its first out-of-state acquisition, Associated Mortgage Company, which was renamed PENNAMCO. Over the next three years, it added four finance company acquisitions to the mix in such diverse places as Denver, New Orleans, San Juan, Puerto Rico and Frederick, Maryland.

In 1970, it also had entered the REIT business with the formation of Associated Advisers that was to be the advisor of the newly-formed First Pennsylvania Mortgage Trust. For First Pennsylvania, this was a major misstep as the REIT stumbled badly when interest rates rose sharply in 1974. In fiscal 1975, which included half of 1974, the REIT lost about $19 million. This was almost half of First Pennsylvania's total earnings in its last good year. The bank's earnings fell from $43.1 million in 1973 to $18.3 million in 1975.

First Pennsylvania never recovered from this disaster, which can be partly attributed to the continuing poor performance of its nonbank real estate activities. Its earnings did not get back to $43 million for the rest of the decade, and they never got above $30 million. In 1979, earnings were only $16.5 million, and its problems were mounting. Bunting was forced to resign in 1979; the bank had fallen from 20th in size in 1970 to 40th in 1980; and in 1980, it might have failed without federal assistance.

In March 1980, the regulators had to decide between closing the bank, arranging a federally-assisted sale to another bank or giving it the finances to continue. The favored choice was a sale, but under the laws of the time, this would have required the buyer to be a Pennsylvania bank. Mellon was the only bank in the state large enough to absorb First Pennsylvania, and the FDIC was reluctant to put so much of one state's banking resources in a single institution. Ruling a sale out, the FDIC was left to choose between closing the bank or giving it the funding to proceed, and it chose the latter.[6]

As part of this bailout, First Pennsylvania reduced its exposure to non-traditional bank activities. It packaged PENNAMCO, which by then was the country's third largest mortgage bank—a spot ahead of Citicorp's Advance Mortgage—with its consumer finance subsidiary, and then sold the entire package to Manufacturers Hanover for $106.5 million.

First Pennsylvania's performance improved when it got back to the basics and was able to pay back the FDIC, but it was no longer the pre-eminent Philadelphia bank, and its assets fell from $9 billion in 1980 to less than $7 billion in 1989. It had experienced near failure and the passing of the mantle of local leadership to Philadelphia National Bank. In 1989, it was acquired by that bank, which by then had taken the CoreStates name, for less than $1 billion. This was about 40% of what Georgia's Citizens & Southern was sold for in the same year in a nonpremium equal merger, a bank that was 80% of its size in 1980.

Maryland National—The Follower

Maryland National Corporation was another holding company in the NCNB mold in that it had followed a similar growth pattern. In 1960, its primary subsidiary was a Baltimore bank with 28 branches in the immediate Baltimore area, and its name, Fidelity-Baltimore National, reflected its single city orientation. In the 1960s, it made a series of acquisitions across the state and, to reflect its broader coverage, changed the name to Maryland National and formed a holding company, Maryland National Corporation.

By 1970, Maryland National was the largest bank in Maryland with assets of $1.2 billion, and in order to continue growing rapidly, it had to either intensify its coverage in the Washington suburbs or go beyond traditional banking. It decided to do both, and its experience with nonbank expansion in the 1970s was typical of most mid-sized banks.

This was my introduction to banking as one of my responsibilities at Maryland National was to identify out-of-state nonbank opportunities. One of my first steps in doing this was to visit NCNB and First Pennsylvania to learn firsthand what they were doing.

This was uncharted waters for Maryland National, just as it was for NCNB and First Pennsylvania, and, like them, in its eagerness to proceed, it ignored some of the cardinal rules of acquiring. These include a) never buy into a business that is not at least as good as the existing core business, and preferably better; b) buy based on product and market, not management, since acquired management usually departs shortly after being acquired, *and*, most important; c) only buy businesses that one understands. Banks were not alone in ignoring these rules as the disappointing results of the industrial conglomerate merger mania in the 1960s made quite evident.

At Maryland National as well as at NCNB, First Pennsylvania and the other banks choosing this path, there was little concern shown about buying businesses better than banking. If there had been such a concern, there would have been very few nonbank acquisitions since there were, and are, few businesses better than banking.

A representative of another Baltimore financial company, Commercial Credit, expressed his amazement to me at the interest of banks in getting into its business, which was commercial finance. Its management would have traded their operation for a banking franchise without a moment's thought. This is what happened 14 years later when Sandy Weill became CEO of a then failing Commercial Credit and used it to trade up until he was where he wanted to be—buying and then running Citigroup.

Nonbank expansion, though, was the 1970's "new, new thing" and logic was not to get in the way. Maryland National, like the others, wanted "one of each," and off it went. Its primary interests may have been reaching the same level of branch coverage in the Maryland suburbs of Washington as it had in the Baltimore area and taking a unique credit card opportunity as far as it could, but nonbank expansion was high on the "to do" list—and real estate *seemed* to be the area that met the criteria of "as good or better" than what Maryland National already had. Real estate, of course, also included an REIT.

In 1973, Maryland National began the nonbank expansion process by establishing two *de novo* nonbank subsidiaries—Maryland National Realty Investors, a mortgage bank, and Maryland National Leasing; acquiring Bethlehem Acceptance Corporation, a consumer finance company with 18 offices in eastern and central Pennsylvania; and entering into a joint venture with a Florida-based mortgage bank to establish Commonwealth National Advisers. The latter was to be the advisor to Commonwealth National Realty Trust, an REIT.

In 1974, Maryland National opened two more nonbank subsidiaries. The first was Maryland National Industrial Finance Company, an asset-based lender. The second was Redwood Capital Management, Inc., an investment advisory firm.

It was also in 1974 when interest rates hit their first historic high and real estate loan risk escalated quickly. This was when Maryland National learned the hazards of operating a real estate business far from home. The joint venture partner advising Commonwealth National Realty Trust was a Florida-based mortgage banking firm that did the on-site managing while Maryland National's primary role was warehousing the loans. On top of all the other real estate problems at the time, one Friday in early 1974, the partner borrowed funds from the REIT for needs within its own mortgage banking business. By Monday, interest rates had moved so quickly that it could not repay, and the mortgage bank and the REIT were in deep trouble from which neither would recover.

This is an oversimplification, but as the solvent partner, Maryland National had to accept total responsibility, which included a $5 million loss. Fortunately, as Maryland's leading commercial lender, the rising interest rates were a plus for its traditional business, and the loss did not stand in the way of a strong year-to-year earnings gain.

Maryland National did not maintain the unbroken earnings gain throughout the turbulent 1970s, as the real estate market caught up with it in 1976 and 1977, but by the end of the decade, nonbank activities contributed 11% of earnings. In 1980, there was no more REIT in the mix, but Maryland National still had nine nonbank subsidiaries.

The 11% of earnings from nonbank activity did not accomplish much, though, for Maryland National's overall growth. From 1960 to 1972, when its emphasis was on branching and buying banks, it rose in the national asset rankings from 76th to 59th. In the rest of the 1970's, when nonbank expansion was a high priority, it moved up only three positions. In the next decade, with its growth fueled primarily by branch expansion in the Washington area and its credit card, it rose to the 36th spot.

Maryland National's credit card was a new, if not a nonbank, activity, but if it was included with the nonbank activities, then Maryland National's nonbank record changes dramatically. Maryland National was the largest credit card bank in the state in the 1970s, and by the late 1980s, it had the nation's fifth largest bank-owned credit card. At that time, it was operated as a Delaware-based subsidiary under the name of MBNA.

MBNA was spun-off in 1990 to "pay some bills" when Maryland National was sinking under the weight of excessive nonperforming assets, and the rest is history. Before being acquired by Bank of America in 2005, MBNA had joined Citigroup and JPMorgan in consolidating the credit card business into a big three that left all others far behind.

MBNA was one of Maryland National's two major contributions to the consolidation process. The other was its selling of itself to NCNB, or NationsBank as it was then called, which delivered the largest deposit share in Maryland and second largest in the District of Columbia to what would become the nation's largest retail bank. Ironically, MBNA would later be bought by the same banking organization.

Nonbank Expansion Impact

The time and effort commercial banks spent on expanding through holding company nonbank subsidiaries, both organically-developed and acquired, could be dismissed as "much ado about nothing" if measured by what it added to commercial bank earnings, assets and market capital. These ventures were not nearly as profitable as anticipated, and First Pennsylvania was not the only bank to be badly hurt by such expansion.

The impact, though, was significant even if it could not be readily defined in dollar and cents. It took banks across state lines; separated those that were adept at operating away from home from those that were not; and it set the stage for 1990's sweeping inter-industry consolidation that had a major impact on the consolidation process.

During the 1970s, banks, though, had successfully used their market clout in at least one nonbank industry, mortgage banking. As the decade ended, seven of the ten largest mortgage banking firms were owned by banks. The leader, Lomas Nettleton, was still independent, but the mortgage banks ranked second through sixth in 1979 were subsidiaries of Philadelphia National, First Pennsylvania, Citicorp, Norwest and Wells Fargo. Pittsburgh National and First Union also had subsidiaries among the top ten.

Leading Mortgage Banking Companies, 1980

Mortgage Bank	City	Mortgages Serviced (in millions)	Parent
Lomas Nettleton	Dallas	$6,708	-
Colonial Mortgage	Philadelphia	3,725	Philadelphia Nat'l.
PENNAMCO	Washington	2,885	First Pennsylvania*
Advance Mortgage	Southfield, MI	2,357	Citicorp
Banco Mortgage	Minneapolis	2,828	Norwest
Wells Fargo Mtge.	San Francisco	2,702	Wells Fargo
National Home	Lafayette, IN	2,653	-
Mason McDuffie	Berkeley, CA	2,649	-
Kissell Company	Springfield, OH	2,518	Pittsburgh National
Cameron Brown	Raleigh, NC	2,483	First Union

Note: Western Bancorporation's mortgage operation would have ranked 8th if it was a separate subsidiary.
*Sold to Manufacturers Hanover in 1980.
Source: American Banker, October 15, 1979.

Despite having seven of the top ten mortgage banks, this did not add up to a large, combined national market share for the participating bank holding companies as this was still a fragmented industry. The largest mortgage bank, Lomas Nettleton, serviced a little less than $7 billion in mortgage loans, and even factoring in inflation, this was a long way from the $1 trillion plus being serviced by the 2006 leaders, Countrywide and Wells

Fargo. The latter was the outgrowth of the 1980 mortgage banks ranked fifth and sixth that were owned by Norwest and Wells Fargo.

First Pennsylvania sold its consumer finance and mortgage banking operations in 1980 to a larger bank, Manufacturers Hanover. For a brief time in the 1980s, Manufacturers Hanover, which would be acquired by Chemical in 1991 and eventually became part of JPMorgan, was the largest mortgage banker in the country.

Specialty consumer finance was the second most pursued target for nonbank and out-of-state expansion, but this business was dominated much more than it is today by the captive finance companies of the auto and appliance companies and large independents like Household Financial, Beneficial Finance, Associates and CIT that remained independent until the 1990s, or in the case of Household Finance, even later. The only banks with holding company subsidiaries ranking among the fifty largest noncaptive finance companies in 1979 were First Pennsylvania, NCNB, Security Pacific and Chemical.

These nonbank acquisitions did not directly have much impact on bank consolidation, but it was the proverbial "camel's nose under the tent." Some very aggressive banks had gotten a taste of going beyond their home markets, and they liked the expanded opportunities.

Consolidation On Hold

D espite all of the nonbank expansion, from a traditional banking perspective in the 1970s, consolidation was on "hold." Most of the banks that had wanted to go statewide and were not constrained by local laws already had done so, and interstate banking was still a distant dream. The national deposit shares of the biggest banks were showing some gains, but this came almost totally from corporate and offshore sources as the large money center banks were slow to show an interest in retail banking, and, in some cases, were constrained by state laws from doing so. The dominance of banks also was threatened by the S&L rate advantage on savings accounts and increased interest in branching as well as an increasing flow of funds out of banks *and* thrifts at the end of the decade because of higher rates available from money market funds and other investment options.

In the 1970s, not only was consolidation on "hold," but it started to appear that when, and if, consolidation moved forward it might not be dominated by the banks. Two other persistent fears were that ATMs would make branches obsolete and that interest would be permitted to be paid on checking accounts with a devastating impact on bank earnings.

There were good reasons to consider banks under siege in the 1970s with regulations making banks compete with "one arm tied behind their backs" in the pursuit of deposits. This mentality was a major reason banks spent so much time trying to cross state lines even if the businesses they were entering were not as good as banking. In addition to the geographic expansion, banks also wanted the right to compete with a wider range of financial services, but at that time, the expansion of powers and coverage seemed to be a one-way street favoring thrifts and brokerage firms. The emergence of the ATM also raised the specter of various types of retailers taking a backdoor route into banking at the expense of bank branches. Adding to the problems was investor disinterest in bank stocks after 1972.

Thrift competition, particularly from S&Ls, was a major concern. Historically, thrifts had not competed directly with banks for deposits since they could not issue checking accounts, which was the primary bank deposit prior to 1970. They also were required by regulation to limit their lending to home mortgages. The *quid pro quo* for thrifts was that they could pay a rate of 3.25% on savings accounts, while banks were not allowed to pay more than 3%. This was not an issue in a low interest rate environment when market-determined rates were below 3%, but it became a big disadvantage for banks as they became more dependent on nonchecking deposits as interest rates were rising in the 1970s.

The difficult economic environment of the 1970s added to these myriad of concerns, particularly the extreme volatility of interest rates. It was the interest rate increase more than anything else that made the 1970s so threatening to banks. Ironically, it was these same high interest rates at the end of the decade that resulted in legislative changes that shifted the balance of power in favor of banks in the 1980s in ways that could not have been imagined a few years earlier, such as bankrupting the thrift industry.

The two oil-driven interest rate spikes were key economic events in the 1970s as far as banks were concerned, and each had a different impact. The first followed the Mideast's Yom Kippur War that threatened the oil supply and came with little warning, and had a much more negative impact on bank earnings, asset quality and stock prices than the second rise, despite its much lower peak. The negative impact put an end to most holding company expansion and had banks talking about getting back to the basics. The second interest rate rise was much more dramatic, and, although it accelerated the flow of deposits out of the banks and into brokerage-run money market funds, banks were better situated the second time around. Asset quality was not a problem this time, and the benefit of wider margins as loan yields rose faster than deposit costs outweighed the negative impact of losing some of their deposit share. By then, bank stock prices also had been down so long that low multiples of earnings or capital, much like a high rate of inflation, had gained an almost begrudging acceptance.

While banks were better prepared for the second interest rate "spike," there was no way thrifts whose loans were primarily long-term fixed-rate home mortgages could fully-adjust. With cheap deposits being replaced by rising rates on savings deposits and high cost CDs, many of the thrifts were dealing with funding costs that were higher than their yields. This was the origin of the thrift crisis that dominated the business headlines in the 1980s.

Continuing Branch Growth

A continuing decline in the deposit share of the large banks between 1970 and 1980 was not a surprise, nor did it necessarily mean that the big banks were losing strength, but it did reflect that their primary business, large corporate lending, was not growing as fast as retail banking. The movement of banking activity from Wall Street to Main Street and from downtown to the suburbs continued, and the money center banks were reluctant participants. In the 1970s, there was little reason to expect that reluctance to disappear.

The big banks in New York and Chicago, along with three or four retail banks in what had become the most populous state, California, were still by far the largest banks in the country. Their customers, though, were large corporations and governments, and they were as ready to do business in Buenos Aires and Madrid as in Buffalo and Peoria. The New York City banks' branches also were primarily in markets experiencing a population outflow, and the Chicago banks were still not allowed to have branches. Thus, it was inevitable that the big New York and Chicago banks would be losing domestic deposit and retail lending share.

Banks, Branches and Large Bank Deposit Share, 1970 and 1980

Year	Number of		All Offices		Ten Largest Deposit Share
	Banks	Branches	Number	Change	
1980	14,434	38,738	53,172	17,822	17.2%
1970	13,511	21,839	35,350	11,668*	18.8

*Since 1960.
Source: FDIC, Historical Statistics on Banking and Report of Condition data as of December 31, 1980.

This inevitable loss of deposit share by the big money center banks to retail banks was furthered by the bank branching mania of the 1960s continuing into the 1970s to which was added an unusual increase in the number of banks. The net increase in full-service banking offices did not double as it did in the previous decade, but the almost 18,000 net new banking offices in the 1970s were about 50% higher in absolute numbers.

The greater emphasis on branching was universal except in those states that clung to unit banking laws, and leading the way was a new breed of banks that were accumulating substantial bulk, but whose growth was constrained by state lines. They were not part of the industry's upper echelon in the 1970s, but they were better prepared to be winners when interstate banking arrived than the money center banks. The 1980s and 1990s would belong to NCNB, First Union, Norwest, First Bank System,

Bank One, Fleet, KeyCorp, PNC, SunTrust, Sovran and a few others that would be referred to as superregionals, but that was unimaginable in 1970, or even in 1979.

A difference in the traditional banking structural pattern in the 1970s from what came before *and* after was in the number of new banks opened and banks disappearing through merger or failure. Despite a difficult economy, many more banks opened in the 1970s than were sold or closed. This was marginally the case in the 1960s, but this relationship was in stark contrast with all other ten year intervals since 1920.

The 2,200 new banks in the 1970s were part of the movement of people and retail activities into the suburbs, particularly in states where banks were not allowed to branch. The flow of banking activities to the suburbs was an acute problem for existing banks in unit banking states as they could not branch anywhere, let alone in the fast-growing suburbs. By comparison, in the 1940s and 1950s, when the memories of the Great Depression were still fresh in people's minds and the move to the suburbs had just begun, there were far fewer banks opened.

New Banks, Mergers and Failed Banks, 1940 to 1999

Period	New Banks	Mergers	Failed Banks
1990–99	1,315	5,047	455
1980–89	2,700	3,465	1,030
1970–79	2,224	1,316	73
1960–69	1,552	1,375	43
1950–59	763	1,416	24
1940–49	621	698	87

Source: FDIC, Historical Statistics on Banking.

The 1980s would see more banks opened than in the 1970s, but because of an increased number of mergers and failures, this did not result in a net gain in the number of banks. In the 1970s, there were about 800 more banks opened than were merged out of existence or failed. Conversely, in the 1980s, there were almost 1,800 *more* bank mergers and failures than openings.

Merger activity also was constrained in the 1970s by loan quality concerns throughout much of the decade and the low bank stock prices that made it difficult for buyers to pay a price that would induce banks to sell.

Thrifts

The competitive impact of thrifts, and particularly S&Ls, was a major bank concern in the 1970s. S&Ls had been around for a long time, but it was not until after World War II that they became major bank competitors in the pursuit of deposits. In the 1950s, S&Ls had spectacular growth and increased their share of deposits from about 8% to almost 19%. This gain was produced primarily by single office institutions as the 6,320 S&Ls operating in 1960 had less than 2,000 branches.

S&L Branch Growth, 1960 to 1980

| Year | Number of | | All Offices | |
	S&Ls	Branches	Number	Change
1980	4,613	16,733	21,346	11,359
1970	5,669	4,318	9,987	2,056
1960	6,320	1,611	7,931	–

Source: United States League of Savings Institutions, Chicago, Illinois, *'83 Savings and Loan SourceBook.*

The S&Ls continued to increase their overall share of deposits in the 1960s, but unlike in the previous decade, it was by only a modest two percentage points. The slowdown in the deposit share gain reflected the delay in joining banks in the proliferation of branches. In the 1960s, S&L branches more than doubled, but with a decline of more than 600 S&Ls, the total increase in offices was only a little over 2,000. Collectively, there was still less than one branch per S&L.

This conservative approach to branching by S&Ls was reversed in the 1970s. Thrift branches almost quadrupled in the decade, and even with almost 1,000 fewer S&Ls, there was a net S&L gain of more than 11,000 offices. This was an increase from less than one to almost four branches per S&L.

This branching binge and aggressive deposit pricing in the high interest rate environment rekindled the S&L's rise in deposit share. Even with about a 1,600 reduction in numbers by the end of the decade, S&Ls increased their share of depository institution assets from about 21% to a little more than 24% between 1970 and 1980. Some of the gain came at the expense of banks whose collective share declined from almost 68% to 66%.

Asset Share by Type of Institution, 1970 and 1980

Year	Percent of Deposits			
	Banks	Savings & Loans	Savings Banks	Credit Unions
1980	66%	24%	7%	3%
1970	68	21	9	2

Source: United States League of Savings Institutions, *'83 Savings and Loan SourceBook.*

Their fellow thrifts, the mutual savings banks, who differed from S&Ls primarily by being insured by the FDIC rather than FSLIC, did not share the S&L gain and had an even steeper asset share loss than banks. Their share of depository institution assets fell from a little over 9% to about 7% in the 1970s. This reflected the slow growth of the markets they served since almost all mutual savings banks were, and are, in the Northeast.

Credit unions continued to grow rapidly with their asset share rising from 2% to 3% during the 1970s. They were still, though, minor players in the overall banking mix.

Bank of Commonwealth[1]

In the 1970s, banks also had to face a nearly forgotten reality—big banks could fail. An inevitable corollary to banking in a difficult economy is that it brings with it higher risk, and if the risk is combined with banks reaching beyond their traditional skills and experience, the results can be disastrous. This was apparent in the REIT problems of the mid-1970s that hurt the earnings of several banks and was a major reason why the FDIC was forced to rescue First Pennsylvania.

First Pennsylvania, though, was the last of four large banks to either fail or require government assistance during this period, and its rescue sent far fewer shock waves through the industry than the near failure of Detroit's Bank of Commonwealth in 1971 and the failures of United States National Bank in San Diego in 1973 and Long Island's Franklin National in 1974. By the time First Pennsylvania was rescued by the FDIC, the thrift crisis had surfaced and the rapid rise in interest rates had many banks taking unusually large securities losses. Thus, its rescue was consistent with the times. The early 1970s, on the other hand, followed almost 40 years of extreme banking stability, and a large, or even a medium-size, bank failing was a totally unanticipated event.

The problems of the first of these banks that required regulatory intervention, Bank of Commonwealth, did not occur overnight. The bank had been acquired in a highly-leveraged proxy fight in the mid-1960s, but because Michigan was neither branching "friendly," nor permitted bank acquisitions statewide, its new owners used a system referred to as "chain banking" to expand. In other words, to cross county lines, they would buy control of several banks, but had to operate the banks independently. The problem was not the "chain banking" concept, but a dangerous mixture of leveraging that flowed from this ownership mode and operating plans oriented toward playing the rate game with securities rather than making loans.

Interest rates increased slowly in the late 1960s and early 1970s, but Bank of Commonwealth's management "bet" on interest rates declining. This structuring of the securities portfolio to make money only if interest rates declined became an acute problem in 1969 as interest rates and the unrealized losses on the securities portfolio not only continued to rise, but the "bet" was increased to try to solve the problem. Highly-leveraged and without the capital to absorb the unrealized securities losses, Bank of Commonwealth was at the mercy of its creditors and regulators.

A few years later, a solution to Bank of Commonwealth's problems might have been a quick, assisted sale to a larger bank. However, with $1.2 billion assets in a market in which the three largest banks held 77% of the deposits; being in a state whose laws barred the entry of banks from another market; and since the concept of an "emergency" lifting of legal barriers had not yet surfaced, a sale was not an option due to legal constraints. The regulators also were not ready to let the fourth biggest bank in Michigan become the first large bank failure since the 1930s, and in 1972, they took a third approach—a bailout. This was short-hand for the government providing the money needed to allow a company to continue to operate.

Bank of Commonwealth also was the reintroduction of regulators to large troubled banks since it was almost 40 years since the last large bank failure. As a result, it was not surprising that the outcome of the Bank of Commonwealth bailout was disappointing.

Irvine H. Sprague, one of the FDIC Commissioners involved, in his book, *Bailout,* said that "One vital ingredient was missing—confidence. That was the biggest mistake we made—thinking we could cure the bank simply by putting enough money into it. The fact was that government money seemed to have made the bank suspect in the eyes of the depositors and private investors. Rather than restoring confidence among the public, the federal assistance seemed to have had the opposite effect."[2]

This loss in confidence not only slowed Bank of Commonwealth's growth and ability to absorb its debt, but the bank actually got smaller. When it was sold a dozen years later, its assets were $300 million less than in 1972, and further assistance was needed to complete its sale to Comerica, one of the Detroit banks that a decade earlier was considered "off limits" as an acquirer because of its negative impact on concentration in the Detroit banking market.

Franklin National

Bank of Commonwealth is noteworthy because it was the first big bank since the Great Depression to need regulatory assistance to avert its failure, but it did not have the "shock" effect of the 1974 failure of Long Island based Franklin National Bank. Franklin National was not only much larger—it was the country's 20th largest bank—but it was next door to the financial capital of the world. Also, in 1972, it was bought by Michele Sindona, "an Italian financier with reputed connections to the Mafia and Vatican banking."[3] Thus, its failure raised concerns about the stability of worldwide banking in a year when interest rates, inflation and asset quality were all moving in the wrong direction.

The negative impact of Franklin National's failure was further magnified by the failure of a mid-sized German bank, Herrstatt, a few months earlier. Its failure was the result of miscalculations in trading foreign currencies, and Herstatt's funding included large loans from other banks. This raised the specter of a "domino effect" with international implications. Despite being a Long Island bank, Franklin National through ownership and sources of business, raised the same fear on a larger scale.

New York was more amenable to a sale solution than Michigan, and although Franklin National was allowed to fail, most of it assets and liabilities were assumed by a consortium of European banks—Deutsche Bank, Societe Generale of Belgium, ABN AMRO and Midland Bank—through a New York-based joint venture, EAB Bank. EAB received less than the $3.7 billion assets of Franklin National prior to its failure, but it was the start of a wave of foreign entry into retail banking in America even before interstate banking was allowed for domestic banks.

The failure of the $1.3 billion United States National Bank in San Diego in 1973 did not get the attention of Bank of Commonwealth and Franklin National. It was not the first big bank in the decade to either fail or need assistance to avoid failing, and it was much smaller than Franklin National. It was another sign, though, of an increasingly difficult banking environment.

There were no other large bank failures throughout the rest of the 1970s, but the list of banks considered to be "troubled" was growing. This would be a major ingredient in the acceleration of the consolidation process.

Bank Stock Prices

Another reason consolidation was on "hold" in the 1970s was bank stock prices. Whether it was the surprising reappearance of troubled banks, and some of the biggest ones were receiving very negative press for loans to emerging countries that were not really "emerging," or just investor aversion to financial stocks when interest rates were rising, the mid- and late-1970s were not good for bank stocks. The 45% drop in the Dow Jones Industrial Index in 1973 and 1974 did not exempt banks nor were bank stocks quick to recover. Low bank stock prices also meant an unattractive acquisition currency.

Maryland National was typical of banks in stock price movement. In the early 1970's, investors liked its growth and the potential of its nonbank subsidiaries. In those "good days," its stock sold at 14 to 15 times earnings and for more than two times book.

It continued to show good earnings gains through 1975—earnings went from $2.02 per share in 1972 to $2.86 per share in 1975—and this seemed sufficient to at least maintain existing price levels, but in 1973, Maryland National's stock followed the market down. By 1974, the average of its high and low for the year was only 8.5 times earnings and 121% of book. A year later, Maryland National's stock price was 6.8 times earnings and 114% of book, but, by then, real estate loan problems provided some justification for a reduced value.

Maryland National Stock Price, 1970 to 1980

Year	Stock Price*	Times Earnings	Percent of Book**	EPS
1980	$16.50	3.9X	54%	$4.29
1979	16.88	4.8	61	3.49
1978	17.38	5.9	69	2.96
1977	18.00	6.8	75	2.63
1976	21.88	9.8	102	2.24
1975	19.50	6.8	114	2.86
1974	21.50	8.5	121	2.52
1973	29.50	12.6	185	2.34
1972	31.00	15.3	216	2.02
1971	28.50	14.9	219	1.91
1970	24.00	12.5	205	1.92

*Average of highs and lows.
**Average book value per share for year.
Source: Maryland National Corporation annual reports.

By the mid-1970s, the investor love affair with banks was clearly over. Maryland National's earnings per share rose from $2.24 in 1976 to $4.29 in 1980, a double-digit annual percentage increase, but despite this, the average of its annual high and low stock prices from 1978 through 1980 did not exceed six times earnings or 70% of book. In 1980, the average price was 3.9 times earnings and 54% of book. The net result was that by the end of decade, its stock was selling at less than $17 per share, or about $7 per share less than in 1970, despite doubling its earnings per share during that period.

This type of bank stock performance was the norm in the late 1970s, and it contributed greatly to putting traditional bank consolidation on "hold" after 1973. It is not easy to acquire banks with a stock selling at 50% to 60% of book.

Structural Stability

The negative impact of stock prices, as well as state line constraints, kept the large banks from enhancing their position in the industry while every one else was much smaller and kept aggressive regional banks from gaining ground on the money center banks, even though the money center banks were losing deposit share against the all bank universe. In fact, this deposit share loss of the big banks was a little misleading as they looked elsewhere for funding and looked to other countries for lending opportunities. If share was measured by assets rather than deposits, the big banks actually gained share in the 1970s.

This stability at the top, collectively, can be seen in the national rankings of banks or bank holding companies during the 1970s. There was little change in the positions of the largest banks between 1970 and 1980, and there also were few signs of upward momentum for mid-sized banks except in Texas, and these were not gains for regional retail banks since the Texas banks were not allowed to branch. They, in effect, had become regional money center banks serving the oil-and-gas industry.

The static structural situation can be seen in the lack of change among the nation's nine largest banks. In 1970, the top nine included six banks from New York City, two from California—BankAmerica, the holding company for Bank of America, and First Interstate—along with the Chicago-based Continental. Ten years later, the nine largest banks were the same nine. Citicorp had moved ahead of BankAmerica at the very top, but only Continental had upward momentum, moving from ninth to sixth place; an ill-conceived momentum it would pay for in 1984 by becoming the biggest corporate bailout of all time. Losing ground was First Interstate that fell from fifth to ninth despite the benefit of being one of the very few banks grandfathered into multi-state operations and having most of its branches in fast-growing California. Chase Manhattan, Manufacturers Hanover, Chemical and Bankers Trust held the same positions in 1980 that they had in 1970, and J.P. Morgan moved up just one spot.

Further down in the rankings, where more position changes would be expected because of less size disparity, the bank holding companies ranked tenth through 16th also were unchanged from 1970 to 1980. These seven banks included three from California—Security Pacific, Wells Fargo and Crocker National—and four regional money center banks—First Chicago, Marine Midland, Mellon and First National Boston. There was some change within the seven, though, as Wells Fargo and Crocker National used their retail orientation in a large, rapidly-growing state to move up a couple of places.

Rounding out the 1980 top twenty were the two Minneapolis banks, Norwest and First Bank System, and the only new entrant, Dallas-based InterFirst. Norwest and First Bank System were little changed in ranking from a decade earlier, but InterFirst jumped from 31st to 19th with more than a six-fold asset increase. Most banks had large asset gains because of the high inflation rates in the 1970s, but only Continental among the very largest banks came close to matching InterFirst's percentage increase.

To put this continuing structural stability between 1970 and 1980 in the broader context of what would happen later, of the twenty largest banks in 1980, only Citicorp, Chemical and the two Minneapolis banks are still around. This assumes the Travelers acquisition of Citicorp is considered more of a management change than a true acquisition. The big banks with the most momentum in the 1970s, Continental and InterFirst, did not even make it through the 1980s as they were casualties of the meltdown in the oil patch. They were joined on the sidelines by Crocker National, Charter and Marine Midland, which were acquired during the 1980s.

The rapid growth of InterFirst in the 1970s followed by disaster was mirrored by other large Texas banks. Republic, Texas Commerce and First City were just outside the national top twenty in 1980, ranking 21st through 23rd, and Texas Commerce and First City were not even in the top fifty in 1970. They either failed or were sold when failure seemed imminent in the late 1980s.

Texas Banks and Future Superregionals, 1970 and 1980

Bank	Assets		National Rank	
	1980	1970	1980	1970
	(in billions)			
Texas				
InterFirst	$13.8	$2.1	19	35
Republic	11.9	2.6	21	31
Texas Commerce	11.3	1.4	22	52
First City	11.3	1.3	23	56
Other				
NCNB	$ 7.2	$1.5	28	46
PNC	6.2	1.9	31	37
Fleet	3.5	1.0	61	79
First Union	3.3	1.1	68	69
Bank One	2.8	.5	80	na

Source: American Banker, April 20, 1982 and 1971 *Polk's Bank Directory.*

Among the superregionals that would have leading roles in the 1990s consolidation process, only NCNB and PNC were even close in size to the banking leaders in 1980. NCNB had assets of about $7 billion at that time, and it had risen from 46th in 1970 to 28th in 1980. PNC had a little over $6 billion assets as the 1980s began and was 31st in the rankings.

Fleet, First Union and Bank One were still local banks with assets in the $2 to $4 billion range when the 1970s ended and were not even among the sixty largest in the country. Bank One, though, while still a local bank, had come a long way. In 1970, it had assets of about $500 million and was nowhere to be found in the national rankings.

The 1970s also did not have the large mergers that would result in immediate jumps in national, or even regional, concentration, and when a large bank was sold, the buyer was usually a foreign bank. Franklin National, a top twenty bank, failed in 1974 and was sold by the FDIC to a consortium of European banks. Union Bank in Los Angeles and National Bank of North America, which ranked 22nd and 28th, respectively, in 1970, were sold to British banks. The regulators, when faced with the failures of Bank of Commonwealth and First Pennsylvania, chose to "bail" them out with government funds rather than let buyers cross state lines or in-state buyers greatly increase their local market shares.

The biggest bank to be acquired by another domestic bank in the 1970s was Security National on Long Island. It had assets of about $2 billion when it was acquired by Chemical in 1975.

Product Change

There also was minimal change in the traditional banking product mix on the loan side in the 1970s, but the transformation of the deposit mix away from checking accounts continued. Noninterest-bearing demand deposits, or checking accounts, fell from a little over half of bank deposits in 1970 to 36% in 1980. This was a long-term downward trend that would continue for years to come, but the 1970s slippage was accelerated by high interest rates that shifted funds of all types into high priced CDs. This increased the CD share from 28% to 47% of bank deposits. The bank savings account share was not down as much as demand deposits, but the impact of not being competitive in rates with S&Ls and the movement to CDs was apparent.

Bank Deposit Mix by Type, 1970 and 1980

Year	Deposits			Deposits/ Assets
	Demand	Savings	CDs	
1980	36%	17%	47%	80%
1970	51	21	28	85

Source: FDIC, Historical Statistics on Banking.

Along with the shift to CDs as interest rates went into double-digits, there also was a movement of money to brokerage firm-run money market funds. Between 1978 and 1980, cash in money market funds grew from $10 to $76 billion and would reach $150 billion a year later before leveling off.[4] This contributed to banks relying less on deposits for their funding as deposits fell from 85% to 80% of assets in the 1970s, but the major reason for a lesser use of deposits was large banks finding alternative, and often cheaper, sources of funding, such as commercial paper, which was short-term, unsecured promissory notes issued by bank holding companies.

It also was in the 1970s that the ATM became a standard part of the banking delivery system. The number of ATMs grew from only about 100 in 1970 to almost 14,000 in 1979, and as the decade wound down, it was no longer whether ATMs could be cost-justified, but whether a bank could be competitive without them.[5]

Different Levels of Concern

For all the bank concerns as the 1970s came to an end, particularly relative to S&Ls, the flow of funds out of the banking system and being unable to cross state lines, the bank problems were far less than those of others. The high interest rates were not only hurting S&Ls, but they were about to set them adrift in a "sea of red ink." This emerging thrift disaster would provide major impetus for interstate banking, and with it, a big step in the consolidation process. The investment banks and their money market funds would remain a competitive factor, but would be more of a nuisance than a concern.

1980: Beginning of a New Era

Bankers generally were glad to see the 1970s end as they were hard, frustration-filled years. Overly restrictive regulations limited growth, and at the time, it appeared that banks were losing ground to competitors that were either not regulated or at least had the benefit of more favorable regulations. While bank asset size increased rapidly for most, this was a bit deceptive because of the impact of an unusually high inflation rate—i.e., real growth was less than what was reported—and asset growth did not always correlate with improved earnings. To add insult to injury, investors appeared to have written off banks as "not worth the effort," and it seemed that having a good bank management position had more prestige than wealth impact.

The arrival of 1980 did not immediately suggest much improvement or even a meaningful change in direction. Interest rates were still rising, and, although rising rates helped earnings at a time when noninterest-bearing checking accounts were more than one-third of bank deposits, money that would normally be put into bank deposits increasingly was going into the brokerage-managed money market funds. There also was no reason to believe that investor interest in bank stocks would improve any time soon.

Even the rising thrift losses, instead of being a competitive plus for banks, were a major nuisance. The need for thrifts to pay-up for deposits to match below-market loans that they had to keep was making deposits more costly for everyone. This was a problem that would prevail throughout the 1980s.

No matter what it looked like to bankers at the time, in the evolution of American banking, 1980 would be a year that stood out as the beginning of a new era. Prior to 1980, how banking was done was changing rapidly, particularly with ATMs and the growing importance of credit cards and CDs, but there was little change in who was delivering banking services. Regulations limited competition between banks and other types of financial institutions, and banks were still not allowed to cross state lines. In 1980, these constraints began to erode, and by the mid-1980s, the erosion turned into a landslide.

This dismantling of barriers between banks and thrifts and between the various states in the 1980s had its roots in a series of regional and industry crises, most of which were the result of interest rates in 1980 and 1981 reaching double-digits. These rates had put thrifts in a much more tenuous position than anyone could have anticipated and were the cause of a farm crisis that plagued the Upper Midwest in the early 1980s. High interest rates did not cause the oil-and-gas industry collapse that devastated banking in the oil patch states, but the rise in oil prices that contributed to the high interest rates created a false, long-term optimism as to the future of that business.

The 1980s also differed from the previous decade in the amount and importance of the banking legislation that was passed and judicial rulings rendered. Most of it was crisis-driven, but the result was to take down the walls between banks and thrifts and clear the way for interstate banking.

The initial legislative response to the problems that were building within the banking industry was a law passed in 1980 removing the caps on rates paid on savings accounts to help stem the flow of money out of banks and thrifts into unregulated investment alternatives. This legislation, the Depository Institutions Deregulation and Monetary Control Act, put thrifts in direct competition with banks by taking the caps off rates paid on savings deposits, which allowed thrifts to be fully competitive in deposit pricing and also let thrifts make commercial loans and offer checking accounts. Coming when it did with interest rates at record heights, this legislation also contributed to the decline of an independent thrift industry as the resulting higher rates paid on deposits were not matched by similar high rates on their primary loan type, home mortgages.

In 1982, there was additional legislation, the Garn-St. Germain Act, which further narrowed the difference between banks and thrifts. This Act and its impact are discussed in the next chapter, but what it did was create an environment that encouraged rapid thrift growth in areas in which thrifts had no expertise. It was a period of a strong belief in deregulation, and thrifts and their regulators bought into deregulation in a big way with what proved to be disastrous results.

There also were interstate acquisitions in 1982 that would help set the stage for full acceptance of interstate banking. These acquisitions were either very small or the result of a bank or thrift failure, and, by themselves, did not amount to much, but the size and nature of the buyers—Citicorp, NCNB and BankAmerica—were to change the thinking relative to interstate banking.

The third governmental action that made the 1980s different than the 1970s was aimed directly at interstate banking. In June 1985, the Supreme Court ruled that the regional interstate compacts in the Southeast and New England that allowed mergers across state lines into consenting states within those regions were legal. Interstate banking had always been allowed if a state did not explicitly prohibit out-of-state banks from buying banks in their state, but in the early 1980s, only Maine permitted this. Even in Maine, for an interstate merger to occur, it was necessary that banks in other states have similar local, reciprocal banking laws to be eligible to merge with a Maine bank. These regional interstate compacts were intended to create this type of interstate merger reciprocity on a limited regional basis.

This regional backdoor approach to interstate banking reflected the primary deterrent to interstate banking historically, which had been the fear in small states of domination by banks in large states, particularly the banks in New York. The regional compacts were a way around this since when states in New England and the Southeast passed reciprocal interstate banking laws—i.e., you can buy banks in my state if we can buy banks in your state—they included geographic constraints that left New York on the outside. This did not sit well with the big New York banks, particularly Citicorp, who would challenge these constraints in the courts, but with the 1985 approval of the exclusionary constraints by the Supreme Court, interstate banking cleared a major hurdle.

Another piece of legislation in the 1980s that was to play a major role in the consolidation of the once highly-differentiated thrift and banking industries was the Financial Institutions Reform, Recovery and Enforcement Act of 1989, or as it is was better known, FIRREA. This was a response to the disastrous second stage of the thrift crisis and, among other things, it abolished the Bank Board and FSLIC, put all thrifts under the regulatory authority of the Treasury Department and shifted their deposit insurance authority to the FDIC. With the same regulators and insurers as for banks, the "turf" impediments to banks buying thrifts, and vice versa, even under non-emergency situations, would soon disappear.

The role that the regional economic downturns played in the 1980s relative to consolidation was immense, and they greatly contributed to the passage of the three major pieces of banking legislation. The 1980s are often considered to have been good years, particularly when compared to the economic turbulence of the 1970s, but being good years did not apply to the whole country or to all industries. There were several regional recessions in the 1980s, two of which were caused by problems within an industry that was a primary source of income for a region. These regional recessions had a negative impact that contributed to the consolidation process.

The first regional economic downturn in the 1980s was a farm crisis resulting from the combination of low prices for agricultural products and high rates on farm loans dictated by the interest rate environment. The negative impact of the farm crisis on banking, though, was limited, to small banks in rural areas. There were no big mergers caused by the farm crisis, although it did slow the growth of the two large Minneapolis banks, Norwest and First Bank System.

A more serious regional and banking problem had its genesis in the oil price increases in the 1970s that ultimately peaked in 1981. When oil prices collapsed in the mid-1980s, the oil-and-gas industry and the economies of the states that were dependent on it, primarily Texas and Oklahoma, went from robust to "bust." The region's banking industry was ill-prepared to adapt to this changed economic climate, and, as a direct result, eight of the forty largest banks in the country disappeared.

At the tail-end of the 1980s, a softening national economy and excess real estate capacity became a serious banking problem in the Northeast and in California. This was more of a 1990s than a 1980s problem, and by then, the radical structural change of the 1980s within the banking industry had made major strides, but this real estate-driven bank disaster resulted in more than 1,500 bank and thrift failures.

Some bank problems in the 1980s came from outside United States. In the mid-1980s, many less-developed countries in the world, particularly in Latin America, were forced to default on their loans and among the major holders of what were referred to as LDC loans were American money center banks. The losses from these loans were so severe that there was concern that a big New York City bank would collapse under the burden.

No money center bank failed, but the LDC loans had totally stopped BankAmerica's growth, and some of these banks never recovered from the losses incurred. By the mid-1980s, the big money center banks were limited in their ability to make large acquisitions, and their plight worsened when large commercial real estate losses in the Northeast and California came on the heels of the LDC problem.

The number of failing financial institutions resulting from the 1980s regional and thrift crises was so substantial that the small bank concern over the possible loss of local control of banking was easily put aside by the regulators because of their need to solve the failing bank situations with as little cost to the government as possible. There were not always in-state buyers for the larger thrifts that had failed, and when Texas banking collapsed, the impact was so widespread that the rescuing banks had to come from other states. Regulators could only ignore the McFadden Act prohibitions against pre-empting state laws on out-of-state bank entry in emergency situations, but in the 1980s, there were a lot of "emergencies."

If state prohibitions against out-of-state bank takeovers could readily be put aside to the benefit of the country's biggest banks, as they were in the early 1980s, then it also was an easier sell for regional banks that were so disposed to get state laws changed to allow them to cross state lines as well. This "sale" became even easier when the Supreme Court ruled in 1985 that state legislation that allowed interstate banking could set geographic limits as to the states that could participate.

As a result of these crises and the introduction of interstate banking, banking by the end of the 1980s looked quite different from what had existed in the 1970s. The money center banks were tottering, and a new breed of regional banks, the superregionals, was moving forward with great haste. Three of the banks that now dominate banking—Bank of America, Wells Fargo and Wachovia—came from the ranks of the superregionals.

The impact of these crisis-driven changes on the banking structure in the 1980s was not immediately apparent in the upper echelons of American banking. Citicorp, BankAmerica, Chase Manhattan and most of the other leading New York City money center banks were so far ahead of everyone else in size that they could not lose their high rankings in just ten years. Except for Citicorp, though, the gap between the 1980 leaders, and the fast-growing superregionals would be greatly reduced. BankAmerica had fewer assets in 1990 than it did in 1980, and Chase Manhattan's assets grew by only 25% in ten years. Meanwhile, Security Pacific almost tripled its assets and moved from eleventh to fifth place nationally, and NCNB had a nine-fold asset increase as it rose from 28th to seventh in the rankings.

The money center banks were on the decline in the 1980s as they were culturally not well-suited to benefit from either branch or interstate growth and were crippled by LDC loans and then commercial real estate lending at the end of the decade. BankAmerica, Chase Manhattan, Manufacturers Hanover and Continental were in dire straits come 1990, or at least had been a few years earlier. BankAmerica had to fend off an unfriendly takeover during this period; Manufacturers Hanover would give up the fight and sell to Chemical in 1991, a fate that awaited Chase Manhattan a little later; and Continental disappeared in 1994.

In the 1980s, interstate banking concerns about future viability of some banks and almost all thrifts and high bank stock prices—something that seemed to be little more than a dream as the decade began—resulted in a merger explosion that was new to banking. Despite this, asset and deposit share of the largest banks actually declined during those ten years as the gains of NCNB, Security Pacific, First Union, Fleet and other superregionals were cancelled out by share losses of BankAmerica and the money center banks. The ten largest banks held almost 31% of bank assets going into the 1980s, and that share was down to about 26% at the end.

What the 1980s would do, though, was to bring a different banking culture to the forefront; create regional banks with this new culture that were large enough to undertake large interstate mergers; and set the stage for the megamergers and consolidation of the next fifteen years. That next stage of the banking consolidation would show up in the numbers in a big way.

How this shift from a money center to a superregional retail culture occurred in the 1980s and its impact on consolidation is a story with many parts and variations. It includes a thrift crisis, troubles in the oil patch, the impact of LDC loans on the money center banks, high stock prices and, most of all, interstate banking, all of which are discussed in the next few chapters. The proliferation of branches that built pressures to go beyond state lines in the 1960s and 1970s slowed in the 1980s, but it had become, in any event, a secondary issue with interstate banking having emerged as the primary impetus for bank expansion and consolidation.

CHAPTER 6

Thrift Crisis: Early Stages

O f all the structure-changing events in the 1980s, the thrift crisis attracted the most attention, and deservedly so as it was a story that moved beyond the business pages. It was a financial disaster of epic proportions that not only devastated an industry, but brought with it considerable personal suffering. The financial impact on taxpayers of solving the thrift crisis is estimated to have been more than $200 billion, and maybe even more than $300 billion. By the time it was through, the crisis also removed thrifts as significant bank competitors in many parts of the country, the Northeast and West Coast being the major exceptions.

The thrift crisis also got the consolidation process rolling in the early 1980s and provided an impetus for interstate banking to be permitted sooner than it might have been otherwise. To limit government losses, regulators initially felt compelled to find homes for some of the earliest large thrift failures, and the only buyers that could absorb the biggest failed thrifts were the largest of the banks. Citicorp, in particular, was allowed to take over failed thrifts in California, Florida, Illinois and the District of Columbia. With that, interstate banking had arrived and others wanted the same privilege.

To understand the thrift crisis and how it impacted consolidation, it helps to divide this crisis into two parts—a) the immediate damage done to the thrift industry as it existed before 1980 and b) the inflation of industry assets after 1982 in response to misguided legislation and regulation. The immediate damage was the failure of numerous thrifts, some of which were quite large, despite the willingness of the regulators to relax accounting rules relative to capital to give these failing institutions time to recover. This was the impetus for interstate banking through the sale of thrifts to large banks. It was the second part—the inflation of industry assets fueled by relaxed accounting rules—that played out so disastrously in the late 1980s that was the focus of the media coverage and primary source of much of the more than $200 billion government outlay to end the thrift crisis.

These two segments of the thrift crisis can be seen in the changing number of S&Ls and their assets. In 1980, there were 3,993 federally-insured S&Ls in the country with a combined $604 billion assets. In the next two years, S&L losses soared and the number of federally-insured S&Ls fell by about 700, or by 18%.

FSLIC and FDIC Insured Thrift Assets, 1980 to 1989

Year	Savings and Loans		Savings Banks	
	Number	Assets (in billions)	Number	Assets (in billions)
1989	2,878	$1,252	489	$280
1988	2,949	1,349	492	284
1987	3,147	1,249	484	262
1986	3,220	1,162	472	237
1985	3,246	1,068	394	217
1984	3,139	976	373	206
1983	3,146	814	391	194
1982	3,287	686	428	174
1981	3,751	640	442	176
1980	3,993	604	460	172

Source: FDIC, *History of the Eighties—Lessons for the Future*, and National Council of Savings Institutions, *1990 Fact Book of Savings Associations.*

Despite the industry being virtually devoid of capital, S&Ls took advantage of reduced capital standards and lax regulation to raise assets from $604 billion in 1980 to more than $1.3 trillion in 1988. This was more than a doubling in size, and it significantly increased the S&L share of total deposits.

In Texas alone, S&L assets rose from $35 billion to $111 billion between 1980 and 1988.[1] That $111 billion assets pales besides the $373 billion assets of the California S&Ls in the latter year, but with much of the Texas growth coming from S&Ls that rose from near obscurity when investors took advantage of the easy access to banking these institutions provided through lax regulations and low capital requirements, this $111 billion would be the source of many abuses associated with the thrift crisis. The rogue thrifts in Texas that filled their loan portfolios with commercial real estate would become the centerpiece of a second, and even more disastrous, phase of the thrift crisis.

There also were 590 state-insured S&Ls in 1980 with combined assets of $12.2 billion in Maryland, Massachusetts, North Carolina, Ohio and Pennsylvania.[2] They were a small part of the total, but the limited resources of the states standing behind them resulted in mini-crises in Maryland and Ohio in 1985 that foreshadowed what was to come a year later nationwide.

Most of the post-1982 S&L asset increase took place in California, Texas and Florida, and it is a fascinating story well-chronicled in other books, one of the best of which is Martin Mayer's *The Greatest-Ever Bank Robbery*. This rise and fall of the rogue thrifts, however, did not have the same impact on bank consolidation as the failure of long-established, large S&Ls and mutual savings banks.

The mutual savings banks performance followed the same pattern as the S&Ls in the 1980s, but without the extremes. The number of mutual savings banks declined from 460 in 1980 to 373 in 1984, a slippage of 19%. Their asset inflation was less than for the S&Ls, but still substantial, rising from $172 billion in 1980 to $284 billion in 1988. Nevertheless, the mutual savings banks might have slipped through with little damage after the early 1980s if a real estate-driven recession had not hit so hard in the early 1990s in the Northeast where most of them were located.

The two parts of the thrift crisis stretched over more than a dozen years, but it was only in the late 1980s that it produced front page headlines. The extensive length of this crisis meant that it began before interstate banking and was not resolved until interstate banking had become a national reality. Thus, to put the decline of the thrifts in its proper perspective, it needs to be interspersed among other industry changing, and often interrelated, events.

An Industry of the Past

The thrift crisis was a disaster waiting to happen. S&Ls and mutual savings banks were a good idea whose time had passed, but like a lot of good ideas that outlive their usefulness, many of the people who were involved did not want to give up or make the necessary changes until it was too late.

S&Ls and mutual savings banks were initially cooperative community endeavors. The overwhelming majority did not issue stock, legally were owned by depositors and operated with minimal capital. Their business model was to take in savings deposits at low customer-acceptable rates, and then lend that money out to finance the purchase of homes. Historically, they did not compete directly with banks since most did not offer checking accounts until the early 1980s, and banks did not become highly-interested in savings accounts and home mortgages until the 1960s. Without equity ownership, thrifts did not have to make a profit, and if they did, it often was distributed to depositors, and throughout most of their history, thrifts were not taxed.

The first thrifts date back to the early 1800s and operated successfully using this simple business model until the 1930s and the Great Depression, when millions of depositors lost their savings and about 2,000 thrifts, mostly S&Ls, failed.[3] This, though, was not a failure of the business model, but rather a lack of capital and the stresses of the time. Like bank customers, beleaguered Great Depression thrift customers withdrew much needed funds and many defaulted on their mortgages.

With the thrift model not in question, the governmental response to the thrift failures in the 1930s was to impose regulatory oversight and offer deposit insurance. For most S&Ls, this was the establishment of the Federal Home Loan Bank Board ("Bank Board") for regulation and the Federal Savings and Loan Insurance Corporation ("FSLIC") for deposit insurance. Some states, most notably Maryland, Massachusetts and Ohio, established their own supervisory and insurance systems for state-insured thrifts. The mutual savings banks shared regulators with commercial banks and were insured by the FDIC.

There were many similarities between mutual savings banks and S&Ls, but there were some important differences. The mutual savings banks were not tied to home mortgage lending, and the large ones in New York City tended to be more oriented toward commercial real estate and multi-family mortgage loans rather than single family home loans. From a regulatory perspective, there were higher capital standards for mutual savings banks than for S&Ls, which reflected their more diverse lending and the shared regulation with commercial banks.

Better regulation and deposit insurance after the Great Depression may have been good ideas at the time, but they also contributed to what proved to be a faulty business model in a high interest rate environment. In the 1960s, this regulatory assistance included the interest rate that thrifts could pay on savings deposits being capped at .25% higher than the 3% rate at which banks were capped. This was a competitive advantage for thrifts, but it removed rate flexibility for their entire deposit base. For banks, a cap on deposit rates was less of a flexibility problem and since most of their deposits were noninterest-bearing checking accounts, they benefited if rates increased.

S&Ls also were restricted in their lending to only fixed-rate home mortgages, and most mutual savings banks, even though not similarly restricted, had the same loan concentration. Capped deposits supporting long-term fixed-rate home loan portfolios worked fine for thrifts as long as interest rates stayed low, which was the case for more than 30 years, but those days ended in the mid-1970s.

There also was an attempt after the Great Depression to have S&Ls and mutual savings banks maintain more capital as a cushion against future problems, but since home mortgages were not high risk loans, capital was never required to be at the same level as banks. The target was 5% of assets, but even that was not rigidly enforced, particularly with the S&Ls.

As interest rates began to climb in the late 1960s, it became harder for thrifts to attract funds with their 3.25% interest rate cap on savings deposits. The introduction of CDs eventually provided the rate flexibility necessary to attract funds even as interest rates increased, but while CDs made it easier for thrifts to attract deposits, they also increased the overall cost of funds and reduced the spread between loan yields and money costs.

Fortunately, the first interest rate peak in the 1970s was neither so high nor of sufficient length to create serious margin-related earnings problems. Thrift lending still was almost totally oriented toward long-term fixed-rate home mortgages, but at least the new mortgages booked were made at higher, market-determined rates.

In 1976, when interest rates started up again, the rates levels went so high, and stayed there so long, that they were disastrous for thrifts. By 1980, interest rates were in the double-digits, and as might be expected, new high-yielding home mortgages were far-and-few between, and to support existing long-term fixed-rate mortgages, thrifts were forced to pay high rates on their CDs. For many of them, buying money to meet existing loan obligations meant an average cost of funds that was higher than the average yield on loans. The result was that the thrift business model was busted, and a thrift crisis was on its way.

Disastrous 1981 and 1982

The mismatch between the average cost of funds and average yield wiped out almost all S&L earnings in 1980, and then in 1981 and 1982, resulted in a collective loss of almost $9 billion for the federally-insured S&Ls. This reduced industry tangible capital from 5.3% of assets in 1979 to less than 1% in 1981. If all S&Ls were viewed as a single firm, the industry had, in effect, failed. In 1981, 28 S&Ls with total assets of $11.5 billion actually did fail, and in 1982, the number of failures grew to 73 with total assets of $22.2 billion.[4] To put this in context, the assets of all banks that had failed from 1934 through 1979 was a little over $10 billion.[5]

Thrift Income and Capital, 1979 to 1983

Year	Net Income (in millions)	Return on Avg. Assets	Capital/ Assets*
Savings and Loans			
1983	$1,969	.26%	.3%
1982	(4,270)	(.64)	.4
1981	(4,632)	(.73)	.5
1980	765	.13	4.0
1979	3,619	.67	5.3
Savings Banks			
1983	$(125)	(.07)%	5.1%
1982	(1,263)	(.72)	5.0
1981	(1,438)	(.83)	5.5
1980	(207)	(.12)	6.4
1979	741	.46	6.8

*Tangible capital for S&Ls.
Source: National Council of Savings Institutions, *1988 Factbook of Savings Institutions.*

From 1980 to 1982, there also were 493 voluntary mergers and 259 supervisory mergers of S&Ls.[6] These were technically failures in which the government loss was deferred by providing the acquirer with assistance in making the acquisition. In other words, the negative impact on the deposit insurance funds was being pushed into the future.

The S&L failures from 1981 through 1983 included some of the country's largest thrifts. First Federal Savings & Loan of Chicago was the nation's ninth largest S&L; Fidelity in San Francisco was 19th; and Miami's Biscayne Federal was in the top fifty.

The mutual savings banks did not fare much better than the S&Ls, but they were helped by higher capitalization. Between 1980 and 1982, they lost about $3 billion. This was a slightly higher percentage of assets than for the S&Ls, but with equity capital at 6.8% in 1979, and adequate tangible capital, the losses still left the mutual savings bank, collectively, in much sounder condition. Failures were fewer than for the S&Ls, but the FDIC still had to deal with 11 failed mutual savings banks in 1981 and 1982 with combined assets of $14.8 billion.[7]

In some respects, the early stages of the thrift crisis looked even worse for the mutual savings banks than the S&Ls based on near-term results. Four of the 13 largest mutual saving banks—New York Bank for Savings, Western Savings Fund Society of Philadelphia, Dry Dock Savings Bank and Greenwich Savings Bank—failed between 1981 and 1983 and were sold by the FDIC in federally-assisted transactions. Five others among the fifty largest met a similar fate. Seven of the nine biggest assisted mutual savings banks sales in this first round of the thrift crisis involved New York savings banks.[8]

The FDIC, however, took a much harder line relative to the mutual savings banks than the Bank Board and FSLIC did toward the S&Ls. They dealt immediately with the most troubled savings banks, and, unlike their S&L counterparts, did not push most of the problems into the future.

There were some successes among the federally-assisted thrift sales, but, in many cases, it was merely merging a failed thrift into a larger, but still troubled, thrift that would later become a casualty in the next round of failures. Two of the seven large failed savings banks in New York were sold in federally-assisted transactions to Buffalo Savings, which would change its name to Goldome, switch to an S&L charter and then turn several years of rapid growth into one of the largest S&L failures. The purchase of Western Savings of Philadelphia had a similar result as part of PSFS and is discussed later in this chapter.

Massive losses and thrift failures in 1981 and 1982, however, were just the tip of the iceberg. Neither legislators nor regulators wanted to see many more thrift failures, and they played games with the accounting rules to buy time for struggling thrifts to recover. The thinking was that lower interest rates and expanded lending powers would restore margins and profitability to levels that would allow troubled thrifts to work their way out of their predicament. It was an understandable reaction, but interest rates did not fully cooperate, and the relaxed accounting rules and expanded lending powers led to other problems.

Legislative Reaction

The need for changes in the laws governing thrifts and commercial banks was obvious in 1980, not only because of the thrift losses, but because of the flow of funds out of banks and thrifts. With the prevailing high interest rates, money was shifting from deposits, particularly deposits constrained by caps, into money market funds run by brokerage firms and other investments.

The initial legislation was the Depository Institutions Deregulation and Monetary Control Act of 1980. It phased out the caps on rates paid on deposits; raised the amount of coverage on insured deposits from $40,000 to $100,000 per account; and expanded deposit powers to include checking accounts for all thrifts.

Passed in 1980, this legislation came before the full realization of the extent of the thrift losses had materialized. Thus, while the removal of deposit rate caps may have been a much needed move to help banks and thrifts compete with the money market funds, it was a mixed blessing for the thrifts. They were better able to compete for money, but competing meant paying market rates for deposits while almost all of their loans were long-term fixed-rate mortgages with yields far below market deposit rates.

The Act's increased coverage of insured deposits from $40,000 to $100,000 per account had its drawbacks. It made deposits safer and increased customer confidence in banks and thrifts, but if a bank or thrift failed, it greatly increased the financial exposure of the deposit insurance funds. That concern in aggregate, though, seemed minimal in 1980.

The Garn-St. Germain Depository Institutions Act of 1982 was aimed specifically at the thrift problems. Garn-St.Germain expanded the lending powers of all thrifts by allowing 30% of their assets to be in commercial loans and to write loans at 100% of appraised value. It also gave states the authority to provide additional incentives to S&Ls and mutual savings banks, including investing in real estate projects. The latter proved to be extremely damaging as California, Texas and Florida, in particular, made it legal for S&Ls, and in these states almost all thrifts were S&Ls, to invest in real estate developments of various types and in other high risk businesses. The intent of this Act was to reduce thrift dependence on long-term fixed-rate mortgages, but diversification into high risk investments and loans only made a serious problem worse.

Capital Dilemma

For thrifts and their regulators, the lack of capital became a major problem in 1982. After two years of large losses and a substantial erosion of capital, the industry, in general, and a majority of individual thrifts needed more capital. Conversely, if capital requirements were enforced as they were for banks, the number of failed thrifts would greatly increase. Thus, the regulators had a dilemma, and in their efforts to solve it, they tried to have it both ways. They encouraged thrifts to raise capital by converting to a stock form of organization and selling assets, but, at the same time, the minimum allowable capital was reduced to 3% of assets for S&Ls. This reduced the margin for error while encouraging growth. The mutual savings banks, because they shared regulators and deposit insurers with banks, were held to higher capital standards, but often even this was still not high enough.

The capital level for all thrifts was further "softened" by allowing them to operate outside of generally acceptable accounting principles. The two most notable exceptions were deferring losses on loans and intangible assets, particularly the "goodwill" generated by an acquisition of a failing thrift, with regulatory capital notes that would count as additional capital from a regulatory perspective.

Goodwill contributing to capital was turning the accounting rules upside down. Goodwill is an accounting term for the approximate difference between the price paid for an acquisition and the capital of that acquired company. It was supposed to be a *deduction* from equity capital, but under thrift regulatory accounting practices, or "RAP" accounting, the goodwill, indirectly, was an *addition* to capital. The goodwill still had to be written off against earnings over a set period of time, but to make this less of a burden, the time was extended from ten to forty years.

It was not anticipated in 1982 that virtually every aspect of the thrift capital problem and supposed solutions eventually would contribute to consolidation, but that is what happened. Shifting from a mutual to a stock form of organization made converting thrifts easier to acquire, and, in fact, made their acquisition a probability. Counting goodwill-related capital notes as capital not only promoted acquisitions, but helped regulators sell failing thrifts rather than liquidate them. The relaxed capital standards were less direct in their consolidation effect, but, at best, all they did was delay the day of reckoning for a large portion of the thrift industry.

Management and Board Weaknesses

What legislators, regulators and trade association lobbyists did not take into account when they passed these laws to reduce accounting and capital standards was the inability of most thrift managements and boards to handle major changes while under duress. What looks good on paper often does not relate to the real world. The new laws also made it easier for the less scrupulous to abuse the system.

It is human nature to think it is "greener on the other side of the fence," but in the 1980s for thrifts, it was. Thrift managements and boards were understandably envious of the favorable position banks had because the majority of their deposits were interest-free checking accounts that help earnings when loan yields rise in high interest rate environments and that most bank loans had yields that adjusted with interest rate changes. Banks that suffered in 1980 and 1981 were primarily those with large fixed-rate securities portfolios that were "under water" because of the rapid increase in interest rates.

Operating in "greener pastures," though, requires an understanding of how business is done "over there," and even if allowed, asset and loan portfolios cannot be changed overnight. The conglomerates of the 1960s had learned the pitfalls of businesses they did not understand, and their managements and boards generally had better business acumen than those of most thrifts.

The inadequacy of the boards of directors of most thrifts may have been a bigger problem than management shortcomings. Management at least could be, and frequently was, changed or enhanced by knowledgeable outsiders, but boards were turf-oriented, susceptible to bad advice and frequently far overestimated their capabilities.

The origin of the board problem was another example of the good ideas of the past outliving their usefulness. Most thrifts in 1980 were nonstock mutual organizations, and, as a result, the directors did not have a financial stake in the business. Their mutual status also did not attract the most skilled businessmen as directors. A typical thrift board was composed of local politicians, doctors, lawyers, hospital and school executives, pharmacists and the like. They were well-intended, community-oriented individuals, but they often lacked rudimentary business skills. It also was common for representatives of the law firm that handled the thrift's real estate-related business to sit on the board, and they were usually among the most powerful board members.

To make matters worse, most thrift boards did not have a mandatory retirement age. Since most thrift directors were not wealthy and enjoyed the board meetings, there was no incentive to leave the board because of their increasing age. Also, after retirement from their own jobs, they had more time for meetings and the monthly check looked bigger. Unfortunately, as people age they do not become more receptive to change.

One of my first acquaintances with a thrift board in the early 1980s was a prime example of the lack of receptiveness to change. When going in to meet the board of a $1 billion Midwest thrift to discuss strategy options, it was stressed by management that the word "association" not "bank" should be used because the directors were proud of their thrift heritage *and* did not like to be referred to as a bank even though the intent was to become more like a bank. Needless to say, change was not something that board really wanted.

The sophistication of thrift boards varied by size and proximity to major cities, but there were elements of the above in even the largest thrifts. As thrifts got bigger, the directors also were less likely to feel they had to listen to outsiders. When the directors of thrifts of all sizes did listen, the advice they usually took was what they wanted to hear, not what they really needed to do.

It also was inevitable that thrifts would get bad advice mixed in with the good, but what was particularly damaging was that so much of it came from their regulators. The common regulatory theme in advising thrifts in the early stages of the thrift crisis was to grow rapidly with loans and investments other than fixed-rate home mortgages and, in so doing, not to worry about reducing capital as a percent of assets.

This type of bad regulatory advice was personally experienced in the Midwest, but with a different thrift, while sitting through a presentation by a representative of the Bank Board. The advice was the common Bank Board theme at the time of growing rapidly to reduce the amount of low-yielding, fixed-rate home mortgages as a percent of total loans and assets. The Bank Board representative was telling the board of this $400 million thrift with no lending skills beyond home mortgages to make loans they did not understand and further reduce capital as a percent of assets.

This advice not only had the stamp of approval of the regulators, but it was what most thrift directors and managements wanted to hear. Going slow and cutting costs, which would have meant firing employees, was not nearly as pleasant as growth. This board, like many others, also felt they *had* to listen to their regulators, and many of the thrifts had passed the point where they could do anything else.

Conversion Process

Conversion from a mutual to stock form of organization was one of the more interesting side-effects of the response to the financial problems of thrifts in the early 1980s. It provided new capital to replace lost capital; helped support rapid growth; and was a process chosen by a much higher percentage of large thrifts than small ones. It also created merger potential that was profit-driven—an incentive that did not exist as a mutual.

Conversion to stock organizations also subverted the principle that thrifts were owned by their depositors. This caused considerable legal and regulatory machinations since few depositors had any idea that they were "owners," and it was an outdated concept. Depositors were constantly changing, and a depositor of fifty years was technically no more of an owner than the customer that made his initial deposit that very day.

Since the need for capital was so strong for thrifts, most conversion applications were approved by the regulators. The *quid pro quo* was that depositors were given the first opportunity to buy the stock. This began a new investment game that continues to this day of potential investors putting deposits in thrifts they think will convert so that they are assured of being able to buy the stock in the initial public offering.

The conversion process was virtually nonexistent in the 1970s and started slowly in the 1980s, but by the mid-1980s, it had become a mini-industry for lawyers and investment bankers. In the 1970s, the total gross proceeds from public equity offerings in mutual-to-stock conversions were less than $300 million. From 1980 through 1982, a similar amount was raised by converting thrifts in a difficult market. Then from 1983 through 1987 the conversion business exploded and about $7.8 billion was raised of which $5.4 billion was raised in just two years—1983 and 1986.[9]

Converting to a stock organization, though, did not change the board composition or management. The result was stock thrifts with a mutual mentality and investors taking a far greater risk than they imagined. It also meant more mergers and more costly thrift failures.

PSFS

There was no better illustration of the extent of the thrift problem and the solutions tried in the early 1980s than the saga of the nation's oldest thrift, the Philadelphia Savings Fund Society, or PSFS as it was commonly-known. It was the largest banking organization in Philadelphia when measured by deposits; the biggest mutual savings bank in the country; and the fourth largest thrift of any type. At the end of 1980, it had assets of about $7 billion; capital of $424 million, or a healthy 6% of assets; was profitable; and, presumably, had been profitable in most previous years. There were also many previous years since PSFS was founded in 1816.

When interest rates rose sharply and the industry-wide mismatch in the cost of funds and yields occurred, all that history did little for PSFS. It lost about $40 million in 1981 and $124 million in 1982, and its capital had fallen to about 4% of assets.

PSFS's Financial History, 1980 to 1992

Year	Assets	Capital	Net Income	
			Call Report	As Reported
	(in millions)		(in millions)	
1992*	$ 5,026	–	$ (93)	$ (145)
1991	5,975	$ 146	(103)	(61)
1990	6,520	191	(106)	(209)
1989	12,640	304	(91)	(56)
1988	17,172	359	(227)	(210)
1987	19,016	569	(74)	(396)
1986	18,447	970	(18)	23
1985	17,143	954	(13)	65
1984	13,723	894	(12)	72
1983	11,922	823	(22)	26
1982	10,105	428	(124)	(174)
1981	7,424	389	(40)	(33)
1980	7,063	424	12	21

*September 30, 1992.

Source: Meritor call reports and annual reports.

With the assistance of its regulators, PSFS improved its capital base, but at a high price. In 1982, it acquired the failed Western Savings, which prior to its demise was Philadelphia's second largest thrift with assets of about $2 billion. Western Savings added $796 million of goodwill to the PSFS balance sheet that was accompanied by $500 million in capital notes that counted as regulatory capital. By standard accounting practices, the goodwill incurred from the Western Savings purchase had technically made PSFS a failed institution as its goodwill exceeded equity capital, other than the FDIC-issued capital notes, by more than $300 million. This goodwill also would be a future earnings burden as it had to be written off over forty years in equal annual payments that began immediately.

In September 1983, PSFS converted from a mutual to a stock form of organization. This added another $335 million to its capital base, and it also made PSFS marginally solvent by lifting its true equity capital above the amount of goodwill on its books. With these moves, PSFS increased its capital as reported in its annual reports from $424 million in 1980 to $970 million in 1986.

The capital increase was a positive step, but PSFS also followed the thrift growth pattern espoused by the regulators. Between 1980 and 1986, it increased its assets from $7 billion to more than $18 billion, and two years later, its assets were $19 billion. PSFS reported profits between 1983 and 1986, but these were accounting profits that deferred actual losses. PSFS also tried to bury the past by changing its name to Meritor.

This was the thrift rescue game played at the highest level with one of the nation's largest thrifts, and in the immediate post-1982 period, it looked like it might succeed. PSFS was Philadelphia's biggest bank or thrift in 1980 when its troubles started, and by 1986, as Meritor, it was far larger than any local rival. It also was profitable under RAP accounting.

Unfortunately, the PSFS story did not end in 1986. Interest rates started up again in 1987 making its deferred losses harder to defer and the goodwill write-offs overwhelming. In 1987, it restructured its balance sheet and wrote off much of its goodwill and, in so doing, reported a loss of almost $400 million. From 1987 through 1992, PSFS, or Meritor, lost almost $1.1 billion. The losses included the goodwill write-offs, but they also were net of income received from selling assets as it reduced assets from $19 billion at the end of 1987 to $5 billion in 1992.

What happened after 1986 goes beyond the thrift crisis' early stages, but the losses that led to the FDIC closing Meritor in 1992 were partly caused by loan quality problems that accompanied the rapid asset expansion. At the quarter-end prior to being closed, almost 10% of Meritor's assets were not producing revenue.[10]

Meritor's demise also contributed to the consolidation process. It began as the biggest bank of any type in the Philadelphia area, and in the end, all of its Philadelphia area branches were acquired by Mellon, one of Pennsylvania's largest banks. These branches eventually would be sold to a subsidiary of the Royal Bank of Scotland, one of the world's largest banks and one of two large foreign banks that were contributing to the increase in the control of American banking by a small number of very large banks.

Short-term Recovery

Meritor's temporarily improved earnings performance from 1983 through 1986 was typical of the thrift industry, and by 1986, the surface numbers looked quite good. From 1983 through 1985, S&Ls as a group were profitable, albeit using dubious accounting methodologies, and in 1985, the industry's earnings reached $2.6 billion. This was only .26% of average assets, but it was a profit. During this period, S&L assets also grew from $686 billion to almost $1.1 trillion, and about 300 new S&Ls were chartered.

Thrift Income and Expense, 1983 to 1987

Year	Net Income (in millions)	Return on Avg. Assets	Tang. Capital/ Assets
Savings and Loans			
1987	$(7,070)	(.59)%	.7%
1986	(1,472)	(.13)	1.2
1985	2,646	.26	.8
1984	956	.11	.3
1983	1,969	.26	.4
Savings Banks			
1987	$1,924	.79%	7.6%
1986	2,265	1.00	7.3
1985	1,265	.60	5.6
1984	1	–	4.9
1983	(125)	(.07)	5.1

Source: National Council of Savings Institutions, *1988 Factbook of Savings Institutions.*

S&L tangible capital, however, was still less than 1% of assets, and the worst was yet to come. In 1987, the industry lost $7.1 billion. In the next two years, the total loss was $31 billion, but that is a story for a later chapter.[11]

The deteriorating situation also had outrun the ability of the insuring agency to solve the problem without outside assistance. At year-end 1984, FSLIC had reserves of only $5.6 billion to pay off the depositors when an S&L failed while the number of insolvent S&Ls, even under phony RAP accounting, had assets of almost $15 billion. Two years later, the assets of insolvent thrifts were $68 billion.[12]

The mutual savings banks, as a result of higher starting capital and the less forgiving approach of its regulators, performed better. Their renewed profitability continued through 1987, and in 1985, reached 1% of average assets. With an abundance of capital, it seemed likely that these mostly-Northeast institutions would weather round two of the thrift crisis, but they would be exchanging one crisis for another. With a heavy orientation toward real estate and a much expanded exposure to commercial real estate, the mutual savings banks, albeit many of them were no longer mutual, were among the biggest losers in the real estate-driven recession of 1989 through 1992 that devastated banks as well as thrifts.

Thrift Crisis and Interstate Banking

The initial stages of the thrift crisis had helped banks accomplish what they had been trying to do for so many years—crossing state lines with full-service banking. With an entire thrift industry suffering from the mismatch between cost of funds and loan yields, it was extremely difficult, if not impossible, to find thrift buyers for all large failed thrifts, even using capital notes for capital relief as was done when PSFS bought Western Savings. The only alternative to a costly liquidation, in some cases, was a sale to a bank, even if this meant a violation of McFadden Act prohibitions against crossing state lines with full-service banking, or at least nearly full-service banking.

The regulators took this step in 1982, and the recipient of their largesse was Citicorp. It not only assumed the liabilities and good assets of a $2.9 billion failed S&L, but that S&L, Fidelity, was located in one of the country's most attractive banking markets, San Francisco. What Citicorp had been trying to do for fifteen years, cross state lines with traditional banking, became a reality, and this was just the beginning.

Citicorp acquired three more failed thrifts in 1984 through federally-assisted transactions that had combined assets of about $4 billion in other large, attractive markets. In March 1984, it took over Biscayne Federal in Miami and First Federal Savings & Loan in Chicago. In August 1984, it added National Permanent in Washington, DC to its trophy case. In a little over two years, Citicorp had added branch networks in California, Florida, Illinois and the Washington, DC area to its New York base.

These assisted thrift acquisitions by Citicorp revived the concerns of the early 1970s of a New York domination of American banking. Small banks and state bank associations had to accept the *fait accompli*, but the early 1980s thrift acquisitions by Citicorp had the dual effect of making large regional banks in other states want the same opportunity to cross state lines, yet limit further expansion by the big New York banks.

The primary impact of the early stages of the thrift crisis on bank consolidation was the sale of these four S&Ls to Citicorp and the incentive that it provided for interstate banking. Three of those four S&Ls were among the 35 largest in the country in 1980, and First Federal Savings and Loan of Chicago was the ninth largest.

Countering these Citicorp acquisitions was the rapid asset growth of the S&Ls after 1982 that temporarily had reduced the bank share of total assets and deposits. This increased S&L share, though, was a "bubble" and only the beginning of the thrift crisis. The worst was yet to come.

Trouble in the Oil Patch

T he thrift crisis and interstate banking were the headline stories of the 1980s, but for impact on consolidation, they had to share the stage with the troubles in the oil patch. During these years, a sharp drop in oil prices and a small rogue bank in Oklahoma City were catalysts that forced eight of the country's forty largest banks to be sold. Of these eight, four are now part of Bank of America; three were bought directly, or indirectly, by JPMorgan and its Chemical predecessor; and the eighth is now Wells Fargo's Texas franchise.

The problems in the oil patch, though, were far more than just a big bank problem. In Texas, 425 banks failed in the 1980s, and, in the latter part of the decade, nine of its ten largest banks either failed or were sold in anticipation of possible failure. In 1988 alone, 175 Texas banks failed with assets of $47 billion, which was 25% of the state's banking assets at the end of the preceding year.[1]

This was in stark contrast to the 1970s and early 1980s when there seemed to be no limits as to how high the Texas banks could go and oil was a source of wealth, not disaster. When most banks were worrying about the negative impact of oil-driven high interest rates on deposit inflow, banks in Texas, and throughout the Southwest, were prospering. They may have been hobbled by state laws that prohibited branching, but when an economy does well, banks benefit, and the high oil prices that drove up the interest rates in the late 1970s and into the early 1980s, created a strong economic environment in markets dominated by the oil-and-gas industry.

Texas and its two largest cities, Dallas and Houston, were the major beneficiaries of this oil "boom," but times were also good in Denver, Tulsa, Oklahoma City and other oil-and-gas centers. Oil patch millionaires were seemingly created overnight; their status embellished by two top-rated TV soap operas, *Dynasty* and *Dallas*; and the region's banks, particularly those in Texas, were rapidly rising up among the ranks of the nation's largest. At the time, there seemed to be no end in sight for the oil patch, its millionaires or its banks.

This "go-go" reputation was something Texas and Oklahoma bankers relished. It was a different world, and just how different was hard for those who did not live or work there to imagine. My first taste of this "go-go" attitude came in 1979 with a call from a small bank in suburban Houston. Its CEO wanted to meet soon and was thinking about lunch the next day. He did not see why I could not catch a morning flight out of Washington and fly back that night. With this "get it done fast" attitude at a very conservative, small Texas bank, it was not hard to envision the big bank Texas lending culture of that era.

Unfortunately, a "go-go" attitude cannot totally change business cycle patterns, and it may be a bit of a cliché to say that "what goes up must come down," but much to the dismay of the oil patch, this applied to oil prices, the local economy and the fortunes of local banks. Oil prices rose from $2.75 per barrel in 1973 to almost $37 per barrel in 1981 and then fell to $10 in 1986.[2] The oil patch economy and bank profits followed the oil prices in the downward slide.

When oil prices were at their peak in 1980, there were 1,467 Texas banks that, collectively, were highly profitable, and they only had to make modest contributions of just over $300 million to loan loss reserves. These were good times for the oil-and-gas industry and Texas banks, and over the next five years, the number of banks increased by about 500.

Texas Banking Statistics, 1980 to 1990

Year	Number of Banks	Pre-tax Operating Income	Contribution To Reserves
		(in millions)	
1990	1,184	$757	$885
1989	1,318	(646)	2,337
1988	1,501	(2,032)	2,714
1987	1,772	(2,757)	3,566
1986	1,972	(1,706)	3,471
1985	1,936	948	1,921
1984	1,854	1,455	1,338
1980	1,467	na	318

Source: FDIC, Historical Statistics on Banking.

In 1986, when oil prices hit bottom, the number of banks in Texas peaked, and the earnings and loan loss contributions were telling a different story. The annual $318 million loan loss reserve contribution of 1980 had grown to almost $3.5 billion, and the combined pretax net operating loss was $1.7 billion. In the next three years, Texas banks would lose over $5 billion on a pretax basis, and by 1990, the number of banks was reduced by about 800, or 40%. These were not the expectations of the Texas bankers.

The extent of this banking disaster in Texas and the contiguous states of Arkansas, Louisiana, New Mexico and Oklahoma was well-documented and succinctly summarized in the FDIC's *History of the Eighties: Lessons for the Future*, which at the beginning of its chapter on *Banking Problems in the Southwest* stated that "of the total failure-resolution costs borne by the FDIC from 1986 to 1994, half ($15.3 billion) was accounted for by southwestern bank failures. This included losses of nearly $6.3 billion in 1988 and $5.1 billion in 1989—91.1% and 82%, respectively, of total FDIC failure-resolution costs for those two years. From 1987 through 1989, 71% of the banks that failed in the United States were southwestern banks (491 out of 689), and so were some of the most significant failures such as banks within the First City Bancorporation, First RepublicBank Corporation and M-Corp holding companies."[3]

The area's banking problems went beyond the banks. The Southwest was one of the areas hit hardest by the S&L crisis, which is chronicled in chapter nine. Texas, alone, would account for almost 30% of the federal expenditures for solving the S&L crisis.[4]

Republic Bank

The rapid rise, and subsequent fall, of the large Texas banks was epitomized by the fortunes of one of its biggest, Republic. This Dallas-based institution was founded in 1920 and had become the largest bank in the state by 1948, but was still small by national standards.[5] In 1960, it barely made it into the top 100 nationwide, but was helped by being in a state with a rapidly-growing economy. Even though Republic could not open branches because of Texas banking laws, by 1970, it had become one of the fifty biggest banks in the nation. By 1980, it had formed a holding company, and, in that year, Republic took advantage of a change in Texas banking law that allowed the intrastate acquisition of banks by acquiring Houston National Bank.

With this acquisition, Republic had become a force in both of Texas' largest cities, Dallas and Houston, and by 1984, it was the 19th largest bank holding company in the country, and the fifth largest not based in New York, California or Illinois. The aura of invincibility, though, was gone, and four years later, Republic was part of one of the largest failures in American banking history.

Even as its fortunes diminished, Republic would continue to rise in the rankings. A desperation-driven merger in 1987 with the second largest Texas bank, InterFirst, to form First RepublicBank Corporation would make it the country's 13th largest bank holding company. This, though, was the combining of banks with similar problems in a deteriorating economy, and it was the end for both banks. Republic is best remembered as the federally-assisted sale to NCNB that highlighted the disappearance of big-time Texas banks *and* the vehicle that allowed NCNB to become more than a regional bank—and more on that later.

Penn Square Bank

The oil patch did not have to wait for the price of oil to drop sharply to create problems for the banking industry nor did all the damage start in Texas. Oil was still king when little Penn Square Bank in Oklahoma City was sowing the seeds that would lead to the failures of two large banks far removed from the area and threaten the viability of one of New York City's largest, Chase Manhattan. Its failure in 1982 took place a few years before the oil-and-gas industry collapsed and there was widespread concern about the viability of the big Texas banks, but it was a reminder of the downside of the oil-and-gas industry—a downside that had brought us the Teapot Dome scandal in the 1920s and would give us Enron in 2002.

The Penn Square saga began quietly enough in 1975 when William Jennings bought a small bank in Oklahoma City's Penn Square Shopping Center with $2.5 million borrowed from a local bank and little equity.[6] At the time, the bank had assets of $46 million and capital of $4 million, and even at its peak in 1981, its assets were only $436 million. Size, however, did not constrain its lending.

What Jennings did with Penn Square was sell the glamour and high yields of its speculative oil-and-gas industry loans to banks in other parts of the country that were starved for high-yielding loans in an environment that had seen the cost of funds reach record levels. Penn Square's strategy was to make loans to oil-and-gas companies far beyond its legal lending limit and then participate those loans out to large banks around the country. The large banks included Continental, SeaFirst and Chase Manhattan, and the reputation of the participating banks became an endorsement of the quality of the loans. Unfortunately, the partner banks seemed to have done inadequate checking on their own.[7]

In the late 1970s, Penn Square accelerated its lending, and it did not have to do much marketing. As a source of much-desired high-yielding loans, it could off-load virtually every loan it made. This reduced the incentive for Penn Square loan officers to do their homework and paperwork on the loans they were making. This style of lending could only go on so long, and in 1982, Penn Square collapsed.

Without its many loan participants, the collapse of a still small bank in Oklahoma would have been a local story. It became a major story when some of the upstream banks had losses relating to Penn Square that ran into the hundreds of millions of dollars. Chase Manhattan, Continental and Seafirst were hit the hardest, and, in the case of Continental, it had about $1 billion in Penn Square-originated loans.[8]

Chase Manhattan was large enough to survive with only its reputation impaired, but SeaFirst and Continental were not so fortunate. The Seattle-based SeaFirst was the largest bank in Washington and 28th largest in the country, but the Penn Square-related losses were sufficient to force its sale to BankAmerica. Continental, the sixth largest bank in the country and the largest in the Midwest, did not immediately succumb to its Penn Square problems, but the damage to its reputation was more than it could handle, and in 1984, the FDIC was forced to rescue it with a $4.5 billion bail-out. This was, and remains, the nation's most expensive bank rescue.[9]

Continental, like Bank of the Commonwealth and First Pennsylvania before it, never recovered from its FDIC bail-out. It was totally eclipsed in the Chicago market by its long time rival, First National Bank of Chicago, and by 1990, it was not only no longer one of the ten largest banks in the country, but it did not even make the top twenty-five. In 1994, Continental, like SeaFirst before it, was acquired by BankAmerica.

Penn Square may have done more to further bank consolidation than any bank, big or small, in the country, and it might even be argued that its impact on consolidation rivaled that of the thrift crisis. Bringing down the biggest banks in Illinois and Washington and causing each to become part of BankAmerica was no small feat.

Continental

The failure and subsequent FDIC bail-out of Continental was a result of the Penn Square loans, but it also reflected the aggressive lending attitude of Continental and a general laxness of the regulatory system at the time.

Continental was looking for a Penn Square as much as Penn Square was looking for Continental.

In the late 1970s, Continental became an extremely aggressive lender. Between 1976 and 1981, commercial loans not secured by real estate grew from about $5 billion to more than $14 billion. This made it the nation's largest commercial lender and helped lift its assets from $21 to $45 billion. By more than doubling its size in five years, its growth was much faster than that of any of the other national banking leaders.

Ten Largest Bank's Asset and Loan Growth, 1976 to 1981

Bank	Assets		C&I Loans*		Annual Asset Growth
	1981	1976	1981	1976	1976–
	(in billions)				1981
1. Bank of America	$119	$73	$12.1	$7.1	10.6%
2. Citibank	105	62	12.5	7.7	11.3
3. Chase Manhattan	77	45	10.0	9.2	11.4
4. Manufacturers Han.	55	30	9.5	4.4	12.8
5. Morgan Guaranty	54	29	5.6	3.1	13.5
6. Continental	45	21	14.3	5.1	16.1
7. Chemical	45	26	10.8	4.7	11.6
8. Bankers Trust	33	22	5.2	3.1	8.7
9. First Nat'l.-Chicago	33	19	5.6	4.0	11.8
10. Security Pacific	31	16	5.9	2.5	13.5

*Commercial and Industrial loans not secured by real estate.
Source: FDIC, History of the Eighties—Lessons for the Future, page 237.

As is so often the case, rapid growth was greeted with more praise than concern, which can add to the desire to grow rapidly. In response to a question at a meeting I attended relative to how he anticipated where the next big bank problem might occur—William J. Seidman, who headed the FDIC for a tumultuous seven years starting in 1985—answered all too correctly in words to the effect of "I would just check to see who was last year's banker of the year."

Continental fit this role. According to the FDIC's *History of the Eighties-Lesson for the Future*, "Continental's management, the bank's aggressive growth strategy and its returns were lauded both by the market and by industry analysts. A 1978 article in *Duns Review* pronounced the bank one of the top five companies in the nation; and an analyst at First Boston Corp. praised Continental, noting that it had 'superior management at the top, and its management is very deep;'" (and) in 1981, a Salomon Brothers analyst echoed this sentiment, calling Continental 'one of the finest money center banks going.'"[10]

By late 1981, Continental's luster had started to erode. Its second quarter earnings declined, and some large credit gambles were going awry. Among others, it had a $200 million loan to a nearly bankrupt International Harvester. It also was a major participant in loans to developing countries, the infamous LDCs that were a major problem for money center and large California banks in the 1970s and 1980s.[11]

Continental's slide had begun, and with $1 billion in loans from Penn Square that failed in July 1982, it was no longer an investor favorite. Its stock price dropped by more than 60% the month the Penn Square failure was announced.

A bigger problem, though, was the depositors. As a money center bank in a state that allowed only token branching, Continental's local core deposits were only a small part of its deposit base. Thus, it had to buy deposits across the country and even in foreign countries. This was bought money with above-average costs, and, with the lack of confidence instilled by the Penn Square failure, Continental's ability to find new funding was made more difficult and the cost of funds increased significantly. As its troubles mounted, it was only a matter of time before there would be a "run" on deposits, and this threat was increased by the type of depositors it had and their ability to use electronic transfers to withdraw deposits.[12]

The "run" began in earnest in the spring of 1984, and the FDIC had to find a buyer, put in sufficient federal funds to keep Continental operating or let it fail. Continental's problems were so severe that there were no buyers, and its salability also was hindered by its lack of a branch network. The only options were a bailout or failure, and Continental was deemed "too big to fail," a concept that was to stir a lot of controversy. This left only the bailout option, and in 1984, the FDIC bought its bad loans and inserted new capital at a total cost of about $4.5 billion.[13]

Texas Bank Collapse

Penn Square and Continental were precursors of things to come in the oil country. The "go-go" banking Penn Square carried to an extreme was still in effect after Penn Square failed, and it had spread beyond the oil-and-gas industry. Dallas, Houston and a host of other cities in the Southwest were growing at a rapid pace, and one result was that commercial real estate loans became a major lending emphasis of the area's big banks—a focus reinforced by the still-existing prohibition against branching.

The problems of the big Texas banks also were complicated by some typical board reactions. Bank boards do not like to lose market share, and for Dallas and Houston banks, a natural response was to push their lenders to make more oil-and-gas and commercial real estate loans.[14] Much of this pressure was based on a widely-held belief that the price of oil would go as high as $60 per barrel.

A price of $60 per barrel was excessive, but this was an economic "boom" built on oil price expectations, and when oil prices fell, an economic collapse was inevitable. Oil-and-gas may have been a great business in 1981 when the price of oil was close to $37 per barrel, but it was a disaster at $10 in 1986. As went oil, so went commercial real estate and banking. Between 1980 and 1987, office vacancy rates in Dallas rose from 8% to 17%, and in Houston they went from 11% to 37%.[15]

Republic was not alone in riding this wave of oil prosperity and the resulting optimism into the upper ranks of American banking. In 1984, Republic and four other Texas bank holding companies—Texas Commerce, InterFirst, M-Corp, the holding company name for Houston's Mercantile Bank, and First City—were the nation's fastest growing large banks and ranked among the country's twenty-five largest. They were larger than NCNB, Bank One or any of the superregionals that were to become such familiar names. Even Allied Bank, the sixth largest Texas bank, was bigger than Bank One.

At the time, it seemed as if nothing could stop these banks, and that interstate banking was likely to spread the reach of these Texas institutions throughout the South and West. With the close banking links between banks in Texas and Chicago, a move in that direction also seemed possible.

A year later, the Texas economy collapsed, dousing the dreams of the state's banks in a torrent of nonperforming loans and red ink. Republic and InterFirst tried to survive through the cost savings of an ill-fated equal merger. Texas Commerce and Allied were sold to large out-of-state banks while they were still technically viable organizations—Texas Commerce to

Chemical and Allied to California-based First Interstate. For the Republic-InterFirst combination, referred to hereafter as First RepublicBank, First City and M-Corp, the outcome was far worse.

Largest Texas Banks, 1984

Bank	Assets (in bill.)	National Rank	Outcome	Eventual Owner
1. InterFirst*	$22	18	Failed	Bank of America
2. Republic*	22	19	Failed	Bank of America
3. Texas Commerce	21	21	Sold	JPMorgan
4. M-Corp	21	22	Failed	Bank of America
5. First City	17	24	Failed	JPMorgan
6. Allied	10	36	Sold	Wells Fargo
7. Texas American	6	63	Failed	JPMorgan
8. Cullen Frost	3	–	As is	Cullen Frost
9. National Bancsh.	3	–	Failed	Bank of America
10. BancTexas	2	–	Failed	Various

Republic and InterFirst merged in 1987.
Source: American Banker, March 19, 1985

Despite the collapse, out-of-state banks were still enamored with the long-term potential of Texas, and the struggling Texas banks did not lack for buyers before or after failing. Chemical and First Interstate took their chances early-on with the 1987 and 1988 acquisitions of Texas Commerce and Allied Bank, respectively, without federal assistance and, for awhile, they may have questioned their wisdom in doing so. Time, though, proved their acquisitions to have been good ones. NCNB made the biggest move by acquiring First RepublicBank from the FDIC in a tax incentive-laden 1989 deal that cost taxpayers $3.9 billion. Bank One would follow suit later that year with its assisted purchase of M-Corp, which, although only half the size of First RepublicBank, resulted in a public outlay of $2.8 billion.[16]

First City, which was the fifth largest bank in Texas when the deluge began, was the first large Texas bank to need federal assistance, albeit it was the last to surrender its Texas' roots. It was taken over by an investor group in April 1988 with FDIC-assistance, which meant it kept its name and was still a Texas bank, but this just delayed the inevitable. Without the help of a larger bank, First City, found itself back looking for federal assistance again, and in 1993, First City was sold in parts with the majority going to Chemical and its Texas Commerce subsidiary.

BankAmerica did not acquire any of the leading banks in Texas as it had its own problems with LDC loans, but it was not left completely out of the Texas sell-off. By 1990, its financial condition had improved, and it added $3.7 billion in assets in the assisted purchase of Sunbelt Savings. In 1993, it added $6.9 billion assets when it acquired First Gibraltar, the largest Texas S&L. First Gibraltar, or Gibraltar as it was then called, also was the largest thrift in Texas in 1982, and would merge with the third largest, First Texas, in the mid-1980s.

First City

It would be the NCNB rescue of First RepublicBank that would be the most noteworthy of the big Texas bank failures as it was the biggest bank in the state. This was a key, if not *the* key, step in NCNB's rise to a lead position in the American banking structure, but the uniqueness and double-failing of First City was an equally important part of what was happening in Texas at the time. The alternative to an assisted sale to a larger banking organization was investor capital, and, if available, even if it meant losing control, was often more attractive to those in charge of the failing bank in that it might preserve more jobs and reduce the embarrassment locally by maintaining a headquarters in the home city. First City took this route, which resulted in a continuing, and unpleasant saga that ran for a few years.

First City, like all of the large Texas banks, was slipping fast in 1987, and in the middle of the year, it approached the FDIC with a request for what was called open bank assistance. This, in essence, was providing the same relief with an investor group relative to bad loans and investor claims that would be given to a bank acquirer in an assisted merger. An outside investor group headed by A. Robert Abboud, the former chief executive of First National Bank of Chicago, was proposing a plan that would inject $500 million in new capital into First City through a stock offering. Abboud was well-connected and well-respected, and in September 1987, the FDIC gave First City and Abboud the go-ahead with a March 1988 deadline to complete the transaction.[17]

Raising the funds proved to be more difficult than Abboud expected, particularly since a month after getting the go-ahead, the stock market had its biggest one-day drop ever. This "spooked" investors, and there also was the problem of getting existing shareholders and bondholders to go along with considerable loss to their original investment. As of March 1989, the money had not yet been raised, and First City was much closer to failing.[18]

The FDIC granted the Abboud group another month, and during that time the imminent demise of First RepublicBank, the state's largest bank had become more apparent, which helped get the deal done as it became quite clear that if nothing was done, all would be lost. In April, Abboud and his investors put in $500 million in new capital, which gave them control, and the FDIC provided a note for $970 million dollars that would also serve as capital. In return, the FDIC received warrants that could at a later date give it 15% of the common stock.[19]

Unfortunately, that was not the end of the story. After some initial success, First City's began to slide downward again, and in 1990, it had a loss of $180 million. In early 1991, the First City board replaced Abboud as chief executive, but that did little to halt the downward drift, and in 1991, the loss was $252 million. By early 1992, it was obvious that First City was going to fail for a second time. At the end of October, the FDIC effectively took control of the First City banks, and in November, the holding company filed for bankruptcy protection.[20]

In January 1993, the FDIC announced the sale of the First City banks to twelve different financial institutions, but Chemical's subsidiary, Texas Commerce, got by far the lion's share. Its portion included the Dallas and Houston banks and 73% of the assets.[21] Because of the improved banking climate in 1993, the FDIC was able to get out of this second failure of First City with no additional losses, but its total loss attributable to First City over the entire period was $1.1 billion.[22]

NCNB-First RepublicBank

First RepublicBank did not stay in the headlines for nearly as long as First City, but it was the "poster-boy" for the Texas bank collapse. It was not only the biggest bank in Texas to fail, but it was also the largest American bank to fail and the most costly resolution for the FDIC for a failed bank at $3.9 billion.[23] Continental cost the FDIC $4.5 billion, but that Chicago bank was "rescued" and never actually failed.

The NCNB federally-assisted takeover of the bank subsidiaries of First RepublicBank also was the first large assisted bank transaction done with tax incentives, and it moved NCNB into the top tier of American banks. Prior to this purchase, NCNB was the nation's 18th largest bank with assets of $28.6 billion. It was smaller than Shawmut, First Fidelity and even First RepublicBank and only slightly larger than First Union and Sovran. After the transaction was done, NCNB was the seventh biggest bank in the country.

NCNB had been one of the most aggressive regional banks for some time. In the 1970s, it was a leader among banks in crossing state lines with nonbank acquisitions. Then when limited interstate banking was permitted in the 1980s, its expansion focused on the Southeast, particularly on Florida. It increased its assets from $7.2 billion in 1980 to almost $29 billion in 1988 through a series of mid-level Florida bank acquisitions— Ellis Banking, Pan American Banks, Exchange Bancorporation and Gulfstream Banks—along with the purchase of South Carolina's second largest bank, Bankers Trust.

These acquisitions made NCNB the biggest bank in the Southeast, but it did not have the capacity to easily absorb the purchase of a failed bank the size of First RepublicBank. Citicorp and Wells Fargo also were on the short list of likely buyers and Citicorp had significant size advantages.[24] BankAmerica likely would have been on that list as well if it was not temporarily side-lined by LDC problems.

The appeal of Texas and its growing list of troubled banks had caught the attention of NCNB management as early as 1986, but it was not likely that they were thinking as big as First RepublicBank at that time. In 1986, NCNB had invested $6 million in Charter Bank of Houston and had used the Charter base to acquire a failed Houston Bank, which gave it a 40% ownership of a $500 million Texas bank. This small acquisition put NCNB in Texas and gave it a familiarity with the FDIC sale process.

Going from a $500 million acquisition to the purchase of a $33 billion bank bigger than itself was a big step, and NCNB had neither the capital nor ability to raise the funds to pull off such a transaction. These were obstacles, but they did not prove to be insurmountable.

NCNB and its CEO, Hugh McColl, in particular, saw First RepublicBank as a unique opportunity and were determined to give it a try. Giving it a try meant convincing the FDIC that NCNB provided it the best of all worlds in solving one of its biggest headaches—i.e., the expertise to handle the bad loans and running First RepublicBank at the least cost for the FDIC. Because of its size, this would require the FDIC to become a partner and let NCNB buy it on a "pay as you go" basis with a key element being able to use the accumulated losses as future tax deductions against bank earnings.[25]

The resolution of the FDIC's First RepublicBank problem was much faster than that of First City, which partly reflected the size, but also the timing. The FDIC had to move on First RepublicBank in March 1988, six months later than it started the process with First City, and the numbers were getting worse for the Texas banks as each quarter ended.

NCNB was particularly aggressive and innovative. The keys to its eventual success were two rulings from the internal revenue service that NCNB would receive approximately $1 billion in tax benefits if it acquired First RepublicBank. In essence, it was told that it could acquire First RepublicBank in a tax-free exchange and carry forward the losses from the failed organization to offset future income. This allowed NCNB to bid higher than others since the others did not realize this potential benefit— and the FDIC chose not to tell them on the basis of all bidders' information being confidential.[26]

What NCNB was proposing was to acquire 20% of about $25 billion in acceptable assets for $210 million and manage a pool of about $5 billion in bad assets that technically would still belong to the FDIC. It would buy the other 80% from the FDIC over time out of the tax loss carry-forwards that First RepublicBank had accumulated; would legally be protected from suits or damages connected with First RepublicBank's past; and would get a small percentage on any gains realized in the reduction of the pool of bad assets.

Acquiring $25 billion of good banking assets for about $1 billion of which all but $210 million could come out of tax credits sounded too good to be true. The FDIC did not immediately jump at this arrangement and continued to discuss other rescue opportunities with Citicorp, Wells Fargo and a group associated with First RepublicBank management group. It may have had internal doubts as to whether NCNB could really pull this off, but this also was procedural.

In the end, those concerns did not ultimately deter the FDIC, which accepted NCNB's proposal as being the least costly to the taxpayers, and, in no small part, this was the result of a sales effort by McColl and others in the NCNB team as to their ability to make this work. It proved to be a correct call on the FDIC's part, and NCNB, overnight, became the biggest bank in Texas and one of the ten largest in the country.

Bank One-M-Corp

The FDIC was through with large Texas rescues for 1988, but 1989 was to bring one more to the table, M-Corp, the holding company for the Mercantile banks in Texas. As 1988 began, it was the second largest bank holding company in Texas with assets of about $29 billion, and it had been losing money since the fourth quarter of 1986. It avoided joining First City and First RepublicBank as FDIC wards in the spring of 1988, through the sale of technology and consumer lending subsidiaries that netted some $400 million in cash.[27] These moves, however, were only buying time.

By late 1988, the FDIC was actively involved with "supervising" M-Corp's activities, and in March 1989, the closing and subsequent sale process began. Among the bidders were NCNB, the recapitalized First City, Chemical and Bank One.[28] For NCNB and First City, this raised antitrust competitive concerns and raised questions about just how much "bad bank" business they could handle. For Chemical that already had taken over Texas Commerce, there was the competitive overlap consideration. Bank One was the obvious choice.

In June 1989, the FDIC agreed to a deal with Bank One that had a total resolution cost of $2.8 billion and hoped it had closed the door on rescuing large Texas banks.[29] Unfortunately, it had not seen the last of First City.

The Oil Patch Legacy

The impact of the problems in the oil patch on the consolidation of banking and its contribution to interstate banking are impressive. Of the forty largest banks in 1982, eight were forced to sell or were sold by the FDIC because of oil patch-related problems.

Penn Square's collapse alone took down two of them. The largest bank in the state of Washington, SeaFirst, was sold to BankAmerica in a 1983 assisted transaction. The sale of Continental was slower in coming, but its need to sell began with the bad Penn Square loans, and in 1994, ten years after being rescued by the FDIC, it also was bought by BankAmerica.

The other six were casualties of the decline in oil prices in the mid-1980s and the resulting collapse of Texas real estate values. The two largest Texas banks, Republic and InterFirst, after their merger and subsequent failure had become part of NCNB. Chemical bought Texas Commerce and most of First City, numbers three and five; Bank One acquired M-Corp from the FDIC; and First Interstate bought Allied Bank.

Two of the other failed top ten Texas banks that ranked seventh and ninth, Texas American and National Bancshares, also ended up as part of major out-of-state acquirers. Texas American's franchise was sold to Bank One, and, as a result, would eventually be part of the JPMorgan franchise. The nine of the twelve National Bancshares banks sold to NCNB belong to Bank of America. Cullen Frost in San Antonio, the ninth largest bank in Texas in 1986, was the only top ten bank in the state to survive.

Although not of the same importance to the consolidation process as the disappearance of eight of the forty largest banks in the country, the three Texas S&Ls that ranked among the country's forty largest S&Ls in 1982 also were sold during this period. As will be described in more detail in a later chapter, the 22nd ranked Gibraltar acquired the 40th ranked First Texas in 1987 and changed its name to First Gibraltar, and then it, too, was bought by BankAmerica in 1993. The 31st ranked University Savings failed in 1989, and its branches were acquired by NCNB.

These sales made Bank of America and JPMorgan the big winners in the oil patch banking disaster and gave Wells Fargo its stake in Texas. Directly or indirectly, Bank of America ended up with the two largest banks in Texas, Republic and InterFirst; the ninth largest, National Bancshares; and the state's three largest thrifts. JPMorgan, on its own, albeit it was called Chemical at the time, bought the third largest bank, Texas Commerce, and most of the fourth largest in the state, First City, and then through the acquisition of Bank One, inherited the fifth and seventh largest Texas banks, M-Corp and Texas American. When the original Wells Fargo bought First Interstate in 1996, it also bought the Allied Bank franchise.

The impact of these moves on consolidation also went beyond just what was acquired. Republic, InterFirst and Texas Commerce were likely to have become major players in interstate expansion, and their forced sale eliminated potential rivals to the five banks that now dominate American banking. In 1984, in fact, the three leading Texas banks seemed likely, or even more likely, to be major players in the interstate banking expansion and consolidation than NCNB, First Union, Bank One or Norwest.

Interstate Banking Gathers Momentum

B y the late 1970s, even before there were thrift and oil patch crises, there was a growing sense of the inevitability of interstate banking, but that "inevitability" always was at least a couple of years away and without good answers as to how the protectionist attitude toward small banks would be overcome. As technology improved and ATMs proliferated, it was totally illogical that in a business as important as banking a state line would decide whether a bank could maximize its ability to provide optimum service. Logic, though, often comes in a distant second when the protection of local businesses is the prime obstacle whether it is banking, steel or the benefits of free trade.

For one living in the Washington area, state line constraints seemed particularly ludicrous as the central city and its two main suburban areas, the Maryland suburbs and Northern Virginia, were three different banking markets, each with its own set of banks. A customer working in Washington and living in the suburbs could not use the same bank where he or she worked *and* lived. Even the area's one bank holding company with multi-state coverage, First American, had to operate its banks totally independent of each other in the different political jurisdictions.

Prior to 1982, the inevitability of interstate banking also was more of an intellectual argument than an actual movement. The large New York banks, particularly Citicorp, and regional banks such as NCNB were pushing the concept, but there was little support in most state legislatures or state banking associations. There was a real concern at the time that interstate banking would lead to the takeover of banking in small states by the big banks in New York and California and, to a lesser extent, Texas.

In this hostile environment, if interstate banking was to become a reality, it was going to have to take a backdoor approach and probably with the courts playing a major role. It was a classic "David versus Goliath" battle, and the votes in this battle were, at least initially, for the combatant with the sling shot.

By 1982, three areas of vulnerability to the interstate banking barriers had surfaced, and each was to play a major role in its undoing. The most obvious was a growing thrift crisis accompanied by large thrift failures that would force their regulators to look to out-of-state banks and/or thrifts as buyers to minimize the negative impact on the deposit insurance funds. This happened in December 1982, when Citicorp was permitted to buy a large, failed thrift in San Francisco. Not so obvious, but also destined to play major roles were NCNB's mid-1970s acquisition of a Florida trust company, and Maine opening its doors to out-of-state bank acquisitions in 1975.

The oil patch problems in the Southwest also had interstate banking implications as early as 1982, but the impact was muted by geography. The regulators had little choice but to approve the sale of a failing SeaFirst, the largest bank in the state of Washington and a Penn Square casualty, to BankAmerica on an "emergency" basis. With both seller and buyer being West Coast banks, though, this acquisition did not have the same impact on the interstate banking battle that was being played out primarily on the East Coast of a Citicorp buying out-of-state thrifts even if the acquired thrift also was on the West Coast.

Citicorp was the source of most local bank fears, and it was on the East Coast that the initial interstate banking battles would be fought. The West Coast was more receptive from the beginning, and in much of the Midwest, banks were still battling to get in-state branching.

NCNB's Florida Incursion

If one event stood out above all others in pushing aside the interstate barriers in 1982, it was NCNB using a previously acquired trust company to buy its way into traditional banking in Florida. This was an unforeseen fortuitous circumstance being used to change the direction of an industry. Without NCNB's early 1970s acquisition of a small trust company in Florida, interstate banking might have been delayed for several years in the Southeast and elsewhere.

If interstate banking had been delayed, NCNB would not have had the size to buy the failed Republic and InterFirst banks in Texas, and without these purchases, it is unlikely that there would be a Bank of America based in Charlotte today. NCNB might have found other stepping stones, but the path would have been more difficult and the end result would have looked more like today's Wachovia than the trillion dollar plus Bank of America.

In the 1970s, NCNB, however, *did* buy the Trust Company of Florida as part of its effort to cross state lines with nonbank acquisitions. It would have liked to expand across state lines with traditional banking as well, but this was long before that type of expansion was possible. A trust company, though, was a natural extension of a nonbank strategy even if the trust company technically had to have a bank charter to operate.

How much of a role chance can play in an industry altering event was evidenced by this trust company acquisition. In his biography of Hugh McColl, Ross Yockey provided some relevant dialogue to this point as this acquisition took place even without the chairman and CEO at the time, Tom Storrs, being there. According to Yockey:

"Hugh McColl (an EVP at the time) was in the middle of a discussion in Luther Hodge's office when Bill Dougherty (NCNB's president) came in and told them about the Orlando opportunity. Dougherty had just got off the telephone with a former associate who was now CEO of Pittsburgh National Bank. He told them, 'This guy wants to know if we are interested in buying a little trust company down in Florida.'

'How much money is it losing?' McColl wanted to know.

'No, no, it's not that,' Dougherty protested. 'It seems he forgot to ask his board if he could buy it and now they want him to get rid of it. He says he will sell it to us at cost. And Mr. Storrs (NCNB's chairman) is out of town.'

McColl and Hodges (also an EVP) looked at each other.

'Why not?' asked McColl.

'Sure,' Hodges agreed. 'Go ahead and buy it.'

So Dougherty bought it. The Trust Company of Florida had only $35 million in assets, pocket change to a bank like theirs, but it might get larger someday, especially with Walt Disney building that new tourist attraction down there."[1]

For better or worse, NCNB had acquired an entry vehicle into Florida banking, but it is unlikely in 1972 anyone fully realized the magnitude of this possibility. In fact, a couple of years later when NCNB was struggling with real estate problems, some of its executives suggested selling the trust company.[2]

Trust Company of Florida may not have been a traditional bank, but even in 1972 its purchase by an out-of-state bank raised a few hackles down in Florida, and legislation was subsequently passed to keep other out-of-state banks from doing the same thing. As time would show, the legislation did not keep out-of-state banks already there from expanding throughout the state via traditional bank mergers.

In 1981, NCNB decided to see if it could take advantage of this legal opening and use its trust company presence to buy one of Florida's bigger banks. It talked to most, if not all, large banks in the state and was most enthused about the possibility of buying the $2.5 billion asset Florida National Bank in Jacksonville. The major impediment was getting this bank, and presumably other large banks as well, to agree to a merger not knowing if the legislative loophole that NCNB was counting on to get a merger approved would materialize.[3]

To remove this uncertainty, NCNB reached an agreement with the owners of First National Bank of Lake City, Florida, a bank with assets of about $30 million. This was to be NCNB's test case to see if it could get Federal Reserve approval of a bank acquisition in Florida based on its trust operation. In December 1981, the Lake City acquisition was approved and the deal was closed on January 8, 1982. NCNB was finally in the traditional banking business in Florida and able to buy other Florida banks.

Even with this approval, NCNB was unable to convince any of the larger Florida banks to accept an offer to be acquired; but before 1982 was over, it had bought two mid-sized banks, Gulfstream Banks in Boca Raton and Exchange Bancorporation in Tampa. By year-end 1982, NCNB had Florida assets of almost $2 billion and had become the state's seventh largest bank; and this was only the beginning. It was a major player in Florida and had at least a couple of years' head-start on other out-of-state banks.

NCNB's success in Florida could have been an isolated event with minimal effect on the consolidation process, but it had an impact on the thinking of other banks that went far beyond its increased size in the state. The leading banks in the Southeast were both delighted with and envious of NCNB's Florida moves, and, as a result, they became much more proactive in supporting legislative change in favor of interstate banking. It was a "breach in the dike," and the urgency of going further was building.

The Maine Event

Meanwhile, at the far other end of the East Coast in Maine, a second 1982 interstate merger announcement would open the door to interstate banking even further. Maine was an unlikely place for a major interstate event to occur, since unlike California and Florida where Citicorp and NCNB had made their moves, it was not on the wish list of many banks. Maine's primary interest to bank acquirers was more likely to have been the scenery and second homes rather than banking. The old political adage of "as goes Maine, so goes Vermont" would pretty much sum up the out-of-state banking interest.

In fact, Maine had opened its doors to out-of-state banks as early as 1975 when it passed a law allowing out-of-state banks the right to buy banks in

Maine if the partner's home state extended similar privileges to Maine banks—a process known as reciprocity. This opening for interstate mergers, however, received so little attention that even banks in Maine had not given it much thought.

The low level of concern in Maine about being inundated by out-of-state banks was evident in a 1982 planning meeting of one of the state's largest bank holding companies, Northeast Bankshares, a bank holding company I was working with at the time. The primary subject of discussion was statewide expansion by Northeast, not the possible entry into the state by out-of-state banks. The only person at that meeting even thinking about the ramifications of the 1975 legislation was Northeast's inside counsel.

The counsel reminded the attendees that New York had just passed reciprocal legislation, and that the structure of Maine banking could be in for big changes. His comments were not ignored, but neither did they raise much concern. There was not much Northeast could do about it, in any event, and selling the bank was not a consideration, or at least it was not thought to be a consideration, at that meeting.

A few months later, a telephone call from the Northeast president, Roger Castonguay, presented a very different picture. Peter Kiernan, the president and CEO of Norstar, an Upstate New York regional bank based in Albany, had visited with Castonguay and made an offer of 1.35 times book—a good price at the time—to buy the bank, which Castonguay felt might be too good to refuse. The price did not seem "too good to refuse" to me, but interstate banking in northeastern United States was on its way.

The pricing was of little importance relative to the impact of the sale of this bank on the bank consolidation process, but it was an interesting sidelight as to just how low bank sale prices were at the time. My response to Castonguay was that the bank was worth at least 1.5 times book, and he asked me to make that case in writing. This was done and shown to Norstar, and in a conversation I will long remember, Castonguay called and said

"You and I are not too smart. I showed your memo to Kiernan.

He took a quick look and said, 'will you shake on this.'

I guess we should have asked for more."

Whether or not it was a good price, Northeast had agreed to sell to Norstar. Regulatory approval was forthcoming, and by June 1983, the first true interstate bank acquisition in the United States since the 1930s was a done deal. A few months later, Depositors, a second bank holding company in Maine, was acquired by another Albany bank, KeyCorp.

As in Florida, the importance of the initial interstate acquisitions in Maine was not the impact of the actual purchases, but the response they evoked. Maine may not have been a large, or even an attractive, banking market, but it did not sit well in the bank boardrooms in Boston to see New York bank holding companies buying banks in what they considered their own backyard.

Regional Compacts

The responses to NCNB's acquisition in Florida and Norstar's in Maine were the same—regional interstate banking compacts. These were agreements between states to allow interstate banking on a reciprocal basis within a specified geographic area. What had happened in Florida and Maine as well as Citicorp's acquisition of a failed thrift in California—followed by similar thrift acquisitions in Florida, Illinois and the District of Columbia—would make interstate banking a reality and move the inevitability of interstate banking from an intellectual discussion to, "What was the proper strategic response?" The challenge for states and banks was no longer how to stop interstate banking, but how to use it to their benefit.

Two underlying and interrelated concerns that shaped the general response to the coming of interstate banking were the fear of domination by the large New York banks and the time needed for regional banks to build the necessary mass to compete with the New York banks, which was thought by some to be as long as ten to fifteen years. Banks in California and Texas also were of concern because of size, but on the East Coast, their proximity made them less likely threats than the large New York banks, particularly Citicorp. An answer to these concerns was regional compacts that excluded banks in New York, California and Texas.

The regional banking compact idea was not a new one. NCNB had proposed legislation in North Carolina in 1979 that would permit interstate mergers between banks in North Carolina and southeastern states on a reciprocal basis, and similar legislation was being considered in Florida. This proposed legislation, though, did not garner support from the state banking agencies and other leading banks in either state and, as a result, never even made it to a vote.[4]

Five years later, it was a totally different banking environment, and NCNB did not have much trouble making the Southeast banking compact a reality. In 1984, Florida, Georgia, North Carolina and South Carolina all signed on, albeit with a one-year waiting period. It would only be a matter of time before other states in the region would join.

The same process was played out in New England with the Boston and Hartford banks taking the lead. In 1984, bank legislation was passed in Connecticut, Massachusetts and Rhode Island to form a New England banking compact that allowed mergers between banks in the participating states. Since Maine had full interstate banking already on its books as long the other state had reciprocity, banks in any of the southern New England states could merge with banks in Maine. Rhode Island also included a "trigger"—i.e., a set date— that would take reciprocal interstate banking nationwide in 1987.

In both regions, some large banking combinations were announced fairly soon after the regional compacts were in place. The biggest proposed merger in the Southeast was the original Wachovia and First Atlanta, a combination that would create a bank larger than NCNB. In New England, Boston-based Bank of New England announced its intention to merge with CBT, Connecticut's largest bank and Bank of Boston agreed to buy Casco Northern in Maine, RIHT Financial—the initials stand for Rhode Island Hospital Trust—in Rhode Island and Colonial Bancorp in Connecticut. Interstate banking and consolidation in the Southeast and New England was off and running.

There was one problem, New York was excluded from both of the regional compacts, and this did not sit well with the large New York banks. Not only would the compacts allow the largest Florida banks to be acquired by out-of-state banks without New York banks being able to participate, but nearby Connecticut, whose southwest corner is part of the New York metropolitan area, also would be off-limits. Citicorp as the primary target of the exclusion responded by filing suit to stop the restrictive legislation.

Citicorp's suit put interstate banking on hold, and the case made it all the way up to the Supreme Court. This was a much anticipated court ruling without an overwhelming consensus as to what the outcome would be. It is an open question as to what the states involved would have done if the Supreme Court had ruled against regional compacts, but they did not have to face that decision. In June 1985, the Supreme Court ruled in favor of the regional compacts, and with that approval, interstate banking was not only permissible, but an irresistible force.

In New England, which is separated from the rest of the United States by New York, the geographic limits to the New England compact were near their final form right from the start. New Hampshire and Vermont opted out initially as they did not want to have their banking dominated by the big Boston banks, but they are a small part of the New England banking market. Banks in Connecticut, Maine, Massachusetts and Rhode Island were free to merge, and merge they did.

In the Southeast, the Supreme Court's approval of regional interstate banking had a geographic broadening effect. In 1985, Maryland and Virginia joined the original four states—Florida, Georgia, North Carolina and South Carolina. The District of Columbia had technically become a member that year by permitting interstate banking nationwide, but its banks were only of interest to neighboring states. By 1987 Alabama, Mississippi and Tennessee also were members of the Southeast regional compact.

North Carolina Domination

Looking back at the Southeast regional banking compact, it is easy to view it as a one-sided agreement that allowed North Carolina banks to dominate banking in the region and to eventually become national banking powers. This was not the intention, and despite the intense early merger activity of NCNB and the Wachovia-First Atlanta merger, it was not that one-sided at the beginning.

In 1984, and prior to the Supreme Court decision, NCNB had used its early entry into Florida to become the biggest bank in the Southeast with assets of $16 billion. The only other bank in the area with assets of more than $10 billion was Barnett in Florida with $13 billion. This was a good start for NCNB, but three years later, it was still just barely first among near-equals.

Largest Southeast Banks, 1987

Bank	Assets 1987 1984 (in billions)		1984 Rank	Eventual Owner
1. NCNB	$29	$16	1	Bank of America
2. First Union	28	7	8	Wachovia
3. SunTrust	27	9	4	SunTrust
4. Barnett	23	13	2	Bank of America
5. Sovran	21	8	6	Bank of America
6. Citizens & Southern	20	8	7	Bank of America
7. First Wachovia	19	9	5	Wachovia
8. MNC	17	7	9	Bank of America
9. Southeast Bkg.	13	10	3	Wachovia
10. Signet	11	4	19	Wachovia

Source: American Banker, March 29, 1985 and March 29, 1988.

By the end of 1987, NCNB had almost doubled in size to $29 billion in assets with more Florida mergers and the acquisition of Bankers Trust, the second biggest bank in South Carolina, but it was only slightly larger than First Union and SunTrust. First Union had been active in the interim with the acquisition of First Railroad & Banking in Georgia, Northwestern Bank in its home state of North Carolina and Florida's Atlantic Bank. These deals had lifted its assets from $7 billion in 1984 to $28 billion three years later. SunTrust, an Atlanta-based combination of Trust Company of Georgia and SunBanks in Florida, had 1987 assets of $27 billion.

There were three other banks—Barnett, Norfolk-based Sovran and Citizens & Southern in Atlanta—that had assets in 1987 in excess of $20 billion, and First Wachovia, the combination of First Atlanta and the original Wachovia, had just missed that cut-off with assets of $19 billion. Add in Maryland's MNC with assets of almost $17 billion, and there were eight Southeast banks with the size and momentum to be candidates for regional leadership.

It was during this period that the term "superregional" was first used to describe banks that were regional in scope, but of substantial size. When it came to superregionals, the Southeast had more than its fair share.

In 1987, though, it would have been hard to believe that of the ten largest banks in the Southeast, only three would be left twenty years later. Five are now part of Bank of America, and four are major components of Wachovia. SunTrust alone of the non-North Carolina banks in the Southeast managed to maintain its independence.

New England Impact

New England was a much smaller region than the Southeast, and the elimination of state line restrictions in four of the six New England states led to a much greater degree of local concentration with four Boston banks— Bank of Boston, Bank of New England, Fleet and Shawmut—and two in Hartford, CBT and Hartford National, leading the way. Bank of Boston was by far the largest bank in New England in 1984, but despite starting off much larger than other banks in the area and several interstate acquisitions, it could not maintain its earlier dominance. Others used their new geographic freedom to close much of the size gap.

Bank of New England, the name taken in 1982 by what had formerly been New England Merchants, was the most aggressive of the New England banks in using the regional compact to its advantage. It increased its assets from about $7 billion to almost $30 billion between 1984 and 1987, most of which came from a supposedly "equal" merger between

Bank of New England and CBT. Equal, in this case, meant that the headquarters was in Boston; management came from CBT; and the Bank of New England name was utilized. Being initially the most aggressive, though, did not lead to success, as Bank of New England in the early 1990s would become the second largest failure in banking history.

Largest New England Banks, 1987

Bank	Assets 1987 1984 (in billions)		1984 Rank	Eventual Owner
1. Bank of Boston	$34	$22	1	Bank of America
2. Bank-New England	29	7	3	Bank of America
3. Fleet/Norstar	25	6	6	Bank of America
4. Hartford National	16	6	5	Bank of America
5. Shawmut	11	7	4	Bank of America
6. BayBanks	9	5	7	Bank of America

Source: American Banker, March 29, 1985 and March 29, 1988.

Another Boston-Hartford equal bank merger, Shawmut and Hartford National in 1988, would create a major player in the region. It also would take away Hartford's last bank of any size.

The key player in New England bank consolidation would be Fleet, or Fleet/Norstar as it was temporarily called, the product of another of these "supposedly" equal mergers in 1987. This one was between Rhode Island's biggest bank Fleet and Norstar, the Upstate New York bank that had put the interstate process in New England in motion when it acquired a bank in Maine in 1983.

Fleet, a bank holding company whose origins go back to 1791, was the dominant partner from the beginning with the headquarters staying in Providence even though Norstar's Peter Kiernan was named chairman and CEO. The Fleet dominance was made even more so when Kiernan died within a year of the merger.

Fleet, which would subsequently drop the Norstar name, increased its assets from a little less than $6 billion in 1984 to about $25 billion by the end of 1987. Its CEO, Terry Murray, would be one of the most successful of the new breed of superregional leaders, and over the next twelve years, he would make Fleet pre-eminent in the region. The six biggest banks in New England in 1987, starting with the failed Bank of New England in 1991, would become part of Fleet by 1999, and subsequently part of Bank of America when Fleet took that larger bank's $49 billion offer in 2004.

LDC Crisis

Interstate banking and the rise of the superregionals began in earnest with the approval of the regional banking compacts in June 1985. By the end of 1987, several East Coast banks had tripled in size and were on their way to becoming much bigger banks. This, though, was only part of the story in the mid-1980s as the largest banks in the country were not enjoying these years. While NCNB, First Union, Fleet and others moved toward bigger and better things, the money center banks struggled to survive. In fact, they struggled so much that it may not have made much difference to the future industry structure if the New York banks had not been excluded from the regional compacts.

The problem for the big banks was the loans to the less-developed-countries, or as it was commonly called, the LDC debt crisis. This crisis began in August 1982 when Mexico announced it would be unable to meet its obligations to service an $80 billion debt. By October 1983, there were 27 countries owing $239 billion that had rescheduled their debts. The largest portion of this debt was in Latin America, an area in which American money center banks were the primary lenders. The eight largest banks in United States were major holders, and LDC loans constituted 147% of their combined capital and reserves at the time.[5]

There was no "quick fix" to the LDC problem, and in 1987, Citicorp, Chase Manhattan, BankAmerica, Chemical and Manufacturers Hanover had a combined loss of almost $5 billion. It was not just a BankAmerica and big New York bank problem either as California-based First Interstate and First Chicago added another $1.1 billion to the 1987 losses. Continental, Mellon, Marine Midland and Charter also had big losses that year.

Concern about the health of these large banks also severely impacted their credit ratings. In the late 1970s, they were all triple-A credit banks, but in 1987, only JPMorgan even had a double-A rating. BankAmerica, Chase Manhattan, Chemical and Manufacturers Hanover were B-rated, which was just above junk bond status.

Largest Domestic Banks, 1987

Bank	Assets 1987 1984 (in billions)		Net Income (in mill.)	Long-Term Debt Rating*
1. Citicorp	$204	$151	$(1,138)	A1
2. Chase Manhattan	99	87	(895)	Baa1
3. BankAmerica	93	118	(955)	Ba3
4. Chemical	78	52	(854)	Baa1
5. J.P. Morgan	75	64	83	Aa1
6. Manufacturers Han.	73	77	(1,140)	Baa3
7. Security Pacific	73	46	16	na
8. Bankers Trust	57	45	1	A1
9. First Interstate	51	46	(556)	na
10. First Chicago	44	40	(571)	A3

*Moody's ratings.
Source: American Banker, March 29, 1985 and March 29, 1988.

The LDC problem also greatly slowed the growth of these big banks. Between 1984 and 1987, BankAmerica and Manufacturers Hanover had their asset size decline, and Chase Manhattan, J.P. Morgan, Bankers Trust, First Interstate and First Chicago had only modest gains.

Citicorp went against the slow growth trend with a $53 billion asset gain during these three years, some of which came from its multiple thrift purchases. This made it more than twice as big as the second largest bank, Chase Manhattan, but was not a sign of good things to come as Citicorp would be only modestly larger in 1990; still losing money; and would drop out of the world's twenty largest banks as measured by assets. Ten years earlier, it was number one in the world rankings.

With these problems, the ability of the money center banks to play a major role in the early years of interstate banking would have been severely limited even if they had not been excluded by the regional compacts, and they were not alone on the sidelines. The LDC crisis coincided with, and was aggravated by, the sharp decline in oil prices that would devastate the big Texas banks. As a result, the money center banks were forced to watch smaller regional banks close the size gap. The Texas banks did not even last long enough to watch.

Even with their problems, on size alone, some money center banks participated in interstate expansion in areas other than New England and the Southeast, but were limited to rescuing seriously troubled or failed banks and thrifts. In 1982, BankAmerica crossed state lines to buy a failed SeaFirst in Seattle under the "emergency rules" that permitted interstate acquisitions if there were no in-state buyers; Citicorp bought failed thrifts in three different states and the District of Columbia in 1982 and 1984; and, in 1987, Chemical rescued a near failing Texas Commerce. When a buyer was desperately needed, the regulators would look the other way if there were no better alternatives, but a healthy bank was unlikely to sell to a bank with marginal bond ratings.

Midwest Reaction

The leading Midwest banks, except First Chicago and Continental, were not hobbled by the LDC crisis, but they were latecomers to interstate banking. In a region where many states had not removed the barriers to statewide branching, enthusiasm over interstate banking was, as would be expected, generally quite low.

By 1987, though, the most easterly of the Midwest states—Ohio, Indiana, Michigan and Wisconsin—had passed reciprocal interstate banking laws that had no regional restrictions. This meant that banks in these states could merge with one another and with banks in Kentucky to the immediate south of Ohio and Indiana, which had by then joined the interstate banking parade. In 1988, an adjoining state, Pennsylvania, would opt into interstate banking, leaving Illinois as the only the major hold-out among large states in the Midwest or geographically close to the Midwest.

This was about a two-year delay in interstate banking in the eastern part of the Midwest relative to New England and the Southeast, and since it did not include all of the Midwest, the regional impact in the initial years was far less than in those other regions. The different starting dates for interstate banking for the states within the Midwest also shifted the balance of power in favor of the banks in states like Ohio and Michigan vis-à-vis banks in the states further west, particularly Illinois and Minnesota.

The Midwest banks quickest to take advantage of interstate banking were Bank One and National City in Ohio. Bank One acquired one of the biggest banks in Indiana, American Fletcher, in 1987. A year later, it bought one of Wisconsin's largest banks, Marine. In so doing, it increased its assets from about $13 billion in 1986 to more than $25 billion in 1988 and moved from seventh to third in asset size in the Midwest. National City did not improve its area ranking immediately, but its acquisition of First Kentucky, the biggest bank in Kentucky, was the major reason its assets went from $14 billion to almost $22 billion during this period. This gave National City near parity in size with all of the leading Midwest banks except First Chicago.

Largest Midwest Banks, 1988

Bank	Assets 1988 1986 (in billions)		Rank 1986	Eventual Owner
1. First Chicago	$44	$39	1	JPMorgan
2. Continental	31	33	2	Bank of America
3. Bank One	25	13	7	JPMorgan
4. First Bank Syst.	24	28	3	U.S. Bancorp
5. NBD	24	21	5	JPMorgan
6. Norwest	22	22	4	Wells Fargo
7. National City	22	14	6	National City
8. Boatmen's	15	10	11	Bank of America
9. Harris	11	10	9	Bank of Montreal
10. Comerica	11	10	10	Comerica

Source: American Banker, April 16, 1987 and April 11, 1990.

Even with only modest growth, First Chicago was still much larger than other Midwest banks in 1988. Its $44 billion assets was about 45% more than any other bank in the region despite being in a state that still prohibited branching and interstate banking.

Its crosstown rival, Continental, and the Minnesota banks were not as fortunate and lost some of their edge in the immediate years after interstate banking was allowed. Continental, which had its customer "confidence" problem after being bailed-out by the FDIC as well as unfriendly home state banking laws, had its assets fall by about $2 billion. It was still number two in the region in assets in 1988, but within two years, it would be passed by Bank One and Norwest and be only slightly ahead of Detroit's NBD. First Bank System, with an unusually large asset decline between 1986 and 1988 that would continue into 1990, fell from third to fourth place and would eventually slide all the way to seventh before reversing its momentum.

More important than the individual bank performance in the Midwest relative to consolidation was that in this large geographic area, there were only seven banks in 1988 with assets over $15 billion. This included the two banks in Chicago that were still constrained in their growth by state laws. This slowed consolidation in the Midwest relative to the Southeast and New England, and regionally stacked the deck in favor of the Ohio and Michigan banks, particularly Bank One, NBD and National City. Soon, though, economic problems in other parts of the country in the post-1989 era eventually would work to the advantage of all Midwest banks relative to comparative growth, and particularly favor those banks in the states with an interstate banking head-start.

Middle Atlantic Dilemma

Caught in a "no man's land" in interstate banking were banks in New Jersey and Pennsylvania. These states were slower than other East Coast states to enact interstate banking legislation, primarily because they did not fit geographically into either the Southeast or New England regional banking compacts, and for these two states to accept interstate banking would be an open invitation to New York dominance of their local banking. Using the "contiguous state" wording to limit the interstate banking geographic area did not accomplish anything since New York was a contiguous state. The big New York City banks may have been limited in what they could do in the mid-1980s because of the LDC loans, but that did not lessen the fear in nearby states of a New York takeover if interstate banking was allowed.

Nevertheless, Pennsylvania and New Jersey had interstate legislation on their books by 1987. This included New York, but except for a couple of mid-sized acquisitions by Chemical in New Jersey, the New York banks, troubled by LDC loans, stayed home.

The only Pennsylvania bank that took advantage of the introduction of interstate banking in the late 1980s was Pittsburgh's PNC. It used proximity to the Midwest to move into Kentucky and Ohio in 1987 and 1988. This lifted its assets from $22 billion in 1986 to almost $41 billion in 1988, which made PNC by far the biggest bank in Pennsylvania. It also was much larger than any bank in the Midwest except First Chicago, and for PNC with its Pittsburgh base, the Midwest was as natural an expansion area as eastern Pennsylvania and New Jersey from a geographic perspective.

Starting from a smaller base, two New Jersey banks, First Fidelity and Midlantic, also used interstate acquisitions to improve their regional status. First Fidelity's acquisition of one of Philadelphia's largest bank holding companies, Fidelcor, helped it almost double its assets from just over

$15 billion in 1986 to almost $30 billion in 1988. Midlantic, with a series of smaller mergers, had a similar percentage increase going from nearly $12 billion to almost $20 billion with much of the increase coming from the acquisition of four Upstate New York banks from one of the smaller New York City money center banks.

Largest Middle Atlantic Banks, 1988

	Bank	Assets 1988 1986 (in billions)		Rank 1986	Eventual Owner
1.	PNC	$41	$22	2	PNC
2.	Mellon*	31	34	1	Bank of New York
3.	First Fidelity	30	15	3	Wachovia
4.	Midlantic	20	12	5	PNC
5.	Corestates	16	15	4	Wachovia

*Sold retail branches to Royal Bank of Scotland.
Source: American Banker, April 16, 1987 and April 11, 1990.

Sitting on the sidelines in the early years of interstate banking were the largest banks in Pittsburgh and Philadelphia, Mellon and CoreStates. Mellon, which was in a battle for survival with an overdose of LDC loans, saw crosstown rival PNC, not only go past it in size, but leave it far behind as Mellon's assets fell by $3 billion between 1986 and 1988. CoreStates also lost ground between 1986 and 1988, but would make up for lost time in 1990 with the in-market purchase of First Pennsylvania. The latter had not recovered from its problems in 1970s that led to its bailout by the FDIC.

The West

Interstate banking in the western part of the country was not resisted and, in fact, had become a necessity in parts of the region because of the oil patch problems. As noted earlier, BankAmerica had acquired the biggest bank in Washington, SeaFirst, in 1982 under "emergency" conditions after the latter's overdose of Penn Square's oil-and-gas loans, and Texas had no choice but to endorse the concept to facilitate exits for its largest banks when its economy collapsed in 1986. First Interstate already was in many western states as a result of its "grandfathered" status when it was spun off from A. P. Giannini's Transamerica in 1958.

The openness of the West to interstate banking worked primarily to the benefit of banks in California after the biggest Texas banks had been eliminated. BankAmerica had made its move into Washington before stumbling; First Interstate was among the out-of-state acquirers of failed or failing Texas bank leaders; and Security Pacific had bought the second largest bank in Washington, Rainier Bancorporation.

Largest Western Banks, 1988*

Bank	Assets 1988 1986 (in billions)		National Rank	Eventual Owner
1. BankAmerica	$95	$104	3	Bank of America
2. Security Pacific	78	63	5	Bank of America
3. First Interstate	58	55	8	Wells Fargo
4. Wells Fargo	47	45	11	Wells Fargo
5. Valley National	12	11	45	JPMorgan
6. Bancorp Hawaii	7	5	72	Bank of Hawaii
7. United Banks	6	4	82	Wells Fargo
8. First Security	5	5	85	Wells Fargo
9. City National	4	3	90	City National
10. First Hawaiian	4	3	98	BNP Paribas

* Includes Southwest and Rocky Mountain states.
Source: American Banker, April 16, 1987 and April 11, 1990.

The original Wells Fargo stayed in California, but was by no means silent. It greatly increased its size in the 1980s with the acquisition of a struggling Crocker National that in 1980 had been the nation's 13th biggest bank.

In fact, as the 1980s were coming to a close, it was not a stretch to think of the largest California banks as future leaders internationally as well as nationally, notwithstanding BankAmerica's problems. These were the years when Japan was riding high, and being located on the Pacific Rim was considered to be a stroke of good fortune. First Interstate, Wells Fargo, Security Pacific and a recovering BankAmerica stood to be the beneficiaries. At the end of 1988, they were the third, fifth, eighth and eleventh largest banks in the country. The next largest bank in the West was Valley National in Phoenix, and it had assets of a little under $12 billion and was not among the forty largest banks nationwide.

Unfortunately, neither the Japanese nor the West Coast economies were able to maintain their momentum into the 1990s, and, in fact, both went into reverse. As a result, a California banking collapse, and not a national bank ascendancy, became the big banking story out of the West in the early 1990s and a major contributor to the consolidation process—a story that is told in a later chapter.

Going National

This seemingly imminent interstate potential of the big California banks in the late 1980s, regardless of what was to happen later, and the rise of superregionals in the Southeast, New England and parts of the Midwest, created a banking environment far different than what had existed in 1980. Less than five years after the 1985 Supreme Court approval of the regional compacts that took interstate banking beyond emergency situations, most states had either accepted national interstate banking or were about to do so.

As the 1990s began, the stage had been set for American banking to follow the course of industries that had not been segmented by artificial barriers. Interstate banking's impact on consolidation, though, would be muted from 1989 through 1992 because of the most serious crisis banking had faced since the Great Depression. Banks and thrifts had been far too eager to lend to developers, and the result was a crash in real estate values, particularly commercial real estate, throughout much of the country with disastrous results.

Many of the problems that were to come, however, had their roots in the thrift crisis and the regulatory response to the massive thrift losses of the early 1980s. It is easy to say that banks and thrifts had been far too eager to lend to developers, but the thrifts were encouraged to do so by the regulators and, in many cases, banks were either responding in order to remain competitive or were just swept up in the real estate hysteria of the late 1980s. As the 1980s progressed, the thrift crisis, interstate banking and the regulatory response would be increasingly interrelated.

Thrift Crisis: Changing the Landscape

By the time interstate banking had moved into its national phase, the thrift crisis had entered a very painful second stage. In this stage, the focus shifted almost entirely to S&Ls, rather than mutual savings banks, as the number of insolvent S&Ls ratcheted upward dramatically, particularly in the Southwest. By 1987, FSLIC, the S&L deposit insurer, had exhausted all of its reserves, and in 1989, the situation would deteriorate to the point that legislation was passed that eliminated FSLIC; shifted the insuring of S&L deposits to the FDIC; and took S&L regulation away from the Bank Board and placed it in a new agency, the Office of Thrift Supervision, or OTS, that would report to the Treasury Department.

Mutual savings banks or just savings banks as they had come to be called since so many had forsaken mutuality, also struggled in the late 1980s. Most savings banks, though, remained viable until at least 1989 when real estate values in the Northeast, particularly commercial real estate, declined as a result of overbuilding and a softening of the economy. By then, it was difficult to sort out just what was a continuation of the 1980s' thrift crisis or part of a new, and in many ways, even more devastating, banking problem if measured by the number of bank and thrift failures.

What happened to undo the progress that seemingly was being made by thrifts after 1982? For awhile, it looked like the gamble the regulators and legislators had taken in trying to prop up the S&L industry with phony accounting, relaxed capital standards and diversification had succeeded. In 1983 and 1984, the "band-aids" seemed to be working as most S&Ls were profitable, busy diversifying assets and raising capital. It was a high risk period, but a couple of years of profitability and the willingness of investors to literally throw money at thrifts through stock conversions created a false sense of optimism.

For the regulatory and legislative gamble to work, though, three things had to happen. Interest rates had to go down sharply, and stay down; there had to be an extended period of economic stability; and thrifts had to avoid the temptation to abuse the relaxed supervision and capital standards. This was asking a lot, but at least there was a sharp drop in interest rates between 1981 and 1986 with only modest increases in the next couple of years. If lower interest rates were all that was needed, then the gamble might have worked.

An extended period of economic stability also was a lot to expect after the turbulence of the 1970s. Optimists could dream in the early 1980s about the economically calm years after World War II through to the mid-1960s as to what was possible, but those were different times. The collapse of the economy in Texas and other oil patch states in 1986 would put an end to those dreams.

As for the good behavior on the part of S&Ls, there were too many of them and too much temptation in a "go-go" era for there to be little in the way of corporate malfeasance. Most thrifts, S&Ls and savings banks, made a sincere effort to adjust to a changed environment without going across the line, and some of those that did were doing so at the urging of the regulators. The introduction of stock ownership also brought with it incentives to take advantage of the relaxed supervision and the low cost of buying S&Ls for personal gain. The result was a lot of rogue thrifts that made a bad situation even worse and contributed to giving S&Ls, in general, a bad name.

Thus, in 1983 and 1984, whatever optimism there was about limiting the damage to the thrift industry would prove to be false optimism. An early sign of this came in March 1985. A "run" on the Home State Savings in Cincinnati occurred, followed shortly by a "run" on Baltimore's Old Court Savings & Loan. They were state-insured thrifts, but their actions and the effect on their state insurance funds were precursors of what was to happen nationally a year later.

Home State and Old Court

Home State Savings was not the first S&L closed in the 1980s, nor even the first one since 1983, but it holds a special place in the annals of the thrift crisis. Prospects, as noted above, were looking better for thrifts as interest rates declined, profits returned and investors re-capitalized almost any sizeable thrift that was willing to convert from a mutual to a stock form of organization. Then, in March 1985, came the Home State fiasco.

The $1.4 billion Home State was the largest S&L in a state-insured banking system, and, as such, it took down the entire Ohio deposit insurance fund with it. To make matters worse, its failure was preceded by a highly-publicized depositors' "run" that was based on fraudulent behavior. Its owner, Marvin Warner, and nine others connected with Home State went to jail as result of its failure.[1]

Home State's collapse was brought on by its investments, not by bad loans or a margin-overhead mismatch. The trigger was the failure of ESM Government Securities, Inc., a firm with a long-time, close relationship with Home State. The Florida-based ESM was deeply in debt, a fact it had been hiding with misleading reports, and in March 1985, it was closed after being charged with fraud. When it was revealed that Home State was a big holder of ESM bonds, its depositors rushed to get their money. After a deposit withdrawal of $150 million, twice the amount of the reserves of the Ohio deposit insurance fund, the state had no choice but to step in and close it.[2]

This was not the end as deposit runs began at five other Ohio-insured S&Ls. Nine days after Home State failed the governor of Ohio felt compelled to call a "thrift holiday" on March 15th and closed all state insured thrifts for a day. On the following Monday as a direct result the dollar fell relative to other currencies and the value of gold rose $50 in a day. This made Home State more than just a local problem.[3]

The only good news in the Home State story is that recoveries by the state were able to repay the initial cost of the bailout that was about $130 million. The recovery, though, took more than fifteen years to complete.[4]

Two months later, the Home State story was rerun in Maryland as another state-insured S&L, Old Court Savings & Loan in Baltimore, started down the same path. As early as 1978, its owner, Jeffrey Levitt, had been accused of diverting funds for his own use, but again the triggering event for its demise was not a direct theft of funds, but rather the failure of a bond seller. When news of the negative impact of the Old Court's bond losses became known in May 1985, as with Home State, a run on deposits began that spread from Old Court to other Maryland-insured S&Ls, and nearly caused a collapse of the Maryland deposit insurance fund. It was almost two years before Old Court's depositors got all of their money back.[5]

Old Court was the second widely-publicized case in early 1985 of management misdeeds at an S&L. Besides investing badly, Levitt also was convicted of stealing $14.7 million of Old Court depositor's money and spent seven years in prison.[6]

Problems at just two S&Ls were enough to bankrupt the state deposit insurance funds, and put 121 state-insured S&Ls in Maryland and 71 more in Ohio at risk. Most Ohio and Maryland's state-insured S&Ls survived and qualified for federal deposit insurance, but these crises exposed the potential for problems elsewhere. Home State and Old Court were the public's initial exposure to thrifts playing fast and loose with depositor money, but they were far from the last.

At the time, though, the statewide thrift crises in Maryland and Ohio were generally dismissed as special situations that occurred only because they did not have the weight of the federal government behind them. Many on the inside knew better, but they were still hoping for the best.

Post-1985 Slide

The "best," though, was not to be, and with the collapse in 1985 and 1986 of the economy in Texas and other oil patch states, any hopes for a "soft landing" disappeared. Nationally, S&L profits fell from $3.7 billion to little more than breakeven in 1986, and the S&Ls that failed that year were large enough to wipe out all existing FSLIC reserves. Two years later, FSLIC's reserve deficiency reached $75 billion.

S&L Decline, 1985 to 1989

Year	Savings and Loans*	Net Income	Assets of Failed Thrifts (in billions)	FSLIC Reserves
1989	2,878	$(17.6)	–	–
1988	2,949	(13.4)	$142.7	$(75.0)
1987	3,147	(7.8)	20.8	(13.7)
1986	3,220	.1	16.2	(6.3)
1985	3,246	3.7	6.3	4.6

*FSLIC-insured only.
Source: FDIC, History of the Eighties—Lessons for the Future.

The number of S&Ls also began to decline, including even those kept open under government receivership, and the assets of failed thrifts were rising rapidly. From 1985 to the end of 1989, the number of FSLIC-insured S&Ls fell from 3,246 to 2,878, and in 1988, assets of failed S&Ls had reached $143 billion. These were not good times for S&Ls and those who regulated and insured them.

FIRREA

By 1989, the thrift crisis reached such a serious state that a radical restructuring of the industry and its oversight was needed. This resulted in the passage of Financial Institutions Reform, Recovery, and Enforcement Act, or FIRREA, in February of that year. This legislation shifted supervision of S&Ls from the Bank Board to a new regulatory agency, the OTS that would report to a Treasury Department that also had authority over national banks. It abolished the S&L insurance fund, FSLIC, as well and replaced it with the FDIC-administered Savings Association Insurance Fund, and created the Resolution Trust Company, or RTC, under the management of the FDIC to handle insolvent S&Ls. Finally, FIRREA imposed stricter accounting, capital and lending standards.

From a consolidation perspective, FIRREA was the end of the long-time autonomy of the S&Ls. Their supervision and deposit insurance had been placed under the same federal authorities that handled banks, which made it inevitable that inter-industry mergers would be allowed even for healthy thrifts. FIRREA also required thrift capital, loans and investments to meet the much stricter bank requirements, which immediately reduced the viability of many S&Ls, including some of the largest, and sped up the closing of failed thrifts.

Regional Progression

Despite the dire circumstances of FSLIC as early as 1986 and 1987, the second stage of the thrift crisis had not then reached all parts of the country even though the overreaching and inadequate capital was fairly universal within the industry. In the Ohio and Maryland mini-crises, the state-insured coverage was such that the misdeeds of a couple thrifts could take down the local thrift insurance funds, but the panic had not spread to the federally-insured thrifts in those states. In most states, Texas being an exception, it took a sharp downturn of the local commercial real estate market in the late 1980s to push the local thrift industries over the edge.

In 1986 and 1987, thrifts in big states other than Texas had problems as well, but they trailed Texas by two to three years in maximum impact. The Florida thrifts had a dip in earnings in 1986, but their peak loss year was 1989. In Pennsylvania, thrift losses would start in 1988 and peak in 1989. California and New York thrifts generally remained profitable until 1989 when those states began to suffer from overbuilt real estate markets.

Thrift Industry Losses in Selected States, 1984 to 1992

Year	Texas	Florida	Pennsylvania (in millions)	New York	California
1992	$704	$309	$270	$764	$637
1991	236	58	57	(711)	251
1990	126	(403)	(166)	(596)	(1,115)
1989	(499)	(712)	(497)	(1,383)	(665)
1988	(4,423)	(437)	(156)	728	715
1987	(7,122)	(105)	207	1,258	113
1986	(3,219)	95	334	1,493	1,025
1985	476	159	271	758	1,258
1984	280	37	119	(239)	(123)

Source: FDIC, Historical Statistics on Banking.

Texas S&L Debacle

The catalyst for FIRREA, the legislation that was intended to bring closure to the S&L portion of the thrift crisis, was Texas. Its S&Ls carried to an extreme the "grow and diversify" mantra preached by regulators and, collectively, lifted assets from $35 billion in 1980 to $111 billion in 1988. Texas was not only first out of the gate in the second stage of the crisis with large losses and widespread failures, but by being first, its S&L losses, alone, were enough to bankrupt FSLIC. These S&Ls were part of the "go-go" attitude of the state that accompanied the oil boom of the 1970s and early 1980s, and when that boom ended and the economy collapsed, like the Texas banks, the S&Ls were stuck with overwhelming amounts of bad loans.

By the end of 1986, Texas noncurrent S&L loans were $11.3 billion and a year later were $14 billion. This resulted in a collective loss of about $15 billion from 1986 through 1989, and in 1987, the total capital of all Texas S&Ls was a negative $7.8 billion. By year-end 1987, Texas S&Ls accounted for 62% of S&L losses nationwide.[6] With these results, it was not surprising that the number of S&Ls in the state would fall from 281 in 1986 to 68 in 1991.

Texas S&L Slide, 1985 to 1991

Year	Number of S&Ls	Assets	Net Income	Equity Capital	Noncurrent Loans
			(in billions)		
1991	68	$48.9	$.2	$2.4	$.3
1990	80	58.6	.1	2.1	.3
1989	116	68.8	(.5)	1.4	7.3
1988	205	110.9	(4.4)	(4.1)	10.7
1987	279	99.1	(7.1)	(7.8)	14.0
1986	281	96.3	(3.2)	(1.0)	11.3
1985	273	91.3	.5	3.0	3.7

Source: FDIC, Historical Statistics on Banking.

Also helping to make Texas the centerpiece of a controversial second round of phony accounting was the 1988 Southwest Plan. This was an effort by an already bankrupt FSLIC to conserve its cash by consolidating failed thrifts into clusters, and then selling them with capital notes, future loss coverage guarantees and tax credits. This was a rushed rescue project as the law that allowed S&L losses to offset other taxable gains, the key attraction to buyers, was to expire at the end of that year.

By being the first state to have widespread S&L failures and the focus of the Southwest Plan, Texas became forever linked with the worst abuses of the thrift crisis, which was somewhat unfair. Popular books written about the crisis at the time placed a lot of emphasis on how the Texas S&Ls had robbed the taxpayers, but those who argued that what happened to the S&Ls in 1986 was no different than the simultaneous collapse of the Texas banks, were not wrong. Texas S&L failures were part of the oil patch meltdown, but these S&Ls had more than their fair share of shady characters, albeit many were not from Texas.

With the oil patch economy still booming in the 1980 to 1982 period, Texas S&Ls actually had come through the first part of the thrift crisis in better condition than thrifts elsewhere and believed like the banks that there was no stopping the Texas economy. Their subsequent rapid growth was facilitated by the relaxed capital and lending standards, but those growing rapidly did not expect to fail, and most of their owners took large personal losses when an S&L did fail. There were exotic investments that make good reading and look bad in retrospect, but what brought the Texas S&Ls down was the same decision that hurt the local banks—lending on commercial real estate in Dallas, Houston and the other large Texas cities.

Something else that was different about the S&Ls in Texas that was to contribute to their spectacular growth from 1982 to 1985 and their equally spectacular fall after 1985, was that so many of its thrifts were already stock organizations in 1980, including most of the large ones. Thus, when rules were relaxed relative to capital required and acquiring new capital, many Texas S&Ls did not have to convert from mutual to stock in a process that required regulatory oversight and kept unqualified individuals from gaining control. These S&Ls were ready for immediate sale, and, unfortunately, the buyers included some of the more notorious corporate raiders of the day using the junk bond financing of Michael Milken of Drexel Burnham & Lambert.

Gibraltar

Gibraltar Savings, the largest thrift in Texas with about $3.3 billion assets in 1980, was typical of what happened and why there were so many bad headlines. It was a stock thrift before the S&L crisis began, and, in the early 1980s, was acquired by Saul Steinberg, a well-known corporate raider and long-time beneficiary of the Michael Milken-Drexel Burnham junk bond financing.[7]

Steinberg was one of many characters involved in Texas S&Ls who liked the headlines. He was a big-time art collector and spender, and a Liz Smith *New York Magazine* column in 1989 lends flavor to his life and the times describing a party Steinberg's wife threw for his 50th birthday. In this column Smith says it "was reported that she spent her own money (estimated at from $250,000 to $1 million) to impress her husband and some 250 guests." Smith went on to note that "the Steinberg beach house overlooking the Atlantic rocked and rolled with hundreds of flickering terra cotta pots, identical twins posing as mermaids in the pool, dancers in seventeenth century garb, heralds and banner wavers .... He (Steinberg) joked about that his wife had done a lot for the economy and 'anyone that is talking about recession—well forget it.'"[8] This was in 1989 when concerns over the cost of the thrift crisis were at their peak.

Steinberg, though, had been smart enough to sell Gibraltar in 1984 to a holding company that also controlled the state's third largest thrift, First Texas, and he and the other owners of Gibraltar were allowed to take out $268 million in cash as part of the sale.[9] This was not the only source of wealth that made his 1989 birthday party possible, nor was Gibraltar the investment most associated with him—that would be Reliance Insurance—but this was the type of story that added so much to the luster of the Texas portion of the S&L crisis. As was so frequently the case, the person adding the luster, Steinberg, was not from Texas.

After the sale to the holding company, Gibraltar and First Texas were operated separately, but by 1988, both had failed. At that time, Gibraltar, First Texas and a few other insolvent thrifts in the words of Martin Mayer in his book, *The Greatest-Ever Bank Robbery,* "were stitched into one $12 billion S&L by FSLIC in 1988 (part of the Southwest Plan) and sold to Milken's friend Ron Perelman of Revlon (for $315 million). To make the deal satisfactory to Perelman, the FSLIC had to provide a subsidy that has been estimated as high as $5 billion, some of it in the form of notes guaranteeing as much as ten years of high return on loans that were usually in default some part of it in the form of tax credits." Mayer went on to say that "for $315 million (of which $240 million was borrowed). . . he (Perelman) got tax deductions valued at $897.3 million. For calendar 1989, Perelman's new First Gibraltar reported payments from the government of $461 million and net profits to Perelman (all tax-free) of $129 million."[10] In 1993, Perelman sold First Gibraltar to BankAmerica for $110 million.

Perelman was another New Yorker dabbling in Texas S&Ls, and he was colorful and seemed to enjoy publicity as much as Steinberg. His bald head, ever-present cigar and the beautiful women at his side, four of whom he married, were frequently on display in the society pages, including this billionaire's most recent ex-wife, the actress Ellen Barkin.

The notoriety of and financial gains by investors like Steinberg and Perelman gained more attention as the cost of resolving the S&L crisis rose, which added to the public concern. The cost, excluding interest payments, of the failures of Gibraltar and First Texas was calculated to be $5.4 billion. Add in Vernon S&L, also in the Southwest Plan's First Gibraltar package, and the cost goes up to $6.4 billion.[11]

The stories of a couple of others among the five largest Texas S&Ls, University and Sunbelt, only vary from those of Gibraltar and First Texas in that they did not merge with another large S&L prior to their 1987 or 1988 failure. They were also put into RTC receivership, and then sold by the RTC—University as branches to NCNB and SunBelt to BankAmerica. The total pre-interest cost of resolution was $3.8 billion for SunBelt and $2.5 billion for University.[12]

The differences between the failures of the large oil patch S&Ls and those of the big Texas banks were more in how they were handled by their regulators than the actual monetary cost to the insurance funds. The FDIC moved a lot quicker, but its cost of selling FirstRepublicBancorp to NCNB and M-Corp to Bank One was a hefty $5.6 billion. From a consolidation perspective, the end result was similar to Gibraltar, First Texas, Sunbelt, University *and* First RepublicBank with all ending up as part of Bank of America.

Beyond Texas

Texas accounted for 14 of the 25 largest RTC bailouts, but it was far from alone in costing the taxpayers billions of dollars. California had four of the 25 largest RTC bailouts, including the most expensive, American Savings & Loan in Stockton, which had a resolution cost of $5.7 billion, as well as one of the most famous S&L failures, Lincoln Savings & Loan. Lincoln was owned primarily by Charles Keating, and gained particular notoriety when the names of five U.S. senators, including John McCain and John Glenn, were bandied about as having possibly provided assistance in keeping the regulators at bay. They became known as the Keating Five, but it appeared that they did little more than make the normal inquiries that congressmen make on behalf of constituents.

Among the other states, Arizona had two of the 25 costliest S&L bailouts; and New Jersey, Arkansas, New York, Louisiana, Colorado and Florida had one each. The Arkansas S&L was not Madison Guaranty of Whitewater fame, but the one that failed in Colorado was Silverado whose board included Neil Bush, son of the first George Bush who was president at the time. The cost of closing and selling Silverado was estimated to be $1.3 billion.

New York's contribution to the list, Buffalo-based Empire FSB, was unique in that it started as a mutual savings bank, and then after going public and being allowed to buy two failed savings banks, Empire switched to what it considered a more favorable S&L charter. As an S&L, it was closed by the RTC and sold to various buyers at a cost to the government of about $1.6 billion.

Winding Down

The passage of FIRREA in early 1989 was the beginning of the end of a thrift crisis distinct from an overall banking problem. The RTC would be selling failed S&Ls and S&L assets for several more years, but by the end of 1991, the extent of the damage was measurable. The damage that was done, both in terms of money and what it did to the S&L business, though, would be long remembered.

From 1981 through 1991, FSLIC and the RTC sold 891 S&Ls with federal assistance and closed another 242. This was 1,133 failed S&Ls with combined assets of $461 billion, and at the end of 1991, the RTC still had 46 S&Ls in receivership with assets of $15.2 billion. This was almost one-third of the total number of thrifts that existed in 1980, and more than three-fourths of 1980 S&L assets.

S&L Assisted Mergers and Closings, 1981 to 1991

Year	Assisted Mergers	Closings	Total	Assets Involved (in billions)
1991	153	78	231	$89.0
1990	246	68	314	112.6
1989	54	6	60	31.1
1988	207	26	233	142.7
1987	56	17	73	20.8
1986	34	20	54	16.2
1985	22	10	32	6.3
1984	17	9	26	5.8
1983	33	6	39	16.5
1982	46	1	47	19.8
1981	23	1	24	na
Total	891*	242	1,133	$460.8

* Does not include 46 S&Ls still in RTC receivership with assets of $15.2 billion as of December 31, 1991.
Source: Sheshunoff S&L Quarterly, December 1986 and 1991.

The assisted mergers and closings per year from 1981 through 1989 showed just how the regulators had delayed solving the problem before the economic collapse in the oil patch turned a serious situation into a crisis. From 1981 through 1985, there were just 27 S&Ls closed and 141 merged with federal assistance. This was not a lot of closings and assisted-mergers compared to what was coming. Assets involved were not much more than 10% of what would eventually be sold or closed by FSLIC and the RTC.

By 1987, it was obvious that the "band-aids" had not solved the S&L problem and the economic collapse in the Southwest had become a major complication, but FSLIC did have the funds to deal with the situation. In

1986 and 1987, the S&Ls closed or merged with federal assistance were still a relatively modest 127 with combined assets of $37 billion.

Going slow ended in 1988, but with FSLIC still short of funds, it had to find methods other than closing an insolvent thrift. The next attempt to delay the inevitable was to use federally-assisted mergers with notes, margin guarantees and tax benefits—the infamous Southwest Plan. This was once again pushing the problem into the future, but FSLIC managed to sell off 207 S&Ls with total assets of about $140 billion with a minimal immediate cash outlay. There were 26 S&Ls closed in 1988, but these were mostly small and had combined assets of only a little over $3 billion.

In 1989, FIRREA and a well-funded RTC replaced FSLIC, but it took time for the RTC to become fully functional. As a result, it was a year of insolvent S&Ls being taken over by the RTC, but not many were closed or sold. There were only 60 S&Ls with assets of about $31 billion that were put out of their misery in 1989.

In 1990 and 1991, the RTC was fully operative, and it sold or closed 545 S&Ls with assets of more than $200 billion. The primary assistance was the RTC keeping the bad assets, and by 1992, it moved from being the manager of troubled S&Ls to being a manager of troubled assets.

The cost of the S&L portion of the thrift crisis has been estimated to have been anywhere from $200 billion to more than $300 billion with the difference between the high and low estimates normally being the interest paid on the initial cost. It is likely that the direct cost was over $200 billion, but that does not begin to cover the cost of the problems created by S&Ls and savings banks liberally supplying developers with funds to build offices, malls and hotels that were not needed. This led to large real estate losses for banks, thrifts and investors that put the country into a depressed economy that lasted from 1989 to 1992. Thus, while it is impossible to definitively measure the real cost of the thrift crisis, $300 billion is a modest estimate.

The savings banks contributed to the overbuilding in the late 1980s, but with almost all of them being in the Northeast, there were few savings bank failures between 1983 and 1990. Syracuse Savings was the only one with assets in excess of $1 billion to be closed and sold by the FDIC during this period.

RTC Sales

With FSLIC having been replaced by the FDIC and the RTC in 1989, all constraints about selling failed S&Ls to commercial banks disappeared, and in the massive sell-off in 1990 and 1991, banks were the primary buyers. As a result, a large part of what was once an autonomous S&L industry was transferred by acquisition to banks, and much of it went to BankAmerica and the superregionals.

BankAmerica, which had survived its LDC loan problems and moved away from its flirtation with money center bank activities, was by far the most aggressive acquirer of failed S&Ls. It bought nine large failed S&Ls with collective assets at the time of assumption of $31.5 billion and this understates BankAmerica's total gain from RTC sales. It acquired Security Pacific and First Gibraltar in 1992 that together had bought five failed S&Ls with combined assets of about $22 billion that would become part of the BankAmerica franchise. Thus, its total assets bought from the RTC, direct and indirect, were about $53 billion.[13]

Bank One, NCNB and First Union were other bank buyers of multiple large S&Ls from the RTC. Each had S&L asset purchases in excess of $5 billion.

The eventual big winners from the RTC sales were Bank of America and Washington Mutual. Among just the deals in which buyers of S&Ls added total assets of $2 billion or more from purchasing S&Ls with assets in excess of $500 million, about $62 billion is now part of Bank of America's franchise and almost $34 billion is in the Washington Mutual network. Wachovia was a distant third with $13 billion of such RTC assets finding their way into its hands.

That Bank of America and Washington Mutual ended up with more thrift franchises as a result of RTC sales than the other big banks was at least partially because of location. Bank of America's two main components, BankAmerica and NCNB, and Washington Mutual had much stronger interests than other banks at the time in the areas where the largest failed thrifts were—Texas and California.

Consolidation Impact

The impact of the thrift crisis on consolidation had as much to do, or more, with how the crisis changed the banking landscape than the increase in the size of banks resulting from the thrift assets they acquired, directly or indirectly. From a consolidation perspective, what the thrift crisis had done beyond these acquisitions was:

- Help pave the way for interstate banking, primarily through the impact of Citicorp's early 1980 thrift acquisitions;
- Reverse the upward momentum of thrifts;

- Bring on the consolidation of the regulatory and insurance agencies of both thrifts and banks under the Treasury Department and FDIC to create a more unified banking industry; and,

- Create more expansion opportunities for superregionals than for the once dominant money center banks.

Thrift Crisis Summary

The FDIC's *History of the Eighties—Lessons for the Future* is good reading for anyone who wants an objective and detailed, view of the bank and thrift problems of the 1980s, and it summed up the second stage of the thrift crisis, or S&L crisis as the FDIC preferred to call it, in a thoughtful and concise two paragraphs.

Its summation was that "the S&L crisis overlapped several regional banking crises in the 1980s and at first was similar to the crisis involving mutual savings banks. However, in contrast to FSLIC, the FDIC had both the money to close failing mutual savings banks and the regulatory will to put others on a tight leash, while allowing some forebearance in the form of the Net Worth Certificate Program. To be sure some mutual savings banks later got into trouble with poor investments and failed, but the cost of those failures pales in comparison with the costs of the failures in the S&L industry, which was encouraged to grow and engage in risky activities with little supervision. When the Bank Board realized that its strategies had failed, it attempted to correct the problems through regulation. In contrast, federal bank regulators used supervisory tools and enforcement actions to limit growth and raise capital levels at commercial banks and mutual savings banks. But both banks and S&Ls, and their regulators, got caught up in boom-to-bust real estate cycles."

"In the 1980s a 'go-go' mentality prevailed, along with the belief in many regions that the economies in those regions were recession proof. In both the Southwest and New England, the high growth strategies pursued by many S&Ls increased the competition for deposits and therefore raised the interest expense for both banks and thrifts. This situation persisted and worsened as deeply insolvent S&Ls remained open because FSLIC lacked reserves. Banks also faced competitive pressures from the thrifts that aggressively entered commercial mortgage lending markets and aggravated the risk taking already present in commercial banking."[14]

In retrospect, there is little doubt that once the damage had been done in 1980 through 1982 to thrift viability, the thrift crisis, particularly the S&L

portion, was a series of mistakes by the regulators made worse by regional recessions and a "go-go mentality" that made sure the "band-aids" did not work. Thrifts most severely damaged in the early 1980s' "sea of red ink" would not survive, and few of the thrifts that were insolvent in 1982 were around a dozen years later.

The thrift crisis also caused problems for other banking organizations. The desperate effort by so many thrifts to grow rapidly and diversify had them bidding aggressively for deposits that drove the cost of funds up for all banking organizations, as noted in the FDIC analysis, and they made funding too easily available for developers that seldom saw a vacant lot that could not use a building. Much of the real estate overbuilding on the two coasts and in the Southwest could be traced to unwise lending by thrifts and the competitive desire of the banks not to be left behind.

The FDIC, in its comments, was a bit self-serving in exonerating itself. Meritor was the biggest savings bank insured by the FDIC, and it used the phony accounting, relaxed capital standards and rapid growth as eagerly as any S&L, albeit there did not appear to be any management chicanery involved. Also, to blame S&Ls for the excesses in New England is wrong considering the predominance and actions of savings banks in the region. The primary differences between the Bank Board, FSLIC and the regulators and insurers of the savings banks was that the latter *had* the reserves to cover the losses of failed institutions and were under less industry pressure to look the other way when things went wrong.

1980s in Retrospect

T he 1980s were a period of dramatic change in banking led by the arrival and spread of interstate banking. It would have been hard to imagine as the decade began that in just ten years, a bank in North Carolina would be among the leaders in states as large and far away as Florida and Texas or that Bank of Boston would be among the most common signage in Maine, Connecticut and Rhode Island. Conversely, by 1990, it was hard to recall that a few years earlier customers in the suburbs of New York, Washington and the other cities that straddled state lines had to use different banks if they wanted to utilize a banking office near their home *and* downtown. Change did not arrive evenly across the country as some states like Illinois still had few bank branches, but for most of the nation it was a very different banking environment in 1990 than what had existed ten years earlier.

A period of change in how a product is delivered almost by definition results in more structural change within an industry than in a period of calm, and when accompanied by an event such as high interest rates that favor one sector of an industry over another, the degree of change is magnified. The 1980s favored a retail banking culture over a money center culture and also favored the depository institutions that had the most flexibility in product pricing. Thus, banks able and willing to follow their customers with offices and that had flexible loan yields improved their competitive status relative to banks with money center cultures, banks in states with limited branching and thrifts that could branch freely, but had relatively inflexible loan yields.

The advantages of the unencumbered retail banks were further aided by the LDC debt crisis and collapse of the oil-and-gas industry negatively impacting most banks without retail cultures, which were primarily in hostile branching environments like Texas and Illinois. Thrifts with their business model that required stable or declining interest rates had little chance of keeping pace with more favorably situated banks.

With much of the country moving into a recession in 1989 and almost 500 banks failing in the next three years, the 1980s' losers would not be alone in questioning the benefits of change. The bottom line, though, was that no matter what happened negatively from 1989 to 1992 in banking, the 1980s' winners were in better shape to go forward when the economy improved than those who had not fared as well.

In retrospect, interstate banking was clearly the change in the 1980s that had the biggest impact on consolidation, but there were other, often interrelated, changes that also played major roles in the transformation and increasing levels of concentration. Among the most important of these were:

- The rise of superregionals with a retail culture and seemingly endless desire to expand;
- The reversal of the thrift momentum of the 1960s and 1970s;
- A slowdown in the opening of branches;
- The diminished importance of checking accounts; and,
- The growth of loan securitization.

Except for the rise of the superregionals and the thrifts' reversal of fortune, these changes were not headline grabbers, but when viewed over time, were dramatic in their own right. Checking accounts that were more than 50% of bank deposits in 1970 and 36% in 1980, were only 20% of deposits by 1990, and this was at a time when deposits of all types were declining as a source of bank funding. The securitization and sale to third parties of home mortgages that represented more than half of the nation's private debt rose from 12% of home mortgages in 1980 to 37% in 1990. The decline in the importance of checking accounts raised questions about the need for branches, while the big increase in the securitization of home mortgages did the same about the need for thrifts.

Rise of the Superregionals

The usurping of center stage by the superregionals in the 1980s was an outgrowth of interstate banking, but their rise was greatly assisted by the problems of others. Playing major roles in the growth of regional banks based outside of New York City were acquisition opportunities that came with the collapse of the Texas banking system; the inactivity of the money center banks throughout most of the decade because of the LDC problems; and the diminished position of thrifts.

Largest Domestic Banks, 1990

Bank	Assets* 1990 1980 (in billions)		Asset Share** 1990 1980		Banking Offices
Money Center Banks					
1. Citicorp	$217	$115	5.6%	5.7%	322
2. BankAmerica	111	112	3.4	5.9	1,295
3. Chase Manhattan	98	76	2.9	4.1	344
4. J.P. Morgan	93	52	2.2	2.7	5
5. Chemical	73	41	2.2	2.2	369
6. Bankers Trust	64	34	1.7	1.8	4
7. Manufacturers Han.	62	56	1.7	2.8	220
8. First Chicago	51	29	1.4	1.5	1
9. Bank of New York	45	10	1.4	.6	243
10. Bank of Boston	33	16	.9	.8	267
Subtotal	$847	$541	23.4%	28.1%	3,070
Superregionals					
1. Security Pacific	$84	$28	2.2%	1.4%	1,001
2. NCNB	65	7	1.9	.4	924
3. Wells Fargo	56	24	1.6	1.3	575
4. First Interstate	51	32	1.5	1.7	1,057
5. C&S/Sovran	51	3	1.5	.1	1,009
6. PNC	46	6	1.4	.3	511
7. First Union	41	3	1.2	.2	768
8. SunTrust	33	3	1.0	.2	625
9. Fleet	33	4	1.0	.2	538
10. Barnett	32	4	1.0	.2	599
Subtotal	$493	$114	14.3%	6.0%	7,607
Total	$1,340	$655	37.7%	34.1%	10,677
Ten Largest***	$923	$589	25.4%	30.7%	

* *Holding company assets.*   *** *Includes Continental in 1980.*
** *Bank assets only.*   *Source: American Banker, April 20, 1982 and February 8, 1991.*

In 1990, the ten largest superregionals had combined assets of almost $500 billion and more than 14% of bank assets. This was more than a fourfold increase in assets in ten years and almost a tripling in asset share. NCNB, First Union, C&S/Sovran, SunTrust and Fleet had ten year asset gains in excess of 900%, and the largest superregionals—Security Pacific, NCNB and Wells Fargo—moved into the top ten in asset size nationwide, ranking fifth, seventh and tenth, respectively, in 1990.

The superregional growth came primarily from equal mergers and buying smaller banks, but their share gains were facilitated by the slowed growth of money center banks. While the ten biggest superregionals were recording more than a 400% increase in assets in the 1980s, the ten largest money center banks had a collective gain of just 56%. As a result, the money center share of all bank assets fell from about 28% to a little over 23% between 1980 and 1990.

The nation's second largest bank, BankAmerica, was the big loser as it struggled with an internal culture conflict. It had long been the country's largest retail bank, but in the late 1970s, began acting like a money center bank. As a result, it was severely hurt by the LDC debt crisis. Despite being in rapidly-growing California, BankAmerica sat on the merger sidelines from 1982 through 1990; was almost acquired in the mid-1980s in a hostile takeover attempt by the much smaller First Interstate; and had an asset decline between 1980 and 1990.

BankAmerica would put its focus back on retail banking, but there was no making up for the ground lost in the 1980s. If it had not strayed from its retail roots, it would have had substantial in-state growth and most likely would have been a major buyer of banks in Texas during the oil patch crisis. In this mode, BankAmerica almost certainly would have been by far the biggest of the superregionals in 1990—probably with $200 billion plus assets instead of $111 billion. Considering how acquisitive it became after 1990, if it had started from this larger base in 1990, BankAmerica would not have been vulnerable to a less than equal merger eight years later that kept the name, but moved the headquarters and control from San Francisco to Charlotte.

While BankAmerica was the most illustrious of the big bank losers in the 1980s, it was far from alone in its ill fortune. Continental was no longer in the top ten; Manufacturers Hanover had annual asset gains of only 1% per annum; and Chase Manhattan did not do much better at about 3% annually. They all would be gone by the mid-1990s.

It was not all bad for the money center banks in the 1980s. Citicorp, despite being stung by LDC losses and falling out of the top twenty in the world in earnings and assets for the first time in 1990, increased its domestic dominance. With $217 billion assets in 1990, it was almost twice as large as its closest rival, BankAmerica. Chemical also did well holding its market share and becoming a leading player in Texas.

Two of the smaller money center banks, Bank of New York and Bank of Boston, improved their status by moving away from the traditional money center mode of operation. Bank of New York began a strategy of abetting money center banking with processing activities that generate large amounts of fee income, a strategy that continues to serve it well. Bank of Boston benefited from the New England interstate banking compact and took a page out of the superregional playbook by acquiring banks in Connecticut, Maine and Rhode Island.

The isolated money center bank successes, though, would not slow the changing of the guard, an occurrence that became particularly noticeable in terms of numbers of banking offices. Security Pacific, First Interstate and C&S/Sovran had more than 1,000 banking offices in 1990, and each of the ten biggest superregionals had at least 500 offices. BankAmerica also had more than 1,000 branches, but all of the real money center banks had fewer than 400 branches. This was a cultural variance that favored superregionals in a national interstate banking environment.

Despite the dramatic increase in asset share of the superregionals in the 1980s, the overall share numbers obscured the ongoing consolidation of banking. The share of the ten largest banks fell between 1980 and 1990, but this reflected the fortunes of the money center banks that dominated the top ten in both years. The consolidation that really counted, and a forerunner of what was to happen in the 1990s, was the rise from 6% to the more than 14% of bank assets by the ten largest superregionals.

Merger Mania

Interstate banking also had set in motion a quest for size led by the superregionals that triggered an unprecedented merger spree in the 1980s. From 1980 to 1989, there were 4,271 bank acquisitions. This was more than three times the number of bank mergers in the 1970s, and slightly more than the number of sales that took place in the twenty years from 1950 through 1979. Unfortunately, about 800 of those mergers were assisted transactions involving failed banks.

Bank Mergers in the 1980s

Year	Mergers			New Charters
	Unassisted	Assisted	Total	
1989	411	175	586	192
1988	598	173	771	229
1987	543	136	679	219
1986	341	101	442	257
1985	336	87	423	331
1984	330	62	392	391
1983	314	33	347	361
1982	256	25	281	317
1981	210	5	215	198
1980	126	7	133	205
Total	3,465	804	4,269	2,700
1970–79	1,316	50	1,366	2,224

Note: There were 226 banks closed in the 1980s and 50 closed in the 1970s.
Source: FDIC, Historical Statistics on Banking.

Merger activity also increased steadily as the 1980s progressed with 1987 and 1988 being by far the busiest years. The decade began with 133 bank mergers in 1980, but by 1985, there were more than 400 in a single year. That number jumped to 679 in 1987, and then peaked in 1988 at 771 before being slowed by deteriorating economic conditions. Some of the increase in merger activity in the mid-1980s can be attributed to interstate banking, but a rise in bank stock prices also was a big contributor.

Most mergers in the 1980s also used pooling accounting, which is an exchange of stock that combines the balance sheets and income statements of the two merging entities as if they had always been together and without punitive accounting adjustments. With pooling, a bank could buy another bank at a price times the seller's earnings plus after-tax cost savings equal to its existing market price times earnings without incurring any earnings per share, or EPS, dilution. If a selling bank's earnings were increased by 50% because of cost savings, then a buyer with stock selling at 14 times earnings could pay 21 times earnings without EPS dilution. If a bank's stock price went up, it could pay more, and if the price went up significantly, then it often could pay a price that could not easily be refused.

When the 1980s began, bank stock prices were low, and it was hard for a bank to buy another bank using pooling accounting for much over book value without sustaining excessive EPS dilution. As a result, there were few bank mergers, and those that occurred were often cash purchases rather than an exchange of stock that required the use of purchase rather than pooling accounting.

In purchase accounting, the acquirer does not keep the seller's equity and has to put the approximate difference between the price paid and capital of the seller on its books as a nonearning asset commonly referred to as goodwill, which was discussed briefly in the chapter on the early stages of the thrift crisis. As a result, purchase accounting not only constrained the price that could be paid, but it usually required the buyer to be much bigger than the seller because of capital constraints. Not being able to include the seller's capital in a cash transaction usually reduced the buyer's capital-to-asset ratio, and often below acceptable regulatory levels.

Stock Price Gains

In 1982, the prices of stocks, in general, and bank stock prices, in particular, began a six year rise after almost a decade of languishing in the doldrums. This was a necessary ingredient in the merger spree of the mid-1980s that contributed so heavily to the rapid growth of the superregionals.

Good bank stock indices were not readily available in the 1980s, but the movement of the stock of one of the high-fliers of that decade, Fleet, was indicative of the stock price trends of this period. Its major difference from the stock movements of other large Northeast banks was that Fleet's value lasted through 1989 since it was not overwhelmed by commercial real estate problems quite as early as most others in the region.

In the early 1980s, Fleet's stock, like most bank stocks, struggled to get above six times earnings and 100% of book. It was not until 1983 that it was able to finish a year above both those levels—and even then, a stock priced at 6.8 times earnings and 117% of book was not making anyone rich. This type of pricing made it difficult for banks to pay a high price for an acquisition in an exchange of stock, and, if cash was available, it usually was a better alternative as acquisition currency. At that time, there also was a lot of acquiring being done using debt instruments, and, in some cases, having the seller own the securities behind the debt to facilitate the transaction.

Fleet Stock Price, 1980 to 1990

Year-End	Stock Price*	Times Earnings	Percent of Book	EPS
1990	$ 11.00	–	62%	$ (.51)
1989	26.13	7.9X	131	3.30
1988	25.50	8.5	143	3.01
1987**	27.13	10.4	187	2.62
1986	23.25	9.7	179	2.50
1985	13.72	6.3	na	2.17
1984	14.28	7.1	125	2.03
1983	11.94	6.8	117	1.80
1982	8.95	5.6	101	1.60
1981	7.28	5.5	91	1.33
1980	5.83	5.1	82	1.15

Adjusted for all stock splits through 1990.
** June 30, 1987 or six months ended June 30, 1987.
Source: Moody's Financials, various editions.

It was in 1986 that bank stock prices finally experienced some good gains, and Fleet's stock almost doubled in value between year-ends 1985 and 1986 reaching $23.25 per share. By mid-1987, the price was above $27 per share, 10.4 times earnings and 187% of book. These were high multiples for the time, albeit well below what would come a decade later.

This also was the high point for bank stock prices in the 1980s, and it made prices paid for banks above two times book commonplace. After years of stock prices below book, this type of pricing was a strong inducement to sell, and higher stock prices coinciding with the advent of interstate banking led to a surge in unassisted mergers in 1987 and 1988.

Bank stocks fell along with all other stock prices in the October 1987 market crash, but bank acquisition activity stayed at a high level for a year after the stock price peak. This reflected deals in the planning stage prior to a fall-off in stock prices and the desire of some sellers who wanted to sell before prices fell even further.

Fleet's stock price ended 1989 only slightly below its June 1987 high, but the impact on multiples of earnings and book was not as favorable. Its

EPS and capital continued their upward movement, and, as a result, its year-end 1989 stock price was only 7.9 times earnings and 131% of book. This was not much above where it was in 1983 and 1984.

A year later, Fleet would be caught up in the regional collapse of the real estate markets, and its stock would be back at 1983 levels and selling at only 62% of book—and even that was better than many bank stocks. This, though, was the beginning of the 1990s, and part of a New England banking debacle that will be discussed in the next chapter.

Branch Growth

Surprisingly, even as large branch networks became more important to a bank's success and market value, the branch explosion of the 1960s and 1970s did not carry-over into the 1980s. There were many reasons for this including so many branches already having been opened that there was no longer the same customer need for additional offices, growing concern that the proliferation of ATMs would eventually make branches obsolete and the poor financial condition of so many banks and thrifts. Mergers also played a role as many overlapping offices were closed. In the 1960s and 1970s, there were few branch closings to offset the branches being opened.

There were still a lot of branches opened by banks in the 1980s, but the net gain in bank offices of 9,601 was only a little more than half the net gain in the 1970s and about 2,000 fewer than in the 1960s. The slowdown was even more pronounced when the increase in number of offices is viewed as a percent. The net gain in banking offices in the 1980s was 18% compared to a 50% increase in both the 1960s and 1970s.

The change in the number of offices for the troubled S&Ls was more dramatic. In the 1970s, S&L offices grew from just under 10,000 to 21,346, a gain of 114%, even as the number of S&Ls fell by about 1,000. Between 1980 and 1984, when S&Ls were losing money, there was a slight decline in number of offices.

In the mid-1980s, changes in the reporting of numbers of thrifts and thrift branches created some "apples and oranges" in comparing the early 1980s with the latter part of the decade. The FDIC took over the insuring of S&Ls in 1989 and only takes its historic thrift data back to 1984, and then between 1984 and 1987, the state-insured thrifts either disappeared or joined the FDIC system. As a result, the FDIC undercounts S&Ls and all thrifts in 1984 and had an unusual increase between 1984 and 1987 as state-insured thrifts moved into its system.

Bank and Thrift Branches, 1970 to 1990

Year	Number of Institutions	Branches	All Offices	
			Number	Change*
Banks				
1990	12,347	50,406	62,753	9,601
1980	14,434	38,738	53,152	17,802
1970	13,511	21,839	35,350	11,668
Thrifts**				
1990	2,815	18,795	21,610	(3,896)
1987	3,622	21,884	25,506	1,430
1984	3,418	20,658	24,076	–
Savings and Loans Only				
1984	3,391	17,949	21,340	(6)
1980	4,613	16,733	21,346	11,359
1970	5,669	4,318	9,987	2,056

* Preceding ten years for banks and S&Ls only in 1970 and 1980 and banks in 1990; preceding three years for thrifts in 1987 and 1990; and preceding four years for S&Ls only in 1984.
** Federally-insured thrifts only and increase between 1984 and 1987 is primarily a shift of state-insured S&Ls to federal charters. Total thrifts in 1984 were 3,993.
Source: FDIC, Historical Statistics on Banking and United States League of Savings Associations' 85 Savings and Loans Sourcebook.

From 1987 through 1990, when the "apples and oranges" problem disappeared, the decline in thrifts and thrift branches was substantial. In those three years, there was a reduction in S&Ls and savings banks of about 800 and a decline in the number of thrift offices of almost 4,000. Some of the disappearing branches found their way into the bank numbers as a result of bank acquisitions of thrifts, but this did not change the net impact on all banking offices.

Bank/Thrift Mix

The decline of the thrifts in the 1980s was more apparent in fewer branches, S&L failures and reported losses than in lost asset share. After having increased their share of assets from about 8% in 1950 to 23% in 1980, the S&L upward momentum ended, but only after 1985 and the slippage in the latter part of the 1980s was not of seismic proportions.

Depository Institution Asset Share by Type, 1980 to 1990

Year	Banks	Savings and Loans	Savings Banks	Credit Unions
1990	68%	22%	5%	5%
1985	66	26	5	3
1980	68	23	6	3

Source: FDIC, Historical Statistics on Banking; National Council of Savings Institutions, *1988 Fact Book of Savings Institutions*; and 1990 Credit Union Annual Report.

The S&L share of depository institution assets rose from 23% in 1980 to almost 26% in 1985, but by 1990, the S&L asset share had slipped to 22%. Thus, the S&Ls ended the decade pretty much where they began.

There was slippage, though, if their thrift brethren, the savings banks, were combined with S&Ls. Savings banks did not place nearly the same emphasis on growth during the 1980s as S&Ls, and their share of depository institution assets fell from a little above 6% in 1980 to less than 5% in 1990. This slippage reflected their problems, but it also was a reflection of the low growth in the Northeast where most of the savings banks were located—and that some of them chose to adopt a more lenient S&L charter. In so doing, their assets moved from the savings banks to S&L universe.

The banks had little change in asset share in the 1980s as they mirrored the S&Ls in reverse. The banks started the 1980s with a 68% asset share; fell to 66% in 1985 as S&Ls went on their desperation growth binge; and then were back at 68% in 1990.

The credit unions were the big winners as they rose from an asset share of less than 3% in 1980 to almost 5% in 1990. This put them only a year away from moving from fourth to third among depository institutions, ahead of the savings banks, in asset share. In many respects, they were filling a void left by the decline of thrifts, and particularly by the reduced number of mutual thrifts, which, like credit unions, had the competitive advantage relative to pricing of not needing to produce substantial earnings.

Asset share is far from a perfect measurement of the relative status of depository institutions, but deposit shares were increasingly understating the position of the big banks, including the superregionals that were gaining the upper hand in the battle for supremacy among financial institutions. This was because large banks were increasing their dependence on borrowings and decreasing their utilization of deposits for funding.

Product Mix

The shift away from deposits for funding also reflected the reduced importance of noninterest-bearing checking accounts. In 1950, they were 76% of all bank deposits; by 1970, they had fallen to 51%; ten years later, they were 36%; and by 1990, just 20%. As the majority of funding shifted to interest-bearing funds, the big banks weighed the relative cost of deposits against borrowings. The overall decline in deposits as a percent of assets was fairly modest, but was much larger for the large bank segment.

Bank Deposit Mix by Type, 1970 to 1990

Year	Percent of Deposits			Deposits/ Assets
	Demand	Savings*	CDs	
1990	20%	34%	46%	78%
1980	36	17	47	80
1970	51	21	28	85

* Includes MMDAs, NOW accounts and regular savings.
Source: FDIC, Historical Statistics on Banking.

The 1980s also saw a broad customer acceptance of money market demand accounts, or MMDAs. Passbook savings were becoming a thing of the past, and in the 1970s, the combination of all interest-bearing accounts other than CDs fell from 21% to 17% of all deposits. In the 1980s, instead of declining, these deposit types doubled their share to 34% of all deposits with most of the increase reflecting the growth of MMDAs.

CDs, which had their "day in the sun" when interest rates were in double-digits in 1980 and 1981, held their status well throughout the rest of the decade. The CD share of all deposits jumped from 28% in 1970 to 47% in 1980, and in 1990, were still 46% of deposits.

The shift in bank loan mix was equally dramatic in the 1980s and a clear break with the past. The major changes were a greater commitment to lending overall; a shift away from unsecured commercial loans toward real estate-secured lending of all types, albeit the shift had as much to do with an increase in real estate lending as it did an actual decline in commercial lending not secured by real estate; and the rise of the credit card.

Using real estate as a vehicle to increase loans as a percent of assets was symbolic of banking in the 1980s and the source of many of the bank problems. Loans went from 56% of assets in 1980 to 63% in 1990, and commercial real estate jumped from 11% to 19% of loans. Too many of these were bad commercial real estate loans in California, Texas and the Northeast, and by 1990, the banking industry was already paying for this increased commercial real estate orientation and the poor credit standards associated with so many of these loans.

Bank Loan Mix by Type, 1970 to 1990

Year	Percent of Loans					Loans/ Assets
	Home Mtg.	Other Real Estate	Com- mercial*	Consumer		
				Credit Card	Other	
1990	19%	19%	29%	6%	13%	63%
1980	14	11	38	3	15	56
1970	14	10	38	2	20	52

*Not secured by real estate.
Source: FDIC, Historical Statistics on Banking.

The impact of the credit card was not that noticeable in relation to loans, but these numbers understate the reality. In the 1980s, credit cards grew from 3% to 6% of loans, but credit cards were much more important than this by 1990. Credit card loans held in bank portfolios were only a little more than half of all credit card debt, and about 20% of credit card loans were securitized.

Securitization

Securitization, the packaging of loans to be sold as securities, came into its own in the 1980s. Being able to make loans, but not having to hold them, meant that the number of loans a bank could make was no longer limited by capital and locally-generated deposits. A bank could generate as many conforming mortgage loans as its lenders could produce and sell them to third parties—primarily Fannie Mae, Freddy Mac and Ginnie Mae—that would then package them and sell as securities.

This radically changed the home mortgage market in the 1980s as the mortgage pools replaced thrifts as the primary holder of mortgage loans. When the 1980s started, thrifts held almost 50% of all residential mortgages in their portfolios. By 1990, their share was down to 28%. Conversely, the mortgage pools' share had jumped from 12% to 37%. Not only did thrifts have earnings and capital problems in the 1980s, but their reason for existing had been undermined.

Holders of Residential Mortgage Debt, 1980 to 1990

Year	Mortgage Pools*	Thrifts	Banks	Govt. Agency	Others**
1990	37%	28%	16%	5%	14%
1985	26	38	15	8	13
1980	12	49	16	6	17

  * *Includes Federal National Mortgage Association, Federal Home Loan Mortgage Association and Government National Mortgage Association.*
  ** *Includes individuals, credit unions, mortgage companies, REITs, pension funds and life insurance companies.*
  Source: Federal Reserve Bulletins.

Securitization is an often overlooked factor in the consolidation of banking, but in the 1980s, it was a major lament of small banks and thrifts. The relationship that went with holding a mortgage or owning the credit card in a customer's pocket was an important element of small bank and thrift success, a plus that securitization was taking away. In the 1990s, almost all fixed-rate mortgages were sold to third parties, and credit cards were well on their way to domination by MBNA and two or three large banks.

New England "Miracle" Ends

T he 1980s took banks from the dark ages into the modern era in the midst of a national thrift crisis, a near meltdown of the money center banks and problems in the oil patch that devastated local banking industries, but it was 1989 to 1992 that would decide which banks fell by the wayside and which ones might prevail in the consolidation process. During these years, a national real estate-driven recession would contribute to the failure of more than 1,500 banks and thrifts; push many of the superregionals of the 1980s to the brink of failure—sending one, Bank of New England, over the brink; and add to the woes of the already staggering money center banks. These were difficult years for banks and thrifts, and by the time the "dust had cleared," the direction of the consolidation process had been totally altered.

During these years, the problems were no longer just at the big banks that the local bankers did not like very much anyhow; or with thrifts that banks felt were unfairly poaching on their territory; or even far away in Texas, which was "far away" for everyone not living in Texas, Arkansas, Oklahoma or Louisiana. Now problems were nationwide, but particularly on the East Coast from Maine to Florida and in California, as asset quality was deteriorating and being a banker was no longer the safe, pleasant occupation it had once been.

This was a shock to most banks since the 1980s, other than for the money center and Texas banks, had been good years until 1989. High interest rates in the early 1980s may have been a disaster for thrifts, but they sent money rolling into banks, widened margins and benefited earnings. Interstate banking had become a reality, bank stock prices were once again moving up and bank salaries were rising as well. For most bankers, the 1980s really were Reagan's "morning in America," and the bad days of the 1970s were a fading memory.

It is easy to look back at the 1980s and realize that it may have been too much of a good thing in much the same way that the oil boom in Texas was in the years preceding 1985. These good times revived the investor interest in bank stocks, but at the same time, producing double-digit earnings gains to keep stock prices rising began to override other considerations. The only way to do this seemed to be to lend, lend and lend some more, and with the optimism that existed throughout most of the decade, there always seemed to be a need for another office building or condominium. If banks did not make the loans, there were plenty of thrifts that would and customers would be lost. The real estate lending fever had reached the stage in one small "hot" state, New Hampshire, that if the employment gains in banking and construction were removed, there was no growth at all.

By 1987 and 1988, though, there was a growing concern about the future and the "bubbles" that were arising in parts of the economy. Most of the concern was about rising home prices and excess commercial and retail space, but much like in the late 1990s technology bubble, even the "bears" were not expecting anything more than a period of modest adjustment. If there were asset quality problems on the horizon, the feeling was that it was still primarily a thrift problem.

The full extent of the adverse banking trends in 1989 was not widely recognized immediately, and even as the clouds darkened as the year moved on, it was easy to rationalize that it was just another regional problem— New England and Florida falling into the Texas trap of overbuilding based on false optimism. Concerns that loan quality problems would spread to New Jersey, Washington, North Carolina's Research Triangle and then on to California was a year away. The 1989 to 1992 banking crisis would hit hardest in the "boom" areas where overbuilding was easy to justify, but in the search for double-digit earnings gains, banks from all over the country were putting money into these areas.

The impact of these four years from the beginning of 1989 through 1992, or from 1990 to 1993 in California, on the future structure of banking went far beyond what anyone could have imagined at the time. In New England, these were the years when Fleet moved away from the crowd and Royal Bank of Scotland gave its recently acquired Citizens subsidiary the backing to go from being a fringe competitor to an emerging powerhouse. Elsewhere on the East Coast, NCNB and First Union took advantage of the problems of others to build the bulk needed to become the Bank of America and Wachovia of today. On the West Coast, BankAmerica and Washington Mutual were the main beneficiaries of the consolidation that flowed from these difficult years. In New York City, the woes of the money center banks went from bad to worse as lingering international loan problems were compounded by delinquent commercial real estate loans.

The idiosyncrasies of the structural changes in the four most affected regions—New England, the Southeast, California and the New York area— are such that each deserves its own chapter. New England was the first to see its economy and banking industry falter during this national recession, and it is the logical place to start.

New England Overview

In the 1980s, New England was home to the "Massachusetts miracle" that launched the presidential candidacy of its Governor, Michael Dukakis, and had made Route 128, the highway that encircles Boston, synonymous with "high tech." New Hampshire, with its proximity to the Massachusetts technology base and lack of an income tax, was growing even faster than Massachusetts. Digital and Wang were the "hot" high tech companies; the Reagan military build-up had revitalized Raytheon and a host of small defense industry suppliers; and Harvard and MIT were a source of endless management and technological skills. At least in 1988, that was what everyone thought.

The region's largest banks, particularly Bank of New England, got caught up in the euphoria and went on acquisition binges facilitated by the arrival of interstate banking that greatly increased their size, but along with the enhanced size, came greater risk. Shortly after the Supreme Court blessed the New England interstate banking compact in 1985, Boston-based Bank of New England completed an "equal" merger with Connecticut's largest bank, CBT. Two years later, another Boston bank, Shawmut, went the same route with Hartford National, Connecticut's second largest bank. That same year, Fleet, in nearby Providence, used Rhode Island's 1987 "trigger" opening the state up for national interstate banking to move into Upstate New York and Maine with another so-called "equal" merger—this one with the Albany-based Norstar. In each case, the surviving holding company was headquartered in either Boston or Providence.

Bank of Boston was too big for an "equal" merger within the confines of New England, and unlike Rhode Island, Massachusetts was several years away from letting its banks expand beyond New England. Bank of Boston did what it could, though, to expand, and, in the 1980s, bought the largest banks available in Connecticut, Maine and Rhode Island.

In 1989, the "miracle" started to unravel in Massachusetts and throughout New England. Digital and Wang were making yesterday's products, a common ailment in the high tech business, and the fall of the Berlin Wall spelled the end of the defense spending boom. Suddenly, instead of wondering where they would find workers, companies in New England were letting people go, and an abundance of new office space and luxury

149

condominiums went from a sign of prosperity to a drag on the economy. This economic slowdown hit first in the Merrimac Valley in Massachusetts and southeastern New Hampshire where Wang and so many of the high tech and defense companies were based, and within a year, it had spread to all of New England. Digital, in particular, seemed to have a plant in almost every corner of the region.

New England Asset Quality Change, 1988 to 1992

Year	CT	ME	MA	NH	RI	VT
NPAs/Assets						
Banks						
1992	3.78%	2.02%	2.36%	2.82%	3.60%	3.75%
1991	5.89	3.79	3.55	4.27	5.99	4.69
1990	8.95	3.85	6.62	5.65	6.25	2.93
1989	4.53	2.12	3.81	3.06	2.58	1.77
1988	1.35	.75	1.57	1.15	1.53	1.12
Thrifts						
1992	5.60%	3.42%	3.25%	3.09%	5.54%	4.46%
1991	6.96	4.55	5.22	4.51	8.03	5.91
1990	6.98	5.76	5.95	8.55	6.62	4.27
1989	2.92	3.98	3.88	4.42	2.27	2.45
1988	1.24	2.15	2.31	1.67	1.58	1.85

Source: FDIC, Historical Statistics on Banking.

By the end of 1989, nonperforming assets had become a big banking problem throughout New England. Between year-ends 1988 and 1989, bank nonperforming assets in Massachusetts had jumped from 1.57% of assets to 3.81%. In Connecticut, they went from 1.35% of assets in 1988 to 4.53% in 1989. In each state, Bank of New England was a major contributor to the decline in asset quality. In New Hampshire, even without a Bank of New England contribution, the amount of assets not performing increased from 1.15% of all assets in 1988 to 3.06% in 1989. A year later, nonperforming assets were 6.62%, 8.95% and 5.65% of all bank assets, respectively, in Massachusetts, Connecticut and New Hampshire.

As 1990 came to an end, nonperforming assets exceeded tangible capital for banks in Connecticut, Massachusetts, New Hampshire and Rhode Island and had a similar negative relationship with thrifts in Connecticut, Maine, New Hampshire and Rhode Island. Nonperforming assets for Connecticut banks and New Hampshire thrifts were more than 200% of tangible capital. The negative asset quality impact on banks and thrifts was generally similar with the major variances coming from the negative effect of Bank of New England on Connecticut and Massachusetts bank numbers in 1989 and 1990 and the abundance of capital that the thrifts in Massachusetts had going into the period as a result of the stock conversions of so many of the state's largest savings banks.

Statewide totals, of course, are just that—totals—and many banks and thrifts were doing much worse. As a result, banks and thrifts began failing in large numbers in 1990, but it was 1991 that was the year of reckoning with more than 50 New England bank and thrift failures. In 1991, failed banks were 25% of the prior year-end banking assets in New Hampshire, 18% in Connecticut, 15% in Maine and 12% in Massachusetts.[1] These 1991 failures included Bank of New England and New Hampshire's five largest banking organizations.

In one of my *New England Banking Reports* at the time I wrote that "New England banking hit its low point in the first quarter of 1991 when the Bank of New England was seized and nonperforming assets climbed above 7% of total assets. At that time, New Hampshire's banking leadership was on its 'last legs,' and obituaries were being written for Bank of Boston, Shawmut and BayBanks."[2]

The opening line of that winter's *New England Banking Report* was "'Somebody said things couldn't get worse, but they did.' Those were bleak days for New England banking, and before the year ended (1991), 53 banking organizations with more than $40 billion in deposits had failed."[3]

From a bank consolidation perspective, the big New England stories in these troubled times were the failure of Bank of New England, the demise of New Hampshire's banking leaders, the rise of Fleet to preeminence and the opportunism of a Rhode Island thrift, Citizens, with foreign ownership. Superior management may have been the main reason that Fleet and the Royal Bank of Scotland's subsidiary, Citizens, benefited from the problems of others, but they were helped by banks in New York and New Jersey having their own problems and not being able to take advantage of the opportunities in New England.

Bank of New England

The biggest banking story in New England in the 1980s was Bank of New England. It was a "rags to riches" saga with a disastrous ending that was played out in less than a decade. In May 1982, Boston's $3.8 billion New England Merchants announced its biggest acquisition up to that point, T.N.B. Financial in the western part of the state, and then changed its name to Bank of New England. It was eager to be something more than a second-tier bank in Massachusetts and by the end of 1988, Bank of New England was no longer second-tier. Its assets had topped $32 billion, and it was almost as large as Bank of Boston. The dream was to end two years and six days later when Bank of New England went into FDIC receivership.

The big step for Bank of New England in moving from $3.8 billion to over $32 billion in assets was its equal merger with CBT, the largest bank in Connecticut. This deal was announced in 1984, but delayed by Citicorp's legal objection to its being excluded from buying New England banks until the Supreme Court ruled in June 1985 that states could exclude New York and thereby Citicorp from their interstate banking region. Three months later the merger was consummated. As part of the merger agreement, the Bank of New England name was retained and the headquarters stayed in Boston. Leadership from CBT led by Walter Connolly, however, assumed management of the combined banks whether that was the original intent or not. Within a year of this merger, Bank of New England acquired mid-sized banks in Maine and Rhode Island.

As a result of these acquisitions, Bank of New England raised its assets from a little less than $4 billion in 1981 to almost $23 billion by 1986. It was already second only to Bank of Boston in New England, and was rapidly closing the size gap between the two.

In 1987, Bank of New England received a "gift" from Fleet that would contribute to its sudden decline. Fleet made an unsolicited offer in late 1986 to the Conifer Group, Inc., a bank holding company in Worcester with assets of almost $4 billion and bank subsidiaries stretching from Cape Cod to the Berkshires. Conifer, a client of mine at the time, angrily felt this letter had "put it in play" and looked for buyers other than Fleet. Bank of New England was a logical alternative, and it outbid Fleet with what at the time was considered an astounding price at 18.6 times earnings and 303% of book.

The Conifer acquisition proved to be a bad deal for Bank of New England and the Conifer shareholders. One of Conifer's banks, Union National, was in the heart of the high tech country and would be a major source of bad loans. As for the Conifer shareholders, they would soon wish they were holding Fleet rather than Bank of New England stock.

In early 1989, the first bad vibes about Bank of New England began to surface. It was one of several banks with loans to a leveraged Chicago firm that was in danger of defaulting on its loans. Bank of New England's exposure was not that big, but the Chicago loans raised questions about its lending habits as this was a long way from home.

In December 1989, Bank of New England sent shock waves across New England and beyond when it announced, under pressure from the FDIC, that it was increasing loan loss reserves by more than $700 million. It put much of the blame on the loan portfolio of Union National even though Union National did not even have assets of $700 million. Bank of New England would report a loss for the fourth quarter of 1989 of $1.1 billion, and in early 1990, its CEO, Walter Connolly, was forced to resign. He would be replaced a few months later by Larry Fish, who would later prove to be one of the country's most capable bank CEOs, but by then, it was too late for Bank of New England.

Bank of New England's losses caused the regulators grief as well, and in Phillip L. Zweig's book on Wriston and Citicorp, he stated that "under the gun for the belated handling of BNE (Bank of New England), regulators came on like gangbusters on institutions throughout the country, virtually cutting off credit for real estate transactions." He quoted Citicorp's then president, John Reed as saying "That just killed the market. . . and from then on you couldn't sell buildings for love or money." According to Zweig, "If the credit crunch and the recession that it triggered needed a starting date, the 1989 examination of Bank of New England was it."[4]

Zweig and Reed were not alone in blaming the regulators for the real estate loan quality problems of the banks and thrifts in the post-1980 era. The regulators, though, had a tough choice. They could do what they did in the early 1980s with the thrifts, which was "close their eyes and hope for the best," or "get tough." The former approach had been a costly mistake, and it is hard to blame the regulators for not wanting a re-run of the thrift crisis.

Whatever its effect on the rest of the banking industry, Bank of New England was finished. It spent 1990 trying to find a partner and selling assets to maintain its capital adequacy, but by the end of the year, its time had run-out. On January 6, 1991, its banks in Massachusetts, Connecticut and Maine were declared insolvent and went into FDIC receivership. The FDIC had to find a buyer on the best terms possible. One possible buyer was Citicorp, and BankAmerica was believed to have a strong interest.

In April 1991, the FDIC made its decision and decided to stay local, accepting a Fleet offer for all three banks that was partially financed by the leverage buyout specialist, Kohlberg, Kravis, Roberts & Co. ("KKR") of "Barbarians at the Gate" fame—a best-selling book that told the story of how KKR won a widely-publicized hostile takeover of RJR Nabisco in 1988. This time around, KKR provided $283 million of the $683 million capitalization increase that Fleet had promised in order to obtain regulatory approval of the Bank of New England acquisition. Fleet would later repay KKR and have sole control of Bank of New England. The total cost to the FDIC was $889 million.[5]

With this transaction consummated, the big four of New England banking was down to three, and Fleet had become the largest bank in the region. At the end of 1991, Fleet had assets of $46 billion compared to $33 billion for Bank of Boston and $23 billion for Shawmut.

New Hampshire Impact

Bank of New England was the headline story in New England's early 1990s banking disaster, but what happened in New Hampshire was more devastating in its local impact. Much like the economic collapse in Texas a few years earlier, this banking crisis completely annihilated the largest New Hampshire banks and thrifts and let out-of-state banks gain preeminence in this small, but attractive, banking market. Most of this out-of-state takeover occurred on a single day in October 1991.

Like Texas, New Hampshire is a state with a strong independent streak, and in the 1980s, it was growing rapidly and prospering. The state's lack of an income tax along with a business friendly environment, attractive lifestyle and proximity to a Boston-centered high tech and defense industry boom had attracted businesses, second homes and retirees. As in Texas pre-1986, there was a strong feeling of invulnerability in New Hampshire.

New Hampshire also did not join Massachusetts, Connecticut, Rhode Island and Maine in their early endorsement of interstate banking. The out-of-state takeover of banking that occurred in Maine was viewed as inevitable in New Hampshire under similar circumstances, and the state legislators resisted opening its doors to out-of-state banks until 1988 when it felt it had no other choice. When the doors opened, two of its three largest banks, First New Hampshire and Indian Head, were sold to Bank of Ireland and Fleet, respectively. They were the only ones thinking "sell," and they proved to be the smart ones.

154

In 1989, New Hampshire still had five local banking organizations with assets in excess of $1 billion—Amoskeag, New Hampshire Savings, United Savers, BankEast and Numerica. While historically reluctant to sell, these five were in a race against the clock in a rapidly declining economy, and asset quality uncertainties had eliminated even the possibility of a sale. It was a race, unfortunately, that they were destined to lose, and on October 10, 1991, the FDIC closed all five. Amoskeag and BankEast had the most attractive franchises and were packaged together and sold to the Bank of Ireland. The others—New Hampshire Savings, United Savers and Numerica—were also sold as a package to an investor group as there was little interest from banking organizations. The investors, New Dartmouth Bank Group, contributed $38 million and the FDIC contributed $61 million to insure that there was adequate capital. The investor sold this package to Shawmut in 1993. The total cost to the FDIC was $891 million.[6]

These closings and sales dramatically altered the New Hampshire banking structure. Of the seven biggest banking organizations in the state when the economic downturn began, four became part of Bank of Ireland, two were acquired by Shawmut and one was bought by Fleet. A couple of years later, Royal Bank of Scotland, through its Rhode Island-based affiliate, Citizens, would purchase majority ownership of the Bank of Ireland's New Hampshire operation and Fleet would purchase Shawmut. Thus, by 1996, Fleet and Royal Bank of Scotland had, directly or indirectly, acquired all of New Hampshire's largest banks and thrifts.

Fleet[7]

Fleet's success in New Hampshire was only a small part of one of the more remarkable success stories in American banking. The bank's origins go back to 1791 with the founding of Providence Bank. In 1951, it became the Providence Union Bank following a local merger, and in 1954, merged with Industrial Trust Company and became Industrial National. In the 1970s and early 1980s, Industrial National was an active buyer of mortgage banks and other nonbank financial companies, and by 1982, it had assets in excess of $5 billion. In that year, it also changed its name to Fleet.

When interstate banking was allowed, Fleet responded quickly with some small bank acquisitions in Connecticut, but its big move came when it was allowed to go beyond New England in 1987 and announced an equal merger with Norstar. This merger took Fleet into Upstate New York and Maine; made it one of New England's four largest banks; and temporarily resulted in the cumbersome Fleet/Norstar name. Few, though, would have anticipated in the late 1980s that the Providence-based Fleet, and not one of the leading Boston banks—Bank of Boston, Bank of New England or Shawmut—would be the last big bank standing in New England; have the largest retail deposit share in the Northeast; and then sell to Bank of America for an imposing $49 billion.

The Norstar merger was a big step in Fleet's ascendancy, but equally important was how Fleet navigated the treacherous waters from 1989 to 1992, particularly having the courage to undertake the Bank of New England acquisition. Fleet was not immune to asset quality deterioration—in 1991, its NPAs were almost 5% of assets—but it did not slip as far as Bank of Boston, Shawmut or Bank of New England, and apparently it impressed the FDIC with how it was dealing with its problems. Fleet's willingness to take on Bank of New England in 1991 was a surprise, but even more surprising was the FDIC's willingness to let it do so.

Fleet's purchase of Bank of New England in 1991 instantaneously made it the largest bank in New England and kept a large competitor out of the region. Neither Bank of Boston nor Shawmut were in a position to assume what was left of Bank of New England, and if Fleet had not come up with a creative acquisition proposal, the FDIC almost certainly would have turned to BankAmerica or some other out-of-state bank. If they had done so, Fleet might not have been able to afford Shawmut and then Bank of Boston, and even if it could, it was likely to have been outbid by a much larger potential acquirer.

Citizens

The other bank that benefited greatly from the troubles of others in New England during this period was Royal Bank of Scotland, which in 1988 acquired Citizens Financial Group, a Rhode Island holding company whose primary subsidiary was a Providence-based savings bank with assets of $2.6 billion. Citizens was one of many New England thrifts in 1988 in the $1 billion to $4 billion range and did not seem to be nearly as good an entry vehicle as First New Hampshire, which had been acquired by Bank of Ireland. They were about the same size, but First New Hampshire was a commercial bank in a much more dynamic market. A less dynamic market, though, was a plus as Citizens, unlike First New Hampshire, was profitable every year from 1989 through 1992 and had relatively modest asset quality concerns.

Thus, Citizens was not an embarrassment to its foreign parent, Royal Bank of Scotland, and with the parent's muscle behind it, Citizens was able to buy when others were on the sidelines. In 1990, it bought the $1.2 billion

Old Colony Trust Company in Rhode Island from Bank of New England prior to the latter's failure, and in 1992, moved into Massachusetts with the acquisition of a failed savings bank in Plymouth.

In 1992, Citizens also made a management change that would give it the leadership to move to the next level. Larry Fish, a top executive at Bank of Boston and the man who tried to save Bank of New England in its dying days, knew the New England banking market well and became Royal Bank of Scotland's "man in America."

Fish kept the Citizens acquisition machine rolling. In the next two years, Citizens bought three more thrifts from the FDIC with combined assets of $2.5 billion, two of which were in Connecticut. The recession was over in 1993, but there were few buyers with an appetite for New England thrifts that were still struggling with the scars of the previous years. In 1993 and 1994, Citizens acquired three Boston area savings banks with combined assets in excess of $3 billion. By 1996, Bank of Ireland had enough of New England and sold a majority interest in First New Hampshire to Citizens.

By the time Royal Bank of Scotland integrated First New Hampshire into its system, it had become a major New England player. Its regional assets were in excess of $15 billion; it had significant presences in Rhode Island, Massachusetts, Connecticut and New Hampshire; and it was third in New England deposit share behind Fleet and Bank of Boston.

Aftermath

In 1993, New England bankers could breathe a sigh of relief as the economy and asset quality improved, but it was a badly-shaken local banking industry. In the preceding four years, about 100 New England banks and thrifts with combined assets in excess of $55 billion had failed, and this was only the assets at the time of failure. The assets involved if counting what the failed institutions' assets were a couple of years earlier would have been at least $75 billion. In addition to Bank of New England, the 1989 to 1992 casualties included at least a dozen banking organizations with assets in excess of $1 billion.

If the recession had lasted another six months, there would have been several more large failures as recapitalizing troubled banks required investor confidence. This was something that would only come when a turnaround was in sight, and there were a lot of banks and thrifts just barely making it.

The "near death" experience also had a psychological impact on the willingness to remain independent, particularly among stock thrifts. In 1990 and 1991, there were no unassisted thrift sales in New England because of asset quality problems for both sellers and buyers, and there was only one in 1992, albeit a large one—Society for Savings in Hartford. It was the ninth largest banking organization in New England when the recession began with assets of $4 billion and was acquired by Bank of Boston in 1992. It was a different story in 1993 and 1994 when 21 stock thrifts were sold, including seven of Massachusetts' ten largest with Fleet and Citizens buying five of the seven.

Of the four big banks in New England when 1989 began, Bank of Boston, Fleet and Shawmut were still there in 1993, but the order had been changed. Fleet had replaced Bank of Boston as the leader, and Fleet's going forward while the Bank of Boston and Shawmut stagnated had ramifications that went far beyond 1993. Fleet had the momentum and would soon have the market capital and investor support to acquire Shawmut in 1995 and Bank of Boston four years later.

Largest New England Banks, 1993

Bank	Assets 1993 1988 (in billions)		1988 Rank	Eventual Owner
1. Fleet	$ 48	$ 29	3	Bank of America
2. Bank of Boston	41	36	1	Bank of America
3. Shawmut	27	28	4	Bank of America
4. State Street	19	8	6	State Street
5. BayBanks	10	10	5	Bank of America
6. Citizens	7	3	–	Royal Bk.–Scotland
7. People's	6	6	8	People's
8. Northeast Savings	4	8	7	Bank of America
9. Peoples Heritage*	3	2	–	Toronto-Dominion
10. NBB	2	1	–	Bank of America
Bank of New England	–	32	2	Bank of America
Society for Savings	–	4	9	Bank of America
Home Owners	–	4	10	–

* Changed name to Banknorth in 2000.
Source: *American* Banker, April 11, 1990 and April 14, 1994 and SNL Financial, Charlottesville, Virginia.

State Street and BayBanks did not have the size of New England's three largest banks, but they were much larger than all other banks in the region in 1988 *and* 1993. State Street more than doubled in size during those five years with assets reaching almost $19 billion by the end of 1993, but even before 1988, it was exiting traditional banking, concentrating instead on asset management and selling its trust servicing capabilities to other financial institutions. State Street's much increased size reflected its trust and trust-related businesses. BayBanks, Massachusetts' most consumer-oriented bank, slipped badly during the early 1990s and was acquired by Bank of Boston in 1995.

The rest of the top ten banking organizations in New England in 1993 were thrifts—Citizens, People's, Northeast Savings, Peoples Heritage and NBB—two of which, Citizens and Peoples Heritage, would successfully make the transformation from thrift to bank and become Fleet's primary competition throughout most of New England. Peoples Heritage eventually would do so under a name it took from one of its acquisitions, Banknorth. By 1995, Northeast Savings, a Hartford-based savings and loan, had been sold to Shawmut, and NBB, a New Bedford savings bank, acquired by Fleet. People's, a Bridgeport savings bank, was still around in 2007, but it had not moved far beyond its Connecticut base.

The ultimate beneficiaries of the consolidation in New England that was triggered by the real estate-driven recession from 1989 to 1992 were Bank of America and the Royal Bank of Scotland. The five largest banking franchises in 1988 and seven of the ten largest would be part of Fleet ten years later and delivered to Bank of America in 2004 when it acquired Fleet. Royal Bank of Scotland's Citizens affiliate was able to assemble the mass to eventually become the second largest banking organization in the region.

Charlotte's Web

T he negative effect of the real estate-driven recession that began in 1989 and stretched through the early 1990's was not nearly as damaging to banking in the Southeast as it was in New England, or for that matter in California, the subject of the next chapter; but the recession's Southeast impact on bank consolidation nationally, and regionally, was much greater. Two of the five banks that were to buy nearly 50% of America's largest business came from this region, and it was in these years that NCNB and First Union became more than just a couple of ambitious southern banks.

In 1989, if asked to name the banks most likely to be among the handful of banks that would dominate banking 18 years later, few would have put NCNB on the short list even after its purchase of the Republic and InterFirst banks in Texas, and it is unlikely anyone would have included First Union. The obvious choices were the traditional leaders—Citicorp, BankAmerica and Chase Manhattan. Despite recent problems, they had been among the largest banks over most of the last sixty years and were still the three biggest. Chase Manhattan's money center culture seemed to be more of a growth impediment than it was for Citicorp, but it was logical to assume that Chase would solve that problem by buying a large superregional when it had its finances back in order. Beyond these three long-time leaders, Security Pacific and First Chicago were more likely to have been mentioned than NCNB and First Union as future dominant banks. First Interstate, PNC and Bank One were others that would have been considered.

Security Pacific was the most obvious choice beyond the big three to be in that handful of dominant banks 18 years later. It was the largest bank in Los Angeles; a likely beneficiary of the booming Pacific Rim fueled by strong growth in Japan; and had jumped from 11th to fifth in asset size since 1980. There was no indication at the time that the California economy would soon be reeling and Security Pacific would have such serious asset quality problems that its sale would be a matter of survival as early as 1992.

First Chicago, or a successor, was another strong candidate to join the big three at the top based on location. Illinois banking laws still discouraged branching and interstate banking, which limited First Chicago's ability to grow, but despite being smaller than NCNB, it seemed logical that when national interstate banking law superseded state laws that some large bank would want to be headquartered in the Midwest's commercial center. This theory looked prescient in 1995 when NBD, the alphabetized name for what used to be National Bank of Detroit, acquired First Chicago in one of those equal, but not really equal, mergers and took its management and holding company name to Chicago. Three years later Bank One in Columbus, Ohio made the same move after acquiring First Chicago-NBD. In 2003, when there were six, rather than five, banks with almost 50% of the banking assets, one of those six was a Chicago-based Bank One.

Why not NCNB after what it had accomplished in the 1980s? It had been a primary force in breaking down interstate barriers and had increased its assets from $7.2 billion to $66 billion in just nine years. In so doing, it had moved from 28th to seventh in size among the nation's banks, and moving up a couple more places would have been a normal progression. Nevertheless, NCNB had its doubters.

There were many reasons for not believing totally in NCNB in those days. One of the most common criticisms was that it was better at buying banks than running them. In 1989, the rumblings out of Texas were that NCNB was driving away customers by the droves, and it was jokingly being said that its initials really meant "no credit for nobody." There was some truth to this as its Texas loans were less than 40% of assets in 1990. As time would show, though, NCNB was right to worry more about the bottom line than market share in the early 1990s, and by the end of 1994, its Texas bank loans were in excess of 70% of assets.

NCNB's acquisition activity also was primarily buying smaller banks and failed institutions auctioned by the regulators. It was a bold and ready acquirer, but the banks it most wanted to buy usually chose another option. The three biggest banks sold in Florida in the 1980s—the prime target state for NCNB—chose someone other than NCNB. A much courted First Atlanta picked Wachovia over NCNB, and in 1989, an unsolicited offer to Citizens & Southern, Georgia's largest bank, was rebuffed with bitter words. An exception was Bankers Trust in South Carolina that had close board ties to NCNB, but it was only number three in a relatively small state.

A major reason why NCNB was not a buyer of choice was its CEO, Hugh McColl. NCNB owed its recent successes to McColl's leadership and determination, but his determination had a dark side that did not win over everyone. He had a reputation for being bold, arrogant and abrasive. He was an ex-marine, and proud of it, and he liked to use military terms when talking about acquisitions, which did not always go over well with potential partners.* Making unsolicited public offers to buy banks also was not a common banking practice, particularly in the South.

What may have seemed like weaknesses in 1989, however, would serve McColl and NCNB well in the difficult banking environment that lie ahead. NCNB did know how to run banks as well as buy them, and it was ready to exploit opportunities in a down economy while others were worried about adding risk. In the difficult environment of the early 1990s, NCNB's most desired merger candidates frequently had limited, if any, other options.

First Union, with its more congenial leader, Ed Crutchfield, was able to fill the role of buyer of choice better than NCNB, although neither could match a third North Carolina bank, Wachovia, in that role. Congeniality and money, however, helped First Union acquire banks in Florida and Georgia that put it ahead of NCNB in those states. The latter's Texas acquisitions, though, had put NCNB far ahead of First Union in overall size, which was to be a trump card in the days to come.

Southeast Banking Environment

It was the debilitating impact of commercial real estate lending gone awry in the early 1990s that reshaped the East Coast banking structure from Maine to Florida and provided the opportunity for NCNB and First Union to become more than just large southern regionals. Outside of New England, the degree of the loan quality problems varied greatly, and the fortunes of banks striving for regional leadership were heavily influenced by location. New York City and its New Jersey suburbs looked a lot like New England from a loan quality perspective, but going south and west from that densely populated area, the problems were much more scattered, and, ironically, reflected an area's growth dynamics. The better the market seemed to be for commercial real estate, the worse the loan problems.

---

*In the process of taking over C&S/Sovran, McColl had asked his head of Human Resources to provide a profile of the CEO of C&S/Sovran, Bennett Brown. In response, he also received an internal profile on himself that stated that from Brown's vantage point "McColl was arrogant, crude and ungentlemanly. Moreover, Brown was turned off by McColl's use of words suggesting power."[1]

In a Southeast that included all of the coastal states that were part of the southern interstate banking compact—i.e., from the Mason-Dixon line south—the areas hardest hit were Washington and South Florida. Like New England, these had been hot markets that seemed invulnerable to a serious downturn. As the nation's capital, Washington historically kept growing in good and bad times as the latter usually resulted in expanded government programs. South Florida, with growth fueled by sunshine and retirement homes, seemed equally immune to normal economic cycles.

Another "hot" market that bred builder overoptimism was North Carolina's Research Triangle. The state capital and three large universities—Duke, University of North Carolina and North Carolina State—created a strong growth environment, but being much smaller than the Washington area or South Florida limited the damage it could inflict on North Carolina banks.

In cities with low commercial real estate demand like Baltimore and most cities in the Midwest, the locally-generated loan quality concerns were more of a nuisance than a concern. If there was little need for the first large office building, new mall or condominium, then there would not be multiple developers trying to meet that need.

Atlanta also missed this round of overbuilding, possibly reflecting its earlier experience. In the mid-1970s, it was the focus of a real estate debacle with an emphasis on excess hotels. At that time, Atlanta was emerging as a major airline and convention center with a need for more hotel space. With little going on in most of the rest of country, this need was met with too much developer enthusiasm, and a few hotels too many were built with bank loans. It was hard to generate the same lending enthusiasm a second time around.

These regional loan quality variations coming at a time when banks were in a race for size and able to move across state lines had a tremendous effect on how that race evolved. The real-estate driven recession of the early 1990s favored banks in Charlotte and Atlanta over banks in Washington and Miami. Banks in Baltimore as well as in Southeast and Central Virginia also would suffer because of their proximity to Washington as some of the larger banks in those areas had major subsidiaries in the Washington area.

NCNB, with its boldness and creativity, may have done well under any set of circumstances, but if the playing field had been level in the early 1990s, or tilted the other way, Sovran and MNC, instead of NCNB and First Union, might have been poised to become national banking powers. Real estate woes, unfortunately for Sovran and MNC, are fickle in geographic orientation. In the mid-1970s, it was Atlanta and the Carolinas that were the primary sources of bad loans in the region. This time around, it was the Washington area and South Florida.

The unevenness of the asset quality in the Southeast in the early 1990s can be seen in the percent of assets not performing. At one extreme, banks in the District of Columbia, collectively, had nonperforming assets rise from less than 1% of assets at year-end 1988 to more than 7% two years later, and then move above 10% at the end of 1991. This was higher than in any New England state. Conversely, even at the peak of the crisis, in Georgia, North Carolina and South Carolina bank nonperforming assets were less than 2% of all assets.

Southeast Asset Quality Change, 1988 to 1992

State	NPA/Assets				
	1992	1991	1990	1989	1988
District of Columbia	7.00%	10.06%	7.09%	1.07%	.86%
Maryland	3.05	3.95	3.54	.96	.71
Virginia	2.34	3.45	2.34	.68	.65
Florida	2.21	2.82	2.95	1.93	1.82
South Carolina	1.74	1.95	1.36	.77	.63
Georgia	1.34	1.90	1.68	1.13	.97
North Carolina	1.17	1.80	1.50	.70	.56

Source: FDIC, Historical Statistics on Banking.

Banks in Maryland, Virginia and Florida did not have as many bad assets when measured as a percent of all assets as the District of Columbia, or the New England states, but their statewide numbers do not reflect the depth of the problem in parts of these states. Banks in the Maryland and Virginia suburbs of Washington and in South Florida may not have reached double-digits percentage in nonperforming assets, but were at least in the 5% to 7% of assets range of the New England states.

Since the extent of the asset quality concerns of the large Southeast banks during this recession reflected its commitment to the most troubled markets, Southeast Banking and MNC were the most vulnerable big banks. Southeast Banking was Miami-based and had the biggest commercial real estate commitment in South Florida. MNC, despite being headquartered in

Baltimore, was not much better off since it owned one of the two largest banks in the District of Columbia, American Security, and its Baltimore-based flagship bank, Maryland National, had almost 100 branches in the Maryland suburbs of Washington. MNC was second behind Sovran in Washington area deposit share.

Sovran, which would soon be C&S/Sovran, was the largest bank in the Maryland-Virginia area and vulnerable as well, but its Washington area assets were a smaller part of its overall asset base than for MNC. Its asset quality deterioration might have been little more than a bad memory if C&S/Sovran had been given time to work through its loan problems. Its problems, though, would be NCNB's opportunity.

First American, Washington's largest locally-based bank, also would be hit hard. Its troubles, however, went far beyond the local economy due to its ties to an overseas criminal banking organization, BCCI, discussed later in this chapter.

For banks in Georgia and the Carolinas to have troubled loans rise above 1% of assets, let alone 2%, was not something they were accustomed to, or liked, but relatively speaking, they did not have asset quality concerns. For the bigger banks in these states, other than NCNB and First Union, the response to even a modest increase in bad loans, though, was one of extreme conservatism. Wachovia and SunTrust were risk-adverse even when it meant forsaking better loan yields, an attitude shared by Citizens & Southern prior to its being pushed into a merger with Sovran in late 1989.

Southern Banking in 1989

Entering these troubled times, NCNB had a big size advantage over other banks in the South stemming from its acquisition of the Republic and InterFirst banks in Texas in 1988, but it was not an advantage that assured its position as a market leader. These purchases had made NCNB more than just first among near-equals in the South, but the Texas banks were outside NCNB's home area, the Southeast, and a merger between two of the other large Southeast banks could create a bank that could rival NCNB. As for First Union, it was still part of the crowd and had temporarily even lost its number two position in asset size to SunTrust.

The differences between banking in Texas and the Southeast alluded to above also reflect a regionalization that prevailed in the South in 1989. Interstate banking was only four years old, and the initial step for a bank in crossing state lines was usually to buy a bank in a neighboring state. Thus, although the southern interstate banking compact stretched from Maryland to Texas, there were still four distinct banking markets in the South—a true Southeast of Florida, Georgia and the Carolinas; the Middle Atlantic states of Maryland and Virginia plus the District of Columbia; a Mid-South of Alabama, Louisiana, Mississippi and Tennessee; and Texas whose oil patch problems had thrown its banking open to all comers.

North Carolina's NCNB and First Union were an integral part of a four-state "true" Southeast that not only had common geography, but also was bound together by the common objective of the area's largest banks to expand into Florida because of its size and growth potential or, if already there, concentrate on in-state expansion. NCNB's interest in Florida had been the impetus for interstate banking in the South, and by 1989, NCNB and First Union were among the five largest banks in that state measured by deposit share. Two of Georgia's three biggest banks, Citizens & Southern and Trust Company of Georgia, also had extensive Florida coverage. Trust Company's merger with Florida's third largest bank, Sun, would create SunTrust, which despite the semblance of equality in the name would be headquartered in Atlanta. The biggest remaining independent Florida banks, Barnett and Southeast Banking, had neither the need nor desire to move north into slower growing states.

In 1989, Florida's banking structure had undergone a major change when First Union announced its acquisition of Florida National. It was the third largest bank headquartered in the state; the prime target for NCNB when it entered Florida in 1982; and for awhile had an agreement to sell to Chemical contingent on New York banks being allowed into Florida, which was not to be in the 1980s. The Florida National acquisition put First Union in second place in deposit share behind Barnett in Florida.

The fourth state in the Southeast, South Carolina, was much smaller than the other three, and its banking was destined to go the way of banking in most small states—absorption by big banks in bordering states. Its largest bank, South Carolina National, was acquired by Wachovia in 1991, and the next three in size had been bought by Citizens & Southern, NCNB and First Union prior to 1989.

The intertwining of banking in these four Southeast states was further enhanced by two inter-region mergers that tied North Carolina and Georgia closer together. In 1985, First Atlanta spurned the overtures of NCNB and announced an equal merger with Wachovia to form First Wachovia with dual headquarters in Atlanta and Winston-Salem. A year later, First Union acquired Georgia's fourth largest bank, First Railroad.

Thus, NCNB had greatly increased its size by its acquisitions in Texas, but it was falling behind in its home market. Wachovia, it would drop the

"First" that had come with the First Atlanta merger, was the most respected bank in North Carolina; had the second largest deposit share in Georgia; would soon become the leader in South Carolina; and was the area's real buyer of choice. First Union was number two in Florida; number four in Georgia; and had a solid presence in South Carolina. NCNB was only number three in South Carolina; falling behind in Florida; and just a fringe player in Georgia. This was not what NCNB had in mind when it opened the door in the South for interstate banking.

In fact, it appeared that NCNB had misplayed its hand close to home in 1989, and that its Texas acquisitions had merely given it size while others were building better franchises. A heavy-handed and hostile approach to a merger with Citizens & Southern, Georgia's largest bank, would drive that bank into a marriage of convenience with Virginia's biggest bank, Sovran. This would create a bank almost as large as NCNB, and with a far more cohesive franchise, or at least, so it seemed.

The formation of C&S/Sovran was 1989's big merger—nationally as well as in the South—but it was not the only Southeast merger to impact the regional balance of power. First Union's purchase of Florida National had made it the second biggest bank in Florida. Further north, MNC bought one of its chief Maryland rivals, Equitable, and with that transaction moved far ahead of all banks, other than Sovran, in an area that had better growth potential than the Carolinas.

Thus, as the 1990s began, NCNB may have greatly increased its size with its Texas acquisitions, but it was still stuck with the rest of the pack in a southeastern big nine. This would change over the next three years as not only did fortune favor NCNB, but it had a leader in McColl who was not one to pass up opportunities presented to him.

In the early 1990s, NCNB would become the preeminent bank in the South with its purchases of C&S/Sovran and MNC, and First Union would become a solid number two with what was left over—Southeast Banking in Florida, Dominion Bankshares in Virginia; the Washington-based First American; and several large thrifts. Of the region's nine largest banks in 1989, Citizens & Southern, Sovran, MNC and Southeast Banking were gone by 1993, and Barnett, SunTrust and Wachovia were left to play catch-up in an environment in which "catch-up" would be no easy task.

NCNB—Citizens & Southern

NCNB's transition from being one-of-many in the Southeast to the dominant force in the entire South in just four years did not come easily. As would be the case in this and any other consolidation process, though, one move tended to beget another. Crossing state lines in the 1970s had brought NCNB into Florida with a small trust company, the vehicle it then used to be the first outside bank to make a real bank acquisition in that state. The size and experience gained from its Florida ventures gave NCNB the credibility to accomplish the acquisition of two failed banking leaders in Texas in 1988. With Texas came size and the ability to make an unsolicited offer to buy a bank that had a year earlier been its equal, Citizens & Southern. When it finally succeeded in that endeavor in 1991, MNC would be "easy pickings" a year later.

The "one step begets another" sequence was severely tested in 1989 when NCNB tried to use its size to force an acquisition that would make it the largest bank in the Southeast. Its target, Citizens & Southern, was the largest bank in Georgia—an obvious gap in NCNB's coverage—and also had a sizeable presence in Florida and South Carolina. It was an ideal fit, and McColl began the pursuit by calling Citizens & Southern's president, Bennett Brown, to arrange for merger discussions. When that failed, NCNB made an unsolicited offer of $2.4 billion, which would have been the highest price ever paid for a bank up until that time.[2]

What seemed logical and desirable to NCNB, however, did not meet with a favorable reception at Citizens & Southern. A war of words was followed by both sides hiring some of the top law firms and investment bankers in the country. Three weeks later, NCNB recognized the inevitable and withdrew the offer, but this was only the beginning.

The history of hostile takeovers in banking did not favor NCNB in its first use of the tactic. McColl's belief that he had a chance to succeed may have reflected his having beaten strong odds in convincing the regulators to sell him failed banks in Texas that, collectively, were almost as large as NCNB. Hostile takeovers only succeed, though, when three key factors are in alignment—the aggressor is strong and competent; the target is underperforming; and there are no comparable alternatives, often referred to as white knights, available. NCNB was a strong, competent bank, but Citizens & Southern was not underperforming; and it had white knights. These white knights may not have been able to top the NCNB price, but they might have been sold to investors as better long-term alternatives, even if this may have been a stretch.

Hostile transactions, although far-and-few-between in banking, have been part of the consolidation process. Norstar, the Upstate New York bank that made the first interstate acquisition in Maine, and subsequently merged with Fleet to form Fleet/Norstar, had one of the more notable hostile merger successes in its pursuit of Security New York in Rochester in 1983. This was the city I had left when I first got into banking, and when I was asked to participate, my initial reaction was that Rochester takes care of its own, and that Norstar and its CEO, Peter Kiernan, were wasting their time.* A visit with Kiernan, however, made a believer out of me.

In Norstar-Security New York, unlike NCNB-Citizens & Southern, the conditions for a successful hostile takeover were there. Norstar was a strong bank with a highly-respected CEO; Security New York was an underperformer with limited investor support; and there were no better buyer alternatives. There were other buyers, but even within Security New York, the thinking was that if a sale was necessary, Norstar was the lesser of evils—and the best outcome for shareholders.

Despite not having matched Norstar's success, NCNB's aborted hostile takeover was not the end of its efforts to buy Citizens & Southern. If a mistake had been made, it was not NCNB's hostile bid, but Citizens & Southern seeking a partner in order to survive. In September 1989, it announced a merger with Sovran, Virginia's largest bank. Sovran was a good partner choice based on 1989 circumstances, but Citizens & Southern's timing could not have been worse.

Sovran had become Virginia's number one bank after a merger of Virginia National and First & Merchants, the market leaders in Norfolk and Richmond, respectively. It subsequently acquired the largest bank in the Maryland suburbs of Washington, Suburban Trust, and then in 1987, bought Commerce Union, the third largest bank in Nashville, Tennessee. Sovran also had purchased a small bank in the District of Columbia. By 1989, it was by far the biggest bank in the Middle Atlantic states south of the Mason-Dixon line as well as being a factor in adjoining Tennessee's best market, Nashville.

The merger of Sovran and Citizens & Southern created a bank almost as large as NCNB and one with a more cohesive franchise. The combined banks were number one in Virginia and Georgia and among the top six in Florida, Maryland, South Carolina, Tennessee and the District of Columbia. Its less abrasive leadership also made it appear more suited than NCNB to make the next big acquisition in the area.

*In 1968, Taylor Instruments, one of Rochester's larger firms, was recipient of a hostile tender offer from a Latin American-based holding company. The Rochester firm for which I was working at the time, Ritter Pfaudler, was the successful white knight in a spirited acquisition battle and preserved the Rochester roots of Taylor Instruments. After the merger, the name of the firm was changed to Sybron as Ritter Pfaudler Taylor seemed a bit much.

There were two flaws, however, in a "live happily ever after scenario" for the newly-formed C&S/Sovran. The economy did not cooperate, and the terms of the deal let the economy be a bigger weakness than it should have been. On the plus side, it quickly abandoned its initial name of Avantor in favor of the longer, but more meaningful, C&S/Sovran.

Sovran was the dominant partner getting 15 board seats to 14 seats for Citizens & Southern, but there was to be dual headquarters in Norfolk and Atlanta. Also, the CEO initially would be Citizens & Southern's Brown, but upon his retirement at the end of 1991, the position would shift to Sovran's president, Dennis Bottorf, who was in his late forties and likely to be around for a long time. The normal sequence in this type of an equal transaction is that the equality disappears with the retirement of the first CEO, and the new CEO's home base, in this case Norfolk, becomes the de facto, if not the legal, headquarters.

Any good feelings related to this merger began to dissipate in 1990, as the economic problems that had surfaced in New England and Florida a year earlier were now hurting other areas and none worse than Washington. By the end of 1990, NPAs of District of Columbia banks had risen from less than 1% of assets two years earlier to more than 7%, and the problems were far more acute in the Washington suburbs than in the city, particularly in a part of Northern Virginia referred to as the Dulles Corridor. The excessive optimism of the mid- and late 1980s had resulted in a glut of empty office buildings financed by bank loans, and the large banks in the area, including C&S/Sovran, were major holders of these loans.

With its geographic diversity, C&S/Sovran was far from the hardest hit by the loan quality crisis in the area, but its nonperforming assets had increased from less than 1% of assets at the end of 1989 to 2% of assets a year later and were still rising. The Virginia portion of C&S/Sovran alone had an increase from 2.23% to 5.87% during 1991 of assets not performing. This was less than some other banks in the area, but was enough to send the stock price plummeting. When the merger was announced in September 1989, Sovran's stock, which C&S shareholders received in exchange for their stock, was selling at about $42.00 per share. By the end of 1990, four months after the merger was completed, the price was down to $15.63, which was about 72% of book value.

The problems were not life-threatening, and the Virginia bank may have done as well as could be expected under the adverse circumstances, but if Citizens & Southern had not merged with Sovran, its stock price would have been a lot higher. SunTrust, the remaining large, independent bank in Atlanta had a stock that was still trading at about two times book. The Citizens & Southern board members and investors were well aware of this, and from their less-troubled Atlanta base, were not shy about letting their disappointment be known. Their concern was heightened by Bottorf being scheduled to replace Brown as CEO at the end of the year.[3]

The problem might have blown over as the economy improved if NCNB had not interfered. C&S/Sovran had a lot of company with its high level of nonperforming assets among large banks on both coasts and not just in its home area. Wells Fargo, Barnett, Fleet, BankAmerica and most of the big New York City banks had high nonperforming asset levels and yet were to have their stock prices increase by multiples of three to four times over the next seven years. For all of these banks, 1991 and 1992 were trying years made much harder by worried regulators reading them the "riot act" and raising the specter of a possible failure.

C&S/Sovran's declining asset quality and stock price, combined with a sharply divided board and regulatory concern, was an opportunity for NCNB to accomplish what it had failed to do two years earlier. In May 1991, McColl placed a call to Brown once more. This time he was not rejected out-of-hand, and negotiations began.[4]

This was not really a hostile takeover as the acquirer was willing to consider the offer, but the offer was not welcomed by the Virginia board members. They almost certainly felt they were victims of something that was beyond their control and that they could survive, but the key elements of a successful hostile takeover were in place. The buyer was a competent, well-respected bank. The target was underperforming no matter what the excuses were, and there were no white knights to come to the rescue. C&S/Sovran was the 12th largest bank in the country; far bigger than any bank other than NCNB in the South; and the large banks in New York and California had their own problems. In any event, the latter were excluded from buying banks in the Southeast because of the regional restrictions on interstate banking that were still in place. NCNB was still not a buyer of choice, but this time the seller did not have choices.

In retrospect, this was a "done deal" as soon as NCNB decided to move forward, but like any transaction of this size, it had a lot of internal machinations. The Virginia directors wanted to stay independent, and most of the Georgia directors, including Brown, wanted to as well, yet the latter were not enthused about seeing control transferred to Bottorf. From an Atlanta perspective, the CEO transfer would have looked like a sale in its own right. There also were the usual concerns about price and pride.[5]

In July 1991, an agreement was reached, and a deal was struck for $4.5 billion, almost twice what had been offered for Citizens & Southern two years earlier despite the asset quality problems. It was a new high for a bank sale price; albeit one that would be eclipsed a month later by

BankAmerica's purchase of Security Pacific. The only negative vote was from the Citizens & Southern side, and it was a symbolic vote against the disappearance of Citizens & Southern's name.[6]

A new name, NationsBank, was chosen for the combined institutions, which would be the nation's third largest bank with assets of $119 billion. In the spirit of equality, Brown became chairman of NationsBank, but it was a victory for NCNB and McColl. There were now few doubters that NCNB, or NationsBank as it was to be called, would be one of the survivors of the consolidation process.

NationsBank—MNC

NationsBank was not through taking advantage of the problems of others. Buying C&S/Sovran made it by far the biggest domestic bank not based in New York or California and gave it the largest market share in the traditional Southeast of Florida, Georgia and the Carolinas as well as in the Middle Atlantic states to the immediate north. All that was missing in the latter was a strong position in Baltimore that was there for the taking along with an increased market share in the Washington area.

MNC, a new name for what was once Maryland National Corporation and whose primary subsidiary Maryland National was the biggest bank in Baltimore, was second in size to C&S/Sovran between New Jersey and the Carolinas. It had greatly enhanced its coverage in 1987 with the acquisition of American Security, the second biggest bank in the District of Columbia, and in 1989, merged Baltimore's third largest bank, Equitable, into Maryland National. By the end of 1989, MNC had assets of $26 billion, including Equitable, and was similar in size to Sovran, Citizens & Southern and Wachovia. It also still owned MBNA, which was the fifth largest bank-owned credit card company in the country. It was a bank on the move, and a much bigger company than the Maryland National Corporation that I had left a dozen years before.

Unlike the newly-formed C&S/Sovran, MNC was not geographically diversified, and as a result had a larger percentage of its funds committed to commercial lending in the Washington area. Its subsidiary, American Security, was second to Riggs in asset size in the District of Columbia, but was the largest lender in the city and had substantial loan exposure in the Dulles Corridor. When the commercial real estate markets collapsed, MNC was the region's most vulnerable large bank holding company.

No large bank between Boston and Miami was hit harder than MNC by the downturn in the real estate markets. Its American Security subsidiary had more than 21% of its assets not performing by the end of 1990, and a year later, it was still near 20%. Its much larger Maryland National subsidiary was not in nearly as dire straits, but with nonperforming assets equal to 7.68% of all assets at the end of 1991, it also was a troubled bank.

Baltimore and Washington Asset Quality Change, 1989 to 1992

Bank	1990 Assets (in bill.)	NPAs/Assets			
		1992	1991	1990	1989
Baltimore					
Maryland National*	$14	4.79%	7.68%	7.51%	1.05%
First National**	7	1.77	2.22	2.05	2.03
Union Trust**	4	3.00	4.75	4.92	1.88
Bank of Baltimore	4	9.37	6.03	2.39	1.03
Washington					
Riggs	$7	6.02%	6.00%	4.71%	.75%
Chevy Chase***	6	10.54	13.26	8.89	5.61
American Security*	4	10.86	19.62	21.40	8.49
First American-VA	4	9.53	10.70	5.05	.93
MNC	27	6.19%	10.83%	7.41%	1.08%

* MNC subsidiary.
** Bank level data.
*** Savings bank.
Source: Ferguson & Company, Irving, Texas.

American Security and Maryland National had a larger percentage of assets not performing than any of the other leading banks in their respective markets. Nonperforming assets as a percent of assets for the four largest banks in each market also showed the depth of the loan quality problem in Washington and how much worse it was in that area than in Baltimore, just 40 miles away. In 1991, three of Washington's four largest banks had more than 10% of assets not performing. A fourth, Riggs, which had never been much of a commercial real estate lender, was at 6.00%. In Baltimore, Maryland National with nonperforming assets at 7.68% of total assets at year-end 1991, led the way, but among the four largest Baltimore banks, it had by far the most coverage in the Maryland suburbs of Washington.

The situation at MNC was further complicated by a commercial paper liquidity crisis in early 1990 that had forced the sale of MBNA. MNC had issued more than $2 billion in commercial paper that came due in 1990 that it would have defaulted on if it did not come up with substantial amounts of new money. Its answer was to sell MBNA in a public offering that raised $992 million. This solved the liquidity problem, averted a possible failure and brought in much needed new capital, but was at the expense of a major source of strength and future value.

MNC changed management in 1990, and the chairman of the recently acquired Equitable, Al Lerner, assumed the CEO role. He was an astute entrepreneur who had built Progressive Insurance into a model for a property and casualty underwriter, but his timing for the Equitable sale to MNC was not one of his finer moments. It was a mistake, though, that was made much more palatable by his acquiring an almost 10% share of MBNA when it was sold to investors. His investment would be worth more than $1 billion a few years later, and this helped Lerner finance his purchase of the new Cleveland Browns franchise in 1998.

The MBNA sale was only a temporary solution for MNC, and even though its prospects were improving by 1992, it was under pressure from the regulators to sell or raise new capital. Since there were no buyers for banks with MNC's problems in 1992, it had to either find new capital or hope it could keep its regulators at bay until the local real estate market improved. In mid-1992, the latter course carried with it more risk than its board was prepared to accept.

For the creative NationsBank, this was an opportunity to solidify its position in the region by becoming as strong in Maryland and the District of Columbia as it was in Virginia. Nationsbank, like other potential acquirers, was not yet ready to take on MNC's problems in 1992, but it sold the MNC board on accepting a $200 million investment that could be used as capital in return for a five-year buyout option at approximately $1.3 billion. This was a low price for a healthy MNC, and in 1993, NationsBank exercised the option.

With the C&S/Sovran and MNC deals, NationsBank had created a southern powerhouse with national potential. Its branch coverage stretched from Baltimore to El Paso, and it had about 10% of deposits in the South. It was first in deposit share in Georgia, Maryland, South Carolina, Texas and Virginia, second in the District of Columbia, third in North Carolina and fourth in Florida.

First Union

NationsBank's crosstown rival in Charlotte, First Union, could not match its moves, but First Union vastly improved its position during this period as others disappeared or sat on their hands. From 1989 through 1993, First Union would acquire four banks with combined assets of close to $40 billion. With these purchases, its assets grew to a little over $70 billion by 1993, and it had become the country's ninth largest bank. In the South, only NationsBank was larger. First Union's target markets were Florida and the Washington area, and by the end of 1993, it was in the top two in each.

Its Florida success was particularly noteworthy in that its acquisitions moved it up to second place in deposit share behind Barnett and gave it the largest deposit share on Florida's Gold Coast stretching from Miami north to Palm Beach. In what had been the primary target state for NCNB, it was First Union that had made the bigger impact.

First Union's first post-1988 acquisition was the Jacksonville-based Florida National, which was the third largest Florida bank behind Barnett and Southeast Banking. It had assets of $7.8 billion when acquired, and Florida National alone would move First Union into second place in the state.

Another Florida purchase by First Union, Southeast Banking, would make it number one in Florida's largest market, Miami, and First Union may have owed this success to NCNB's preoccupation with C&S/Sovran. Miami's Southeast Banking was South Florida's biggest bank with assets of $13.4 billion, but its location and orientation toward commercial lending would be its undoing in a real estate-driven depression. By early 1991, its loan quality and supporting capital had deteriorated to the point that it was unable to raise new capital, sell or survive. In September 1991, Southeast Banking was taken over by the FDIC and put up for sale under the FDIC's assisted-sale program.

NCNB and First Union were among the most interested potential acquirers, but because Southeast Banking had failed, its buyers were not strictly limited to states in the southern interstate banking compact. It was an opportunity for New York banks to gain access to a market that had long been high on their "wish lists." It was an attractive acquisition with most of the risk being taken away by the FDIC, and Southeast Banking's buyer would be the leader in Florida's biggest market.

Fate, though, was to smile on First Union. The New York banks were in their own battle for survival; the most difficult competition within the region, NCNB and C&S/Sovran, were otherwise involved; and Barnett had too much of a market overlap to gain regulatory acceptance unless there were no other alternatives. NCNB was actively pursuing Southeast Banking at the same time it was going after C&S/Sovran, and considering its success in Texas buying

175

failed banks, it had to be a favorite to win in Florida as well. When NCNB won its more desired prize to the north, however, it had to put aside other endeavors. In the end, First Union, SunTrust and Barnett bid on Southeast Banking, and First Union's offer was considered to be the best by the FDIC.[7]

NCNB's acquisition of C&S/Sovran and then MNC did not preclude it from making additional acquisitions in Maryland, Virginia and the District of Columbia, but the practicalities of integrating such large banks into its system were substantial; and, thus, First Union was a logical haven for other struggling banks in those states and the District of Columbia. In 1992, First Union bought the $8.6 billion asset Dominion in Virginia, and a year later, acquired the deeply-troubled First American in Washington, a holding company with banks in Washington as well as in its Maryland and Virginia suburbs. Each of First American's three largest subsidiary banks had more than 9% of their assets not performing at the height of the recession.

First American's acquisition made First Union a leader in the Washington area, a dubious distinction at the time, but Washington was a large market with good growth potential even as its banks faltered. After acquiring First American, First Union had about 9% of the area's deposits, second only to NationsBank.

First Union also was one of the more active buyers of failed thrifts during this time. In 1992, it bought four thrifts with total assets of almost $10 billion. This included the two largest in Georgia with combined assets of $7.2 billion.

First American

In a story about bank consolidation, the travails of First American are more interesting than pertinent, but it is difficult to dismiss First American in just a couple of paragraphs on First Union's acquisitions. The troubles that forced the sale of First American went far beyond the asset quality concerns of other banks in these troubled times and showed that the regulators did not know everything about the banks under their control. In the early 1980s, First American had secretly come under control of the Bank of Credit and Commerce International, or BCCI, an international bank founded by Agha Hasan Abedi, and was not just another foreign bank.

A Senate Foreign Relations Committee report in 1992 stated that "Unlike any ordinary bank, BCCI was from its earliest days made up of multiplying layers of entities, related to one another through an impenetrable series of holding companies, affiliates, subsidiaries, banks-within-banks, insider dealings and nominee relationships. By fracturing corporate structure, record keeping, regulatory review and audits the complex BCCI family of entities created by Abedi was able to avoid ordinary legal restrictions on the movement of capital and goods as a matter of daily practice and routine. In creating BCCI as a vehicle fundamentally free of government control, Abedi developed in BCCI an ideal mechanism for facilitating illicit activity by officials of many of the governments whose laws BCCI was breaking.[8]

"BCCI's criminality include fraud by BCCI and BCCI customers involving billions of dollars; money laundering in Europe, Africa, Asia and the Americas; BCCI bribery of officials in most of those locations; support of terrorism, arms trafficking, and the sale of nuclear technologies; management of prostitution; the commission and facilitation of income tax evasion; smuggling and illegal immigration; illicit purchases of banks and real estate; and a panoply of financial crimes limited only by the imagination of its officers and customers.[9]

The size and scope of BCCI's activities and involvement with a major American bank were sufficient to make its control of First American a front page story that benefited from star power as well. First American's chairman, Clark Clifford, and president, Robert Altman, whose careers became closely tied to BCCI, were far from anonymous figures. Clifford was a well-know advisor to presidents and a former Secretary of Defense. Altman was not as well-known as Clifford, but was the husband of a movie star, Linda Evans of Wonder Woman fame. Prior to assuming their positions at First American in 1981, Clifford and Altman also represented Bert Lance, a well-known adviser to Jimmy Carter, in the sale of Lance's National Bank of Georgia to a BCCI nominee.

Ironically, prior to the coming of Clifford, Altman and BCCI, First American, or Financial General as it was known then, had the inside track on being one of the biggest of the 1980s superregionals. It was one of just seven banks that had been "grandfathered" into operating in multiple states prior to the arrival of interstate banking. It had sold banks in some of these states, but in 1980, it was still active in Maryland, New York, Tennessee, Virginia and the District of Columbia and could have acquired banks in any of these states when others could not. For reasons that are clearer now than they were then, First American chose to concentrate on its Manhattan office and international banking, and the interstate opportunity was lost.

Thrift Decline

The consolidation process in the Southeast was driven primarily by the sale of banks like First American, but also was helped by a decline in the number of thrifts and thrift assets. Some of the fall-off was the clean-up of the thrift crisis of the 1980s, particularly in Florida, but much of it came from some of the region's larger thrifts moving into commercial real estate in the late 1980s and paying a steep price for doing so.

From 1989 through 1993, about 190 of the thrifts in a Southeast defined to also include Maryland, Virginia and the District of Columbia disappeared, but more important was the decline in thrift assets in this region. They were more than halved from $198 billion at year-end 1988 to $92 billion in 1993. In Florida, the asset fall-off was from $89 billion to $33 billion, and by 1993, every one of these Southeast states, except Florida, had thrift assets of less than $17 billion.

Southeast Thrifts by State, 1988 to 1993

State	Number of Thrifts		Thrift Assets	
	1993	1988	1993	1988
			(in billions)	
North Carolina	86	133	$12	$21
Maryland	83	97	17	23
Florida	79	145	33	89
Virginia	43	63	14	30
Georgia	39	21	7	20
South Carolina	38	48	9	12
District of Columbia	2	5	1	3
Total	370	562	$93	$198
Mid-South	110	232	$17	$43

Source: FDIC, Historical Statistics on Banking.

In the rest of the South, other than Texas, thrifts were never much of a factor and became even less so during this period. In the Mid-South states of Alabama, Louisiana, Mississippi and Tennessee, the number of thrifts fell from 232 to 110 between year-ends 1988 and 1993. The most thrift assets in any one Mid-South state in 1993 were the $6.3 billion in Tennessee.

The disappearance of large thrifts was even more dramatic. In the expanded Southeast, there were 44 thrifts at the end of 1988 with assets in excess of $1 billion. Five years later, there were just 15, and by the end of 1995, there were only six. Just two, Chevy Chase and BankAtlantic, were still around in 2007. Florida was by far the most impacted by the sale of its large thrifts. It had 26 thrifts with assets over $1 billion in 1988 and just nine in 1993. The buyers were usually banks, but in Florida, some of the sales were to large West Coast thrifts. Many of these transactions were regulatory-assisted sales of failed thrifts.

Then There Were Two

The change in the Southeast banking landscape caused by the real estate recession of the early 1990s was one of the biggest facilitators of the consolidation process. In 1988, the region had seven banks—NCNB, SunTrust, First Union, Barnett, Citizens & Southern, Sovran and Wachovia—with assets between $20 billion and $30 billion, and two

Largest Southeast Banks, 1993

Bank	Assets 1993	Assets 1988 (in billions)	Rank 1988	Eventual Owner
1. NationsBank	$158	$30	1	Bank of America
2. First Union	71	29	3	Wachovia
3. SunTrust	41	29	2	SunTrust
4. Barnett	38	26	4	Bank of America
5. Wachovia	37	22	7	Wachovia
6. Crestar	13	10	–	SunTrust
7. Signet	12	11	10	Wachovia
8. Central Fidelity	10	5	–	Wachovia
9. BB&T	9	4	–	BB&T
10. First Virginia	7	5	–	BB&T
Sovran	–	23	5	Bank of America
Citizens & Southern	–	21	6	Bank of America
MNC	–	18	8	Bank of America
Southeast Banking	–	16	9	Wachovia

Source: American Banker, April 11, 1990 and April 14, 1994.

others, MNC and Southeast Banking, with assets in excess of $15 billion. Five years later, NCNB, by then NationsBank, had acquired three of these nine banks; had almost $160 billion assets; and was the country's third largest bank. First Union was a distant second in the Southeast with assets of $71 billion, but was the only other large bank in the area that had materially increased its size during these five years.

SunTrust, Barnett and Wachovia were still around in 1993, but with assets in the $37 billion to $41 billion range, had done little more than grow with the rate of inflation. They were still substantial banks and made some acquisitions during this period, but had fallen into banking's second tier regionally as well as nationally and looked more like sellers than buyers. Barnett would be acquired by NationsBank in 1998, and Wachovia was bought by First Union in 2001.

The remainder of the top ten in the Southeast in 1993 was composed primarily of Virginia banks with assets of less than $15 billion. Crestar, Signet, Central Fidelity and First Virginia had survived a bank-damaging recession that had hit close to home, but three of the four would sell within four years and the fourth a couple of years later. Signet and Central Fidelity would become part of the Wachovia banking network. Crestar was acquired by SunTrust, and First Virginia was bought by BB&T that made its first appearance in the Southeast top ten in 1993 while on its way to bigger and better things.

California Dreaming

I t was hard to imagine in 1989 the economic problems that were to bedevil the East Coast banks could soon become an equally negative force in California. Some of the larger banks in that state, particularly BankAmerica, had been hit hard by loans to developing countries, the earlier discussed LDC crisis, but California, and the entire West Coast, was benefiting from a burgeoning Japanese economy and President Reagan's defense build-up. At the time, it seemed like California and its largest city, Los Angeles, were riding an unstoppable wave of growth that would give its large banks and S&Ls national as well as regional preeminence.

In one of my banking reports in 1988, I was enamored enough to write that "it is inevitable that when barriers are removed, money flows to where the action is, and the combination of Japan, the strong economies of the region, the banking weaknesses in other parts of the nation are moving banking in the Far West to the head of the class. The regional allure has drawn eastern banking organizations such as Citicorp, Chase Manhattan and KeyCorp and every major Japanese bank . . . helping to transform Los Angeles into a banking center that threatens to rival New York and London, if not Tokyo."[1]

Today these statements sound almost ludicrous, but in 1988 and 1989 this was a logical assumption. Of the nation's approximately 70 banks and thrifts with assets in excess of $10 billion in 1989, 17 were in California— ten in Los Angeles alone—and just 13 in New York. Of the 15 highest bank or thrift market capitalizations, five were in California and four were in New York. BankAmerica, Security Pacific, First Interstate and Wells Fargo ranked third, fifth, ninth and twelfth in size among banks, and the country's eight largest S&Ls, led by Ahmanson and Great Western, were in California. These institutions, except for BankAmerica and Wells Fargo, had their headquarters in the Los Angeles area.[2]

Three years later, Japan's economy was faltering; the rising star of Far West banking, Security Pacific, was forced into a sale to BankAmerica; and five of the eight largest California banking organizations had more than 5% of their assets not performing, and a sixth just missed. What had looked so promising in 1988 and 1989 seemed ages ago, and any California dreams of domestic banking preeminence were over.

When economic conditions began to improve in California in 1994—the real estate-driven recession that began a year later than on the East Coast also ended a year later—among the big banks, only Security Pacific was gone, but those that remained had been weakened. BankAmerica doubled its size with the Security Pacific acquisition, but along with that purchase came far more bad loans than anticipated. Local S&Ls were hit even harder. Of California's 13 S&Ls with assets in excess of $10 billion at the end of 1988, seven were gone by 1994.

A Different Local Banking Industry

California's rapid descent from such heights was a sad turn of events for a local banking industry that had been at the forefront of banking trends for so many years. The state's size, rapid growth, geographic detachment from the rest of the country and early elimination of in-state prohibitions on branching allowed banks and thrifts to develop the economies of scale that spurred innovation and put California banks years ahead of banks in the rest of the country in retail banking. Bank of America was the "poster child" as early as the 1930s for progressive banking with its large branch network and its pioneering of the bank credit card in the 1960s, but was only the most visible part of a vibrant California banking industry.*

Right up through the 1970s when the ranks of the largest banks were dominated by New York and Chicago money center institutions, Bank of America, Security First, Western Bancorporation, Wells Fargo and Crocker National were the only retail banks that were regular members of the top 25 banks nationwide. They had branch networks in the 1930s and 1940s that banks elsewhere would not match until the 1970s. Transamerica, the Bank of America holding company, owned so many banks outside California that when its banks, other than Bank of America, were spun off into a new entity, Western Bancorporation, it immediately became one of the country's largest bank holding companies with banks in eleven western states.

---

*The continual usage of both Bank of America and BankAmerica in the text is confusing, but factually correct. Bank of America was the name of the biggest California bank from 1930 until it was sold to NationsBank in 1998. In 1968, a holding company was formed as the parent of Bank of America that was called BankAmerica. In 1998, BankAmerica and Bank of America were bought by NationsBank, which chose to use the Bank of America name instead of NationsBank for both its holding company and lead bank.

The rapid growth of California also created an in-state S&L industry that dwarfed what existed elsewhere. In 1980, the country's eight largest S&Ls were in California, and the S&Ls in the state held about 20% of S&L assets nationwide. By the end of 1988, the twelve largest S&Ls were in California and held 31% of the national S&L assets.[3]

California Bank Deposits by Bank Type, 1982 and 1986

Banks	Deposits		Percent of Total	
	1986*	1982	1986*	1982
	(in billions)			
Big Four				
BankAmerica	$ 53	$ 58	27.2%	35.7%
Other three**	72	46	37.1	29.7
Subtotal	$125	$104	64.3%	65.4%
Foreign				
Japanese	$ 21	$ 8	10.8%	5.3%
British	–	21	–	13.5
Other	2	3	1.2	2.0
Subtotal	$ 23	$ 32	12.0%	20.8%
Local	$ 46	$ 21	32.7%	13.8%
Total	$194	$153	100.0%	100.0%

*Includes all mergers completed or in process to date.
**Security Pacific, First Interstate, and Wells Fargo.
Source: FDIC Data Book, Operating Banks and Branches, June 30, 1982 and 1986.

The immense size of the market and interstate banking prohibitions also gave California banking an international flavor in the 1980s as foreign banks flocked to a market that was off-limits to out-of-state domestic banks. Standard Chartered, Lloyds, Midland and Barclays came from England. Bank of Tokyo, Sumitomo, Mitsui and almost every other large bank in Japan were among the foreign entrants, and banks came to California from South Korea, Hong Kong, Italy, France, Canada and Mexico. Some of the foreign banks were serving ethnic populations of their own nationality, but others had bigger goals. In 1981, Midland bought 57% of Crocker National, the 13th largest bank in the country. Another English bank, Standard Charter, owned Union Bank, with assets of $7 billion in 1980 and was California's sixth largest bank. Bank of Tokyo and Barclays had California assets of $3.6 billion and $2.7 billion, respectively, in that same year.

The foreign invasion of California banking peaked around 1982 with about 21% of statewide deposits with the British banks holding almost 14%. In the next six years, the British banks left California with Midland's sale of Crocker National to Wells Fargo and Standard Chartered selling Union Bank to the Bank of Tokyo leading the way. By the late 1980s, the foreign share of California banking had dipped to 12%, almost all of which was Japanese-owned.

The purchase of Crocker National by Wells Fargo was a major step in consolidating California banking in that it changed a big five into a big four, but this acquisition only maintained the big four's statewide deposit share at around 65%. Crocker National being acquired by Wells Fargo and smaller acquisitions by Security Pacific merely offset the lost share of a struggling BankAmerica.

Another dimension in California banking growth was the opening of a plethora of new banks. From 1980 through 1989, the number of banks in the state increased from 281 to 479, and in the four years between 1982 and 1986, the local banks' statewide deposit share increased from about 14% to 33%. This explosion of new banks was another manifestation of the state's booming economy in the 1980s.

Dark Clouds Gather

It is convenient to group the corresponding decline of the California and Japanese economies because of the coincidental timing and combined negative impact on the euphoria that had built up about the Pacific Rim, but the California decline had more to do with Europe than Japan. Southern California had an even bigger stake in the American defense industry than New England, and, like in New England, the Reagan defense build-up of the 1980s was the primary source of Southern California's economic boom. The region's major employers included Northrup, Hughes, Lockheed, TRW, Rockwell, McDonnell-Douglas and General Dynamics. When the Berlin Wall fell in 1989 and the Cold War ended, there was a substantial drop-off in defense spending and Southern California was a big loser.[4]

The percentage of total defense-oriented jobs was never that high in Southern California, but the rapid increase in defense-related employment fueled a growth in home and office building much as the oil and gas boom had done in Texas. Between 1980 and 1990, available square footage of office space in Los Angeles County grew from 68 million to 148 million. When the basis of this growth, the defense industry, began downsizing, the office vacancy rate rose rapidly, and the only good news for local banks was that Japanese banks held about half of the commercial real estate loans. On the housing side, the high demand for living quarters was accompanied by a rapid increase in housing prices, which in turn created a high vulnerability of mortgage defaults if home values were not sustained.[5]

Despite the many negative indicators, belief in the California dream was slow to die. The state had been in a perpetual boom for decades, and all previous downturns had been mild. The feeling then was that this would be the case one more time. No one thought that when employment peaked at the end of 1990, California would lose 752,000 jobs in the next four years—most of which would be in Southern California—or that the unemployment rate would reach 9.5% in September 1992.[6] This just was not supposed to happen in California.

While the reasons for the 1980s economic boom in California were unraveling, the state's big banks were just starting to enjoy a welcome revival. A very competitive market and their ventures into money center activities, particularly LDC loans to Mexico, had resulted in BankAmerica losing money from 1985 through 1987 and First Interstate and Security Pacific reporting losses in 1987. Wells Fargo had lost money in 1983 and 1984. From 1988 through 1990, though, all four were profitable and enjoyed the best overall earnings of the decade, but continued to carry relatively high levels of nonperforming assets—above 2.5% of all assets in 1989. BankAmerica had more than 4% of its assets not performing.

In 1991, nonperforming assets were rising and earnings declining for most banks in the state, and for some, much more than for others. Security Pacific suffered the most among the large banks. It was the biggest bank in Los Angeles and had far more of its assets committed to Southern California than the other large Los Angeles bank, First Interstate, a new name for what was once Western Bancorporation. Security Pacific's nonperforming assets rose from 2.75% of all assets at the end of 1989 to 6.44% at the end of 1991, and in 1991, it lost $775 million. First Interstate, which had almost two-thirds of its assets outside of California, also lost money in 1991, but much less than Security Pacific—albeit still a substantial $288 million. The San Francisco-based Wells Fargo and the Bank of Tokyo-owned Union Bank had big year-to-year increases in nonperforming assets-to-assets in 1991, but continued to make money.

California Asset Quality Change, 1987 to 1992

	NPAs/Assets				
	1992	1991	1990	1989	1987
California					
Banks	4.80%	4.46%	2.78%	2.54%	3.56%
Thrifts	4.02	3.99	2.82	2.10	3.41
Banks					
BankAmerica	3.71%	3.44%	3.21%	4.48%	6.13%
Security Pacific	–	6.44	3.77	2.75	3.45
First Interstate	1.58	3.39	3.55	3.75	3.35
Wells Fargo	5.38	4.79	2.82	2.63	3.90
Union	5.53	4.45	2.71	2.13	2.15
Thrifts					
Ahmanson	5.07%	4.68%	2.67%	2.18%	1.38%*
Great Western	1.33	1.24	.89	.45	.65
GlenFed	4.62	3.31	2.15	1.86	1.51*
Golden West	1.60	1.47	1.02	–	–

*1988.
Source: FDIC, Historical Statistics on Banking and SNL Financial Services Inc., Charlottesville, Virginia.

BankAmerica fared much better than its chief in-state rivals after 1990. Its 3.44% of assets not performing at year-end 1991 was up marginally from the previous year-end, but was well below its 6% plus of the mid-1980s. This was not good asset quality, but BankAmerica had raised its annual income above $1 billion in 1989 and kept at least that level, or better, during the entire recession.

The large California S&Ls generally came into the 1990s with better asset quality than the banks, and the largest among them, Ahmanson, had hardly been touched by the 1980s' S&L crisis. In fact, the large California thrifts had been buyers of failed thrifts in Florida and other states. By 1991, however, most of them were experiencing a rapid increase in nonpeforming assets. California's and the country's largest thrift, Ahmanson, the holding company for Home Savings, had 2.67% of assets not performing at the end of 1990, 4.68% a year later and then moved above 5% in 1992. California and the nation's third largest, GlenFed, followed the same trend from a slightly lower base.

There were, though, some exceptions to their rapid decline of asset quality. Great Western, which was only slightly smaller than Ahmanson, never had nonperforming assets reach 2% of total assets, and Golden West, parent of World Savings, was totally committed to home mortgages and had relatively minimal loan quality problems during the entire period.

Security Pacific[7]

The big story in California banking during these years was the rapid decline of Security Pacific. It was the rising star of West Coast banking in the 1980s, and in 1989, it seemed likely to eclipse BankAmerica. Security Pacific's assets had increased from $28 billion in 1980 to almost $80 billion by the end of 1988; it was based in Los Angeles where the action was; its losses related to LDC loans were far less than for BankAmerica; and it was the fifth largest bank in the country. Security Pacific seemed to be the right bank, at the right place, at the right time.

Security Pacific began as Farmers & Merchants Bank in Los Angeles in 1871 and grew rapidly with its market. In 1929, it became Security First National Bank, and in the 1950s, Security First merged with Pacific National Bank in the northern part of the state and took the name Security Pacific. It had become one of California's largest banks by the 1920s, and since 1940, was close to, if not in, the top ten nationally. By 1960, only BankAmerica and Western Bancorporation had larger branch networks.

In the 1980s, Security Pacific was aggressively taking advantage of opportunities that came with interstate banking. In 1986, it bought Arizona BancWest, the third largest bank in Arizona. A year later, it bought Rainier National, the second largest bank in Washington, and Oregon Bank, the third largest bank in Oregon. In 1989, it added the second largest bank in Nevada, Nevada National. As a result, by 1989, it had 20% of its assets outside of California. This was less than the 60% plus non-California assets of its crosstown rival, First Interstate, but Security Pacific had become more than just a California bank. It also had aggressively expanded into international banking.

The man responsible for this dramatic growth and diversification in the 1980s, Richard Flamson III, would hand the reins over to Robert Smith in 1990 who had promised to boost the stock price and push Security Pacific into a fresh round of acquisitions. Unfortunately, Flamson left behind a slew of problems, and Smith was soon into damage control rather than expanding. Along with a $200 million write-off in 1991, he closed down the international lending and securities trading operations. In the meantime, loans on several highly-leveraged deals were going bad, and its bad real estate loans stretched from Great Britain to Arizona—and this was before California's real estate market began its sharp descent.[8]

By the second quarter of 1991, California real estate loans were about half of Security Pacific's $658 million nonperforming loans, and this was only the beginning of the rapid deterioration of its real estate loan portfolio. There also was speculation that looming loan problems had ended merger talks with Wells Fargo that presumably would have at least had Security Pacific as a nominal equal partner.[9]

In August 1991, BankAmerica was willing to tread where Wells Fargo supposedly was not and trade loan quality risk for franchise enhancement. It paid $4.7 billion for a faltering Security Pacific, and the size of the acquiree lifted BankAmerica's assets to a level just below that of Citicorp, but it was not all roses for the buyer. Security Pacific had $1.4 billion in losses in the three quarters prior to the deal being consummated, and BankAmerica would eventually charge $3.6 billion of the purchase price to goodwill.[10]

BankAmerica paid far too much for a bank that would have been close to failing a year later, but the purchase reduced California's big four to a big three and combined what in 1988 had been the third and fifth largest banks in the country. It was another major step in the consolidation process, but the high cost in terms of price paid and losses incurred may have helped put BankAmerica in a secondary role when it merged with NationsBank in 1998.

Security Pacific was the only large bank forced to sell because of the real estate problems in California, but the number of banks in the state was greatly reduced. Between 1990 and 1994, there were 47 bank failures and 59 acquisitions, many of which were the result of the threat of failure. The largest of these smaller bank acquisitions was First Interstate's purchase of the $2.2 billion San Diego Financial, parent of San Diego Trust & Savings.

S&L Impact on Consolidation

There was no single deal remotely resembling the disappearance of Security Pacific on the thrift side of the California banking industry, but collectively, the damage done to the S&Ls in the state during this period may have had a greater overall impact on the consolidation process. In 1988, there were 13 S&Ls in the state with assets in excess of $10 billion, and five with assets of more than $25 billion—Ahmanson, Great Western, Cal Fed, First Nationwide and GlenFed. The latter were as large as NCNB, First Union, Fleet, Bank of New England and Bank One at the time. By the end of 1994, there were just six independent California S&Ls with assets of more than $10 billion and three with assets of more than $25 billion.

Largest California S&Ls, 1988

Savings and Loans	Assets (in bill.)	Net Income (in mill.)	Percent of Assets		
			Tangible Capital	NPAs	Reserve/ Loans
1. Ahmanson	$40	$203	3.74%	.92%	.13%
2. Great Western	33	248	5.33	1.56	.36
3. Cal Fed	28	135	2.93	2.21	.46
4. First Nationwide*	26	(3)	2.40	–	–
5. GlenFed	25	189	1.69	2.43	.86
6. HomeFed	17	111	4.60	3.27	.58
7. Golden West	17	138	3.34	1.10	.11
8. Great American	16	50	2.60	2.37	.32
9. American Savings	15**	(1)	1.79	–	–
10. Gibraltar	13	(63)	2.33	–	–
11. Coast	13	48	1.92	1.73	.25
12. Columbia	13	65	5.31	.67	.20
13. Imperial	12	15	1.65	3.69	.72

*Owned by Ford Motor.
**Excludes $22.5 billion of former assets put in a new S&L.
Source: Thrift Securities Handbook, Kaplan Smith, April 1989.

Some of the California S&L situation was a carryover of the 1980s thrift crisis, which was both good and bad. On the good side, American Savings had been acquired by Robert Bass in a 1988 FSLIC-assisted deal and was moving forward with new capital and a cleaned-up and greatly reduced balance sheet. Not so good was Los Angeles-based Gibraltar Savings, which would be taken over by FSLIC in March 1989. All of the other large S&Ls, except one, were profitable in 1988. That one, First Nationwide, lost only $3 million and was owned by Ford Motor whose "deep pockets" kept it from being a regulatory concern. The largest S&Ls, Ahmanson and Great Western, each earned more than $200 million in 1988.

Despite having survived the thrift crisis and producing strong earnings in 1988, California's S&Ls were far more vulnerable to a real estate-driven economic downturn than the banks. Eight of the 13 largest California S&Ls had 1988 tangible capital of less than 3% of assets—below 6% of assets is the threshold of regulatory concern—and their reserves were only slowly working their way up from the .10% of loans that was the norm against home mortgages even though much of their lending was now in far riskier commercial real estate. In other words, many of these California S&Ls did not have much of a cushion for dealing with adversity.

Because of their size, the elimination of risk-free FSLIC deals and the real estate problems of the most likely buyers, there were no ready buyers for these large California S&Ls when their loan portfolios put their survival at risk after 1988. Their size also made it very expensive for the RTC that had replaced FSLIC as the repository for failed S&Ls to close a failed S&L and pay off the depositors. Thus, the normal RTC procedure for dealing with failed S&Ls in California after 1989 was to let them continue to operate under RTC receivership until a buyer could be found.

Between 1990 and 1992, three of California's largest S&Ls followed Gibraltar Savings into receivership. All three—Great American, HomeFed and Imperial—were in San Diego, a city that also lost its largest bank in a rescue acquisition by First Interstate during this period.

When economic conditions improved in California, Ahmanson, Great Western and Golden West were still standing with assets in excess of $25 billion and were in a position to be consolidators of what remained of the California S&L industry—a role briefly played by the first two. Golden West was the real success story having come through the bad times without any real loan problems, and as a result, was able to go from seventh to third in asset size in the state while raising assets from $17 billion to $31 billion. Cal Fed and GlenFed, two other California S&Ls with assets over $25 billion in 1988, had survived, but were much smaller in 1993 than in 1988, and struggling.

Another survivor was First Nationwide, which was sold in 1994 by Ford Motor to MacAndrews & Forbes, a holding company controlled by Ronald Perelman. This was the same Perelman that had purchased First Gibraltar, the largest Texas S&L, from FSLIC in one of the controversial Southwest plan deals in 1988, which he later sold to BankAmerica. He would subsequently buy control of Cal Fed in 1996 and GlenFed in 1998, both of which would become part of a holding company called Golden State. In 1998, Perelman had a controlling interest in what ten years earlier were three of California's largest S&Ls—First Nationwide, Cal Fed and GlenFed. Golden State was acquired by Citigroup in 2002.

Consolidation Impact

Unlike the Southeast during the early 1990s, the primary impact on the consolidation process in California, and all of the Far West, was not who made the gains, but rather the failure of any of the region's larger banks to materially improve their positions. The region had no NationsBank or First Union coming out of this difficult environment much stronger than when they went into it. BankAmerica had doubled its size because of the Security Pacific acquisition, but that only brought it back in relative size among big banks to where it had been a few years earlier and with Security Pacific came many problems. Wells Fargo and First Interstate were still big banks, but First Interstate had almost $7 billion fewer assets in 1993 than it did in 1988, and Wells Fargo had not grown much in these five years. These banks were still in the SunTrust-Barnett size category rather than keeping pace with NationsBank and First Union. Bank of Tokyo's deep pockets allowed Union Bank to make it through this period, but with 1993 assets of less than $17 billion, it was strictly a local player.

Among the thrifts, Ahmanson and Great Western had each moved up a position in California when Security Pacific was sold and kept pace with Wells Fargo and First Interstate. They also had been major buyers of thrifts in other states. In mid-1994, Great Western had the largest thrift deposit share in Florida and Ahmanson was second. If there were to be any California thrifts playing a role in the national consolidation process, they were the prime candidates.

On a regional basis, the prospects looked much more positive as the California banks still dominated banking throughout the western part of the country. The only non-California banks in the Far West top ten at the end of 1993 was U.S. Bancorp in Portland, Oregon and Bank of Tokyo, whose American operation was dominated by California-based Union Bank. The California banks and S&Ls had been slowed by the economic downturn, but it seemed possible, and even likely, that they could use their positions in what was still one of the fastest growing parts of the country to regain their momentum.

Largest Western Banks, 1993

Bank	Assets 1993 (in billions)	Assets 1988 (in billions)	Rank 1988	Eventual Owner
1. BankAmerica	$187	$95	1	Bank of America
2. Wells Fargo	53	47	4	Wells Fargo
3. First Interstate	52	58	3	Wells Fargo
4. Ahmanson	51	41	5	Washington Mutual
5. Great Western	36	31	6	Washington Mutual
6. Golden West	28	16	–	Wachovia
7. U.S. Bancorp	21	14	–	U.S. Bancorp
8. GlenFed	17	24	9	Citigroup
9. Bank of Tokyo*	17	15	–	Mitsubishi UFJ
10. American Savings	16	–	–	Washington Mutual
Security Pacific	–	78	2	Bank of America
First Nationwide	16	26	7	Citigroup
Cal Fed	15	25	8	Citigroup

*Union Bank.
Source: American Banker, April 11, 1990.

In retrospect, the California banks and thrifts had lost their momentum for good and were ready to sell if the right offers came along. Within five years, BankAmerica would be sold to NationsBank, Wells Fargo would buy First Interstate and then sell to Norwest and Washington Mutual would roll-up American Savings, Great Western and Ahmanson. Golden State would hold on a bit longer, but in 2002 was sold to Citigroup.

It would not be a total loss for California, though, as after acquiring Wells Fargo, Norwest moved its headquarters from Minneapolis to San Francisco and retained the Wells Fargo name. The lure of the California market was enough to keep one of the five dominant domestic banks headquartered there—even if that bank cannot claim to be totally home-grown.

CHAPTER 14

New York Banking at the Crossroads

T he 1989 to 1992 recession played no favorites based on size and reputation, and New York was certainly no exception. It was the financial capital of the world in 1989, and New York banks were the icons of the industry—at least that was the perception. To most, the term "big bank" meant Citicorp, Chase Manhattan, Chemical, Manufacturers Hanover, J.P. Morgan and one well-known bank on the other coast, BankAmerica. They had been the biggest banks as long as most could remember—albeit their names might have been a little different in earlier days—and the advent of interstate banking had legislators shaping the banking laws of their states to slow the entry of these behemoths forever, if possible, but at least until the local banks had a chance to solidify their positions within their state and region. Even if banks should hit a "rough patch," as would happen in 1989, periods of change historically have enhanced the position of the big banks at the expense of their smaller rivals, and there was no reason to think it would be any different this time around.

The perception of local bankers and state legislators, though, could not have been more wrong, and for New York and its banks, the real estate woes that began in 1989 could not have come at a worse time. Since the late 1970s, New York's big banks had been struggling with nonperforming, or at least underperforming, international loans, most of them to Latin American countries. This slowed their growth throughout the 1980s, and it was these loans, even more than the regional interstate banking compacts, that had kept most of them on the sidelines during the early years of interstate banking. When New York banks were allowed to buy banks in New Jersey in 1989, only Chemical made the effort with a relatively small purchase in the southern part of the state.

The international waters had not only been inhospitable to New York bank loan portfolios in the 1980s, but they also had lost their international preeminence. By 1990, not a single New York bank ranked among the top twenty in the world in assets, and they would have fared no better if the rankings had been based on earnings or market capital. From 1987 through 1992, profits and stock prices were not their strong points.

The decline of the money center banks in New York and elsewhere was nothing new. In chapter two, the large banks' loss of deposit share was discussed in the context of the rapid growth of retail banking after World War II. Only the California banks, because of the immense size of the state and its liberal branching laws, approached the size of the New York banks.

Despite the post-World War II deposit share decline in the 1960s and 1970s, Citicorp, Chase Manhattan and BankAmerica were still the big three of American banking, and in most of those years, Manufacturers Hanover, Chemical, J.P. Morgan and Bankers Trust held the next four places. Charter—which would later change its holding company name to Irving—Marine Midland and Bank of New York were usually just outside the top ten. The dominance of the money center banks was further bolstered by the frequent inclusion among the leaders of Chicago's two money center banks—First National Bank of Chicago and Continental.

Ten Largest Banks by Location, 1940 to 1988

Year	New York	California	Chicago	Other	Total	Percent of Total
Assets (in billions)						
1988	$562	$231	–	–	$860	27%
1980	374	144	71	–	589	31
1960	34	21	3	–	59	22
1940	11	2	3		16	23
Number of Largest Banks						
1988	7	3	–	–	10	
1980	6	2	2	–	10	
1960	6	3	1	–	10	
1940	7	1	2	–	10	

Source: SNL Financial, Charlottesville, Virginia; Polk's Bank Directory; and FDIC, Historical Statistics on Banking.

The perception of potential banking dominance flowing from the streets of Manhattan across United States, though, was still supported by bank numbers as 1989 began. Seven of the ten largest banks were in New York, and the largest, Citicorp, was the country's biggest bank and more than twice as large as number two. J.P. Morgan and Chemical had each moved up a position in the rankings since 1980 to fourth and seventh, respectively. Manufacturers Hanover had fallen from fourth to seventh in asset size, but was still in the top ten. Bankers Trust was number nine, and Bank of New York, fresh off its hostile takeover of Irving, had moved into tenth place. With seven top ten banks in 1988, New York had the same number of top ten banks as it had fifty years earlier, and one more than in 1960 and 1980. The other top ten banks were more than 3,000 miles to the west in California.

The enhanced rankings of the New York banks in 1988 had more to do with the troubles of others rather than their own performances. Between 1980 and 1988, a struggling BankAmerica's assets fell from $112 billion to $95 billion, and Continental had to be bailed out by the government in 1984 because of excessive loan losses. Collectively, the ten largest banks' share of banking assets fell from 31% in 1980 to 27% in 1988. They were still the biggest, but were losing ground.

Thus, when the real estate markets in the greater New York area fell upon hard times, the banks that held the largest portion of the commercial real estate loans were in no condition to just shrug these loans off as short-term problems. To make matters worse, their national reach brought them troubled real estate loans from around the country.

The negative impact of this recession on New York's large banks was the area's big banking story from 1989 to 1993, but the widespread decline in real estate values also hit New York's suburbs and took away any chance New Jersey's banks had of keeping pace with NationsBank and First Union. That state's biggest banks, First Fidelity and Midlantic, would survive, but like so many of their larger brethren in New York, were weaker in 1993 than they were in 1988—and it was only a matter of time before they would be acquired.

It was the New York banks during this troubled period, though, that would alter the direction of consolidation in the dramatic fashion that only their size could produce. Manufacturers Hanover was the lone large New York bank to disappear, but by 1993, Citicorp's once insurmountable size advantage over other banks had been greatly diminished; Chase Manhattan was in a state of decline; and J.P. Morgan, Bankers Trust and Bank of New York had already diversified, or would be diversifying, out of mainstream banking. Only Chemical among these banks maintained anything like its previous status, and that was almost by default. New York City would still have skyscrapers filled with bankers, but unlike in the past, many of those bankers would be working for companies headquartered elsewhere.

In 1989 and the early 1990s, the declining economic fortunes of banks in the greater New York area—money center and otherwise—unlike in most other negatively affected areas, was only tangentially impacted by defense industry cutbacks after the fall of the Berlin Wall. What drives New York City's real estate markets, commercial and retail, and spills over into its suburbs is not manufacturing, but rather the fortunes of financial services companies, brokerage and investment banking firms as well as banks. Beginning with the drop in stock prices in late 1987, the bread and butter of much of the area's financial industry—stock trading and deals—fell sharply, and with them bonuses and employment. This drove high-end housing values down and commercial real estate vacancies up. Ironically, the impetus for the declining economy came from some of the very same firms that would suffer so badly from the results.

An inevitable result of the weakening economy was that the balance sheets of several of the biggest New York banks that were still feeling the negative effects of their international loans went from bad to worse. The added jolt was enough to force Manufacturers Hanover into a sale and raise concerns as to whether Citicorp, Chase Manhattan and Chemical, the first, second and sixth largest banks in the country, would survive.

Asset Quality Decline by Numbers

The negative impact of falling real estate values beginning in 1989 hit Citicorp, Chase Manhattan and Manufacturers Hanover the hardest. By the end of 1990, Citicorp and Chase Manhattan had more than 6% of their assets not performing, and Manufacturers Hanover was just a step behind with 5.80% of its assets not performing. Chemical, Bankers Trust and Bank of New York with nonperforming assets between 4% and 5% of all assets were doing only marginally better, but this was enough for them to have more favorable outcomes.

J.P. Morgan was virtually untouched by real estate problems, but this reflected a corporate strategy that made it look as much like an investment bank as a commercial bank. It still made commercial loans, but almost exclusively to large corporate customers—and it made few commercial real estate loans. Much of its income came from securities offerings, securities trading and financial advisory services, including merger assistance. There were legal limits as to how much of this J.P. Morgan could do, but it made good use of the limited investment banking-type activities allowed.

Large New York Bank Asset Quality Change, 1988 to 1992

Bank	NPAs as a Percent of Assets				
	1992	1991	1990	1989	1988
Bank of New York	2.82%	4.11%	4.00%	2.94%	2.36%
Bankers Trust	3.51	4.74	4.30	2.58	2.31
Chase Manhattan	5.79	5.87	6.04	4.26	4.70
Chemical	4.65	4.73	4.78	4.79	5.28
Citicorp	6.85	6.93	6.55	4.63	4.08
J.P. Morgan	.54	.67	1.18	1.29	1.89
Manufacturers Hanover	–	–	5.80	5.39	5.65

Source: SNL Financial, Charlottesville, Virginia.

Manufacturers Hanover[1]

New York's biggest recession casualty was Manufacturers Hanover, which was acquired by Chemical in 1991. It was the first bank to be sold while in the top ten nationally since the 1930s, but this was a sign of the times and of how consolidation had moved into high gear. Only months later, the fifth largest bank, Security Pacific, was bought by BankAmerica, and the twelfth largest, C&S/Sovran, was acquired by NCNB.

Unlike the other large 1991 acquirees—C&S/Sovran and Security Pacific—Manufacturers Hanover had been on a downward spiral since the mid-1980s and was particularly hard hit by the 1987 suspension of debt payments by Latin American countries. In that year, it made a $2.2 billion contribution to loan loss reserves and had a loss in excess of $1.1 billion. Latin American loans were problematic for all of the big New York banks, but Manufacturers Hanover's contribution to reserves was even higher in dollars than that of the much larger Citicorp. While it was profitable in 1988, the deterioration of the local commercial real estate market sent it back into the red in 1989 with a loss of $518 million.

Manufacturers Hanover was marginally profitable in 1990, but with the deterioration of the real estate markets, loan losses continued to mount. By the end of 1990, almost 6% of its assets were not performing. This was a lower percentage of assets than for either Citicorp or Chase Manhattan, but it had neither the size nor determination to persevere. In July 1991, Chemical acquired Manufacturers Hanover.

Chemical-Manufacturers Hanover, theoretically, was another of those supposedly equal mergers in which the CEO of the acquired bank became the CEO of the combined entity for a year or two after which time the leadership mantle was passed on permanently to the CEO of the acquiring bank, which in this case was Walter Shipley of Chemical. This was the plan in Fleet's merger with Norstar and Sovran's merger with C&S. In this case, though, there was no attempt to include the acquiree's name.

It was a sad ending for one of the great names of New York banking that could trace its heritage back to 1812 when Manufacturers Trust first opened its doors. John Jacob Astor was a founder, and Albert Gallatin, Secretary of the Treasury under both Jefferson and Madison, was its first president. Throughout most of the 19th and 20th centuries, Manufacturers Trust was one of the country's banking elite. In 1960, it was the seventh biggest bank in the country, and a year later merged with Hanover Bank, which was the 14th largest. Following this merger, the new Manufacturers Hanover, or Manny Hanny as it was often called, would be the fourth largest bank nationally in asset size.

Manufacturers Hanover's 1960's post-merger strategy followed the money center mantra of the time of pursuing international loans rather than domestic retail banking. In 1967, 20% of its operating income came from international businesses, and by 1977 had risen to 60%. In the 1980s, this international concentration would become its Achilles heel and not only result in the $1 billion plus loss of 1987, but also reduce its credit rating to almost junk bond status.

In the early 1980s, Manufacturers Hanover attempted to reduce its international dependence by diversifying into nonbank businesses. It bought First Pennsylvania's mortgage banking operation, and for a portion of the decade was the nation's largest mortgage banker. In 1983, it acquired CIT Financial, a commercial finance company for $1.5 billion—the largest price paid up to that time by a bank for an acquisition. This was to no avail and with loan losses rising and capital declining, Manufacturers Hanover sold 60% of CIT to a Japanese bank for $1.3 billion. This was one of many asset sales preceding the merger with Chemical.

Chemical

That Chemical would be the only New York bank to retain its position as a national leader without an ownership change would not have been expected prior to 1990. It was not nearly as well-known as Citicorp, Chase Manhattan and J.P. Morgan, and as the 1980s began, Chemical still trailed

Manufacturers Hanover in asset size. It did not cover itself with glory in the 1980s either. In 1987 and 1989, Chemical lost a combined $1.3 billion, but among the large New York banks, only J.P. Morgan and Bankers Trust came through the decade less-damaged, and they, unlike Chemical, had shown little interest in commercial real estate loans.

Chemical was an active international lender in the 1970s and 1980s like its money center brethren, but differed from the others in its greater interest in retail and branch banking. In 1975, it made the largest bank acquisition of the decade when it bought the Security National Bank on Long Island. In 1982, it agreed to purchase Florida National contingent on interstate bank approvals. This was not to happen, but in 1986, a similar agreement with Horizon Bank in New Jersey became a reality in 1989 when interstate mergers were permitted between New York and New Jersey banks. Chemical's major interstate move was buying the troubled Texas Commerce in 1987 that made it a banking leader in Texas.

When Chemical and Manufacturers Hanover agreed to join forces in 1991, it was a merger based on the assumptions that the cost savings would make the combined entities more profitable than either would have been on its own and that the economy would improve. This was the rationale for the ill-fated Texas merger of Republic and InterFirst four years earlier, but in this case, the economic conditions improved in time for the cost savings to make a difference

Chemical also used the momentum from the Manufacturers Hanover merger to raise additional capital and enhance its status in Texas. It added $1.5 billion in new capital that facilitated the acquisition of the failed First City Bank of Houston in 1993. The First City acquisition combined with the earlier Texas Commerce purchase made Chemical the biggest bank in Texas.

The Manufacturers Hanover acquisition also had made Chemical the third biggest bank in the country, ahead of a faltering Chase Manhattan. It would lose that third position to NationsBank in 1993, but had established itself as the second biggest bank in New York behind Citicorp and a market leader in Texas—positions it would not relinquish.

Chase Manhattan[2]

The downward slide of Chase Manhattan, even without an immediate sale, had almost as big an impact on the direction of consolidation as the sale of Manufacturers Hanover. Its slide would culminate in its falling out of its perennial position as one of the top three of American banking, and the slide was as unexpected as Chemical's ascendancy. It was unexpected, primarily because of its well-known name since Chase Manhattan had been struggling for many years and had large losses in 1987, 1989 and 1990.

The aura of Chase Manhattan was a product of its storied history. Its roots went back to the Bank of Manhattan that was formed in 1799, and it became Chase Manhattan when it merged with Chase Bank in 1955. The latter was founded by, and bore the name of Salmon Chase, Lincoln's Secretary of Treasury and a one-time presidential candidate.

Long before the Chase merger, though, Bank of Manhattan was a big force in the banking business. Bank of Manhattan had greatly increased its size in the 1920s, and in 1930, it bought Equitable Trust, the eighth largest bank in New York City, from John D. Rockefeller. That acquisition made it the biggest bank in the country.

Becoming the biggest bank would magnify the impact of Bank of Manhattan and put it in an unfavorable light in the 1930s when its CEO, Albert Wiggins, made a $4 million profit on a "short" sale on the bank's stock. This was a "bet" that its stock price would decline, and a type of profiteering that did not sit well with politicians or the public in the midst of the Great Depression. This incident would contribute to Wall Street getting blamed for the depression and the passage of the Glass-Steagall Act that was to separate commercial and investment banking for the next sixty years.

With Wiggins' downfall, Bank of Manhattan's leadership moved to the Rockefeller family and its close associates. Winthrop Aldrich, a brother-in-law to John D. Rockefeller, Jr., replaced Wiggins and led the bank until the end of World War II. After the merger with Chase, David Rockefeller, one of John D. Rockefeller's sons, would take the helm of Chase Manhattan and hold it until 1981.

Rockefeller further raised Chase Manhattan's profile with his interest in international affairs, but local leadership was lost to First National City, the Citibank predecessor. By 1980, it was a distant second behind Citicorp, and continued to decline. From 1988 to 1993, Chase Manhattan's assets only grew by about $5 billion, and it fell from second to sixth nationwide. In 1996, it too would be acquired by Chemical.

Citicorp

Citicorp fared better than Chase Manhattan, but 1989 to 1992 were difficult years for the country's biggest bank. It had done much better than most of the New York banks in the 1980s, particularly in the early part of the decade when it expanded into California, Florida, Illinois and the District of Columbia with thrift acquisitions, and it had left BankAmerica and Chase Manhattan far behind in the battle for national leadership. Between 1980 and 1989, Citicorp's assets grew from $115 billion to $231 billion, and by 1989 was larger than BankAmerica and Chase Manhattan combined.

By 1991, though, rumors were rampant that capital was a problem and Citicorp could fail. From 1989 through 1991, it contributed more than $9 billion to its loan loss provision; in 1991, it lost $457 million; and from 1989 to 1993, Citicorp's assets fell by $15 billion. Instead of being twice the size of the second largest domestic bank, its assets were only $30 billion more than those of BankAmerica in 1993, and NationsBank was coming on fast.

Citicorp, however, had more than size going for it. Its international coverage went far deeper than the troublesome Latin American loans, and it had the biggest bank-owned credit card. It needed help, but these strengths plus its past reputation helped it raise the capital it needed including a $643 million capital contribution—15% of total capital—from a Saudi Arabian prince, Alwaleed bin Talal.[3]

From a consolidation perspective, Citicorp was no longer the threat to local banks in other states it once was, nor was it still head-and-shoulders above all other financial services institutions. Its hold on the number one spot in the national banking pecking order was far from secure, and it was no longer too big to be bought. Citicorp's acquisition in 1998 by the less well-known Travelers was a surprise, but this surprise was made possible by the slowed momentum in the early 1990s.

J.P. Morgan, Bankers Trust and Bank of New York

J.P. Morgan had few loan problems and Bankers Trust and Bank of New York had relatively minimal asset quality problems compared to the other big New York banks, and all three were profitable every year from 1989 to 1993. This suggests that they should have gained at the expense of others and improved their national status. They had done better, but in two instances, J.P. Morgan and Bankers Trust, did so because they already had diversified away from mainstream banking. Bank of New York would move in that direction shortly after 1993. Thus, these banks, in effect, withdrew from being part of the full-service regional and national banking scene.

For J.P. Morgan, this withdrawal was consistent with its past. It was one of the most important banks in the world in the 1920s, but had been shorn of its investment banking capabilities as part of the Glass-Steagall separation of banking powers in the 1930s. It continued to be a banking leader thereafter, but its focus was on lending to blue chip corporations across the nation. Unlike its major competitors in the post-World War II era, J.P. Morgan did not try to be a broad-based bank. It did not open branches and had not made many commercial real estate loans.

This proved to be a good decision, but in the late 1980s, "J.P. Morgan was widely thought to be dead in the water. Compared with rivals then eagerly building up loan portfolios, it appeared to have become a sluggish also-ran. Critics said Morgan was too set in its pinstriped ways to survive the rough and tumble of the changing marketplace."[4] What it was doing was becoming more of a hybrid commercial and investment bank—a decision that looked better in 1990 than it did in 1988.

Bankers Trust was a smaller version of J.P. Morgan without the exalted history and long list of *crème de la crème* clients, and unlike other big New York banks, it did not date back to the nation's early days. Bankers Trust opened in 1903 to help other banks with their trust operations. In the 1920s, it broadened its horizons and became a multi-purpose bank, and by 1940 was one of the ten largest banks in the country. In the 1980s, it fortuitously moved away from general purpose banking to concentrate on large corporate customers, its trust operation and a securities business. As a result, Bankers Trust was not as committed to commercial real estate lending in the late 1980s as most other large banks.

Bank of New York's history rivaled that of J.P. Morgan, but differed in that it was still a general purpose bank in 1989, albeit a conservative one. This was consistent with its status as one of the oldest names in American banking having been formed by Alexander Hamilton in 1784. Bank of New York also is unusual among big banks in that it had kept its original name.[5]

In the early 1900s, Bank of New York had fallen behind its New York money center rivals, still it almost made it into the top ten in the late 1980s. This was primarily the result of a hostile takeover of a mid-sized New York money center bank, Irving Trust, in 1988, but Bank of New York had made several smaller purchases to improve its retail coverage as well, particularly on Long Island and in the suburbs north of New York City.

After having survived the trials and tribulations of the 1989 to 1992 recession, Bank of New York would soon move its emphasis away from traditional banking. In 1995, it bought trust services, securities processing and bond administration businesses and became a leader in each. In so doing, it became a profitable financial services company, but would no longer be a factor in bank consolidation other than by enhancing the position of a rival by the sale of its retail banking offices to JPMorgan in 2006.

Across the River

While the problems of the big banks understandably attracted the most attention in this real estate-driven recession, these big banks were far from alone in their suffering in the area. The negative impact of the real estate woes went well beyond New York City, and this could be clearly seen across the Hudson River in New Jersey. Nonperforming bank assets in that state jumped from 1.30% of total assets at the end of 1988 to 2.31% a year later, and by the end of 1990, more than 5% of New Jersey bank assets were not performing. By year-end 1991, the percentage was 5.60%, which was more than a percentage point higher than for New York banks.

Middle Atlantic Asset Quality Change, 1988 to 1992

Year	Banks			Thrifts		
	NJ	NY	PA	NJ	NY	PA
	NPAs as a Percent of Assets					
1992	4.28%	4.22%	1.75%	2.53%	4.78%	1.60%
1991	5.60	4.52	2.31	4.92	5.84	2.94
1990	5.23	4.54	2.17	4.80	4.42	3.30
1989	2.31	3.43	1.34	1.49	1.46	1.03
1988	1.30	3.28	1.41	1.03	1.01	.94

Source: FDIC, Historical Statistics on Banking.

Thrifts in New Jersey suffered a similar asset quality decline. Some of this was a carry-over from the 1980s' thrift crisis that had lifted collective nonperforming assets of New Jersey thrifts above 2% of all assets at the end of 1988. By 1990 and 1991, though, it was real estate loans that had almost 5% of the state's thrift assets not performing. During these years, New Jersey's largest thrift, Howard Savings, would fail despite having had few nonperforming assets going into the period.

Trends were similar, but in more modest proportions beyond the New York metropolitan area in Pennsylvania. Bank nonperforming assets in that state were in the 1.30% to 1.40% of all assets range in 1988 and 1989 and rose to 2.31% of assets by the end of 1991. The thrifts had nonperforming assets climb above 3% of total assets in 1990. These were statewide totals, and banks and thrifts from Philadelphia north to the Poconos experienced a spill-over effect from New York and New Jersey, and had asset quality numbers that were much worse.

New Jersey's two largest banks, First Fidelity and MidLantic, had differing results during this period, but the end result was the same—a loss of momentum and their sales in 1995. Asset quality suffered at both banks, but the larger of the two, First Fidelity, never had more than 4% of its assets not performing. Midlantic was not so fortunate and had over 7% of its assets not performing at the end of 1990, and in 1991 and 1992, the number was above 10%. It was still around in 1993, but this was primarily because of a lack of buyers in the area with the strength to take on its problems.

New Jersey and Pennsylvania Bank Asset Quality Change, 1988 to 1992

Bank	NPAs as a Percent of Assets				
	1992	1991	1990	1989	1988
New Jersey					
First Fidelity	2.70%	3.56%	3.46%	2.07%	1.70%
Midlantic	10.16	10.89	7.10	2.69	1.57
Pennsylvania					
CoreStates	2.67%	3.24%	2.11%	.55%	.56%
Mellon	2.19	3.41	2.88	2.31	3.15
PNC	3.77	5.03	3.11	1.52	1.24

Source: SNL Financial, Charlottesville, Virginia.

First Fidelity's relative success reflected the strong actions taken by a new CEO, Anthony Terracciano. He ruthlessly cut costs and took his losses early. The result was a loss of momentum that was disappointing for a bank that was as big as NationsBank and First Union going into the period and was in a position to do in the Northeast what those banks would accomplish in the Southeast. Instead, it was New England's Fleet that benefited from the disorientation of the New York banks in the 1990s to acquire the largest retail deposit share in the Northeast.

The loss of momentum would result in First Fidelity's sale in 1995, but at least the sale was done from the much improved position produced by Terracciano, and was the best outcome for shareholders. Its $5.6 billion price tag was about four times that of MNC, a bank of similar size in 1990 that was sold out of weakness in 1993.

Pennsylvania's largest banks were outside the New York metropolitan area, but they were lending into the same market and all of them had more than 3% of their assets not performing by the end of 1991. The largest of these, PNC, had nonperforming assets in excess of 5% of total assets. Like with First Fidelity, the decline in asset quality slowed PNC's momentum in the early and mid-1990s, but PNC and Pennsylvania banks overall fared better than the big banks to the north in New York and New England and those to the south in Maryland.

Savings Bank Decline

Other big losers during the region's time of troubles were the once-powerful savings banks that had already been hurt badly in the thrift crisis. By 1988, they were only a pale imitation of what they once had been. There were just six savings banks or S&Ls in New York, New Jersey and Pennsylvania with assets in excess of $10 billion at year-end 1988, and three of these— Goldome, Empire of America and City Federal—had negative tangible capital. A fourth, Meritor, had tangible capital under 1% of assets, and another, Crossland, had tangible capital of less than 3% of assets. Only New York's Dime Savings was truly viable with tangible capital at almost 6% of assets, but it also had 5% of its assets not performing.

Largest Northeast Thrifts, 1988

Thrift	Assets (in bill.)	Net Income (in mill.)	Tangible Capital	NPAs	Reserve/ Loans
			Percent of Assets		
1. Meritor	$17	$(210)	.27%	3.68%	.87%
2. Crossland	15	15	2.83	2.10	.35
3. Goldome	15	(119)	(1.74)	2.86	.48
4. Dime	12	80	5.97	5.39	.25
5. Empire of America	11	(57)	(5.15)	5.98	.82
6. City Federal	11	(12)	na*	na	na

*Specifics not available, but negative.
Source: Kaplan Smith, *Thrift Securities Handbook*, April 1989.

By 1992, all but Dime were gone, and the region's thrifts had become primarily local banking organizations with minimal outreach. Some like Astoria Savings and Queens County Savings had specialties in mortgage servicing and multi-family lending, and by-and-large thrifts would not be challenging the large banks in traditional banking. An exception to this much reduced role was Pennsylvania's Sovereign as it picked up the pieces others had left behind in New England, New York, New Jersey and its home state, to grow to over $80 billion assets by 2007, but in 1993, it had assets of less than $5 billion.

Aftermath

The impact of the recession and declining fortunes of so many of the large banks and thrifts in the New York area was felt both on a regional and national basis. Regionally, the big New York banks remained much larger than other Northeast banks, but their inability and unwillingness to move across state lines was an opportunity for others, particularly Fleet and PNC. As to national preeminence, by 1993, the once preeminent New York City banks had clearly lost their pre-1989 status.

Despite this lost national position in a Northeast that includes New England, the New York banks—Citicorp, Chemical, J.P. Morgan, Chase Manhattan and Bankers Trust—still towered over all other banks in 1993 in relative size, but this size advantage was misleading as to their true regional status. J.P. Morgan and Bankers Trust were out of branch banking. Citicorp and Chase Manhattan had increased assets by less than 6% in the preceding five years and had not meaningfully moved into neighboring states. Bank of New York may have survived relatively unscathed, but had fewer assets in 1993 than in 1988. Only Chemical with its acquisition of Manufacturers Hanover was a larger regional factor in 1993 than it was five years earlier, and Chemical was busy merging the two banks.

From a Northeast perspective, besides Chemical, the winners were the aforementioned, PNC and Fleet—banks that were far-removed from New York City with their primary emphasis. PNC increased its assets from $41 billion to $62 billion during this period and moved from eighth to sixth in the Northeast in asset size. It also moved into the top ten nationally for the first time. Fleet's acquisition of Bank of New England moved it from 13th to seventh in assets and past Bank of New York, Bank of Boston, Mellon and First Fidelity in the process.

Largest Northeast Banks, 1993

Bank	Assets 1993 (in billions)	1988	Rank 1988	Eventual Owner
1. Citicorp	$217	$208	1	Citigroup
2. Chemical	150	67	4	JPMorgan
3. J.P. Morgan	134	84	3	JPMorgan
4. Chase Manhattan	102	98	2	JPMorgan
5. Bankers Trust	92	58	6	Deutsche Bank
6. PNC	62	41	8	PNC
7. Fleet	48	29	13	Bank of America
8. Bank of New York	46	47	7	Bank of New York
9. Bank of Boston	41	36	9	Bank of America
10. Republic	40	25	–	HSBC
11. Mellon	36	31	11	Bank of New York
12. First Fidelity	34	30	12	Wachovia
Manufacturers Hanover	–	67	5	JPMorgan
Bank of New England	–	32	10	Bank of America

Source: American Banker, April 11, 1990 and April 14, 1994.

Nationally, the New York slippage was more noticeable. Citicorp's minimal growth between 1988 and 1993—it actually lost assets after 1989—may not have cost it the number one position, but others were closing the gap. BankAmerica had narrowed much of the difference with its purchase of Security Pacific, and NationsBank and Chemical were each almost three-fourths of Citicorp's size. Chase Manhattan had fallen from second to sixth; Manufacturers Hanover was gone; and Bank of New York was no longer in the top ten.

The New York banks' once dominant position with the only banks of comparable size being in Chicago and California was over by 1993. New York's top ten members had been cut from seven to five; BankAmerica was the only representative from California; and Chicago was not represented at all. With NationsBank in third place and First Union in ninth in 1993, North Carolina had more top ten banks nationally than California.

Largest Domestic Banks, 1993

Bank	Assets 1993 1988 (in billions)		Rank 1988	Eventual Owner
1. Citicorp	$217	$208	1	Citigroup
2. BankAmerica	187	95	3	Bank of America
3. NationsBank	158	30	18	Bank of America
4. Chemical	150	67	6	JPMorgan
5. J.P. Morgan	134	84	4	JPMorgan
6. Chase Manhattan	102	98	2	JPMorgan
7. Bankers Trust	92	58	9	Deutsche Bank
8. Bank One	80	25	26	JPMorgan
9. First Union	71	29	22	Wachovia
10. PNC	62	41	13	PNC
Security Pacific	–	78	5	Bank of America
Manufacturers Hanover	–	67	7	JPMorgan
13. First Interstate	52	58	8	Wells Fargo
16. Bank of New York	46	47	10	Bank of New York

Source: American Banker, April 11, 1990 and April 14, 1994.

The negative impact of real estate problems on New York area banks not only allowed BankAmerica, Fleet and the North Carolina banks to cut into the New York banks once dominant position, but also opened the door for banks in the Midwest. That part of the country had its problems in the early 1990s, but since it did not have a building boom in the 1980s because of a lack of attractive opportunities, there would be no real estate bust. This permitted Midwest banks to continue to grow and acquire in the early 1990s without concern over their own or potential acquiree's asset quality and one Midwest bank, Bank One, had become the eighth largest in the country by 1993.

Midwest's Changing of the Guard

D espite its lack of a decline in real estate values, the Midwest was hit as hard in the early 1990s by the national economic downturn as any part of the country. Jobs were lost and corporate earnings were down, but as noted earlier, since the area had struggled economically through much of the 1980s as well, there had been no earlier commercial building boom or rapid rise in housing values. What did not go up would not come crashing down at the first sign of economic problems; and, as a result, there would be no dramatic increase in the real estate-related nonperforming loans.

Some Midwest banks had problems during this period, but in most cases, the problems came from out-of-area lending. Chicago's two largest banks, First Chicago and Continental, were still burdened with the after-effects of their heavy Texas involvement in the1980s, and in the case of the former, international loans. Michigan National and one of Ohio's largest banks, Ameritrust, also had balance sheets that looked as bad as those of any Northeast bank. For most Midwest banks, though, the recession years only resulted in nonperforming assets moving toward, or slightly above, 2% of total assets. A couple of years earlier this would have been ample cause for concern, but compared to what was happening elsewhere in the early 1990s, 2%, or even 3%, of a bank's assets not performing was well within the realm of acceptability.

This relative calm in Midwest banking allowed the consolidation pattern that would have been expected from the introduction of interstate banking to continue with little concern about out-of-region interference. Problems elsewhere would keep BankAmerica and the New York banks home. The Midwest states allowing interstate banking also had moved beyond the region's east central states—Ohio, Michigan and Indiana—and included Illinois. In fact, the latter opened its doors to interstate banking before fully accepting in-state branching, but this did not lessen the out-of-state interest in the Chicago market.

The biggest changes in Midwest banking between 1988 and 1993 would be the continual slide of the large Chicago banks, First Chicago and Continental, and the rapid growth of Bank One, KeyCorp and Norwest.

The Chicago banks were one-two in asset size in the region in 1988. Five years later, First Chicago would be third and Continental would barely make it into the top ten. Meanwhile, Bank One and KeyCorp, both Ohio banks, had more than tripled in size, and the Minneapolis-based Norwest was not far behind. These rising regional forces also went well beyond the Midwest with their expansion. Detroit's NBD, although not growing as fast as the others, also was of a size by 1993 to be a major player in the next round and was particularly focused on being a significant factor in the Chicago area.

Midwest banking's main attention-grabber in the early 1990s was the spectacular growth of Bank One, but sharing the spotlight with Bank One were the consolidation in Cleveland; the opening of the Chicago market to all comers; and the quiet emergence of a Minneapolis bank, Norwest, whose historic focus had been on the farm states in the north central part of the country. It would be Norwest, not Bank One or a Chicago-based bank, that would become one of five banks that would dominate American banking.

Bank One

While no longer with us, the role played by Bank One in the banking consolidation in the 1990s cannot be overlooked. It had some down days in the mid-1990s, but over the entire decade, it surpassed First Union, Fleet and Norwest in total number of mergers, and by 1999, Bank One had become the fourth biggest bank in the country. Only Citicorp, Chase Manhattan and Bank of America were larger.

This was quite an accomplishment for Bank One, a family-run bank since 1933 and a newcomer to the ranks of big-time banking. In 1935, the Reconstruction Finance Corporation—sort of the RTC of its day— installed John H. McCoy as president of a recapitalized City National Bank & Trust Company in Columbus, Ohio. City National was a small bank in a mid-sized city whose banking was dominated by Huntington and Ohio National, but McCoy was successful in overcoming the odds by countering the bank norm of the time to concentrate on retail rather than commercial banking. In the 1950s, McCoy's son, John G. McCoy, joined City National, and in 1958, replaced his father as its CEO and driving force.[1]

City National grew rapidly after World War II, and in 1967, formed a holding company, First Bank Group, but was still a small factor in the overall Ohio banking market. In 1970, it had assets of about $500 million and was among the 200 largest banks in the country, yet it was only the eleventh largest bank in Ohio and third largest in Columbus.

In the 1970s, First Bank Group made numerous acquisitions in Ohio, and by 1980 had $3.2 billion assets and a place in the top hundred banks nationwide. It also had become the fifth largest bank in Ohio, number two in Columbus and was ready to move onto the center stage. In 1979, the holding company name was changed to the much simpler Banc One.[*]

Bank One made a series of acquisitions in Ohio in the early 1980s, but it was not until the arrival of interstate banking—and a new McCoy, that it moved ahead of other banks in the state. In 1985, John B. McCoy became the third generation to head up this dynamic banking organization, and in 1987, Bank One bought one of the largest banks in Indiana. A year later it acquired a mid-sized bank in Wisconsin and one of the Texas banking leaders, M-Corp, from the FDIC. By 1988, Bank One had assets of $25.3 billion and was the third largest Midwest bank behind First Chicago and Continental. It had almost $4 billion more assets than the second largest Ohio bank, National City.

The meteoric rise of Bank One under the third McCoy through 1988 was only the beginning. In 1989 and 1990, it made three small acquisitions, two of them in Illinois. In 1991, Bank One picked up the pace with three Illinois acquisitions and one in Kentucky with combined assets of about $5 billion. It also bought PNC's southwest Ohio banks, and at the end of the year, Bank One bought a $2.8 billion asset bank in Colorado. Its earlier acquisition of M-Corp in Texas was no longer an isolated expansion beyond the Midwest.

This was all a prelude to 1992 and 1993 when Bank One followed up the Colorado acquisition with the purchase of Valley National, the largest independent bank in Arizona with almost $11 billion assets, and four more acquisitions in Texas. Bank One also acquired the largest independent bank in Kentucky and the second largest bank in West Virginia.

This was a frenetic pace, and by the end of 1993, Bank One was the largest Midwest bank with assets of almost $80 billion and the eighth largest bank in the country. It had not matched the growth of NCNB, but Bank One was bigger than First Union, Wells Fargo and Fleet. It had come a long way in a short time.

---

[*]The term Banc was initially used rather than Bank for the holding company because of legalities relative to use of "bank" in a holding company name. When permitted, the holding company name was changed to Bank One, and that is the nomenclature used throughout this book.

KeyCorp and the Cleveland Consolidation

Bank One's move from its humble Columbus beginnings to being the Midwest's biggest bank overshadowed the jockeying for position in Ohio's biggest city and financial center, Cleveland, but banks in that city would play a major role in Midwest and national bank consolidation; a much bigger role than would have been expected of banks in a rust belt city that had seen better days. Prior to 1980, five of Ohio's six biggest banks—Cleveland Trust, Central National, National City, Society and Union Commerce—were in Cleveland, and the largest, Cleveland Trust, had long been one of the biggest banks outside New York City, Chicago and California.

That Society would emerge from among these five to be Cleveland's biggest bank and second largest in the Midwest by 1993 was as improbable as Bank One's rise a decade earlier. Society's roots went back to 1844, but as a mutual savings bank, not as a commercial bank. It remained Society for Savings and a thrift until 1955 when it converted to a bank charter and became Society National Bank. In 1980, Society was fourth in Cleveland behind Ameritrust—a new name for Cleveland Trust that was intended to give it broader geographic appeal—National City and Central National, and it was not much ahead of Union Commerce in total assets.

Society took a big step forward in the battle for preeminence in the Cleveland area in 1981 when it acquired Central National. By 1985, it had passed a faltering Ameritrust and was second only to National City locally. Society also had become a much more important bank throughout northern Ohio, but in 1988, was just barely in the top ten of Midwest banks and well behind Bank One and National City.

In the early 1990s, Society was not nearly as acquisitive as Bank One, but two of its mergers were larger than any of those of its Columbus rival. In 1991, it bought Cleveland's one-time banking leader, Ameritrust, and in 1993, Society agreed to an equal merger with an Upstate New York bank, KeyCorp. The Ameritrust acquisition gave Society near parity in size with National City and the bulk to deal with KeyCorp on an equal basis.

The KeyCorp-Society merger was unusual in that it really was a near equal sharing between partners. Technically, Albany-based KeyCorp was the acquirer, and its CEO, Victor Riley, became the CEO of the combined banks without a set date as to when he would pass the reins over to a Society person. That, plus the Society name disappearing, suggested that Society had been bought. The *quid pro quo,* though, was that the main office would be in Cleveland, and, if nothing else, this made the new KeyCorp a Midwest bank. Headquarters also usually determines the winner in an equal merger as CEOs move on, and even when they are slow to do so, they become part of the city in which they live.

Merging with KeyCorp made Society more than just a Midwest bank, as well. When Riley took over at National Commerce Bank in Albany, the KeyCorp predecessor and an institution that had been around since 1825, he had ambitions that went far beyond Upstate New York. Riley changed the name to the much catchier KeyCorp and was only a step behind his Albany neighbor, Norstar, in announcing a Maine acquisition in 1982, which also made him an interstate banking pioneer. When KeyCorp was blocked by the New England regional interstate banking compact from following up the Maine expansion with bank acquisitions in southern New England, Riley jumped to the other end of the continent and bought two banks in Alaska in 1985. In 1990, KeyCorp greatly increased its size by buying two failed, but large, thrifts in Upstate New York, and then in 1992, resumed the western adventure with a series of mergers in Idaho, Oregon and Washington.

The KeyCorp-Society combination announced in late 1993 not only created the second largest bank in the Midwest, but also the tenth largest bank in the country with branches stretching from Maine to Alaska. This was an unusual snowbelt strategy that was in sharp contrast to the sunbelt strategies of Bank One and others; but there are advantages in going where the competition is less intense.

National City was the only other large Cleveland bank still around in 1993, and it also had spread its coverage beyond Ohio. It bought banking leaders in Kentucky and Indiana, and by 1993, National City was the sixth largest Midwest bank with $31 billion assets.

Norwest

Norwest, unlike Bank One and KeyCorp, managed to stay out of the limelight with smaller acquisitions, but despite its quieter approach, it was not as much of a surprise in its move toward the upper echelons of regional and national banking. It was a large regional bank going back to the 1920s, and certainly did not start as a thrift and had the benefit of having operated in multiple states for over sixty years. Nevertheless, it would not have been expected that one of today's five dominant banks—Norwest was to eventually take the Wells Fargo name—would have its roots in the plains states.

As discussed earlier, Norwest was formed in the 1920s as a protective association for troubled farm banks in Minnesota, Nebraska, Iowa, Montana and the Dakotas. These states were still its main market in the

1980s and the focus of its acquisition activities. Norwest made 23 acquisitions in nine states with combined assets of $18.5 billion from 1989 through 1993, with the majority being in these core states.

Norwest also was looking to expand beyond the north central states, but its acquisitions beyond its home area typically were natural extensions into neighboring states like Wisconsin, Colorado and Wyoming. The only geographic jumps were eastward into Indiana and westward into a sunbelt state, New Mexico. Its biggest acquisitions were in Colorado and New Mexico.

By the end of 1993, Norwest was the Midwest's fourth largest bank with $51 billion assets and not far behind Bank One and KeyCorp. It also was only warming up its acquisition machine as it would buy 16 banks in 1994, and all but two were in Arizona, Colorado, New Mexico and Texas. Norwest was going south and west into faster growing markets.

Chicago's Diminished Role

The enhanced status of Bank One, KeyCorp and Norwest coincided with the declines of First Chicago and Continental as well as Chicago as a banking center, but the introduction of interstate banking in Illinois had out-of-state banks tripping over themselves to get into the Chicago market. This paradox was the result of downstate legislators protecting their local banks at the expense of the Chicago banks by limiting in-state branching.

Illinois, like Texas, had held out against branch banking longer than other large states. It had a strict prohibition against bank branches until 1976 when banks were permitted to establish a second facility within 3,500 yards. In 1985, this was expanded to allow five banking facilities with one within 500 yards of the bank, which essentially was permission to build a detached drive-in facility; a second within 3,500 yards; and the remaining three in the same county unless the branch was within ten miles of the main office. In 1990, the number of branches allowed was increased to ten in the home county and five in contiguous counties. Not until 1993 were all limitations on in-state branching dropped. This was about twenty years after most other large states had removed their in-state branching barriers.

The use of holding companies and autonomously-operating acquired banks provided some branching relief, but even using Illinois' 1985 branch expansion rules, First Chicago and Continental had less than 20 branches each excluding drive-in facilities in the mid-1980s. By then, BankAmerica and First Interstate each had more than 1,000 full-service banking offices; and Citicorp and Chase Manhattan, even with their money center cultures, had more than 300 branches. Banks in other Midwest states were hampered by local branching regulations, but not nearly to the extent of the banks in Illinois. Society had more than 200 banking offices in Ohio by 1985, long before its purchase of Ameritrust.

The inability to provide full coverage within their home market was a two-fold problem for First Chicago and Continental. It limited their ability to serve consumers and businesses in their own market and forced them to look beyond Chicago and retail banking for growth. This is why they sought loans in the oil patch with disastrous results and First Chicago followed the New York banks into Latin America. The expansion restraints at home not only closed off normal, and generally safer, avenues of growth, but also slowed the development of any semblance of a retail culture.

As if that was not enough, when interstate banking came to Illinois in the late 1980s, First Chicago and Continental did not have much of a head start in their home market. Bank of Montreal and the Dutch-owned ABN AMRO had already used the international immunity from interstate banking prohibitions to buy the third and fourth largest Chicago banks, Harris and LaSalle; and Citicorp used a failed thrift acquisition in 1984 to give it access to Chicago. When the interstate merger prohibitions were removed, banks in Ohio, Michigan, Wisconsin and Minnesota were quick to acquire banks in the Chicago area. As a result, by 1993, ABN AMRO was second only to First Chicago in Chicago area deposits and ahead of Continental. Bank One, Citicorp, NBD and two smaller Michigan banks, Old Kent and First of America, were among the area's ten largest.

Under these circumstances, it was not surprising that First Chicago and Continental had lost their leadership positions in the Midwest by 1993, and that this loss of momentum would lead to their being sold shortly thereafter. Continental was acquired by BankAmerica in 1994, and NBD effectively took control of First Chicago in 1995.

Other Interstate Winners

Besides Norwest and the three Ohio banks—Bank One, KeyCorp and National City—there were other Midwest banks that used interstate banking to greatly enhance their positions from 1989 through 1993. Most prominent among these were Detroit's NBD and Comerica and St. Louis' Boatmen's. Of similar size, but not doing as well in the early stages of this period was the other Minneapolis bank, First Bank System—the future U.S. Bancorp.

NBD had the biggest impact of these banks on consolidation during the early 1990s. Its assets went from $24 billion to $41 billion between 1988 and 1993, which was enough to move from ninth to fifth in size in the Midwest. It was already Michigan's biggest bank, and after three Indiana acquisitions in 1991 and 1992, including that state's largest bank, Indiana National, NBD also became the biggest bank in Indiana. In Illinois, a series of acquisitions made NBD one of the five largest banks in the Chicago area.

Comerica, the second largest Detroit bank, grew even faster than NBD during these years. It almost tripled in size between 1988 and 1993, and its 1993 assets of $31 billion were enough to move it from outside the top ten in the region to number seven. Most of the increase came from a merger with the third biggest bank in Detroit, Manufacturers National, but Comerica also began a sunbelt strategy by acquiring three banks in Texas with combined assets of $2 billion and three in California that were, collectively, almost as large as its Texas acquisitions.

Boatmen's was the most aggressive of the St. Louis banks in the early 1990s. It almost doubled its assets from 1988 to 1993 with ten acquisitions, and with $27 billion assets, Boatmen's was the eighth largest Midwest bank. It, like Norwest, NBD and First Bank System, used the elimination of the interstate banking barriers to move into faster growing markets. Five of Boatmen's ten acquisitions during this period with combined assets of about $1.5 billion were in Oklahoma, which hardly qualified as a faster growing state, but its biggest acquisition, Sunwest, was New Mexico's largest bank with assets of $3.2 billion.

First Bank System did not keep pace with other banks of its size during these years and fell far behind its Minneapolis rival, Norwest. In the late 1980s, it had asset quality and securities problems; lost momentum; and looked more like a takeover candidate than a predator. Between 1987 and 1991, its assets fell by about $10 billion. In 1992, First Bank System was making up for lost ground with two Colorado acquisitions with more than $5 billion in combined assets and one in its home state of Minnesota with $1.2 billion assets. In 1993, First Bank System also joined the crowd in Chicago with an acquisition of a bank in that city with assets of almost $2 billion. By the end of 1993, First Bank System had its assets almost back to the $27 billion it had in 1987, but it had fallen into the Midwest's second tier of banking leaders.

Changing of the Guard

Even though the Midwest had not been surfeited with the bad loans that were plaguing banks on the two coasts, the changing of the guard that took place from 1989 to 1993 was still influenced by asset quality problems that originated prior to 1989. Continental never fully recovered from the Penn Square loans that had precipitated its FDIC bail-out in 1984, and First Chicago and First Bank System had very difficult years from 1987 through 1989. The branching restrictions in Illinois were a problem for Continental and First Chicago, but more because they forced them to look beyond their home market for loans rather than their inability to maximize coverage in the Chicago area.

With First Chicago, Continental and First Bank System—the region's first, second and fourth largest banks in 1988—licking their wounds when interstate banking moved into high gear in the Midwest, the door was left open for others to gain the upper hand in the battle for regional leadership and survival and an opportunity to play a bigger role beyond the Midwest. Bank One, Society, KeyCorp and NBD, in particular, would take advantage of that opportunity.

Largest Midwest Banks, 1993

Bank	Assets 1993 1988 (in billions)		Rank 1988	Eventual Owner
1. Bank One	$80	$25	3	JPMorgan
2. KeyCorp*	60	15	9	JPMorgan
3. First Chicago	53	44	1	Wells Fargo
4. Norwest	51	22	6	JPMorgan
5. NBD	41	24	5	KeyCorp
6. National City	31	22	7	National City
7. Comerica	30	11	11	Comerica
8. Boatmen's	27	15	8	Bank of America
9. First Bank System	26	24	4	U.S. Bancorp
10. Continental	23	31	2	Bank of America
– Michigan National	10	11	10	ABN AMRO

*Includes Society-KeyCorp merger that was announced in 1993.
Source: American Banker, April 11, 1990 and April 14, 1994.

Bank One was by far the most aggressive in numbers of acquisitions and would replace First Chicago as the region's biggest bank, but was not alone in moving past or close to First Chicago in size by 1993. Society was more creative in doing so with its willingness to take on the problems of Ameritrust and give up its name and management preeminence in exchange for geographic diversification and the ability to keep its home in Cleveland. Bank One and Society took different routes, but by 1993, the biggest Midwest banks were in Ohio, not Illinois, and Minnesota's Norwest and Michigan's NBD were not far behind.

The shift of Midwest banking leadership from Chicago to Cleveland, Detroit and Minneapolis in the early 1990s was only the beginning of radical restructuring of Midwest banking. The entry of revitalized banks from the two coasts began in 1994 when Continental was acquired by BankAmerica. A year later, First Chicago would merge with NBD, which was technically a First Chicago acquisition that preserved the Chicago base, but management would come from the Detroit bank. Three years later, Bank One would buy a combined First Chicago and NBD.

Every Other Monday

Interstate banking and economic troubles played major roles in the consolidation of American banking, and the economic downturn from 1989 to 1992 coming so soon after the advent of interstate banking was the single biggest determinant of which banks won and which banks lost, but it was mergers, particularly large mergers, that were the vehicle for consolidation. During these years, the 1,500 bank and thrift failures were disturbing, and Bank of New England being among these failures had a direct impact on consolidation in New England, but it was the billion dollar recession-driven acquisitions by Chemical, NCNB, BankAmerica and First Union that had the national impact. The collapse of Texas banking in 1986 and 1987 was another major direction-altering event, and again, it was large acquisitions of failed or failing Texas banks by Chemical, NCNB, Bank One and First Interstate that made Texas so important to the consolidation process.

Prior to the changes wrought by the widespread economic problems from 1989 to 1992, bank consolidation also was more a matter of perception than reality when measured by bank assets controlled by the largest banks. The failure of so many small banks in the Great Depression caused a big jump in the share of bank assets held by large banks in the 1930s as they were better able to withstand the pressures of an economic downturn in an era when banks were not supported by federally-insured deposits. This big bank share increase, though, was rapidly eroded in the 1940s and throughout much of the 1950s by the return of public confidence in banking in general and an explosion of branches, few of which outside of California were part of the nation's largest banks.

In the 1960s and 1970s, the large bank share of the bank assets was again growing when measured against banks only, but the gain of the ten largest—they went from under 23% of bank assets in 1960 to about 31% in 1980—overstated what was really happening. S&Ls were not included, and this was a period when S&Ls were growing faster than banks. Also, much of the large bank growth was outside traditional domestic banking. Their growth was increasingly being funded by borrowed money and foreign loans were a growing part of their balance sheets.

The rise of the big bank asset share during the 1960s and 1970s would be reversed in the 1980s as the foreign loans became a burden rather than an opportunity—a 31% share of bank assets of the ten largest banks in 1980 fell to less than 26% in 1990—but no one was talking about decentralization of banking. Interstate banking was rapidly moving forward, and banking was being changed locally from dominance by single state banks to dominance by large regional banks, or the superregionals. Small states like Kentucky, Maine, Oregon and South Carolina whose local banks were bought by multi-state banks based in Ohio, Massachusetts, California and North Carolina were experiencing consolidation regardless of what the numbers said about the market shares of a few banks in New York and California. The reduced share of big banks in the 1980s also was greatly influenced by the growth problems of a single institution, BankAmerica.

Large Bank Asset Share, 1960 to 1996

Year	Share of Bank Assets		Bank Assets (in billions)
	Five Largest	Ten Largest	
1996	26.1%	38.3%	$ 4,582
1995	23.1	33.9	4,313
1994	22.7	33.2	4,011
1993	21.2	32.0	3,706
1992	20.6	29.3	3,506
1991	19.4	28.5	3,431
1990	16.2	25.5	3,390
1980	21.0	30.7	1,856
1970	18.0	26.0	570
1960	15.4	22.7	256

Source: FDIC, Historical Statistics on Banking; *Sheshunoff Banking Organization Quarterly;* Federal Reserve, *1980 Bank Holding Company Report; Polk's World Bank Directory*, Spring 1961 and 1971 and SNL Financial, Charlottesville, Virginia.

Thus, while the seeds of bank consolidation go back to the pressures to cross state lines in the 1970s, the thrift crisis and the advent of interstate banking in the mid-1980s, statistically a nationwide increase in the share of bank assets held by a handful of large banks does not show up in the national numbers until 1991. What moved the numbers then were the big mergers, particularly the two large ones announced in late 1991 and consummated in that same year—NCNB-C&S/Sovran and Chemical-Manufacturers Hanover—and the BankAmerica-Security Pacific merger that was announced at about the same time, but occurred in 1992. These acquisitions were of a size not previously seen in banking. In one year, the fifth, eighth and twelfth largest banks were acquired. Occurring during a recession when bank asset growth was slow, this resulted in the asset share of the five largest banks jumping by more than four percentage points in two years—from about 16% to 20.6%—and the ten largest by a little less than four percentage points—from 25.5% to more than 29%. It was an extraordinary two year share gain, and consolidation had become more than a perception.

Megamergers of 1995

The big mergers of 1991 were just a warm-up for the mega-mergers of 1995 that would provide a second major spurt in the consolidation process. In 1995, fifteen bank acquisitions were announced with individual deal values in excess of $1 billion. This was as many billion dollar bank sales than in *all* preceding years. It was a big year for mergers of all sizes, but differed dramatically from other years in the number of large mergers. Take off one month at the beginning of 1995 and add January 1996, and the number of large mergers goes up by only one, but that one, the $12.3 billion acquisition of First Interstate by Wells Fargo, provided a fitting finish to a truly amazing twelve months.

The merger frenzy of 1995 was so intense in that summer that from May through September, it seemed like there was a big merger announced every other Monday. Mergers of this size are usually finalized over a week-end when stock markets are closed and secrecy is easier to maintain and then announced on Monday, or Tuesday at the latest. Ten of 1995's billion dollar bank sales were announced during these five months.

This big merger splurge began innocuously enough on February 5th with a foreign bank, National Australia, announcing the purchase of one of the lingering problems of the earlier recession, Michigan National, in a part of the country that had been relatively untouched by the problems of 1989 to 1992, and ended with the California blockbuster, Wells Fargo buying First Interstate. In between those two deals, the bulk of the big merger activity was in the Northeast with the most noteworthy being Chemical's purchase of Chase Manhattan. There was headline-grabbing action in the middle of the country as well with First Chicago and NBD joining forces.

Large Bank Mergers, 1986 to 1996

Year	Bank Mergers		
	Over $1 Billion*	Unassisted	Assisted
1996	2	554	5
1995	15	609	6
1994	1	548	11
1993	2	481	35
1992	1	428	73
1991	5	447	85
1990	–	393	141
1989	1	411	175
1988	–	598	173
1987	3	543	136
1986	2	341	101

*Deal Value.
Source: SNL Financial, Charlottesville, Virginia and FDIC, Historical Statistics on Banking.

The sudden surge in large mergers was a bit of a surprise since there was only one bank sale in 1994 with a price tag over $1 billion, and that was in January. Thus, for a full year prior to the Michigan National acquisition, there had been no billion dollar bank sales. In the preceding years, 1992 and 1993 combined, there were just three such sales.

Even the one in 1994, BankAmerica's acquisition of Chicago-based Continental, was ten years in the making and certainly not a harbinger of what was to come. After being bailed out by the FDIC in 1984, Continental never regained its momentum, but its ability to sell had first been hampered by Illinois' resistance to interstate banking. Then after the interstate barriers were gone, banks big enough to buy Continental were not interested either because of their own problems or because of better opportunities closer to home. When sale conditions improved, Continental was ready to sell, and it gave BankAmerica its second big acquisition of the first half of the 1990s as well as entry into Chicago.

The Perfect Storm

Why the sudden surge in large bank mergers in 1995? The reasons were enabling legislation, rising stock prices, better asset quality and board fatigue that, collectively, had created a merger environment equivalent of the "perfect storm" made famous in a book and movie bearing that name.[*]

The enabling legislation was the Riegle-Neal Interstate Banking and Branching Efficiency Act of 1994. This was national banking legislation that overrode state restrictions on interstate bank mergers and let national banks operate branches across state lines starting in June 1997. The latter allowed a single bank to have branches in multiple states, which was more cost efficient than a holding company having separate banks in every state. States could opt out of the branching part of Riegle-Neal, but only Montana and Texas chose to do so. If a state did not opt out, then interstate branching was mandated only by merger—individual states could still prevent banks from opening a branch in their state without buying a bank—but states could pass legislation to allow de novo branching across state lines. As a result of Riegle-Neal, interstate mergers were facilitated and cost efficiencies made more attainable.

Another part of the perfect storm creating a favorable large merger environment was better asset quality. Economic conditions had improved rapidly after 1992, but some bank balance sheets were burdened with bad loans long after the recession ended. This was a merger impediment as buyers were reluctant to add loan problems and wanted to get their own asset quality concerns behind them. By 1995, enough time had elapsed to make buyers more comfortable acquiring the loan portfolios of others.

Most important of all to the increased merger activity was rising stock prices. Since the dog days of 1990 through 1995, bank stock prices rose almost 26% per annum, and in 1995 alone increased 50%. These were good years for stocks in general, but better for bank stocks than others. The corresponding stock price gains for the S&P 500 were 13% and 34%, respectively. The much improved stock prices made it easier for buyers to pay a price that sellers would find attractive.

---

[*]*The Perfect Storm* was a best-seller by Sebastian Junger in 1997 about a fishing boat, the Andrea Gail, that sailed out of Gloucester, Massachusetts in the autumn of 1991 and was caught in a rare combination of meteorological conditions that created what was referred to as a "perfect (and extraordinary) storm." The book was made into an equally popular movie in 2000, and the term "perfect storm" has been since used as a description of conditions coming together to create unusual and extreme circumstances, favorable and unfavorable.

Stock Price Index Gains, 1990 to 1995*

Date	Bank Index	S&P 500 Index
Dec. 31, 1995	315	187
June 30, 1995	261	165
Dec. 31, 1994	209	139
June 30, 1994	232	135
Dec. 31, 1993	221	142
June 30, 1993	223	137
Dec. 31, 1992	208	132
June 30, 1992	185	124
Dec. 31, 1991	156	126
June 30, 1991	132	115
Dec. 31, 1990	100	100

*SNL All Publicly Traded Bank Index with 1990 as 100.
Source: SNL Financial, Bank Securities Monthly.

The stock price gains from 1990 through 1995, however, had annual variations that added to the strong sale climate in 1995. Bank stock prices rose rapidly from 1990 to 1993 as the Federal Reserve lowered the Fed Funds rate from a high of 9.75% in 1989 to 3% in 1992. This made bank loans more affordable and bank funding less costly, which investors like. In 1994, inflation became a concern, and the Fed Funds rate was gradually increased until it reached 6% in February 1995. This upward movement of rates took away the market momentum in late 1993 and 1994, and in the second half of 1994, bank stocks as a group lost about 10% of their value.

These declining stock prices lowered acquisition activity in 1994 and early 1995 as it reduced the price buyers would pay while sellers expected the earlier values. As a result, many sales were put on hold until a more favorable merger environment returned in mid-1995 when stock prices were once more rapidly rising.

Last, but not least, in this perfect storm of reasons for a sudden surge in big merger activity in 1995 was board fatigue. Banks on both coasts suffered badly from loan problems in the 1989 to 1992 economic downturn, and accompanying the asset quality problems were regulators that could make life uncomfortable for bank directors. The regulators, themselves, were under pressures from legislators and the media for banking problems, particularly coming on the heels of a thrift crisis, and they could be brutal in how hard they came down on individual banks. In many cases, they were unduly pessimistic, but for directors, who in most cases were not bankers, these were scary times. So scary, in fact, that if they could have done so, many would have voted to sell their banks in the early 1990s. Bad loans and reduced earnings, though, made a sale either impossible or imprudent at the time. Thus, when sales at good prices were again possible, bank directors were ready to move.

Increase in Bank Sale Prices

By mid-1995, the good sale prices had arrived. The $5.6 billion paid by First Union for New Jersey's First Fidelity in June 1995 was a new record high topping what BankAmerica had paid for Security Pacific in 1991. Two months later, Chemical more than doubled that price by paying $11.4 billion for Chase Manhattan. This seemed like a record that would stand for some time, but it lasted only five months. In January 1996, Wells Fargo paid $12.3 billion to acquire First Interstate. These also were offering prices, and since these were all stock transactions, if the buyer's stock price subsequently increased, which was generally the case in this good economic climate, the closing price could be much higher.

The Wells Fargo-First Interstate transaction was almost ten years to the day after the first billion dollar bank sale, also a Wells Fargo acquisition. In February 1986, Wells Fargo bought Crocker National from England's Midland Bank for almost $1.1 billion. Later that year, Chemical's purchase of Texas Commerce would be the second billion dollar transaction.

In 1989 and 1991, the size of bank deals moved to a new level. In the first of those years, Sovran's merger with C&S/Sovran crossed the $2 billion threshold, a level also reached by the Chemical acquisition of Manufacturers Hanover in 1991. A sign of what was to come in pricing came only a week after the Chemical-Manufacturers Hanover deal was announced with NCNB paying $4.5 billion to buy C&S/Sovran. Three weeks later, BankAmerica upped the ante to $4.7 billion with its acquisition of Security Pacific. This price stood as the highest bank sale price for almost four years until it was surpassed by the 1995 First Union purchase of First Fidelity.

The price offered by Wells Fargo for First Interstate in January 1996 would be the highest for more than a year-and-a-half. It was topped by a few billion dollars in late 1997 in acquisitions by NationsBank and First Union, which was to be expected with the steady rise in stock prices during this period. What was not expected was that this gradual increase in bank sale prices would be followed by an almost $83 billion offer to buy Citigroup in 1998, but that is a story for another chapter.

Highest Bank Sale Prices through 1998

Acquirer/Acquiree	Deal Value (in millions)	Date Announced
Travelers/Citicorp	$82,536	5/9/98
First Union/CoreStates	17,104	11/18/98
NationsBank/Barnett	15,523	8/29/97
Wells Fargo/First Interstate	12,310	1/24/96
Chemical/Chase Manhattan	11,358	8/28/95
First Union/First Fidelity	5,555	6/19/95
BankAmerica/Security Pacific	4,667	8/12/91
NCNB/C&S/Sovran	4,457	7/22/91
Chemical/Manufacturers Hanover	2,143	7/15/91
Sovran/Citizens & Southern	2,070	9/26/89
Bank of New York/Irving	1,450	9/25/87
Fleet/Norstar	1,344	3/18/87
Chemical/Texas Commerce	1,092	12/15/86
Wells Fargo/Crocker National	1,080	2/7/86

Source: SNL Financial, Charlottesville, Virginia.

That a majority of the large bank sales in 1995 were in the Northeast—nine of the fifteen—was a logical reaction to the perfect storm. The region's banks suffered extensively from the extreme adverse economic conditions in the early 1990s, and there were more large banks in the Northeast than in other parts of the country. As a result, there also were more large banks in the region suffering from board fatigue. The region's 1995 large mergers were widely spread and left no major Northeast submarket untouched. In most of these mergers, it was not hard to see the impact of the early 1990s recession as a reason for the sale.

New England

Two of the large 1995 Northeast mergers were in New England—Fleet's purchase of Shawmut and Bank of Boston acquiring BayBanks—and were among the most likely to have been at least partially motivated by board fatigue. Shawmut and BayBanks had struggled mightily during the 1989 to 1992 recession and had witnessed up close Bank of New England's failure. The larger of the two deals, Fleet-Shawmut, was announced early in the year when the troubles of the past were still a fresh memory and before the 1995 stock price surge was in full-swing.

Fleet's acquisition of Shawmut also was the first big 1995 merger from a consolidation perspective since a foreign bank acquiring Michigan National had no consolidation impact. This merger combined the first and third largest New England banks; made Fleet by far the biggest bank in the six-state area; and moved Fleet to within one position of being in the top ten nationally.

Bank of Boston's acquisition of BayBanks came ten months later, and may have been motivated by Bank of Boston trying to keep from falling too far behind Fleet and a failed effort to merge with Philadelphia's CoreStates. In the late summer of 1995, Bank of Boston and CoreStates had agreed on an equal merger that would create a $75 billion bank only to receive such a strong negative investor reaction that the merger had to be scrapped. Unlike the Fleet-Shawmut combination that involved banks of similar size, but in the same market, a Bank of Boston-CoreStates merger would have had far less cost savings and either Boston or Philadelphia would have lost a bank headquarters.

Another one-time Boston banking leader, State Street, had moved away from traditional retail and commercial banking, and this combined with the many bank mergers meant that a once banking-rich area had in a little over a decade seen more well-known bank names disappear than survive. Connecticut's banking leaders, Hartford National and CBT, along with Boston's Bank of New England, Shawmut and BayBanks were memories and, State Street was by then playing a different game.

All that remained of New England's leading banks were Fleet and Bank of Boston, and they towered over the local competition. Two banks being so much larger than all others would prove to be an opportunity for the Royal Bank of Scotland's affiliate, Citizens, but in 1995, Citizens was still a long way from challenging them. Fleet had assets of $85 billion by year-end 1995, and with the acquisition of BayBanks, Bank of Boston was close to $60 billion assets. Citizens' assets in 1995 were only $10 billion.

Chemical-Chase Manhattan

In 1995, New York City only had one large merger, but it was by far the Northeast's most important from a consolidation perspective. Chase Manhattan had slid a long way from being one of the big three of banking, but was still one of the biggest names in the industry and its acquisition by the less well-known Chemical was humbling.

Chase Manhattan had been sliding down the ranks of the national leaders for some time and seemed to lack any sense of where it was going. In the 1970s, it was hurt by international loans and the diminishing importance of correspondent banking, which was providing services for other banks. In 1981, David Rockefeller handed the reins over to his handpicked successor, Willard Butcher, and the loan problems continued, particularly international loans, but the oil and gas loans bought from Penn Square also were a major problem. When Thomas Labreque took over in 1990, the situation was such that his first move was to cut expenses; reduce the international coverage; and sell its banking offices in Arizona, Florida and Ohio.

Thus, as others were expanding, Chase Manhattan was retrenching and becoming a declining factor on the American banking scene. In 1988, it was the country's second biggest bank; by the end of 1994, it was number six; and before the Chemical merger was consummated in early 1996, it was number eight. Chase Manhattan's loan problems were by then in the past, but its once sterling reputation was history as well.

In banking, though, names count, and Chase Manhattan could take some solace out of the fact that although it was bought by Chemical, the combined banks would bear the Chase Manhattan name. Not only that, but upon consummation of the merger, the new Chase Manhattan was America's biggest bank.

Pennsylvania and New Jersey

It was in two almost forgotten states in the consolidation process up to this point, Pennsylvania and New Jersey, that the most large merger activity would occur and provide the biggest regional direction shift in 1995. Five of the nine large bank mergers in the Northeast involved banks in these states.

The biggest and most important was the first to be announced—First Fidelity's sale to First Union. First Fidelity was New Jersey's biggest bank; had a large market share in the Philadelphia area; and before it was slowed by the 1989 to 1992 loan quality problems, First Fidelity was bigger than its buyer and almost as large as NCNB. It had lost momentum, however, and presumably had some director fatigue as well, and its sale brought one of the North Carolina banks destined to be a national leader north of the Mason-Dixon line in a big way. The First Fidelity acquisition gave First Union a leadership position in a big Northeast state and a substantial stake in the Philadelphia area—a stake it would turn into dominance three years later when it acquired CoreStates.

In 1995, board fatigue as a motivation to sell went well beyond First Fidelity in New Jersey. A much diminished MidLantic was sold to PNC in that year, and the British-owned National Westminster exited New Jersey with the sale of its American banking business to Fleet. When the dust finally settled in New Jersey, First Union, PNC and Fleet—all out-of-state banks—had three of the four largest deposit shares.

The other major New Jersey merger that year, UJB's acquisition of Summit, was an in-state transaction, but it also had long-term consolidation implications. With this acquisition, UJB replaced First Fidelity as both the biggest New Jersey bank and as number one in statewide deposit share. UJB would take the Summit name after the merger, continue to expand and then sell to Fleet in 2001, which in turn would be sold to Bank of America.

In the Philadelphia area, the large 1995 mergers would also radically change the local banking structure. The local banks had their problems with the early 1990s recession, but the only significant structural change in the Philadelphia area during that period was Mellon's acquisition of a failed thrift, Meritor, from the FDIC. Thus, as 1995 began, Philadelphia's leading banks—CoreStates, Mellon, Meridian, First Fidelity, PNC and Midlantic— were the same as five years earlier. Before the year ended, CoreStates had announced the acquisition of Meridan, PNC had a deal to buy Midlantic and First Union had purchased First Fidelity. Three of the six were gone.

The CoreStates-Meridian merger looked good on paper as it appeared to create a stronger bank and provide Philadelphia with at least one bank with a chance to be a major player. CoreStates was the holding company for Philadelphia National, the area's biggest bank, a position it had solidified a few years earlier by acquiring First Pennsylvania, which in the 1970s had been among the nation's twenty largest banks. In 1994, CoreStates had $29 billion assets, and acquiring Meridian raised its assets to about $44 billion. This did not lift it into a class with First Union or Fleet as the rejected Bank of Boston merger would have done, but CoreStates was still a big bank. The numbers, though, were better than the reality, and the Meridian acquisition was the beginning of the end.

CoreStates was not a skilled acquirer, and the Meridian merger did not proceed smoothly. It was a classic cultural mismatch in which a bank with a money center mentality acquired a retail-oriented bank, and the management battles took away all of the seeming pluses of the combination. The battles raged and the competition had a field day at CoreStates' expense. In 1998, CoreStates would be acquired by First Union and become a major stepping stone in that North Carolina bank's ascent.

Midwest

In the Midwest, 1995 was a big year for large mergers as well with the NBD-First Chicago equal merger and First Bank System, National City and Boatmen's continuing to spread beyond their home states with billion dollar deals. First Bank System bought an Idaho bank holding company, West One, with bank affiliates in Oregon, Washington and Utah as well as Idaho. National City acquired the third largest bank in Pittsburgh, and Boatmen's bought the largest bank holding company in Kansas.

The First Chicago merger with NBD was the centerpiece of the Midwest 1995 merger activity. First Chicago had lost its number one position in the region to Bank One, but was still the big bank in Chicago and, as such, remained a powerful force in the Midwest in which almost any substantial merger would restore its former regional preeminence. First Chicago had been rumored to be talking merger with a number of banks, and in July 1995, announced a $5 billion equal merger with NBD that would regain the top spot regionally and move it back into the top ten nationally.

The new First Chicago-NBD had the largest market share in Illinois, Michigan and Indiana, and with $122 billion assets, First Chicago-NBD was capable of playing a major role in the consolidation process. In 1995, it would have been one of the obvious answers to the hypothetical question posed in an earlier chapter as to who were the most likely banks to be among the five that would dominate banking in 2007.

First Chicago and NBD were a curious mix, however, and how well they would mesh was uncertain. *Business Week* summed it up pretty well in stating that "Apart from being Midwestern bankers, their banks might have been from different planets. Although hurt in the 1980s and early 1990s by lending and trading problems, First Chicago had long been regarded as the preeminent international bank between the two coasts. First's execs viewed their Detroit sidekicks as little more the rubes running a second-tier outfit. NBD saw their new colleagues as East Coast-style gunslingers. And they had very different agendas: NBD wanted to expand beyond its region, while First (Chicago) wanted to avoid being taken over. Such cultural differences had capsized many mergers."[1]

In its efforts to avoid an unwanted takeover, First Chicago had agreed to give a bank two-thirds its size an almost equal amount of shares and an equal numbers of board seats, and was initially viewed as the buyer since the headquarters remained in Chicago and the NBD name came second— and was likely to be dropped in articles and discussions. Fleet/Norstar, FleetBankBoston and JPMorgan Chase are ample evidence of a tendency to drop the last part of cumbersome bank names in conversation and in media reports.

It was NBD's management, though, that prevailed. The president of First Chicago resigned as a result of the merger, and part of the agreement was that NBD's chairman and CEO, Vernon Istock, would be president and CEO of the combined banks and then replace the First Chicago chairman when he retired. This would happen just six months after the merger was consummated. With NBD's Istock running the show, the perception was that NBD was the buyer regardless of who legally bought whom.

What made the First Chicago-NBD important from a consolidation perspective was that it worked well up to a point, but not well enough to maintain its independence for more than three years. In 1998, the same scenario would be rerun with Bank One and First Chicago-NBD agreeing to an equal merger with the headquarters again remaining in Chicago. This time around, the First Chicago and NBD names disappeared, and Bank One was running the show from day one.

Wells Fargo-First Interstate

The Wells Fargo-First Interstate merger in the Far West was almost a rerun of the First Chicago-NBD merger and had the same end result. The acquired, First Interstate, like First Chicago, appeared well-positioned to be one of the top banks in the United States long before interstate banking became widely accessible. When it was divested by Transamerica in 1954, it was the fourth largest banking organization in the country and had banks in eleven western states. Only BankAmerica had more branches, and First Interstate, or Western Bancorporation as it was originally called, had none of First Chicago's branching constraints. With this starting point in the fastest growing part of the country, First Interstate had a franchise to be envied.

First Interstate, though, never lived up to its potential. In 1970, it was still the sixth largest bank in the country, but by 1980, had fallen to ninth, was far behind BankAmerica and only marginally larger than three other California banks—Security Pacific, Wells Fargo and Crocker National. It fared no better in the 1980s even as its home base in Southern California benefited from sunshine, defense spending and a strong Japanese economy. By 1990, its Los Angeles rival, Security Pacific had left it far behind, and

Wells Fargo also had surpassed it in asset size as a result of its purchase of Crocker National. As First Interstate struggled in the 1980s, it had even tried a "hail Mary" pass with a hostile bid to acquire a larger BankAmerica at its low point, but this came to naught.

When the early 1990s recession hit California, First Interstate fared better than its crosstown counterpart, Security Pacific, but it had its share of bad loans and was vulnerable to a takeover. First Interstate's size, the problems of the most likely buyers and an unfavorable sale environment, however, had allowed First Interstate to move into 1995 without any undue pressure to sell. Wells Fargo had been interested in acquiring First Interstate since 1992, but First Interstate dismissed the thought of a merger at least until it had its "house back in order."[2]

By 1995, First Interstate had left its bad days behind, but was still vulnerable to a takeover, and in October 1995, after being rebuffed by First Interstate management, Wells Fargo, which was smaller in assets than First Interstate, but slightly bigger in earnings and market capital, put a hostile offer of $141 per share, or about $11 billion, on the table. In November 1995, its offer of $141 per share was turned down in favor of a friendlier, but lesser, offer of $136 per share from First Bank System.[3] First Bank System was, in effect, a white knight in that it had not precipitated the sale of First Interstate, and as primarily a Midwest bank, would not have much overlap and would make fewer personnel cuts. Wells Fargo, however, did not give up, and in January 1996, its offer of $152 per share, or $12.3 billion was accepted by First Interstate. By the time the transaction closed, a rising stock market had lifted the price to $174 per share, or a little over $14 billion—a nice pay-off for a reluctant seller.

Wells Fargo was the winner, but it was a victory with a bad aftertaste. The merger not only had cultural problems—Wells Fargo was cold and efficient while First Interstate was more customer friendly—and even as a buyer that had overpaid, Wells Fargo was still viewed by First Interstate's management as a hostile acquirer. The result was management defections, unenthusiastic employees, computer glitches and branch closings that led to considerable customer dissatisfaction and a merger nightmare.[4]

Despite the merger problems, an expanded Wells Fargo had assets in excess of $100 billion; was the only large bank with broad coverage on the West Coast other than BankAmerica; and was right behind First Chicago-NBD in the national rankings in eighth place. From a numbers perspective, the Wells Fargo-First Interstate merger looked like a reasonable success. Wells Fargo had been weakened to the point, though, that like First Chicago-NBD, in 1998, it would be acquired by a smaller Midwest bank. In Wells Fargo's case, it would be Norwest.

Big Bang Outcome

One could almost refer to 1995 as banking's "big bang," and until 1998 came along, it was a merger year that went far beyond any other. Some of the names remained, but with the original Chase Manhattan, First Chicago and First Interstate disappearing within a few months of each other, the year was worthy of the "big bang" appellation. On the East Coast, the disappearances of Shawmut and First Fidelity had almost as much of a shock affect as the sales of the aforementioned three.

Largest Domestic Banks, 1995

Bank	Assets 1995* (in billions)	1994	Rank 1994
1. Chase Manhattan	$304	$171	3
2. Citicorp	257	251	1
3. BankAmerica	232	216	2
4. NationsBank	195	170	4
5. J.P. Morgan	185	155	5
6. First Union	132	77	9
7. First Chicago-NBD	122	47	17
8. Wells Fargo	108	53	14
9. Bankers Trust	104	97	7
10. Bank One	90	89	8
11. Fleet	85	49	16
12. PNC	74	64	12
– KeyCorp	66	67	10
– Chase Manhattan	–	114	6
– First Chicago	–	66	11

* Includes large mergers in process and the Wells Fargo-First Interstate merger in January 1996.
Source: American Banker, March 24, 1995 and SNL Financial, Charlottesville, Virginia.

In a single year, the sixth, eleventh and thirteenth largest banks had disappeared; a bank other than Citicorp or BankAmerica was the country's biggest; First Union was the sixth largest bank in the country giving North Carolina two banks among the top six; a Chicago bank was back in the top ten, but with Detroit management; Wells Fargo had rekindled some of its old glory; and Fleet was just one merger away from being in the top ten. It was a new era in banking with some new players with high ambitions and a lot of momentum behind them.

The impact of these big 1995 bank mergers on the asset share of the large banks was substantial, but since so many of the deals closed in the following year, the numerical impact was spread over two years. Between year-ends 1994 and 1996, the asset share of the ten largest banks jumped by about five percentage points from about 33% to a little more than 38%. The share increase of the top five, which came almost totally from the Chemical-Chase Manhattan merger, was not as much, but the increase from a little less than 23% to 26% was surpassed previously only by the 1990 to 1992 gain.

1998: The Superbanks Cometh

The abundance of large bank mergers in 1995 was seen by many as a race for survival, and it was widely expected that the mega-merger mania that surfaced in 1995 would continue into 1996. Wells Fargo's acquisition of First Interstate in January 1996 suggested that the large banks had not lost their interest in getting bigger, and the conditions that had fueled the 1995 activity had not changed. Bank stock prices were still rising—up 35% in 1996 and 48% in 1997;[1] the economy was in high gear; the industry's asset quality was no longer a problem; and banks were enjoying a windfall—the elimination of the FDIC charges for deposit insurance. It looked a lot like 1995, but after the Wells Fargo-First Interstate announcement, the large merger activity slowed to a crawl.

Why this sudden slowdown in large mergers? The reason generally given at the time was that the most active acquirers were digesting what they had already bought. The only noticeable acquirer omissions from the 1995 mega-merger activity were NationsBank and BankAmerica, and the latter was still struggling with its early 1990s acquisitions of Security Pacific and Continental.

This line of reasoning looked even better a few months later when NationsBank, and only NationsBank, moved into action. It could not stay on the sidelines for long, and in August 1996, NationsBank announced that year's only billion dollar bank purchase, other than the Wells Fargo-First Interstate transaction, when it paid almost $10 billion for the Missouri-based Boatmen's. This was a large acquisition that expanded NationsBank's coverage north from Texas into Oklahoma, Missouri and southern Illinois and west into New Mexico, but was an isolated event. In fact, the banks making the billion dollar acquisitions in 1995 were not only non-acquirers in 1996, but they remained inactive through the first half of 1997.

Early 1997 showed some pick-up in large bank mergers with three transactions announced with deal values in excess of $1 billion even with the 1995 acquirers on the sidelines. Except for one, though, these were fairly small, regional purchases. The only one of any size, First Bank System's acquisition of U.S. Bancorp in Portland, also was by another bank that had not made a major acquisition in 1995.

This large merger hiatus ended dramatically in August 1997 when NationsBank struck again and announced it was buying Barnett, Florida's largest bank, for $15.5 billion. It was a new high in bank pricing and made NationsBank number one in the country's fastest-growing big state. Coming so close on the heels of the Boatmen's acquisition, the Barnett deal was a reminder to other large banks that if they sat still for too long, the bankers from North Carolina would be leaving them behind. It can never be known for certain, but some of the large bank merger activity that followed may have been at least partially a response to the moves of NationsBank and its North Carolina compatriot, First Union, in the latter half of 1997.

In November 1997, First Union would "one-up" NationsBank and set another new high for bank sale pricing when it paid a little over $17 billion for CoreStates, Philadelphia's biggest bank. A few months earlier, it had announced that it was buying Signet, a $12 billion asset bank with offices in Virginia, Maryland and the District of Columbia. First Union spent more than $20 billion in late 1997 for banks with about $60 billion in assets and became far more than just another regional bank.

The acquisitions by NationsBank and First Union in late 1997 began a period of large bank acquisitions that would radically alter the structure of American banking and take bank consolidation to another level. The largest mergers during this period were announced in 1998, and as a result, it is the year most associated with this particular merger surge, but this latest wave of consolidation began in earnest in the third quarter of 1997 and ran through the first four months of 1999. When it was over, the dominance of a few—the new superbanks—was readily apparent, and the share of banking assets controlled by five or six banks was well on its way to 50%.

The number of large mergers in 1998 was not that high—there were six fewer billion dollar deals than in 1995—but it was the size of the 1998 acquisitions and what happened in just seven days in April that made the year a watershed for bank consolidation. Between April 6th and 13th, Travelers, an ambitious insurance company, announced an offer of $83 billion for Citicorp, or almost *five times* the previous highest bank sale price; NationsBank continued its furious acquisition pace and nearly matched the Citicorp price when it proposed to buy BankAmerica for $66 billion; and Bank One offered $30 billion to buy First Chicago-NBD. In one week, the country's second, fourth and ninth largest banks with assets of almost $700 billion were in the process of being acquired.

Two months later the consolidation march continued when Norwest announced that it was buying Wells Fargo for almost $35 billion. This was the fourth bank among the nation's top ten acquired in a two month period in 1998, and it was not the last.

In November 1998, another of the nation's largest banks, Bankers Trust, was sold. It was seventh in assets going into 1998 and was acquired by Germany's Deutsche Bank. Since Bankers Trust was bought by a foreign bank, its sale had little impact on consolidation, but with this announcement, half of America's ten largest banks had been sold in 1998.

The sale prices were not only record highs for American banks, but for companies of all types worldwide. The prices for Citicorp, BankAmerica and Wells Fargo ranked one, two, three in sale values for all companies up to that time, and the $30 billion offer for First Chicago was the fifth highest right behind the ill-fated 1998 acquisition of MCI by WorldCom.

The combined announced deal value of 1998's nine billion dollar bank sales was $245 billion. This was about four times the $62 billion combined value of the nine large acquisitions in 1997 and more than five times the $47 billion of the 15 announced in 1995.

Large Bank Merger Value, 1994 to 1999

| Year | Bank Mergers | | | |
| | Deal Value Over | | All | Large Deal Value (in billions) |
	$1 Billion	$10 Billion		
1999	7	2	428	$ 46.2
1998	9	4	567	244.6
1997	9	1	602	61.6
1996	2	1	559	22.1
1995	15	1	615	47.3
1994	1	–	559	2.3

Source: SNL Financial, Charlottesville, Virginia and FDIC, Historical Statistics on Banking.

There were seven more billion dollar bank mergers in the following year, including two with deal values in excess of $10 billion. Total 1999 transaction value of $46 billion, though, also would pale besides the $245 billion of 1998, and none of the acquired banks in 1999 were among the ten largest.

The impact of these deals on bank consolidation was immense. Between year-ends 1997 and 1998, the share of bank assets held by the ten largest banks increased from a little less than 40% to 45.5%. This was by far the largest one year gain since concentration numbers began to rise in 1992.

Large Bank Asset Share, 1990 to 2000

| Dec. 31, | Share of Bank Assets | | Bank Assets (in billions) |
	Five Largest	Ten Largest	
2000	33.2%	46.9%	$6,246
1999	33.0	47.1	5,735
1998	32.9	45.5	5,443
1997	27.4	39.7	5,018
1996	26.1	38.3	4,582
1995	23.1	33.9	4,313
1994	22.7	33.2	4,011
1993	21.2	32.0	3,706
1992	20.6	29.3	3,506
1991	19.4	28.5	3,431
1990	16.2	25.5	3,390

Source: FDIC, Historical Statistics on Banking and *Sheshunoff Banking Organization Quarterly.*

As large as the asset share gain was for the ten biggest banks, it understated the 1998 impact on consolidation as it was not the gains by the ten largest, but rather what was happening among the five largest that was changing the banking structure. By the end of 1998, it was apparent that domestic banking would be dominated by just five or six banks and not ten or more. Between 1997 and 1998, the share of bank assets held by the five largest went from 27.4% to almost 33%. In 1998, five banks had more of the nation's banking assets than the ten biggest had at the end of 1993.

Travelers-Citicorp

It was hard to say which was the bigger transaction in 1998 from a consolidation perspective—Travelers buying Citicorp or NationsBank's purchase of BankAmerica? The Travelers-Citicorp deal was priced higher; came as more of a surprise; and the end result was the biggest American financial institution measured by assets, market capital and earnings. When measured by deposits, loans and banking offices, though, the NationsBank-BankAmerica deal was larger and had the greater direct impact on bank consolidation. The number of combined banking offices was more than 3,000 and dwarfed Citicorp's less than 400 banking offices.

Travelers-Citicorp, though, was a landmark bank acquisition in that it challenged the last remaining barrier for mergers between firms in different parts of the financial services industry—and won. A merger between a bank holding company and an insurance underwriter was not allowed in 1998 nor was it permissible for an investment bank subsidiary to have more than 25% of its revenues generated by products not permissable for commercial banks. This transaction violated both of these rules, and if it were to be approved by the regulators, the rules would have to be changed.

This began a major congressional debate, but in the end, what Citicorp wanted, Citicorp got. In November 1999, the Gramm-Leach-Bliley Act was passed that allowed for mergers between financial services companies of all types.* Thus, by the end of 1999, all national barriers separating banks from these other firms had been removed and the last vestiges of the Glass-Steagall Act muted.

While these nontraditional bank acquisitions did not directly affect the share of bank assets held by large banks, they increased their overall size and market power, and greatly influenced the consolidation process. This is a story told in the next chapter.

NationsBank-BankAmerica

No bank had as much of an impact on the consolidation of American banking as NationsBank; no CEO played a bigger role than Hugh McColl; and NationsBank's acquisition of BankAmerica was the culmination of a more than 25 year march by that institution into national preeminence.

---

*Passage of the Gramm-Leach-Bliley Act created a new holding company type referred to as a financial holding company to accommodate Citicorp, thereafter known as Citigroup, but also opened the door for large nonbanks to establish bank or thrift subsidiaries as part of financial holding companies. Merrill Lynch, MetLife and others were soon operating financial holding companies with newly-created banking affiliates with assets of more than $50 billion, and in some cases, more than $100 billion.

- In the 1970s, NCNB, as NationsBank was known then, was one of the two or three most aggressive bank holding companies in moving across state lines with nonbank acquisitions, and its 1972 acquisition of a Florida trust company gave it a head start with interstate banking.

- In 1982, NCNB used its head start when its trust company acquisition allowed it to circumvent Florida's laws against interstate banking. It created a loophole through which NCNB was able to buy a Florida bank and, in effect, make interstate banking a reality, albeit it took another couple of years to get all the legal approvals.

- In 1988, NCNB made an innovative use of tax credits to buy the failed Republic and Interfirst banks in Texas, and with this transaction, it became more than a regional bank. When these Texas acquisitions were consummated in 1989, NCNB was the country's seventh largest bank.

- In the early 1990s, NCNB used the troubles of C&S/Sovran and MNC to further enhance its status. After the C&S/Sovran deal was finalized, it took the more expansive name of NationsBank and when both of the acquisitions were completed, it had taken another big step forward and temporarily became the third largest domestic bank. In 1995, Chemical's acquisition of Chase Manhattan would push it back to fourth.

- The only part of the consolidation process NationsBank missed was 1995, and it more than made up for that in 1996, 1997 and 1998 with the Boatmen's, Barnett and BankAmerica acquisitions. With these purchases, it became the country's largest bank in terms of domestic loans, deposits and assets, and second largest in overall assets.

The choice of the NationsBank name in 1992 might have been a tip-off to what would happen in 1998. It was an inversion of the BankAmerica name, and NationsBank was well on its way to nationwide coverage. In the mid-1990s, there was considerable speculation that there could be a merger between NationsBank and BankAmerica with Hugh McColl in charge. Thus, the only real surprise when this merger was announced was that it came so soon after the Barnett deal, but there was little time to wait in a frenzied merger climate or BankAmerica might have gone elsewhere.

The BankAmerica acquisition put NationsBank over the top. After the Boatmen's and Barnett purchases, it was once more the third biggest bank in the country and had moved beyond its southern roots. Barnett was an in-region merger that solidified its position in Florida, but Boatmen's was its first venture into the Midwest. With the addition of BankAmerica, it had become number one in the Far West; gained a presence in Chicago; and added more offices in Florida and Texas. NationsBank had clearly become a national bank and a giant even among the large banks.

When the NationsBank-BankAmerica merger was announced there was no question as to who was the acquirer—the headquarters was to be in Charlotte and McColl would be in charge. BankAmerica's David Coulter would be the president and CEO of the bank, but it was clearly a secondary position. Only the name was to be decided later, but even that delay appeared to be a NationsBank decision.

The choice of the Bank of America name for the holding company and consolidated banks was a bit of a surprise, but made good marketing sense. The NationsBank name was retired after just six years, and arguably the best known name in banking, Bank of America, was not only kept alive, but raised to new heights.

For McColl, it had been quite a ride. He had played a major role in the rise of NCNB in the 1970s as an executive vice president, and from 1983 on was the CEO and primary decision-maker. When he took command, NCNB was the 26th largest bank in the country with assets of $12 billion. Upon completion of the BankAmerica merger and at the end of the 1990s, he was running the nation's biggest bank and second largest financial corporation with assets of $633 billion.

NationsBank, First Union and the South

By 1999, the acquisitions of NationsBank and First Union had a national impact, but it was not so long ago that there were still questions about which banks would dominate the South. Even after the Texas banks fell by the wayside in the mid-1980s, there were nine banks in the South with assets between $15 and $30 billion. NationsBank was the largest of the nine and First Union number three, but there was no certainty that they would move away from the crowd and become the biggest banks in the South with far more than a regional content.

After the early 1990s recession and the 1995 merger spree, there were still five large banks in the South—NationsBank, First Union, SunTrust, Barnett and Wachovia—but by then it was the big two of NationsBank and First Union and three others. NationsBank assets were over $180 billion and First Union was up to $140 billion. SunTrust, Barnett and Wachovia had assets between $40 and $50 billion, and long gone were Sovran, Citizens &

Southern, MNC and Southeast Banking. By the time 1998 was over, Barnett was added to the list of missing by acquisition along with Crestar, which had become Virginia's largest bank after the disappearance of C&S/Sovran.

Largest Southern Banks, 1999

Bank	Assets 1999 1996 (in billions)		Rank 1996	Eventual Owner
1. Bank of America	$633	$186	1	Bank of America
2. First Union	253	140	2	Wachovia
3. SunTrust	95	52	3	SunTrust
4. Wachovia	67	47	4	Wachovia
5. BB&T	43	21	8	BB&T
6. Amsouth	43	18	10	Regions
7. SouthTrust	43	26	6	Wachovia
8. Regions	43	19	9	Regions
9. Union Planters	33	15	–	Regions
10. First Tennessee	18	13	–	First Horizon
– Barnett	–	41	5	Bank of America
– Crestar	–	23	7	SunTrust

Source: SNL Financial, Charlottesville, Virginia.

With NationsBank, or as it was now called Bank of America, over $600 billion assets at the end of 1999 and First Union past the $250 billion mark, it was hard to even imagine that ten years earlier these two banks had assets of less than $30 billion and were similar in size to SunTrust, Barnett and Wachovia. SunTrust was still a strong regional factor in 1999 with $95 billion assets—enough to be a third southern bank in the national top ten—and Wachovia at $67 billion was still a highly-respected, multi-state banking operation, but they were increasingly being viewed as acquisition targets, not as buyers.

There were other large southern mergers during this period, but they had little impact on the regional or national banking structure. Three billion dollar 1998 acquisitions, however, created a bit of a stir in the Mid-South, which had been left out of the earlier periods of consolidation. Even after these mergers, though, the acquirers—Birmingham's Regions, Memphis-based Union Planters and First American in Nashville—were still relatively small banks, even when compared to SunTrust. The largest of the three, Regions, had assets of $43 billion.

Norwest-Wells Fargo

When it was announced that Norwest was acquiring Wells Fargo less than two months after the NationsBank-BankAmerica agreement, it seemed like a sad ending for a once vibrant California banking industry—and little chance that California would have a national or multi-regional bank with the stature of NationsBank and First Union or even of a SunTrust. Wells Fargo, BankAmerica, First Interstate, Security Pacific, Crocker National—giants of California banking two decades earlier—had all been sold. To make matters worse, in March 1998, the state's largest thrift, Ahmanson, was acquired by another out-of-state banking organization, Washington Mutual.

The Norwest-Wells Fargo merger, though, was a more equal merger than most mergers that claim that status. Wells Fargo was the bigger of the two banks, but the troubles that flowed from its turbulent 1995 takeover of First Interstate had hurt its reputation and market value. Thus, it was not a surprise that Norwest was the buyer when these banks joined forces and that its management team headed by Richard Kovacevich would be in charge, but part of the deal was that the Wells Fargo name would be retained—a good marketing decision—*and* that the headquarters would be kept in San Francisco. Wells Fargo had been acquired, but California had a bank almost as large as First Union.

Initially, the survival of a San Francisco headquarters was somewhat muted by much of the top management continuing to work in Minneapolis, but as time went by and personnel turned-over, the management gravitated toward the city on the bay. By 2007, only purists thought of Wells Fargo as the successor of Norwest and anything but a California-based bank.

Regardless of who bought whom, Norwest-Wells Fargo was a merger with a major consolidation impact. The new Wells Fargo had more than $200 billion assets and 3,000 branches in 21 states. It ranked in the top three in deposit share in most of the states west of the Mississippi River, and along with Bank of America, was one of the two dominant banking forces in the western half of the country.

The interest that Norwest and Wells Fargo had in generating and servicing residential mortgages also resulted in a national mortgage banking operation with more than 800 offices in 50 states. It was one of the nation's two largest mortgage banks, a business that would grow rapidly in the housing boom that was to come.

Unlike the Wells Fargo-First Interstate merger, Norwest-Wells Fargo would not experience cultural problems. Kovacevich was a highly-respected and competent leader; the overlaps were far less; and the management that survived the turmoil of the Wells Fargo-First Interstate consolidation did not want to see a repeat of that situation. The road forward also was made easier by continuing the Norwest historic pattern of small in-region mergers.

Washington Mutual

Wells Fargo was not alone among western banking organizations to come out of 1998 as much-enlarged and with a national reach. In that year, Washington Mutual, the nation's largest thrift, acquired San Francisco-based Ahmanson, the second largest thrift, which made it the lone thrift to climb into the upper echelons of domestic banking. Ahmanson's purchase did not come cheaply with a price tag of almost $10 billion, but it lifted Washington Mutual's assets to $165 billion at year-end 1998, and for a few months, it was the country's seventh largest banking organization. The Norwest-Wells Fargo merger a couple of months later and Fleet's purchase of BankBoston would push it back to number nine, but Washington Mutual had come a long way and was far from done.

Washington Mutual was, in fact, a success story rivaling those of Bank One, Fleet, First Union and Norwest. In 1980, it was a small S&L in Wenatchee, Washington known as Columbia Federal with assets of less than $300 million. In 1988, it changed its name to Washington Mutual, and in 1992 moved its headquarters to Seattle. At that time, it was still a relatively small S&L with assets of $9 billion and 17 offices, all of which were located in the state of Washington. It was a virtual nonentity in a West Coast thrift industry dominated by large California S&Ls, particularly Ahmanson and Great Western. Luck of location, though, spared it the loan problems of the California S&Ls in the early 1990s, and it had the courage to venture into that huge market when the opportunity arose.

Like most once small banks and thrifts that had moved from relative obscurity to regional and national prominence, Washington Mutual owed its rise to the resourcefulness and determination of one man. In its case, it was Kerry Killinger who came to Washington Mutual as part of an acquisition in 1982 and became its president in 1988. Washington Mutual was struggling in the late 1980s, but with Killinger at the helm, it put its hard times behind and by the end of the 1990s was a national force.

Washington Mutual had not ventured into California until 1996, but when it finally did, it raised a few eyebrows with the purchase of American Savings. With assets of $20 billion, American Savings raised Washington Mutual's total assets to more than $44 billion as of year-end 1996. In 1997, it followed up the American Savings deal with the acquisition of one of the biggest California S&Ls, Great Western. This acquisition not only gave Washington Mutual the largest thrift deposit share in California, but it also put it in Arizona and Florida. By the end of 1997, Washington Mutual's assets were almost $97 billion. In 1998, it completed its California "trifecta" with the Ahmanson acquisition. In 2000 and 2001, it would acquire the biggest thrifts in New York and Texas.

With its S&L roots and large California base, Washington Mutual was challenging the big commercial banks, particularly BankAmerica and Wells Fargo, but was doing so with a large mortgage banking concentration. By 1998, it was already one of the largest originators and servicers of home mortgages. Over the next few years, it would take its mortgage business nationwide and become part of a mortgage banking big three that included Wells Fargo and a mortgage specialist, Countrywide.

This was a model different from most of the big commercial banks, Wells Fargo being a partial exception, but it was a model that depended on the generation of deposits to fund its mortgage banking business. As a result, it was competing with banks of all types in pursuing deposits, and by 2007, Washington Mutual would have almost 2,000 banking offices in 16 states and one of the two largest deposit shares in California, Oregon and Washington. It also had a large presence in Florida and the New York and Chicago metropolitan areas.

Thrifts, as a group, were still major factors in 1998 in most Northeast states and on the West Coast, but Washington Mutual was the only one that became a national factor. The country's second largest thrift after the sale of Ahmanson, Golden State Bancorp, the successor to the Cal Fed and GlenFed franchises, was sold to Citigroup in 2002. In 2005, the Royal Bank of Scotland was still using a thrift charter to expand in the United States, but the parent company certainly was not a thrift. Sovereign in Pennsylvania also was technically a thrift with assets over $80 billion by 2007, but by then it was a thrift in charter only and was not a leader in any of the East Coast's major markets.

Bank One and the Midwest

While Norwest was moving westward in 1998, the other big Midwest banks continued the regional consolidation that began in the late 1980s. The

Midwest, though, was still a fragmented banking market, and despite the efforts of Bank One, this fragmentation did not change much in 1998. Bank One's acquisition of First Chicago-NBD had made it much larger than any other bank in the region, and many of the other Midwest banks that looked like potential consolidators after 1995 either were gone by the end of 1998—First Chicago-NBD and Boatmen's; had moved its base out of the region—Norwest; or had lost momentum—KeyCorp. Only First Bank System, or U.S. Bancorp as it was now called, and National City made even a modest effort to keep pace with Bank One in the Midwest and the large buyers elsewhere in the country.

This relative lack of large merger activity in the Midwest was a little surprising since the branching limitations that had lasted so long in so many of the Midwest states had left a fragmented banking structure and lots of room for consolidation either through mergers of banks in the region or by the entry of outsiders. The outsider threat had not played out as expected, but NationsBank's purchase of Boatmen's and arrival in Chicago through the purchase of BankAmerica were reminders that the region would not be ignored by large, out-of-area banks.

Bank One did its part to consolidate the region, and its acquisition of the larger First Chicago-NBD without corresponding moves by others would create an unrivaled Midwest banking leader. Bank One more than doubled its assets between 1996 and 1999 from $102 billion to $269 billion; was about three times the asset size of the second largest bank based in the Midwest—National City; and was the fifth largest bank in the country.

Bank One also had become far more than just a Midwest bank being among the leaders in Texas, Louisiana, Colorado and Arizona, and seemed well-positioned to join Bank of America as a bank with near-national coverage. It was already there with its credit card operation, First USA, which was one of the three largest issuers of credit cards.

Bank One's acquisition of First Chicago-NBD was the culmination of Bank One's rise from a second-tier bank in Columbus, Ohio to national prominence. Despite some stumbling in the mid-1990s, by 1998, Bank One was back to being a high performer. First Chicago-NBD also had put most of its cultural problems of the 1995 First Chicago-NBD merger behind, but was no longer just a Chicago money center bank. NBD management had prevailed, and although First Chicago-NBD's CEO, Istock, had moved from Detroit to Chicago, his thinking was regional rather than Chicago-centered. To Istock, joining forces with Bank One made good sense in that it created a regional giant with access to high growth out-of-area markets. As a result, for the second time in four years, First Chicago was bought by a bank from another midwestern city, and for a second time, the appeal of Chicago kept the headquarters there.

While this was clearly a Bank One acquisition, it was not the end for Istock. Bank One's CEO, McCoy, was in charge, and Istock had taken a secondary role as chairman, but earnings problems in 1999 would force a McCoy resignation, and Istock would once more take charge. This time, he was thinking about restoring earnings and succession rather than the next big merger.

Largest Midwest Banks, 1999

Bank	Assets		Rank 1996	Eventual Owner
	1999	1996		
	(in billions)			
1. Bank One	$ 269	$ 102	2	JPMorgan
2. National City	87	51	5	National City
3. KeyCorp	83	68	4	KeyCorp
4. U.S. Bancorp	82	36	6	U.S. Bancorp
5. Firstar	73	10	–	U.S. Bancorp
6. Fifth Third	42	21	9	Fifth Third
7. Comerica	39	34	7	Comerica
8. Huntington	29	20	10	Huntington
9. Marshall & Illsley	24	15	13	Marshall & Illsley
10. Old Kent	18	13	14	Fifth Third
– First Chicago	–	105	1	JPMorgan
– Norwest	–	80	3	Wells Fargo
– First of America	–	22	8	National City

Source: SNL Financial, Charlottesville, Virginia.

Two other Ohio banks, National City and Keycorp were second and third in the Midwest with assets of $87 billion and $83 billion, respectively. They were much smaller than Bank One, but with all the large banks that had disappeared since 1995, this was enough size to place them at or near the bottom of the national top ten. U.S. Bancorp and Firstar were the only other Midwest banks with the size to influence consolidation going forward.

Firstar

Other than Bank One's acquisition of First Chicago-NBD, the most intriguing Midwest merger in 1998 involved two mid-sized institutions, Star Banc in Cincinnati and Firstar in Milwaukee. This was the beginning of a series of mergers that would create a contender for being one of the five or six banks that would dominate American banking.

Firstar-Star Banc also was another one of those equal mergers that was based on one partner, Star Banc, having management control and the other the headquarters. In this case, though, Firstar not only had the headquarters, but also kept its name. Neither name nor the headquarters location, however, would be of long duration.

For a brief time, though, the Firstar name would have its day in the sun. The Firstar-Star Banc merger was finalized in November 1998, and the new Firstar had assets of $38 billion and was the fifth largest bank in the Midwest. Five months later, it announced the acquisition of Mercantile Bancorp in St. Louis, and with that merger, more than doubled its size. By year-end 1999, Firstar had assets of $78 billion.

Firstar was still a secondary player on the national stage, but it was gaining momentum, and its president and CEO, Jerry Grundhofer from Star Banc, was the older brother of John Grundhofer, the president and CEO of U.S. Bancorp. In 2000, Firstar and U.S. Bancorp would have a family reunion in another equal merger. Firstar technically was the buyer, but it was U.S. Bancorp's name that was retained and the headquarters was in Minneapolis, not Milwaukee.

Fleet

In New England, there was little room for further consolidation as its banking elite was effectively down to just two—Fleet and Bank of Boston, or BankBoston as the holding company was then called. State Street was still around, but it was a specialty bank with only six banking offices, and the Citizens affiliate of Royal Bank of Scotland was growing rapidly, but still far behind the big two. Short of a Fleet-BankBoston merger or the takeover of one of the two by either the Royal Bank of Scotland or a large, out-of-area bank, the New England role in bank consolidation had pretty much run its course, or so it seemed.

By the second weekend in March 1999, however, another chapter in New England bank consolidation was about to be written. A telephone call from the *Boston Globe* that weekend wanted my views on an impending, and surprising, merger of Fleet and BankBoston. Fleet was completing its improbable run of directly, or indirectly, absorbing almost every bank of any size in New England. By the time it was through, BankBoston, Bank of New England, Shawmut, BayBanks, CBT, Hartford National, Society for Savings, Boston Five and many other locally prominent New England banking franchises were part of the Fleet franchise.

The acquisition of BankBoston, almost doubled Fleet's size in a year. With assets approaching $200 billion, it had moved from eleventh to eighth in size nationwide. Fleet would have to divest some of its New England branches and deposits, but the next largest New England banking organization, Royal Bank of Scotland's Citizens affiliate, was a distant second with American assets of just $23 billion in 1999.

Northeast Impact

As the 1990s wound down, it was a bit unfair to think about Fleet as just a New England bank. It started its move to prominence back in 1987 with an equal merger with Norstar that made it a leader in Upstate New York and gave it offices in the New York metropolitan area. In 1995, Fleet bought NatWest's New Jersey franchise and became a significant factor in New Jersey. With the purchase of BankBoston, Fleet was still much smaller than Citicorp and Chase Manhattan and trailed J.P. Morgan as well, but was a solid fourth in asset size among banks headquartered in the Northeast and was number one in deposit share if large bank main office deposits, which tended to be corporate or government deposits from outside the immediate area, were excluded.

The changing structure in the Northeast during the late 1990s flowed from large mergers by some big banks and a loss of momentum by others. Citicorp and Fleet more than doubled their size through mergers in 1998 and early 1999 while the combined Chemical-Chase Manhattan, the biggest bank in the country in the previous two years, was busy trying to blend together two very complex organizations. As a result, the new Chase Manhattan was not much bigger in 1998 than in 1996 and 1997. J.P. Morgan and PNC were other Northeast banks that did not grow much in the late 1990s.

The major Northeast bank losses by acquisition during these twenty months of frenzied merger activity centered upon 1998 were Bankers Trust, BankBoston and CoreStates. This did not leave much of a second tier behind Citigroup, Chase Manhattan, J.P. Morgan and Fleet in a region that included such large cities as New York, Philadelphia and Boston. The other Northeast banks with assets above $50 billion at the end of 1998—PNC, Bank of New York, Mellon and Republic—were second-tier players with either little momentum or little appetite for traditional banking, and by the end of 1999, Republic was gone.

Largest Northeast Banks, 1999

Bank	Assets 1999 1996 (in billions)		Rank 1996	Eventual Owner
1. Citigroup	$717	$ 310	1	Citigroup
2. Chase Manhattan	406	336	2	JPMorgan
3. J.P. Morgan	261	222	3	JPMorgan
4. Fleet	191	86	5	Bank of America
5. PNC	75	73	6	PNC
6. Bank of New York	75	56	8	Bank of New York
7. Mellon	48	43	11	Bank of New York
8. Summit	36	23	12	Bank of America
9. M&T	22	13	13	M&T
10. Banknorth	14	5	–	Toronto-Dominion
- Bankers Trust	–	140	4	Deutsche Bank
- BankBoston	–	62	7	Bank of America
- Republic	–	53	9	HSBC
- CoreStates	–	45	10	Wachovia

Source: SNL Financial, Charlottesville, Virginia.

The sale of Bankers Trust to Deutsche Bank also was not only a sale, but also was Bankers Trust's final step away from traditional banking. Deutsche Bank, even in Europe was more of an investment bank than a full-service bank, and much of its activity in United States came from its 1996 acquisition of Alex. Brown & Sons, a mid-sized Baltimore-based investment bank. As part of Deutsche Bank, Bankers Trust would fit into that same mode.

National Leaders

The merger activity in 1998 had created two superbanks, Citigroup and Bank of America, and left eight banks and a thrift much larger than all other banking organizations. Mergers announced or completed in 1998 and early 1999 had more than doubled the asset size since 1996 of Citigroup, Bank of America, Bank One, Wells Fargo and Fleet. The smallest of the eight large banks, Fleet, upon completion of its BankBoston acquisition, was more than twice as large as the ninth biggest, SunTrust.

Largest Domestic Banks, 1999

Bank	Assets 1999 1996 (In billions)		Rank 1996
1. Citigroup	$717	$281	2
2. Bank of America	633	186	5
3. Chase Manhattan	406	336	1
4. Bank One	269	102	10
5. J.P. Morgan	261	222	4
6. First Union	253	140	6
7. Wells Fargo	218	80	11
8. Fleet	191	86	10
9. SunTrust	95	52	16
10. National City	87	51	18
BankAmerica	–	251	3
Bankers Trust	–	120	7
First Chicago NBD	–	105	9
Wells Fargo (orig.)	–	109	8
Washington Mutual	$146	22	–

Source: SNL Financial, Charlottesville, Virginia.

Gone from the scene were BankAmerica, Bankers Trust, First Chicago-NBD, the original Wells Fargo, Barnett, CoreStates and BankBoston, and the mighty Citicorp also was acquired. Citicorp, or Citigroup as it is now called, was far from gone, though, as the driving force behind the acquiring Travelers, 'Sandy Weill, saw Citicorp, not Travelers, as the focus of this financial conglomerate. It was not a stretch to say that Citicorp was both the acquired and the survivor. This would be made clear a few years later when Citigroup sold the insurance business of Travelers with minimal impact on earnings.

After the mega-merger mania of late 1997, 1998 and early 1999, American banking was heading into the new millennium with five or six banks well on their way to controlling half of all American banking assets. Citigroup and Bank of America were firmly placed as two of the elite. On size and reputation, Chase Manhattan and J.P. Morgan, were also logical candidates, but they had no momentum at the time, and the latter had not moved toward a more full-service banking mode of operation. Bank One, First Union, Wells Fargo and Fleet had momentum, but still had a long way to go to be ultimate survivors—and were small enough to be bought by Bank of America or Citigroup.

Beyond Traditional Banking

Wat the 1990s brought *new* to bank consolidation was an expansion beyond the traditional. The increase in the share of bank assets held by a handful of banking organizations may have been a dramatic departure from the decline in the 1980s, but this increased share was based on the arrival of interstate banking and the thrift industry collapse in the 1980s. It was then fueled by the negative impact on individual banks of a real estate-driven recession. The increased large bank share may have occurred in the 1990s, but the origins of these gains were in the previous decade.

Legislation allowing banks to reach beyond traditional banking with activities such as investment banking—including underwriting securities, securities sales and selling and underwriting insurance was unique to the 1990s, and ushered in a whole new set of dynamics and the potential for a much broader approach to one-stop shopping for financial services. The outcome expanded the reach of the large banks at the expense of the small, but broader banking powers were cheered by banks of all sizes.

Expansion into previously off-limits segments of financial services was not only new in the 1990s, but its impact on consolidation was abetted by a segmenting of once traditional bank products into sub-industries of their own. Mortgage banking, asset management and credit cards had long been bank services, but they also were specialty services that included nonbanks in the competitive mix.

The emergence of these sub-industries within a broad financial services industry was a much more gradual process than the disappearance of Glass Steagall—the restrictive, hold-over legislation from the 1930s. Originating and servicing mortgages was something banks had been doing for decades, and banks continue to originate and book home mortgages as well as offer trust services and credit cards. By the end of the 1990s, though, small and mid-sized banks, as well as thrifts, were only operating on the fringes of these once traditional banking businesses.

Thus, it was the pressure to eliminate, or at least roll back, the prohibitions of the Glass-Steagall Act of 1933 against banks underwriting and selling securities and insurance that was the 1990s' unique contribution to bank consolidation. There had been considerable movement in this direction even before the Travelers-Citicorp merger, but it was that merger that took down Glass-Steagall and made Sandy Weill, CEO of Travelers and then Citigroup, one of the most important figures in bank consolidation.

One-Stop Shopping

The expansion of bank powers to include investment banking and the sale of securities and insurance initially received a lot of attention as a major step toward one-stop shopping for financial services. It was the benefits of one-stop shopping that had Weill so intrigued with putting into a single organization a commercial bank, an insurance company, an investment bank and a securities brokerage, all with national, or near national, coverage. It may not have worked as well as he anticipated on the retail side, but one-stop shopping remains an important bank objective relative to retail as well as commercial customers.

The concept of one-stop shopping was not new, but most of the earlier efforts had been by outsiders who were not restrained by Glass-Steagall. In the 1980s, it attracted a lot of attention as a result of actions by Sears, the installation of bank branches in grocery stores, and, to a lesser extent, the acquisition of Charles Schwab & Co. by BankAmerica. Not only did one-stop shopping get a lot of attention at the time, but for many bankers, it was as much of a competitive concern as interstate banking.

Sears, in particular, was of concern to bankers. It was still viewed in the 1980s as a retail giant, and its ownership of an S&L, real estate broker, insurance company and credit card brought forth the vision of a powerful marketing force that would have people flocking to Sears to put their money into CDs, buy insurance, make credit card payments, visit an ATM and check out home prices in adjoining kiosks. Only later was it realized that Sears was a fading force in retailing activities of all types.

Bank branches in grocery stores were viewed as an expansion of the bank delivery system and not seen as nearly the threat to traditional banking as the Sears one-stop shopping concept. There was concern, though, that these store branches could morph into the stores owning the branches—a threat that seemed even more ominous with the rise of Wal-Mart.

Combining BankAmerica's large branch network with the Schwab discount approach to trading securities, which was relatively unique at the time, was even further down the list as a competitive threat, but was one more step in the direction of one-stop shopping. Emanating from the biggest retail bank in the country kept it within the confines of the banking industry, but BankAmerica was not just any bank.

Customer resistance and problems at both Sears and BankAmerica greatly reduced the fear of one-stop shopping long before the 1980s had ended. Sears was only a shell of its former self, and the declining fortunes of BankAmerica at the time caused a rift between it and the former owner of Charles Schwab & Co. that ended up with Schwab buying the business back. Grocery store branches continue to exist, but their ownership stayed with banks and thrifts.

What resuscitated the one-stop shopping concept in the late 1990s was the emergence of the internet. It was widely believed as the decade wound down that the internet would make one-stop shopping a viable concept that could be activated from home or work. Like much that had to do with the internet, though, one-stop shopping on the retail side was an over-hyped idea whose immediate, major contribution to bank consolidation may have been the damage it did to one of its prime adherents, Bank One. That bank's commitment to its internet banking subsidiary, Wingspan.com, might have been the difference between it being a survivor and its eventual sale to JPMorgan. Whether one-stop shopping using the internet was truly over-hyped or just ahead of its time is still an open question.

Open question or not, just the probability of one-stop shopping being a deciding factor in which direction customers go was strong enough in the late 1990s to make it an integral part of big bank planning. Deep pockets, large advertising budgets and thousands of branches operated by a single bank had become marketing realities and a strong incentive for banks to get rid of the Glass-Steagall prohibitions and expand their product base.

Fall of Glass-Steagall

When interstate banking barriers fell in the 1980s and rendered the 1920s' McFadden Act obsolete, the 1930s' Glass-Steagall Act that made it illegal for banks to engage in the underwriting of securities in an effort to prevent conflicts of interest—and had been broadly interpreted to keep banks out of nontraditional financial services—was the next constraint that banks wanted to see disappear. Over the years, the prohibition had been modified slightly in areas where there were no apparent conflicts of interest, but the modifications were so minor that as the 1990s began, investment banking and insurance underwriting were still not available to banks.

It was a virtual "given" in the early 1990s that Glass-Steagall would go the way of the McFadden Act. Some of the optimism came from a 1989 ruling by the Federal Reserve that a bank holding company could own an investment bank if no more than 10% of the investment bank's revenues came from services and products not allowable for banks. This permitted bank holding companies to buy or set up specialized investment banking subsidiaries, but the 10% revenue limit on services not allowed to banks was too restrictive for an investment bank subsidiary to have much of an impact on a bank's overall earnings.

This all changed in late 1996 when the Federal Reserve upped the limit for non-allowable investment banking activities to 25% of bank holding company revenues. This provided much more flexibility, and in early 1997, several banks were looking to circumvent the Glass-Steagall Act and test the Federal Reserve's willingness to let this 25% of revenues ruling be its access to a broad-based investment banking effort.

In April 1997, the test case came when Bankers Trust announced it was acquiring Baltimore's Alex. Brown & Sons for $1.7 billion. The price alone was eye-catching, but Alex. Brown was far more than just a regional investment bank. It ranked sixth in the nation in securities underwriting in 1996.[1] Thus, this proposed transaction had the nation's seventh largest bank buying the sixth largest securities underwriter, and if allowed, would be a major contributor to the diminishing of the Glass-Steagall constraints.

In July 1997, the Federal Reserve ruled in favor of Bankers Trust, and in the go-go business environment of the late 1990s, a rush by commercial banks to buy investment banks was anticipated. It would be almost a year, though, before the Travelers-Citicorp merger would propose combining a larger bank and a larger investment banking firm than Bankers Trust and Alex. Brown, but there already had been numerous bank acquisitions of investment banks announced starting in June 1997.

BankAmerica and NationsBank did not wait for the Bankers Trust-Alex. Brown decision before they announced the acquisitions of two of the West Coast's hot, new investment banks. BankAmerica reported its plans to buy Montgomery Securities for $1.2 billion almost simultaneously with Nations-Bank's announcement of its purchase of Robertson Stephens for about $500 million in the summer of 1997. Before the year ended, Fleet, Wachovia, SunTrust, U.S. Bancorp, First Chicago-NBD and Fifth Third were among banks that had deals in place to buy investment banks or securities brokerages. The largest of these transactions was Fleet's acquisition of Quick & Reilly, a nationwide discount broker with more than a million clients.

There was no Morgan Stanley, Merrill Lynch, Goldman Sachs or Salomon Brothers among the to-be-acquired investment banks, but because of the nature of their business, most of the investment banks that were being bought by bank holding companies were well-known, at least locally, and their sales garnered far more attention than their size warranted. This was partly because this was an industry that was fueling the bull market and contributing to the dotcom frenzy of the late 1990s.

All of the bank holding company acquisitions of investment banks in 1997 and 1998 combined, though, did not have near the impact on bank consolidation as a single 1997 merger between an insurance company and an investment bank—a transaction that did not involve a commercial bank. In September 1997, Travelers Insurance announced it was buying Salomon Brothers for more than $9 billion. This was one of the giants of the investment banking industry that would be even larger when combined with the Smith Barney securities brokerage affiliate already owned by Travelers.

The Travelers-Salomon Brothers transaction was closed in November 1997, and with this acquisition Weill, Travelers CEO, had the market clout to consider a merger with Citicorp. Five months later, the Travelers-Citicorp merger would be announced, and with these mergers, Weill had dramatically altered the direction of the financial services industry.

Sandy Weill

No one was more enthralled with the possibilities of financial services one-stop shopping than Sandy Weill, even before he had added Travelers Insurance to his stable of businesses. After buying Salomon Brothers in 1997, his primary objective was to fill the final void in his collection and add a large bank to his holding company. Citicorp was his first choice—he saw no reason not to start at the top—and if Weill had been rebuffed there, he undoubtedly would have found another bank to buy. He was not rebuffed by Citicorp, however, and with that deal, not only did he change the direction of the financial services business, but he also turned himself into a banking and corporate legend.

Unlike other bankers who played leading roles in the consolidation of banking, Weill was not readily identifiable with a single company. Walter Wriston and John Reed were Citicorp; Hugh McColl was NationsBank; and Ed Crutchfield was First Union. Weill would spend just eight years with Citigroup, and his primary contribution to that firm and bank consolidation was the initial act of buying Citicorp. That alone was enough to make him a key player in the consolidation process.

Weill was a well-known figure in financial circles long before 1998 and the Citicorp merger. His career began as a runner for Bear Stearns in 1955, and five years later at the age of 28, he was one of four partners in the newly-formed Carter, Berlind, Potoma & Weill brokerage firm. In 1970, his firm acquired the much better-known Hayden Stone, and in 1973, Weill became CEO of the combined firms. In the next five years, Shearson Hamill and Loeb Rhoades would be added to Weill's growing network of securities brokerage offices. After the last acquisition, what was then called Shearson Loeb Rhoades was second in size only to Merrill Lynch among securities brokerages.[2]

In 1981, Weill took his first step toward one-stop financial services shopping when he agreed to merge his firm with American Express, and in so doing, he also was willing to take the second spot behind the American Express CEO, James Robinson. The combination of American Express and Shearson would create a diversified financial services company that was the leader in travelers' checks and credit cards and second in securities sales, but it was not a happy marriage for Weill who resigned in 1985. Playing second fiddle to Robinson was not as easy as he had thought.

Weill, though, was far from through, and after failing to gain control of BankAmerica, he took over a failing Baltimore business finance firm, Commercial Credit, which would be his new vehicle for buying companies. In 1988, he made a key move when he bought a struggling Primerica, which the year before had acquired Smith Barney, Harris and Upham.

Commercial Credit, Primerica and Smith Barney were only the start of Weill's second career. In 1992, Primerica made a 27% investment in the country's eighth largest insurance company, Travelers, and a year later bought Shearson back from American Express *and* the remaining 73% of Travelers. With the latter, the Primerica name was changed to Travelers. In 1997, Travelers added Salomon Brothers to the mix.

The new Travelers was primarily a collection of once struggling companies, but by 1997, it was a large financial company with revenues of about $38 billion and net income of $3.1 billion—and one of the 50 largest companies in the United States. If it had been a bank, it would have ranked as the largest in revenues and second largest in profits. Only Citicorp had higher earnings. Weill had accomplished this the hard way by initially buying firms with problems and then making the necessary improvements. What he wanted now was a large bank.

Travelers-Citicorp

Citicorp was a big target for Weill, but with the Salomon Brothers acquisition, Travelers was about the same size. In 1997, Citicorp had revenues of $30.3 billion, earnings of $3.6 billion and market capital as of the end of February of $56 billion. Corresponding figures for Travelers were $37.6 billion, $3.1 billion and $64 billion. In Weill's favor were the *Business Week* performance rankings of S&P 500 firms for 1996 that had Travelers fifth behind Intel, Microsoft, Dell and Cisco—heady company at the time. A year later, Travelers had fallen to 16th, but Citigroup, which was in 86th place in 1996, had slipped to 245th in 1997. Thus, when Weill approached Citicorp about a merger in February 1998, he was not coming with hat-in-hand.[3]

That Citicorp, the country's largest bank with a long and illustrious history, would be receptive to overtures from a financial services firm that had been cobbled together in just the last ten years was far from certain, but its CEO, John Reed, was also thinking about the benefits of size and one-stop shopping and was intrigued by the possibility of joining forces with Travelers. In fact, Reed was so intrigued that a merger between Citicorp and Travelers would be announced five weeks later to a generally stunned audience.[4]

Business Week's perception of the transaction was that "perhaps, the best way to describe the Citicorp-Travelers Group Inc. merger is audacious. John S. Reed, America's top banker, and Sanford I. Weill, America's top financial services dealmaker, on April 6 proposed a $70 billion merger that defies existing law. Banks such as Citicorp can't own property & casualty insurers such as Travelers, and are limited in their ability to acquire brokerages. No matter: Reed and Weill believe that by acting aggressively, they can persuade legislators to knock down Glass-Steagall barriers and create a new kind of global financial paradigm."[5]

"In addition to chutzpah, Reed 59, and Weill, 65, are propelled by their shared desire to go out in a blaze of glory. Both are nearing the end of their careers and seem intent on making history by creating the first successful, fully-integrated financial services behemoth. Says a clearly ecstatic Weill: 'The last major thing we are going to do is make this happen.' Adds Reed: 'We don't have to do this. We wanted to create this great enterprise together.'"[6]

Not only was it audacious in challenging existing banking law, but Travelers-Citicorp was the biggest merger in corporate history up to that time. The announced price was $83 billion, not the $70 billion reported in the *Business Week* article. The price took a "hit" as bank stock prices headed down in late 1998, but within two years of closing, two companies that had a combined market value of about $120 billion prior to the merger had a consolidated market value of $256 billion.

The approval risk for a merger that clearly violated existing banking laws was somewhat mitigated by the Federal Reserve not having to approve or disapprove the merger based on its status relative to Glass-Steagall. It could, and did, decide based on normal bank merger criteria, which was contingent on divesting activities that violated banking law if after two years the bank was still in violation of that law. This put the risk on the merging parties, and the Federal Reserve approved the transaction in October 1998.

The risk was there, but relatively slight as Glass-Steagall no longer had a lot of supporters, and 1998 and 1999 was a time when business and mergers were viewed positively by regulators and legislators. Citicorp and Travelers, themselves, also had a lot of legislative power, and the banking industry was behind them as most banks wanted the flexibility of being free of the Glass-Steagall constraints.

The result was the passage of the Financial Services Modernization Act, or as it was technically entitled the Gramm-Leach-Bliley Act, in November 1999. This act created a new type of holding company called simply a financial holding company that in addition to traditional banking could engage in insurance and securities underwriting and agency activities and merchant banking. With this legislation, Citicorp and Travelers were home free, and others were invited to follow their path.

For Citicorp and Travelers, one of the intended outcomes of the merger was one-stop shopping, but an immediate, positive result was an enhancement of Citicorp's competitive status relative to corporations and affluent bank customers. The holding company name was changed, but only slightly, from Citicorp to Citigroup, and Weill, who was to be one of the co-CEOs—Reed being the other—despite coming in as the head of Travelers, was not an insurance man. The reality was that this merger was as much between Citicorp and one of the country's largest investment bank/brokerage operations, Salomon Smith Barney, as it was between Citicorp and an insurance company.

For Weill and Reed, it was a rocky marriage personally as co-CEOs. Reed may have assumed because of age that Weill would be gone not too long after the merger was finalized, and that he would be running the show. This was not to be, and in 2000, Reed would retire instead, leaving Weill in total control, which made the obvious—Weill being in charge—official.

Gramm-Leach-Bliley

An expected reaction to Gramm-Leach-Bliley was that there would be many more mergers between banks, insurance companies, investment banks and securities brokerages that would create new Citigroups or at least mini-versions of it. The numerous merger announcements of banks buying small brokerages and investment banks in 1997 and 1998 made it clear that Citicorp and Travelers were not the only ones thinking along these lines, but the outcome was not what was initially expected.

The Citicorp-Travelers merger and Gramm-Leach-Bliley created a new set of dynamics for banks and other financial services companies, but it did not result in a deluge of mergers between banks, insurance companies and investment banks. Its primary effect would be to help the big banks grow and increase their "deep pockets" advantage over everyone else. As of 2007, the only companies, banks or other, to have benefited significantly from the new law were Citigroup, JPMorgan, Bank of America and Wachovia—four of the five banks that would dominate American banking and overall financial services.

In 2007, eight years after the passage of Gramm-Leach-Bliley, it appeared that:

- Banks had little interest in acquiring insurance underwriters, presumably because of the risks and relatively low growth rates of that business.
- Insurance companies were not buying banks despite banking being a better business, which may reflect an inferior investor status that made them noncompetitive as buyers.
- The biggest banks could expand in these newly allowed areas of opportunity without major acquisitions.

During this period, Citigroup and JPMorgan became world class in investment banking; Bank of America and Wachovia were well on their way to similar status; and SunTrust, KeyCorp and U.S. Bancorp had bought solid regional investment banking presences; but that was about it. By 2007, Citigroup, JPMorgan and Bank of America were the only banks large enough to buy one of the large independent investment banks—Morgan Stanley, Merrill Lynch, Goldman Sachs and Lehman Brothers—but up until then, they either did not feel a need to do so to be competitive or were just not interested.

Banks Versus Investment Banking Boutiques

How did the banks fare versus long-established investment banks like Morgan Stanley, Merrill Lynch, Goldman Sachs and Lehman Brothers after the fall of Glass-Steagall? There is no precise measurement, but if revenues listed in the bank call reports under fiduciary activities, securities trading, investment banking and related activities and venture capital for 2006 were compared to the total revenue of the four large investment banking-securities brokerage boutiques mentioned above, Citigroup and JPMorgan compared favorably just seven years after the enactment of Gramm-Leach-Bliley.

In 2006, Morgan Stanley, Merrill Lynch and Goldman Sachs had total revenues between $30 and $40 billion. This was more than the $23 billion to $26 billion of JPMorgan and Citigroup, but the investment bank numbers include loans that were not included in the traditional bank numbers; and Morgan Stanley's revenues included the Discover credit card that came with its 1997 acquisition of Dean Witter. Since Citigroup and JPMorgan were two of the three biggest card issuers, a similar inclusion would have greatly increased their comparable revenues.[7]

Bank of America and Wachovia were a long way back in 2006 with similar revenues of $12 billion and $7 billion, respectively, but this would still put them solidly in a second tier of investment banks with the likes of Lehman Brothers and Bear Stearns. The overall size and strength of Bank of America, in particular, but also Wachovia, is such that they are almost certain to leave most of the other second-tier players behind and close the gap on the industry leaders. Bank of America buying Morgan Stanley or Merrill Lynch also will be speculated upon until this occurs, they are bought by someone else or become too big to buy.

It could be argued that these nontraditional banking activities were taking the big banks out of mainstream banking and back toward a money center culture rather than adding a marketing advantage over other banks, but that was not the case. Equities and other nondeposit investments had become an integral part of retail, as well as corporate, customer financial activities that competed directly with deposits.

The ability of the likes of Citigroup, JPMorgan, Bank of America, Wachovia and Wells Fargo to use their size to go beyond traditional banking would play a major role in setting five very large banks apart from all others. It was no surprise in 2005 when my Legg Mason investment account was bought by Citigroup and an MBNA credit card dating back to the early 1970s was contributing to Bank of America's revenues.

Securities Brokerage

There is a tendency to group investment banking and the mass sale of securities because of their common emphasis on corporate equities, the New York City domicile of the leading players and Merrill Lynch and Citigroup's preeminence in each. The underwriting of securities and their subsequent sale, though, are not only two different businesses, but the conflict between doing both is such that regulatory authorities insist that when underwriting and sales are both done within the same company that there should be no communication between the sections that do one part and those that do the other—the proverbial Chinese Wall.

The reality, however, is that successful securities underwriting requires a sales arm, and it is easier and more profitable to get this sale assistance "in-house." Anyone who does significant stock purchasing through a broker is well aware of the broker tendency to push stocks that their firm is bringing to market. The excesses of the late 1990s internet and technology booms brought with it a heightened regulatory concern, and combining a bank's lending power with securities underwriting and the sale of securities could be viewed as having actually increased the conflict—and enhanced the ability of big banks to gain customers at the expense of smaller banks.

Selling securities was not new to banks in 1999 as Glass-Steagall had not closed the door on banks selling stocks. If it had, BankAmerica could not have bought Charles Schwab in the 1980s, and in the late 1990s, banks of all sizes were experimenting with selling stocks, particularly via mutual funds, through their branches. Prior to 1998, though, banks were fringe players in the brokerage business, and then came the Travelers-Citicorp merger.

When the Travelers acquisition of Citicorp was announced, most of the attention was on combining of insurance and securities underwriting with the traditional banking activities of a large bank, an obvious violation of Glass-Steagall. That Travelers also owned one of the country's largest securities brokerages, Smith Barney, went relatively unnoticed. Unnoticed or not, with the completion of the Travelers-Citicorp merger, the newly-formed Citigroup became one of the country's largest brokers of securities of all types. Since most stock sales occur in the United States, the merger also made Citigroup one of the largest securities brokerages in the world.

Securities sales did not appeal to all large banks, but one that would follow the Citigroup lead was Wachovia. In 2003, it merged its securities sales business with the extensive brokerage business of Prudential, a large insurance company. Wachovia owned 62% of the combined venture, and it was, in effect, a Wachovia subsidiary operating under the Wachovia name. In 2007, it added to its securities brokerage business paying almost $7 billion for the St. Louis-based A.G. Edwards.

Citigroup and Wachovia may have been alone among the big banks with large brokerage businesses, but even alone, they were enough to put banks at the forefront of securities sales. In 2006, Merrill Lynch was still number one, but Citigroup and Wachovia were second and third in net revenues from the sale of securities and in the size of sales force. The domestic leaders also included a foreign bank, Switzerland's UBS, which in 2000, bought Paine Webber, a large American securities brokerage.[8] When Wachovia completes its A.G. Edwards purchase, it will approximate the size of Citigroup in this business.[9]

The sale of securities also is part of a much larger asset management business since the stock broker who sells securities at least loosely manages the assets of the clients for which he is trading stocks, and often it is more than just "loosely." Firms that managed assets included mutual fund companies, bank trust operations and private banks for the wealthy. Merrill Lynch, Citigroup and Wachovia did all of this, but taking asset management beyond securities sales brought in the likes of Fidelity with its mutual funds; Bank of New York, State Street and Northern Trust with trust operations and related businesses; and the private banking of JPMorgan and others.

Ranking the leading asset managers by amount of assets managed is complex, but a listing in *Barrons* in 2004 for United States put Merrill Lynch first, followed by Citigroup, Fidelity, UBS, Wachovia, JPMorgan and Bank of America. Northern Trust was number nine, and Wells Fargo eleventh.[10] These rankings show that not long after the enactment of Gramm-Leach-Bliley, the banks' role in asset management went far beyond its trust department origins.

Mortgage Banking

Unlike investment banking, mortgage banking did not need Glass-Steagall to disappear in order for the big banks to take over a business that had once been dominated by independent mortgage banks and thrifts. In the 1970s, the Amendments to the Bank Holding Company Act opened the door for banks to either buy or internally establish mortgage banking subsidiaries that could operate across state lines. Citicorp, Wells Fargo, Norwest, First Union and others had bought their way into the top ten in mortgage banking in the 1970s. Being one of the top ten at the time, though, meant having national market shares of less than 2%. Thrifts, not one of which ranked among the leading mortgage companies at that time, collectively, held and serviced about 50% of home mortgages.

What would change mortgage banking in the 1980s and 1990s was the securitization of mortgages that allowed banks and others to originate home loans and sell them to mortgage pools such as Fannie Mae and Freddy Mac. The originator of the loan needed little funding to do this, which opened the door for mass loan originations over a broad geographic region by mortgage banking specialists. This greatly increased the dollar amounts involved and the share of mortgages originated and serviced by the market leaders.

This increase in the size of the mortgage business of a few operations was dramatic in the 1980s on a percentage basis, but the big gains in dollar amounts took place after 1990. In 1980, the largest servicer of residential mortgages was Lomas & Nettleton, a boutique not aligned with a bank that was servicing about $7 billion of mortgage loans. A decade later, Lomas &

Nettleton was still among the leaders with loans serviced of $24 billion, but it had fallen far behind two banks, Citicorp and Fleet, which serviced $63 billion and $46 billion in mortgages, respectively.[11] These numbers seemed big at the time, but 16 years later, Wells Fargo and Countrywide would each be servicing more than $1.2 trillion in home mortgages; Citigroup and Washington Mutual better than $700 billion; and JPMorgan almost $700 billion.

Historic numbers are not as readily available on mortgages originated, but the growth of a handful of originators in the ten years leading up to 2006 was equally astounding. The 1995 origination leaders were Countrywide and Norwest with $35 billion and $34 billion in home mortgages originated, respectively, and they were still the leaders in 2006, albeit Norwest was by then bearing the Wells Fargo name. The difference between 1995 and 2006 was that in the latter year, Countrywide was originating about $450 billion in home mortgages—about a thirteen-fold increase—and Wells Fargo was just under $400 billion.

Home Mortgages Leaders, 1995 to 2006

Bank	2006	2005 (In billions)	1995
Mortgages Serviced			
1. Wells Fargo	$1,342	$1,005	$107
2. Countrywide	1,298	1,111	137
3. Citigroup	751	444	39
4. Washington Mutual	711	747	14
5. JPMorgan	674	604	74
6. Bank of America	419*	368	81
Mortgages Originated			
1. Countrywide	$456	$491	$35
2. Wells Fargo	398	392	34
3. Citigroup	208*	130	5
4. Washington Mutual	196	244	3
5. JPMorgan	178	178	14
6. Bank of America	168	159	11

*Includes subsequently acquired ABN AMRO Mortgage.
Source: American Banker, April 16, 1996 and National Mortgage News, Annual Data Report for 2006.

The size and scope of mortgage banking in the early 2000s favored the large banks, and the only interloper in their dominance of the business was Countrywide, a successful mortgage banking specialist. It was the leader in mortgages originated and second in mortgages serviced in 2006 with $456 billion and $1.3 trillion, respectively.

Countrywide and Wells Fargo were by far the biggest mortgage bankers in 2006 with about 30% of the country's mortgage originations and 31% of the mortgages serviced between them. Citigroup, including ABN AMRO Mortgage that was purchased in February 2007, was third in each category with 7% and 9% of the national totals. Washington Mutual, JPMorgan and Bank of America held positions four through six in home mortgages originated and serviced. Wachovia was eighth in servicing and eleventh in originations.[12]

The impact of the mortgage banking concentration on the overall bank consolidation was substantial. In 1995, Countrywide, Washington Mutual and four banks—Wells Fargo, JPMorgan, Citigroup and Bank of America—collectively, originated only $102 billion in residential mortgages. By 2006, their combined originations were more than $1.6 trillion and 51% of all home mortgage originations, which created a much greater access to a broad customer base than they would have had without this real estate presence.[13]

The numbers on the servicing side were even bigger. In 1995, these same six institutions were servicing $452 billion in home mortgages, and eleven years later, were up to almost $5.2 trillion. This was about 60% of all home mortgages serviced.[14]

Unlike in most other areas of banking, the rise of a handful of firms into dominant positions in mortgage banking was done primarily by internal expansion. The mortgage bankers, themselves, are a fluid employee group, and periodically change jobs without their previous employer being sold. This makes it relatively easy for a well-heeled mortgage bank to enter new markets by acquiring originators.

Nevertheless, mergers have played a significant role. Wells Fargo's position owes a lot to the combination of Norwest and Wells Fargo, each of which had a large mortgage banking business. Bank of America's move into the top six was facilitated by combining the mortgage banking operations of NationsBank, the original Bank of America and Fleet.

Credit Card

Credit cards followed the same path as mortgage banking from being a traditional bank product to a business dominated by the few, but with an even greater level of concentration. Unlike mortgage banking, after 2005, the credit card business no longer had an independent specialist along the lines of Countrywide competing with banks at the top and owed much more to mergers in its consolidation process.

The origin of the bank credit card goes back to the original Bank of America and the BankAmericard in the late 1950s, and in the early years of the card, the bank portion of it was aligned with two card systems, Visa and MasterCard. This made it possible for banks of all sizes to have their own card using their own name. The bank card also had early competition from American Express and retail store cards, including the Sears card that would eventually become the Discover card whose ownership moved from Sears to Dean Witter to Morgan Stanley that in 2007 is in the process of spinning it off to its shareholders.

The credit card, though, benefited more from scale economies than most bank products, and by the time the 1990s began, a few bank cards had become much larger than all others. Citicorp led the way, and other banks among the leaders were Chase Manhattan, BankAmerica, Wells Fargo, First Chicago and MNC with its MBNA subsidiary. The number of nonbank cards also had expanded to include specialists like First USA and finance company cards issued by Household Financial and Advanta.

Largest Credit Card Companies, 2005

Bank	Credit Card Outstandings		
	2005	2004 (in billions)	2001
1. Bank of America	$166	$59	$27
2. JPMorgan	139	135	41
3. Citigroup	137	140	121
4. Capital One	49	49	34
5. Morgan Stanley	47	48	50
MBNA	–	102	83

Source: The Financial Services Roundtable, *The Financial Services Fact Book, 2007.*

By the time the 1990s came to a close, the big bank dominance of the business had been greatly increased. Much of the gain came from mid-sized and small banks selling their portfolios, but some of the increase came from the exiting of a few large players. Bank One bought First USA in 1997, and a year later, Fleet took over the credit card business of Advanta. The bank share gain at the expense of nonbanks was somewhat mitigated by the corresponding success of two bank spin-offs—MBNA from MNC and Capital One from Signet. By 2000, MBNA was part of the credit card "big three" with Citigroup and Bank One.

Like many financial services in the early 2000s, credit cards were soon to be dominated by the nation's three largest banks. Citigroup was already there, and when JPMorgan bought Bank One, it added First USA to its own card business and replaced Bank One as part of the credit card top three. In 2003, Bank of America took a big step in that direction when it announced the purchase of Fleet and its substantial card business. Then in 2005, it bought MBNA—the boutique equivalent of Countrywide in credit cards. This gave Citigroup, Bank of America and JPMorgan well over half of the domestic credit card outstandings.

Insurance

The combination of banking and insurance did not play out quite as expected after the Travelers-Citicorp merger. There were no other major bank-insurance underwriter mergers, and in 2003 and 2005, Citigroup sold its Travelers' insurance underwriting operations. Banks continued, though, to show a strong interest in the sale of insurance, if not underwriting, as banking is by-and-large a distribution business.

The mass sale of insurance had long been a "mom-and-pop" local business, even more so than banking before the interstate era. Some underwriters like State Farm had numerous captive insurance agencies and three large insurance agencies—Marsh & McLennan, Aon and Willis Group Holdings—dominated corporate insurance sales, but the bulk of the retail insurance sales were made by small local firms, which was often an individual operating independently. These small firms had a myriad of state laws protecting them from bank competition.

Banks had long seen the potential for selling insurance through bank branches as a natural adjunct to their banking business, and in some of the European countries, banks sold most of the insurance. Even before 1999, American banks were trying to get around the legal constraints, and by the early 2000s, most of the more serious constraints had been removed.

Even after these constraints were removed, customers did not flock to banks to buy insurance, and the most successful banks in the sale of insurance bought agencies and let them continue to operate as they always had. As banks acquired multiple agencies, though, they began to combine them and sometimes gave them the bank name.

Wells Fargo and BB&T have been the most aggressive banks in the purchasing of insurance agencies, and in 2006, ranked fourth and sixth in insurance sales revenues behind the three agencies mentioned above that specialize in corporate sales. The revenues, however, were small when compared with other nonbank businesses that banks have entered and the sale revenues of retail/wholesale insurance giants like State Farm and Allstate. Wells Fargo had about $1.2 billion in insurance revenues in 2006, and BB&T had insurance revenues of a little over $700 million.[15]

According to an American Bankers Insurance Association survey, in the early 2000s, bank insurance revenues were growing at about 20% a year, but accounted for just 7% of commercial insurance sales and 3% of personal lines. Also, about two-thirds of the revenues banks reported as insurance fees were annuities, a product for which banks accounted for two-thirds of all sales, and annuities are as much an investment product as an insurance product.[16] Banks have a long way to go before they become major factors in the sale of insurance, but insurance is a big business, and the banks are not going away.

Post-1999 Nonbank Expansion Overview

The impact on the consolidation of banking and the broader financial services business from the expansion of the largest banks into related areas such as investment banking, securities sales, asset management, mortgage banking and credit cards after the fall of Glass-Steagall in 1999 was huge. Citigroup and JPMorgan rose to be among the five largest investment banks, and by 2007, were gaining on the leaders as they used their lending prowess to enhance their competitive status. Wachovia and Citigroup had acquired positions right behind Merrill Lynch in securities sales as well as in overall asset management.

The fall of Glass-Steagall had little to do with bank expansion in credit cards and mortgage banking, but the expansion of the large banks in these two businesses coincided rather closely with what was happening in investment banking, securities sales and asset management. The post-2000 credit card purchases by Bank of America and JPMorgan put Citigroup, Bank of America and JPMorgan far ahead of all others in that business. Mortgage banking was not totally dominated by the big banks in 2006 as Countrywide and Washington Mutual were still among the leaders, but the industry was just an acquisition away from having a structure similar to that of the other major nonbank financial businesses.

By 2007, the common perception of a big bank had moved far beyond the bricks and mortar of a branch system, and it takes a lot of resources to go beyond traditional banking. Once that step had been taken, though, those that had made the move had a competitive advantage in brand identification and "deep pockets" in gaining access to all the banking needs of businesses and individuals, particularly affluent individuals.

The fall of Glass-Steagall may have been a trigger that helped move consolidation beyond traditional banking and into its final stages in the early 2000s, but it was the desire of the largest banks to be as dominant in these specialty businesses as they were in their existing businesses that made it happen. This was a desire that had far from run its course by 2007.

And Then There Were Five

T he opportunities offered by the disappearance of Glass-Steagall had changed banking, and as the new millennium began, industry consolidation had reached a level that left few doubts about the degree of dominance of a handful of large banks. The number of American banking organizations with more than regional aspirations was down to eight banks—Citigroup, Bank of America, Chase Manhattan, J.P. Morgan, Bank One, First Union, Wells Fargo and Fleet—and a single thrift—Washington Mutual—and they, like all banks and thrifts, now had the freedom to go beyond traditional banking.

This concentration of so much power in so few hands had come only eighteen years after interstate banking was introduced; sixteen years after it became a legal reality; nine years after the concentration of assets in the hands of the large banks began to gather momentum; and one year after the fall of Glass-Steagall. By 2000, it was apparent that in a few years, five or six banks would control more than half of the nation's banking assets.

These nine banking organizations had survived a winnowing process, but in 2000, they were far from equal. Citigroup and Bank of America were much larger than the others and had momentum. Chase Manhattan with the Chemical management in charge had size, but not momentum. Fleet, Wells Fargo and Washington Mutual were the smallest of the group, but in 2000, they were the stars in performance and momentum. Not doing as well were J.P. Morgan, Bank One and First Union, and each had a different weakness.

J.P. Morgan had an identity problem. It was technically a bank, but it had stayed with the old money center model of being primarily a banker to corporations and governments. As a result, J.P. Morgan had a competitive disadvantage in a role that placed it somewhere between large, full-service banks that offered more options and aggressive investment banking firms that were not as closely regulated. The result was that it was still one of the most respected names in banking, but it was only moderately profitable and was not growing at near the rate of its competition.

Bank One had not lacked for growth after its spectacular run in the 1980s and 1990s, but its rapid growth and high ambitions also brought with them challenges that appeared to be beyond its management capability. It still had an expensive cost structure, and in 2000, Bank One was starting to experience asset quality problems as well. To make matters worse, it, more than any other large bank, was committed to internet banking, and a free-standing internet-banking subsidiary, Wingspan.com, was adding more in costs than it was producing in revenues.

First Union's problems also were a result of rapid growth and, in its case, a flawed acquisition program. In an effort to keep pace with the other emerging banking leaders, particularly NationsBank with which it shared the same hometown, First Union made some questionable acquisitions and its execution was not the best with its quality purchases. Its acquisition of The Money Store in 1998 was a disaster. It was closed two years after being acquired, and as part of the closing, First Union took a $2.8 billion charge.[1] By 2000, it also was still not benefiting the way it should have from the good market position it had assembled in Pennsylvania and New Jersey through the acquisitions of First Fidelity and CoreStates.

With the consolidation of banking having come so far by 2000 and the economy showing signs of weakness as the long stock market rise came to a resounding end, this was no time to be falling behind. J.P. Morgan, Bank One and First Union looked vulnerable as the new century began, and Fleet was beginning to feel the pain of the acquired BankBoston's commitments to Argentina, investment banking in the Silicon Valley and national corporate lending.

J.P. Morgan would not even make it out of 2000, but its name would survive in the new JPMorgan Chase, and by 2001, the gap between the haves and have-nots among the banking elite was immense. Citigroup, Bank of America, JPMorgan Chase and Wells Fargo had the look of winners while it seemed to be only a matter of time before Bank One, First Union and Fleet followed J.P. Morgan out the door. Washington Mutual was doing well, but its size and product mix—heavy mortgage orientation—were constraints in its ability to keep pace with the others.

By 2007, the sorting out was pretty much over, but the first seven years of the new millennium would have its surprises. Bank One and Fleet would be sold, but First Union refused to believe the obituaries being written about it in 2000 and 2001 and stunned industry observers by winning Wachovia away from SunTrust in a spirited acquisition battle. This victory did not immediately win over its doubters as the merger at the time was viewed as two laggards making matters worse by combining, but it gave First Union both a new lease on life and a new name. At the top end of the spectrum, Chase Manhattan continued to add size. It bought J.P. Morgan and Bank One and changed its name to JPMorgan Chase during this period, but its earnings performance was slow to match that of Citigroup, Bank of America and Wells Fargo—or even Wachovia after 2001.

A merger in the first year of the new millennium also brought a new challenger to the fringes of the banking elite—U.S. Bancorp. By combining with Firstar in 2000, it was almost as large as Fleet, Bank One, First Union and Wells Fargo, and has subsequently performed well. U.S. Bancorp, though, has not made another large acquisition, and by 2007, was the leader of a second tier of regional banks that included SunTrust, Capital One, National City, Regions and BB&T, rather than a trailer in the first tier.

Mergers in the Early 2000s

With the elimination of so many of what was already a small group of banks controlling such a large part of the banking industry, it would not be long before the new millennium would begin to take on an aura of being a post-consolidation era. This era had not quite arrived in 2000, though, as the merger-mania of the late 1990s had a year to run. In the first year of the new century, there were eleven billion-dollar bank mergers. These included the sale of J.P. Morgan to Chase Manhattan and the merger of U.S. Bancorp and Firstar. The $81 billion in collective sale value for the big mergers in 2000 was surpassed up to that time only by the $245 billion of 1998.

In the next three years combined, the number of large mergers and their total deal value would be less than in 2000 alone. The low point was 2002 when there was not one billion-dollar merger involving independent banks. M&T bought Allfirst for $2.9 billion, but the Baltimore-based Allfirst was an affiliate of an Irish bank. The quiet period continued through the first nine months of 2003 when there was only one fairly small billion-dollar bank sale announced—BB&T acquiring First Virginia.

A rise in bank stock prices and the lagging momentum of a couple of big banks reignited the megamerger activity in late 2003, and for about ten months, it looked like a rerun of 1998. In October 2003, Bank of America announced the acquisition of Fleet, and less than three months later, JPMorgan agreed to acquire Bank One. These two mergers had a combined deal value of $108 billion and would create the banking big five that would leave everyone else behind. By August 2004, eight more billion-dollar bank sales had been announced with a collective deal value of $47 billion.

This surge in large bank mergers temporarily ended in August 2004. In the last four months of 2004 and through all of 2005, there were just three billion-dollar bank sales with a total deal value of less than $10 billion.

Large Bank Merger Value, 1998 to 2006

Year	Bank Mergers			Large Deal Value (in billions)
	Deal Value Over		All	
	$ 1 Billion	$ 10 Billion		
2006	6	2	305	$ 37.0
2005	3	–	274	8.6
2004	9	3	264	105.8
2003	2	1	226	52.7
2002	–	–	297	–
2001	6	1	363	24.0
2000	11	2	462	81.2
1999	7	2	428	46.2
1998	9	4	567	244.6

Source: SNL Financial, Charlottesville, Virginia and FDIC, Historical Statistics on Banking.

The slowdown in large merger activity, though, was temporary, and although 2006 did not match 2004, it was a busy acquisition year. There were eight bank acquisitions with deal values in excess of $1 billion, and two of them, Capital One's purchase of North Fork and Region's acquisition of AmSouth, had values in excess of $10 billion. The total deal value for the six large bank mergers was $37 billion, which was more than four times the $8.6 billion of the previous year.

Adding to consolidation activity in 2006, albeit not a purchase of an independent bank, was JPMorgan's acquisition of Bank of New York's branch system. JPMorgan bought 338 branches in the New York City area with more than $30 billion deposits, and in so doing, eliminated a major local competitor.

Concentration Impact

The frenetic merger activity in 2000 and 2004 could readily be seen in the rise in the asset share of the five and ten largest banks. With Chase Manhattan's acquisition of J. P. Morgan closing in 2001, the asset share of the five largest banks jumped more than three percentage points from about 33% in 2000 to almost 36% in 2001. For the ten largest, the gain was from almost 47% of bank assets to a little over 48%. In 2004, the increase of the five largest was five percentage points as their share went from about 36% to more than 41%. In that year, the ten largest banks increased their share of bank assets above 50%.

Largest Bank Asset Share, 1990 to 2006

Dec. 31	Share of Bank Assets		Bank Assets (in billions)
	Five Largest	Ten Largest	
2006	46.5%	54.7%	$9,602
2005	43.7	52.5	9,040
2004	41.2	51.0	8,413
2003	36.2	49.3	7,603
2002	35.9	48.9	7,075
2001	35.6	48.2	6,552
2000	33.2	46.9	6,246
1995	23.1	33.9	4,313
1990	16.2	25.5	3,390

Source: SNL Financial, Charlottesville, Virginia and FDIC, Historical Statistics on Banking.

The asset share gains of the top five were not quite as large in 2005 and 2006, but were still substantial. In 2005, their share grew from the little over 41% to almost 44%, and by the end of 2006, they had 46.5% of all bank assets.

In 2007, Bank of America had an agreement to buy the American assets of ABN AMRO that would add another percentage point to the share of the big five. Thus, it is likely that these five banks' share of all domestic bank assets will be approaching 48% by the end of 2007.

The growing importance of five rather than ten banks on the national scene was readily apparent in the diminishing share of the banks that ranked sixth through tenth. Between 1999 and 2006, their share fell from more than 13% of all bank assets to a little over 8%. This was about where it was in the early 1990s when concentration ratios first began to rise.

The growth of the top five at the expense of the second tier of large banks was a continuation of the pattern of the very largest banks buying the biggest banks available. In 1998, five of the ten largest banks were sold. When this big-buying-big type of merger activity occurred after 2000, the impact was greatly magnified by the increased sizes of both the buyers and sellers. When eight banks leave all others behind, and then in the next five years, three of the eight—J.P. Morgan, Bank One and Fleet—are bought by two of the three biggest banks—Bank of America and Chase Manhattan—a large concentration increase is guaranteed.

It was clearly mergers, not organic growth that was driving the bank consolidation. That was evident in the asset share change of the five largest banks in the quiet merger period from the end of 2001 through 2003, which did not include Bank of America's purchase of Fleet that was announced in 2003, but completed in 2004. Their share of bank assets increased in each of these years, but by the end of 2003, their share was only about a half-of-a-percentage point more than it was two years earlier.

JPMorgan

The first large bank out of the blocks with a big acquisition in the new millennium was the one with the least recent momentum, Chase Manhattan. It was the product of mergers in the early and mid-1990s that brought Chemical, Manufacturers Hanover and Chase Manhattan under the same roof with Chemical's management and the Chase Manhattan name. They were all struggling New York money center banks when they merged, and were still struggling in 2000.

The new Chase Manhattan was different from its component banks in size only. It was still a New York bank specializing in national corporate lending with little in the way of retail coverage beyond New York and what Chemical had in Texas. Each of the original banks had suffered badly from their 1970s and 1980s expansion into international lending, and by the late 1990s, even combined they did not begin to match Citigroup's international operations. Bigger it was, though, and in 1996 and 1997, Chase Manhattan was the largest bank in the country measured by assets. At the end of 1999, even with its lack of momentum, it was still the country's third largest bank—and much larger than number four, Bank One.

The announcement in September 2000 that Chase Manhattan would acquire J.P. Morgan sounded like more of the same—a fourth large New

York money center bank being added to the other three, and this time with no retail coverage at all. J.P. Morgan, however, did have an elite national commercial customer list, more investment banking expertise than its acquirer, and Chase Manhattan wanted the merger badly enough to put J.P. Morgan front and center in the holding company name, but the bank would operate as Chase Bank. This merger created substantial size, and upon completion, JPMorgan may not have been as big as Citigroup in total assets or Citigroup and Bank of America in earnings, but it gave a semblance of parity with these banks in a national big three.

While the combination of Chase Manhattan and J.P. Morgan created a third domestic bank of tremendous size, its formation coincided with the exposure of the downside of the 1990s' stock market and merger boom to the detriment of JPMorgan Chase, or just JPMorgan as it is more commonly called, and other large banks. The Enron, WorldCom and similar, lesser mishandlings of corporate accounting were being exposed along with the role the big banks played. The losses for these banks from their involvement would be in the billions of dollars, and JPMorgan did not have the earnings of Citigroup or Bank of America to easily handle this level of loss. The potential losses did not threaten JPMorgan's survival, but they contributed to its earnings being less than those of its primary competitors in the early 2000s. Citigroup did not earn less than $13 billion in any year from 2000 through 2004 while JPMorgan maxed out at $6.7 billion in 2003.

In February 2004, JPMorgan took a big step toward gaining greater true parity with Citigroup and Bank of America when it announced the acquisition of Bank One. This merger reduced the overemphasis on large commercial loans; made it a more complete full-service bank; and, most important of all, increased its earnings potential. The Bank One acquisition was totally out of its past mode of adding money center banks to the fold, and overnight, JPMorgan became one of the country's largest retail banks. Bank One had almost 1,900 branches spread across the midsection of the country and the largest deposit share in the Midwest. It was one of the three biggest credit card issuers, although the quality of its credit card portfolio did not match the standards of the other leaders, Citigroup and MBNA. The credit card had been part of Bank One's problems in recent years.

The Bank One acquisition also had some interesting management implications in that part of the deal was that the Bank One president, Jamie Dimon, would succeed JPMorgan's William Harrison as president and CEO after two years. Dimon had been number two behind Weill at both Travelers and Citigroup before he moved on to take the Bank One job. This merger would bring him back to New York as Weill's counterpart at one of

Citigroup's biggest competitors. This scenario attracted a lot of media attention, but direct competition between the two never really materialized as Weill stepped down from his leadership position shortly after Dimon was in full control at JPMorgan.

JPMorgan made another big move in 2006 with the aforementioned purchase of the retail operation of one of its biggest rivals in the New York metropolitan area, Bank of New York. This took Bank of New York out of the ranks of second-tier American retail banks, and left New York City with only two locally-based banks in the first *and* second tier of banking leaders.

With the closing of the Bank One and Bank of New York purchases, JPMorgan not only solidified its position as the third largest bank in the country behind Citigroup and Bank of America, but became one of three American banks with assets of more than a trillion dollars. It would lag behind the other two in earnings through 2006, but was closing the earnings gap in 2007 and was second only to Bank of America in domestic deposits.

Bank of America

Bank of America was the other big buyer in the post-2000 era, but it was a little slower than Chase Manhattan to swing into action. The 1998 merger between NationsBank and BankAmerica, which instigated the name change, was a big one, and there was a lot of consolidating left to be done. Also in 2001, the man who built this banking empire, Hugh McColl, stepped aside and the reins were passed to his longtime number two, Ken Lewis. Whether Lewis would be as active an acquirer as McColl was yet to be seen.

It would be only a matter of time, though, before Bank of America would be back on the acquisition trail as it still had some work to do. The NationsBank-BankAmerica merger had been hailed as having created the first true national bank with banking offices stretching from the Atlantic to the Pacific Ocean, but this was an overstatement. Bank America had no coverage in the Northeast, and its Midwest banking franchise did not go much north of Missouri. Bank of America also was a secondary player in credit cards, mortgage banking and investment banking.

In October 2003, Lewis showed he was ready to keep the ball rolling and continue the path of McColl when he announced the acquisition of Fleet. It was a pricey $49 billion deal that met with considerable initial criticism, but Fleet was more than just the seventh largest bank in the country. It was the acquisition that could fill the biggest gap in Bank of America's franchise as it had the best retail banking coverage in the Northeast. Fleet was number one in deposit share in New England and New Jersey; had the fourth largest deposit share in New York; and some coverage in eastern Pennsylvania.

There was not a comparable acquisition alternative to Fleet in the Northeast. If Fleet had been bought by Citigroup or JPMorgan, Bank of America might have found other ways into the region—it talked about opening ten to fifteen offices in major metropolitan areas in which it did not have a presence—but this would have taken a long time and the end result would have been far less than what it achieved by acquiring Fleet.

With the purchase of Fleet, Bank of America reached the 10% cap on national deposit share that was part of banking regulation, which was a constraint relative to future large bank acquisitions. At this point, though, the only gap in Bank of America's national branch coverage was in the slowest-growing part of the country, the Midwest, and even there, it was already the market leader in Missouri and had a modest position in the Chicago area.

Bank of America, however, was not through buying. In June 2005, it bought MBNA, the country's largest independent credit card company and one of the three largest bank card issuers. This, added to its existing card business and made Bank of America a challenger for the top spot in a growing segment of the financial services industry.

By the end of 2006, Bank of America had assets of about $1.5 trillion, and in terms of profitability, it stood with Citigroup and the London-based HSBC far above all other financial services companies. Only GE and a couple of large oil companies were in the same earnings class. McColl had built a banking powerhouse, and Lewis had taken it to a higher level.

In early 2007, Bank of America continued to look to expand. It had the aforementioned agreement with ABN AMRO to purchase its LaSalle Bank affiliate that is among the deposit share leaders in Chicago and Detroit. This would fill the Midwest void in Bank of America's coverage and also give it the third largest deposit share in the region behind Wells Fargo and JPMorgan.

Citigroup

Citigroup did as much selling as it did buying in the early 2000s, but this did not slow its momentum. It increased its assets from $717 billion to almost $1.9 trillion between year ends 1999 and 2006, and its earnings rose from $13.5 billion in 2000 to a little over $21 billion in 2006—and this was even with the sale of the Travelers insurance businesses. Citigroup had long since moved beyond being just a New York money center bank, and in 2007, it was arguably the most important financial institution in the world.

This is not to say that everything went smoothly for Citigroup during these years—it did not. Its size was both a blessing and a curse in that its head did not always know what its arms were doing, which was exacerbated by a geographic sprawl that left little of the world untouched. Citigroup was front and center with its involvement in Enron, WorldCom and other large corporate accounting scandals and was accused by Japan and Great Britain of wrongdoings in its financial activities in those countries. Citigroup took an aftertax charge of $5 billion in 2004 for just the WorldCom shareholder suits.[2] In 2004, the Federal Reserve went so far as to prohibit Citigroup from any large acquisitions until it had its house in order.

These problems took more of a toll on management than on earnings and resulted in Weill turning over Citigroup leadership to its chief counsel, Charles Prince, and relinquishing his chairman's role. This was not early retirement, though, as Weill was 73 when he stepped aside in 2006. Some of the top management that had come into Citigroup from Travelers with Weill also left the firm during this period.

The accusations and management changes kept Citigroup in the news, but did little to slow its momentum. A billion-dollar fine was less than two week's pre-tax earnings by 2005, and from 2000 to 2006, Citigroup was in the top two in earnings among all domestic corporations.

The earnings comparisons with its leading competitors were not only favorable, but the contrast in the early 2000s with JPMorgan was substantial. From 2000 to 2004, Citigroup's earnings were between $13.5 billion and $17 billion annually while JPMorgan was averaging about $4 billion a year. The large disparity continued in 2005 when Citigroup's earnings of $24 billion were almost three times JPMorgan's $8.3 billion, albeit that year Citigroup's earnings included some unusual gains. JPMorgan had a large earnings gain in 2006, lifting net income to $14.4 billion. This was still well below Citigroup's net income of almost $22 billion in 2006.

The closing of the gap between Citigroup and JPMorgan's net income that began in 2006, continued in 2007. If first half returns for both banks are indicative of the entire year, the gap will be substantially less in 2007.

Bank of America was far behind Citigroup in earnings as the 2000s began, but was closing the gap even before buying Fleet and MBNA. Its earnings went from $7.5 billion in 2000 to $10.8 billion in 2003, and then with some Fleet earnings in 2004, had a net income over $14 billion. In 2006, Bank of America's earnings were more than $21 billion and only slightly below those of Citigroup.

Citigroup was a banking leader in the early 2000s, but it did not look much like its major domestic competitors. It only had about 1,000 branches, almost all in the New York City area and California. Its strengths were in international banking and a myriad of specialty financial businesses with investment banking, securities sales and credit cards being the most prominent.

Under Weill, Citigroup had shown more willingness to expand its branch network than in the past, although its movement in that direction remained relatively modest. Fleet and Bank One made as much sense for Citigroup to acquire as they did for Bank of America and JPMorgan, instead, though, it chose to buy a $54 billion asset thrift in California, Golden State; a $15 billion asset bank in the New York City area owned by a consortium of European banks, EAB; and a small savings bank in Texas. This was enough to put Citigroup on the potential buyer list for second-tier banks, but the acquisitions did little to change the overall corporate profile.

Citigroup's exiting the insurance businesses through a spin-off in 2002 and the sale of what remained to MetLife in 2005 raised questions as to why the two firms had merged in the first place, but Travelers had brought Citigroup a lot more than an insurance business. The Salomon Brothers investment banking operation and the Smith Barney brokerage business were leaders in their fields and complemented Citicorp's banking business. Travelers may not have brought one-stop shopping to the mix from a retail perspective when it merged with Citicorp, but it had made Citigroup the ultimate in corporate one-stop shopping.

First Union/Wachovia

First Union was a long way from being in the Citigroup or Bank of America size category, although it deserved an A for trying before and after 2000. It had been one of the stars of the 1990s, but by 2000, First Union's acquisition program had run out of steam and was threatening its ability to survive. It was hemorrhaging customers in the Philadelphia area after mishandling its acquisitions of CoreStates and First Fidelity, and the only positive thing that could be said about its Signet acquisition in Virginia was that there were fewer customers to lose. Its $2 billion purchase of The Money Store, a specialty lender, in 1998 had gone beyond losing customers and had cost First Union large amounts of money prior to and as part of its closing. After earning about $3 billion in both 1998 and 1999, First Union reported earnings of just $92,000 in 2000.

It also had become a very unpopular bank with investors, particularly after cutting its dividend in half in 2001, and First Union's stock dropped from an adjusted high of almost $66 per share in 1998 to less than $24 per share in late 2000. After the dividend cut, investor thinking was not when First Union would return to its previous earnings level, but rather what buyer would come to the rescue. The problem with the latter scenario was that there were not many banks large enough to buy First Union, and some of the few that were big enough either had troubles of their own like Bank One; were busy digesting an earlier merger as JPMorgan was doing; or, in the case of Bank of America, had too much overlap to be an acceptable suitor.

Being relatively safe from an unwanted takeover, First Union showed a boldness that surprised almost everyone when it announced in April 2001 that it had agreed to buy Wachovia for $12.7 billion. Wachovia had a long and revered history and was *the* bank in North Carolina when First Union and NCNB were just beginning their rise to prominence. To many in the state, Wachovia was still considered a step above its two much larger rivals. Wachovia, like First Union, however, was stumbling in 2000 and early 2001, which made it susceptible when First Union came calling with a cozy in-state deal in which Wachovia would be treated as a near-equal partner with the new entity operating under its name and with equal board representation. The headquarters, though, was in Charlotte where First Union was based, not in Wachovia's Winston-Salem home, and Ed Crutchfield's successor at First Union, Ken Thompson, would be the CEO.

The joining of these two struggling banks was not greeted with much enthusiasm outside of North Carolina, and Atlanta-based SunTrust thought it had a chance to win Wachovia away from First Union. In May 2001, it made a $13.6 billion hostile bid for Wachovia—$900 million more than the First Union offer. SunTrust hoped a higher offer and better financial position would carry the day. It was more money, but it also was a more complete takeover as the Wachovia name would not survive and the headquarters would be in a much more distant Atlanta. The hostile bid, though, forced First Union to raise its price to $14.6 billion, which SunTrust bettered with a $15.3 billion offer, but how much better was blurred by the true values of the stocks being offered in exchange for Wachovia stock. In the end, First Union prevailed, and in September 2001, the merger was completed and the First Union name was retired in favor of Wachovia.

A "done deal," though, was a different thing than a widely-acclaimed deal, and there were more doubters than believers in the future of the new Wachovia. Earnings of $1.6 billion in 2001 were a big improvement over the near breakeven of 2000, but it was still well below what a much smaller First Union had earned a couple of years earlier.

First Union, however, had learned a lot from its previous mistakes, and the merging of the two banks went smoothly. It was easier to integrate an acquisition in markets in which it was not viewed as an outsider. Yet, it was more than that. By 2002, its performance had improved in the markets to the north, particularly the Philadelphia area, and its earnings were on the upswing. In 2003, the new Wachovia earned $3.6 billion, and a year later, its net income topped $4 billion.

By 2004, Wachovia was ready to move on, and in that year it bought the Birmingham-based SouthTrust for $14.4 billion. SouthTrust had assets of $53 billion; 726 branches stretching from Virginia to Texas; and fit well with Wachovia. SouthTrust and the old Wachovia acquired by First Union were much smaller than Fleet or Bank One, but they were two of the four largest bank acquisitions since 2000.

In 2006, Wachovia continued its national expansion by acquiring Golden West, a California-based S&L and the second largest thrift in the country. Golden West had $128 billion assets and was a family success story—it was almost wholly-owned by Herman and Marian Sandler—and the last of the large, independent California S&Ls.

There was the usual investor furor over the Golden West purchase that accompanied so many of the Wachovia acquisitions as it occurred during a period of declining real estate values, which raised questions as to the shortterm earnings impact. The bottom-line, however, was that by the end of 2006, the new Wachovia had assets of $716 billion; earned $7.8 billion; and when measured by market capital or earnings was one of the dozen largest banks in the world. Not bad for an institution given up for dead by so many five years earlier.

Wells Fargo

Since 2000, there had been no stumbling at Wells Fargo and few big acquisitions. It was an active acquirer having bought sixteen banks since the beginning of 2000, but only the $22 billion, Utah-based First Security went much beyond being a local, community bank. Good internal growth and the numerous acquisitions, though, were enough to raise Wells Fargo's assets from $218 billion in 1999 to about $500 billion in 2006. It had slipped behind Wachovia to fifth in asset size, but that understated its real position.

Wells Fargo loomed larger than its asset size suggested primarily because it was the most consistent earner among the nation's five largest banks in the early 2000s. It earned $4 billion in 2000, increased earnings in each subsequent year and reached $7.8 billion in 2005. This was almost as much as the far bigger JPMorgan earned in that year. It did not keep pace with JPMorgan's large earnings gain in 2006, but Wells Fargo's earnings continued a strong upward pace and exceeded $8 billion.

The growth momentum of much of the market Wells Fargo served, particularly the Southwest and West Coast, helped to generate the good performance, and its commitment to the housing market at a time when that business was sizzling was also positive. In 2006, Wells Fargo was the second largest originator and largest servicer of mortgage loans in the country.

The steady performance was well-received by investors, and Wells Fargo's stock outperformed the other large banks during this period. Its market value in 2007 made it the seventh most valued bank in the world.

How Far the Big Five Have Come

That these five banks had left all others behind was evident in the numbers, and it was amazing how far they had come in 26 years. Citigroup, Chemical and Wells Fargo were big banks by the standards of the time in 1980, but those numbers pale beside what they would be in 2006. Citigroup raised its assets from $115 billion in 1980 to almost $1.9 trillion in 2006—and was over $2 trillion by the end of the first quarter of 2007; Chemical, or JPMorgan as is it now called, jumped from $41 billion to more than $1.3 trillion assets; and Wells Fargo increased its assets from $24 billion to almost $500 billion. What was truly astounding, though, was just how far the two North Carolina banks, Bank of America and Wachovia, had come.

Largest Domestic Banks, 2006

	Assets				
	2006	1999	1993	1988	1980
	(in billions)				
Citigroup	$1,883	$716	$217	$208	$115
Bank of America	1,460	633	158	30	7
JPMorgan	1,352	406	150	67	41
Wachovia	707	253	71	22	3
Wells Fargo	482	218	53	47	24
Total	$5,884	$2,226	$649	$374	$218

Source: SNL Financial, Charlottesville, Virginia and American Banker, April 20, 1982 and April 11, 1990.

In 1980, what was then NCNB had assets of $7 billion, which was a long way from the almost $1.5 trillion of 2006. Despite its relatively small size, it was a well-known bank in 1980 because of its nonbank activities that went beyond the borders of its home state of North Carolina. No one at the time, though, could have imagined that 26 years later, NCNB would be using the Bank of America name and be the largest bank in the country measured by branches or deposits and one of the two biggest banks in the world based on earnings and market capital.

Wachovia was not nearly as large as Bank of America in 2006, but it also had come a long way since 1980 when its predecessor bank, First Union, had $3 billion in assets and was number three in North Carolina. By 2006, it was the fourth largest domestic bank with about $700 billion assets and in the top twelve worldwide in earnings and market capital.

There were eight other domestic banks—U.S. Bancorp, SunTrust, Capital One, Regions, National City, BB&T, PNC and Fifth Third—with assets of more than $100 billion and branch networks in 2006. Of these, only U.S. Bancorp had assets above $200 billion, and just barely so. The growth of most of these second-tier banks was just as explosive as that of Bank of America and Wachovia. In 1980, U.S. Bancorp had assets of $13 billion, PNC $6 billion, National City $5 billion, SunTrust $3 billion and Regions, BB&T and Fifth Third were in the $1 billion to $2 billion range.

Capital One, the nation's eighth largest bank holding company, did not even exist in 1980. It was founded as a credit card operation through a spin-off from a mid-sized Virginia bank, Signet, in 1996, and prior to 2005, would not have even been considered among the second-tier banks. With the acquisitions of Hibernia in New Orleans and the Long Island-based North Fork Bank in 2005 and 2006, respectively, with a combined $80 billion assets, Capital One became more than a credit card bank.

Washington Mutual was still a thrift, but in 2006, was larger than any of the second-tier banks with assets of about $350 billion, but because of its balance sheet mix, was closer in market strength—earnings and market capital—to U.S. Bancorp than to Wells Fargo and Wachovia. Washington Mutual had traveled a particularly long way. In 1980, it was Columbia Federal, a mutual thrift with assets of less than $300 million in the small Washington town of Wenatchee.

Market Coverage

Just how dominant the big five of American banking had become by 2006 can be readily seen in deposit rankings in the four major geographic subdivisions in the United States—the Northeast, South, Midwest and Far West. No bank led in more than a single region with Bank of America, JPMorgan, Wells Fargo and Wachovia dividing the honors, but Bank of America was first or second in three of the four regions, and JPMorgan was in the top five in three of them. This was despite the big banks being less dependent on deposits for funding their loans and investments than small and mid-sized banks and thrifts.

In the Northeast, JPMorgan had by far the most deposits, $301 billion in mid-2006, followed by Bank of America and Citigroup in the $140 billion to $150 billion range. Royal Bank of Scotland and Wachovia rounded out the top five with deposits in the $70 billion to $90 billion range. London-based HSBC was not in the top five, but was a close sixth behind Wachovia.

Deposit Share Leaders by Region, 2006*

Bank	Deposits (in bill.)	Bank	Deposits (in bill.)
Northeast		South	
1. JPMorgan**	$301	1. Wachovia	$234
2. Bank of America	150	2. Bank of America	213
3. Citigroup	144	3. SunTrust	118
4. Royal Bank-Scotland	86	4. JPMorgan	81
5. Wachovia	73	5. BB&T	74
Midwest		Far West	
1. Wells Fargo	$102	1. Bank of America	$208
2. JPMorgan	92	2. Washington Mutual	170
3. U.S. Bancorp	68	3. Wells Fargo	164
4. National City	63	4. Citigroup	48
5. ABN AMRO	60	5. U.S. Bancorp	46

*June 30, 2006.
**Includes acquisition of Bank of New York branches.
Source: SNL Financial, Charlottesville, Virginia.

The Northeast deposit rankings, however, were skewed by out-of-area deposits, particularly foreign deposits held in New York City main offices. If Manhattan was excluded from the region, JPMorgan would fall from first to second place in deposit share, and Citigroup would be out of the top five. With this change, Bank of America was number one as a result of its Fleet acquisition with about $45 billion more deposits than JPMorgan in 2006. Royal Bank of Scotland was third, Wachovia fourth and PNC replaced Citigroup in the top five.

In the South, Wachovia and Bank of America were far ahead of all others with $234 and $213 billion deposits, respectively. SunTrust was a distant third in 2006 with $118 billion deposits. JPMorgan and BB&T were four and five with deposits in the $70 billion to $85 billion range. Wachovia and Bank of America's deposit totals were helped by out-of-area main office deposits, but neither bank had large amounts of foreign funds.

The big banks were not nearly as dominant in the Midwest as they were in the rest of the country. In mid-2006, Wells Fargo and JPMorgan ranked one-two, but being at the top required only a little over $100 billion in regional deposits. U.S. Bancorp, National City and the Dutch-owned ABN AMRO rounded out the Midwest top five with deposits in the $60 to $70 billion range.

The Far West was by far the most concentrated of the four regions with Bank of America, Washington Mutual and Wells Fargo running well ahead of all others with a combined 40% of the deposits. Bank of America was first in 2006 with $208 billion deposits. Washington Mutual and Wells Fargo followed with $170 billion and $164 billion, respectively. Citigroup and U.S. Bancorp were in the top five in the Far West, but with less than $50 billion deposits each, they were far behind the regional big three.

Bank of America leading in only one of the four geographic areas is a bit misleading. Take out the New York City main offices, and it was as far ahead of everyone else in the Northeast as it was in the Far West, and was a close second in the Southeast. Its proposed acquisition of ABN AMRO's American operation will make it number three in the Midwest.

Investor Return

Despite their success in consolidating American banking and gaining tremendous size and stature, the nation's five largest banks have been widely criticized for not having served investors well. Investors might have done better if at some point these banks had been sold instead of being buyers, but this is true of almost any stock firm. Conversely, if all companies were sold before they became too large to be bought, many of the nation's businesses, and most certainly banking, would be dominated by foreign companies that have not been as investor-conscious as their American counterparts.

In any event, those that invested early in these five big banks did not do badly, particularly with Citigroup, Bank of America and Wells Fargo's successor bank, Norwest. A $100,000 investment in Citigroup at the end of 1985 with reinvested dividends would have grown to $2.6 million by the end of 2006—an annual return of 16.9%—and a similar 1995 investment, when Citigroup was struggling, would be almost $1.1 million ten years later for a 24.1% annual gain. A $100,000 investment in NCNB/NationsBank in 1985 and 1995 would have been $1.2 million and almost $500,000 by the end of 2005 for annual returns of 12.5% and 15.2%, respectively. For the Norwest investors, the annual return since 1985 and 1995 on $100,000 invested was a very robust 18% plus in both instances.

Investor Return on the Big Five—1985 to 2006

Bank	2006 Return on $100,000 Invested in*			
	1985		1995	
	Amount (in thous.)	Annual Return	Amount (in thous.)	Annual Return
Citigroup	$2,640	16.9%	$1,075	24.1%
Bank of America**	1,192	12.5	473	15.2
JPMorgan***	423	7.1	403	13.5
Wachovia	651	9.3	205	6.7
Wells Fargo****	3,704	18.8	622	18.1

*Investment made at the end of the calendar year.
**Original investment in NCNB.
***Original investment in Chemical.
****Original investment in Norwest.
Source: Internal calculations from various sources.

Investors did not do as well with Chemical's New York roll-up. The Chemical-led consolidation of the four large New York money center banks—Chemical, Manufacturers Hanover, Chase Manhattan and J.P. Morgan—has just started to deliver any real momentum, but it is also unlikely that any of the component parts would have done better on their own *or* could have found better buyers considering their sizes and conditions at the time of sale. For Chemical, now JPMorgan, an investment of $100,000 at the end of 1985 would have become about $400,000 at the end of 2005, or an annual return of 7.1%. If the investment had been made in 1995, though, when most of Chemical's merger activity was finished and the economy had improved, it would have generated a much better 13.5% annual return; and the dollar value would be almost as much as for a similar investment made ten years earlier.

Wachovia also has not done as well for investors as Citigroup, Wells Fargo and Bank of America. This was primarily due to its slippage from 1998 to 2001 when its stock fell from about an adjusted $66 per share to $24 per share and its dividend was cut in half. Even with this slippage, though, an investment of $100,000 in Wachovia's predecessor bank, First Union, twenty years ago was worth over $600,000 at the end of 2005, equivalent to an annual return of 9.3%. A similar investment in 1995 would have been worth about $200,000, a 6.7% annual increase.

This is not bad collective performance and contradicts what was being said by securities analysts who seem to think the world began in 1998 when bank stocks were at their peak. Bank of America has proved them wrong with its recent Fleet acquisition, and Wells Fargo, Wachovia and JPMorgan are likely to do the same as they move on to bigger and better things.

Foreign Banks

Another phenomenon of the early 2000s has been the resurgence of foreign bank influence in the United States. Other than the London-based HSBC and the Royal Bank of Scotland, the largest banks outside of the United States, foreign banks are not threatening the dominance of the big five of American banking, but could eventually dominate the second tier as the domestic banks in that category dwindle in numbers as a result of acquisitions. Not since the late 1970s and early 1980s has there been such significant foreign bank acquisition activity in the country, and the foreign banks look to have more staying power this time around.

All that is left from the first incursion of foreign banks is HSBC; Bank of Tokyo, which is now Mitsubishi UFJ and almost totally focused on California; Bank of Montreal in Chicago; and the beleaguered ABN AMRO that is selling its American banking business to Bank of America. The British banks that made such a big splash in California during those earlier years are long gone.

Between 2000 and 2004, nine American banks and thrifts were bought by foreign banks with deal values in excess of $1 billion. The combined deal value of these acquisitions was about $27 billion. Go back one day to December 31, 1999 and add in HSBC's purchase of Republic of New York that closed on that day, and the number of big foreign bank purchases rises to ten and the combined deal value to $35 billion. This does not include the 2002 purchase by HSBC of Household Finance for $14.9 billion that was not technically a bank despite being a large consumer lender nationwide.

The large foreign buyers besides HSBC were BNP Paribas of France with four large American bank acquisitions, Royal Bank of Scotland with three and Toronto-Dominion with two. These are substantial banks with a lot of market clout. Royal Bank of Scotland was the second largest non-American bank and fifth largest in the world in 2006 measured by earnings, and BNP Paribas was fifth in earnings among just foreign banks. Toronto-Dominion is not quite in a class with the others, but with 2006 assets of more than $300 billion and market capital of $45 billion, it is a large bank with closer geographic proximity than the European banks.

Foreign Banks in the United States

Bank	U.S. Offices*	U.S. Assets* (in billions)	Country
Royal Bank of Scotland	1,669	$161	United Kingdom
BNP Paribas	669	56	France
Toronto-Dominion	641	40	Canada
HSBC	462	478	United Kingdom
Banco Bilbao**	462	40	Spain
ABN AMRO	411	156	Netherlands
Royal Bank of Canada	348	23	Canada
Mitsubishi UFJ	341	52	Japan
Bank of Montreal	240	43	Canada
Banco Santander	64	9	Spain
Barclays	1	207	United Kingdom
ING Groep	1	53	Netherlands

*December 31, 2006.
**Includes the acquisition of Compass Bankshares, Inc.
Source: SNL Financial, Charlottesville, Virginia and Bloomburg.com.

HSBC with 2006 American assets of $478 billion, 462 bank offices mostly in New York and numerous finance offices across the country, has the potential with the acquisition of a second-tier American bank to turn a big five into a big six. It is rumored to be a potential acquirer whenever a large regional bank is thought to be selling, but it has stayed on the sidelines since its 2001 Household acquisition.

Royal Bank of Scotland has been the most aggressive of the foreign banks in the early 2000s with its $10.5 billion purchase in 2004 of Charter One, a thrift with $41 billion assets and 571 branches focused on Ohio, Michigan and western New York. This helped lift Royal Bank of Scotland's total number of bank office to 1,669 by year-end 2006, which was the eighth largest branch network in United States. With just $161 billion in American assets in 2006, however, Royal Bank of Scotland has a long way to go to move beyond a second tier of domestic banks.

In just numbers of large bank and thrift acquisitions in the United States since 2000, the Paris-based BNP Paribas has been the most active buyer, but its purchases have been smaller than those of HSBC and Royal Bank of Scotland. All of its acquisitions were in western United States, and its 2006 American assets were just $56 billion. Its 669 banking offices, though, is the second most of any foreign bank.

The only other foreign banks with more than 100 banking offices in the United States in 2006 were three Canadian banks—Toronto-Dominion, Royal Bank of Canada and Bank of Montreal; ABN AMRO; and Tokyo-based Mitsubishi UFJ. Toronto-Dominion, with 641 bank offices coming from its recent purchase of Banknorth, is third largest of the foreign banks when measured by number of offices. ABN AMRO, of course, will be off this list when it completes the sale of its offices to Bank of America.

Barclays, a British bank ranked seventh in earnings among banks outside United States, had assets of $207 billion in its American banking subsidiaries in 2006, and was a slightly smaller version of Deutsche Bank that had $431 billion in American banking assets, but this overstates their true banking positions on this side of the ocean. Neither had retail banking offices in United States in 2006, and their bank assets are primarily in investment banking and asset management activities.

Having only one or two banking offices does not, however, preclude a foreign bank from having a major impact on American retail banking. ING Groep, another Dutch bank, has only a single office in United States, but it has used that office to buy deposits nationally. Since entering United States in 2000, it had accumulated almost $50 billion deposits by mid-2006.

Banco Santander, a Madrid-based bank and fifth largest bank outside United States based on market capital, is a potentially significant player in the domestic market. It owns a 25% share of Sovereign, a thrift with deposits of a little over $80 billion in the Northeast. It has the right of first refusal if Sovereign chooses to sell, and its 2004 purchase of the largest British mortgage bank, Abbey National, indicates Banco Santander is not adverse to large acquisitions outside of Spanish-speaking countries.

The early 2000 interest in American banking by foreign banks also was symptomatic of the rising globalization of the industry. In Europe, Canada and Japan, the limited size of the home market prompted banks to look to new markets for expansion. In United States, Citigroup needed no prompting to do so, but as Bank of America and JPMorgan reach regulatory and geographic limits on their domestic expansion, they, too, will face pressure to expand into other countries to maintain their growth momentum as well as trying to keep pace with Citigroup.

CHAPTER 20

Beyond the Big Five

Banking since 1990 has been far more than a few banks getting larger and increasing their share of the banking business and the Gramm-Leach-Bliley legislation removing almost all barriers between banking and other financial services. As might have been expected as a corollary to an increased level of concentration, the number of banks was dramatically reduced, but this did not mean the remaining banks were losing their competitive fervor. Banks of all sizes continued to open branches; new banks were still opening; thrifts, despite their problems in the 1980s and early 1990s, remain significant competitors in some parts of the country; and the credit unions continued to expand their coverage.

Throughout this period, the product mix on both sides of bank balance sheets were in flux, causing margin reductions that were hurting profits. Intense competition for loans and deposits were putting downward pressure on loan yields and upward pressure on funding costs, and the spread between bank interest income and expense has fallen from 3.78% in 1994 to 2.95% in 2006—a drop approaching a full percentage point.[1]

Change in Number of Banks

The reduction in number of banks has received more attention than the increased market share of the large banks. National concentration numbers are of little interest to the general public, but it is newsworthy each time a local bank is sold. Starting in the mid-1980s, and even more so in the 1990s, this was a frequent occurrence. The number of banks in the country hit their post-1920s peak in 1984 at about 14,500, but by the end of the 1980s, the number was down to 12,715 with much of the slippage being driven by regional economic crises. By the end of the 1990s, there were just 8,581 banks, and by year-end 2006, there were 7,402—or about half the number of banks that there were twenty years earlier.

Economic problems contributed greatly to the reduction in number of banks in the late 1990s, but with improved economic conditions of the mid-1990s, the motivation for banks to sell shifted from fear of survival to offers too good to refuse. Whatever the reasons, the "urge to merge" in the 1990s was high. There were 5,413 bank mergers in those ten years, or almost 1,100 more than in the 1980s and four times the total for the 1970s.

Bank Mergers and New Charters Since 1970

Year(s)	Number of Banks*	Mergers			New Charters
		Unassisted	Assisted	Total	
2005–06	7,402	–	–	579	342
2000–04	7,630	–	–	1,597	645
1995–99	8,581	2,750	21	2,771	861
1990–94	10,452	2,297	345	2,642	454
1980–89	12,715	3,465	804	4,269	2,700
1970–79	14,364	1,316	50	1,366	2,224

Note: There were 25 banks that failed from 2000 to 2006; 89 failed and closed in the 1990s; 226 in the 1980s; and 50 in the 1970s.
*End of period.
Source: FDIC, Historical Statistics on Banking.

A high level of bank merger activity continued into the 2000s, but it was not at the frantic pace of the 1990s. In the five years from 2000 to 2004, there were 1,597 mergers, more than 1,000 less than in the preceding five years. In 2005 and 2006, there were 579 bank mergers, a pace that if spread over five years would be 1,450 mergers.

Further exaggerating the impact of the merger activity since 1990 on a shrinking number of banks was a decline in the number of banks opened. It seemed like every merger spawned a cadre of unhappy bank officers who moved on to start their own banks, but the number of start-ups in the 1990s was less than half the number in the 1980s, and only about 60% of the total in the 1970s. There were about 1,300 banks opened in the 1990s compared to 2,700 in the previous decade.

The banks opened between 2000 and 2006 approximated the number of banks opened in the 1990s, but was down from the pace in the post-recession part of that earlier period. In the late 1990s, the annual rate of banks opened was about 170. Since 2000, the average number opened annually was closer to 140.

Share by Institution

Despite the massive reduction in the number of banks since 1990, banks as a group increased their share of depository institution assets, which was at least partly due to thrift problems continuing into the early 1990s. Banks had been losing share to thrifts and credit unions for many years prior to the mid-1980s, and bank share of the combined assets of all depository institutions had reached a low of 66% in 1985. As the thrift problems mounted in the late 1980s, banks asset share reversed its long-time slide and grew to 68% in 1990, 76% in 1995, and almost 80% by 2000. Much of the gain came through the purchase of thrifts.

Depository Institution Asset Share by Type, 1980 to 2005

Year	Banks	Thrifts	Credit Unions
2005	78%	16%	6%*
2000	79	15	6
1995	76	18	5
1990	68	27	5
1985	66	31	3
1980	68	29	3

*Peaked at 6.3% in 2003.
Source: FDIC, Historical Statistics on Banking: National Council of Savings Institutions, *1988 Fact Book of Savings Institutions;* and 1990, 1995 and 2000 National Credit Union Annual Report.

Thrifts were clearly a diminishing factor in the 1990s as their share of depository institution assets fell from 27% to 15%, but the absolute decline in thrift assets ended in 1993, and the share slippage was over in 2000. From 1993 to 2000, thrift assets increased by $217 billion, and then from 2000 to 2005, their share of assets grew from 15% to 16%. This was a little misleading, though, as about 20% of thrift assets in 2005 were part of large insurance companies and bank holding companies.

The strong asset gains of the credit unions that had been going on for decades, and was given a boost by the 15 year slide in thrift share, continued past 2000, but has since ended. In 2005, credit unions had about the same 6% of depository institution assets they had in 2001, but, collectively, since 2003, they have lost share.

Branching in the 1990s

What has not been consistent with five banks gaining almost 50% of the domestic bank assets and a much diminished role for all other banks since 1990 was the continuing expansion in the number of bank offices. In 1990, there were fewer than 63,000 such offices across the country. By 2006, there were more than 80,000 bank offices, and this growth occurred despite a strong belief in the 1990s that ATMs and remote access banking would soon make branches obsolete.

Bank and Thrift Branches, 1980 to 2006

June 30,	Number of		All Offices	
	Institutions	Branches	Total	Change
Banks				
2006	7,402	72,994	80,496	8,102
2000	8,315	64,079	72,394	5,940
1995	9,942	56,512	66,454	3,701
1990	12,347	50,406	62,753	9,581
1980	14,434	37,738	53,152	17,822*
Thrifts				
2006	1,279	12,981	14,260	148
2000	1,589	12,523	14,112	(1,341)
1995	2,030	13,423	15,453	(6,156)
1990	2,815	18,794	21,609	(2,466)
1984**	3,418	20,657	24,075	–

* Increase over 1970.
** First year of comparable thrift data.
Source: FDIC, Historical Statistics on Banking.

In the early 1990s, there were indications of the above starting to occur. From 1990 to 1995, there was a net increase of about 3,700 bank offices, but much of this was purchased thrift offices. The total number of bank and thrift offices *declined* by almost 3,500 during these five years.

Since 1995, and particularly after 2000, whether needed or not, banks began opening branches at a rapid pace. Including thrift offices, the net increase in banking offices between 1995 and the end of 2000 was about 3,000, and from 2000 to 2006, there were more than 8,000 bank and thrift offices opened.

Most of these offices were opened by the shrinking number of small and mid-sized banks. The five banks that control almost 50% of all bank assets had about 16,500 bank offices between them in 2006, or about 20% of the bank total.

Why this surge in branching in recent years in the face of a growing use of remote access banking? The early 2000s had been good years for banks as the stock market crash at the beginning of the period sent money out of the stock market into banks, while declining interest rates made these deposits extremely profitable. This softened the impact of declining loan yields and created a feeling within banking, particularly in small banks, that gathering deposits through branches—or as some would call it "getting back to the basics"—was the best part of the business.

Whether this is true or not is arguable, and rising interest rates and flattened earnings in 2006 and 2007 will cause some rethinking. What is not arguable is that additional bank offices and expanded hours of operation are increasing bank operating costs as margins continue to shrink.

Deposit Mix

The rapid increase in the number of bank offices not only defied the logic of the large increase in bank concentration since 1990, but it also was not consistent with deposit trends. The traditional reason for most visits to bank offices was to cash a check. This was certainly the case in 1970 when more than half of all bank deposits were noninterest-bearing checking accounts, but by 1990, this type of deposit was only 20%. By 2000, noninterest-bearing checking accounts were down to 15% of bank deposits, and by 2006, they were just 9%.

Initially, the shift away from checking accounts was into CDs, but since 1990, the flow has been into money market demand accounts, or MMDAs as they are commonly called. From 1970 to 1990, CDs grew from 28% of deposits to 46% in 1990 before slipping off to 39% in 2006. Savings accounts, which include MMDAs, had been diminishing as a percent of all deposits, much like checking accounts, up until about 1980 when they were only about 17% of the total.[2] This decline was reversed in the 1980s, and by 2006, savings, primarily MMDAs, were 56% of deposits.

Bank Deposit Mix by Type, 1970 to 2006

Year	Percent of Deposits			Deposits/ Assets
	Demand	Savings*	CDs	
2006	9%	56%	35%	66%
2000	15	45	40	67
1990	20	34	46	78
1970	51	21	28	85

*Includes MMDAs, NOW accounts and regular savings.
Source: FDIC, Historical Statistics on Banking.

Since the MMDA had limited checking capabilities, this was not quite the move away from checking accounts that the numbers suggest, but far more than for regular checking, the transferring of money out of MMDAs was done by remote access. MMDAs were not a factor in creating a need for new branches.

Loan Mix

The change in loan mix since 1990 and before also has not benefited small banks with its shift away from consumer installment loans and commercial lending. In 1970, consumer loans, other than credit cards, were 20% of bank loan portfolios. By 1990, this type of loan was down to 13% of total loans, and in 2006, it was 8%. Commercial loans not secured by real estate fell from 38% of total bank loans in 1970 to 29% in 1990, and then down to 19% in 2006. These were the traditional "bread and butter" loans of small banks.

Taking their place in bank portfolios were real estate loans, both commercial and residential. In 1970, home mortgages were 14% of bank loans. In 1990, they were up to 19%, and in 2006, they were almost one-third of all bank portfolio loans. In these same years, other real estate loans rose from 10% of all loans to 19% and then 26%. As a result, in 2006, real estate loans of all types were 58% of bank loans.

Bank Loan Mix by Type, 1970 to 2005

Year	Percent of Loans					Loans/ Assets
	Home Mtg.	Other Real Estate	Com- mercial*	Consumer		
				Credit Card	Other	
2006	32%	26%	19%	6%	8%	59%
2005	31	25	19	7	9	60
2000	24	19	28	7	9	61
1990	19	19	29	6	13	63
1970	14	10	38	2	20	52

Not secured by real estate.
Source: FDIC, Historical Statistics on Banking.

The increased emphasis on real estate loans also is understated by looking at portfolio loans only. Banks and others were making more real estate loans to sell into secondary markets than they were keeping in their portfolios as the rapid growth of the securitization of loans that began in the late 1970s continued beyond 1990. In 1980, the large mortgage pools—Fannie Mae, Freddy Mac and Ginnie Mae—held 12% of mortgage debt. In 1990, their share was 37%, and in 2005, it was 55%. This, as noted earlier, was a process dominated by the large banks—and particularly the big five.

What Next?

I f the last 25 years have taught us anything about the direction of banking, it is that the big banks keep getting bigger and the number of banks smaller. This was hardly surprising since when the artificial barriers that limited bank expansion were removed, it was only natural that banking would evolve toward the structure of most industries—a handful of dominant firms surrounded by specialists supplying services that are difficult for industry leaders to provide. What may have come as a surprise, at least to some, was how far and how fast consolidation moved when the market and product constraints were lifted.

So where does banking go from here? There certainly will be more of the same as additional large mergers give the five largest banks and a couple of big foreign banks 60% to 70% of bank assets, and the 7,000 plus existing banks falls to 4,000 or 5,000. No matter how one feels about Citigroup, Bank of America and JPMorgan, they have reached a size and global importance that suggests they will only get larger and more powerful, and Wachovia and Wells Fargo are fast approaching that status, if not already there. These large banks will have off-years, but are beyond this being more than temporary setbacks.

As consolidation moves forward, the increased importance of remote access banking and the large bank ability to use it to their advantage will be the most significant difference from the past. The specter of a dominating preeminence of remote access banking has long hung over banking and the broader financial services industry, and its time is coming. What is less certain is how remote access banking and the increased scope of the large banks will impact others in the industry.

The accelerated acceptance of remote access banking will be driven by four main elements—and technology is not one of them. The technology is already there, and much of it has been there for a long time. What will be different going forward are:

- More customers being able to fully understand and utilize remote access banking.
- The increased cost burden of operating branches as much extended hours becomes the norm.

- Large banks focusing on internal growth rather than buying market coverage.
- Globalization bringing new thinking along with foreign banks into the market.

Technology is still the major facilitator of change in the banking structure, but the change it brings through the increased use of remote access banking will flow from its interrelation with the above-mentioned customer skills, the growing cost of the existing delivery system and large banks, domestic or foreign, expanding with a lesser dependence on traditional bank acquisitions. Economic crises and investor activism also will be factors in future structural change.

The expectation that the expansion of remote access banking will be the primary change element in the future of banking is reminiscent of predictions in the 1990s of a much diminished branch usage that has not yet occurred, but times change. The natural evolution of banking toward remote access as the primary method of delivery is as natural as the consolidation across state lines that flowed from the introduction of interstate banking.

Remote Access

Remote access banking has always been a potentially important determinant of the industry structure, but as long as branches were the primary mode of delivery, it played a secondary role. Banking, though, is primarily moving numbers from one place to another, and as a result, more susceptible to remote access than almost any other large business since moving numbers does not *need* two pairs of human hands interacting.

Since the technology for greater use of remote access banking and the substantial changes it can bring to the banking structure for the most part already exists, what has been keeping it from being more of a factor in the delivery of bank products and services are consumer fears and the still limited customer technological skills. Much of the fear factor is well-founded because of concern over identity theft, but it is only a matter of time before technology and recognition of limited customer liability minimizes concern. Time and demographics are already reducing the skill shortcomings of customers as a remote access deterrent, and this is a process that will accelerate.

Demographics

The demographics of an aging population will be an important, and perhaps the most important, element in making remote access banking more prevalent in the future through its impact on the customer's ability to use the conveniences remote access brings. An aging population is seldom viewed as being a positive change in the customer base, but in banking, it creates a more technologically savvy customer base that will do what has long been predicted, but has not yet occurred. This is to dramatically reduce the need for banking products and services delivered through branches.

Young customers are more attuned to using remote access for banking whether it is through ATMs or home computers, and as they age, this will not change. If it is assumed that people born after 1965 are the truly internet savvy, then the upper age limit of those with minimal branch needs will rise, reaching 50 years by 2015 and 60 years by 2025. At the other end of the spectrum, an expanding senior customer base that has its social security and retirement payments deposited directly into a bank eliminates their biggest reason for going into a bank branch—to deposit a check. Put those two factors together and there will be far less need for the personal delivery of bank services.

This does not mean the end of bank branches, but suggests there will be fewer of them and that they will be used differently. Offices will still be needed for loan meetings, providing financial advice and doing things that cannot be done by remote access. This suggests that large centralized bank offices that are more meeting-oriented will prevail over the teller station and drive-through focused facilities.

Changing demographics also will accelerate the specialization of small banks. As the mass market moves away from branch usage, banks that specialize in small business lending, recent immigrants and other niches may find themselves in greater demand while small, general purpose banks in urban areas lose their relevance. The words "recent immigrants" are used rather than "ethnic group" because most ethnic groups, once they move past recent immigrant status, prefer the same conveniences of the mass market as everyone else.

These changing demographics may seem to favor a Citigroup model that focuses on remote access, lending and nontraditional banking activities over a branch-laden Bank of America. The Citigroup advantage, though, assumes that Bank of America and others with a similar approach, which is just about everybody else, cannot make as good use of remote access to service a larger customer base as well as making the branches they keep an advantage in customer relationships, particularly on the lending side. This is a dubious assumption.

Delivery System Overhead

Change in the delivery of bank products and services has always been part of the natural evolution of the industry, but the impact of overhead coming from the recent trend toward long hours is likely to be different in the future. The movement toward longer hours pioneered by Commerce in the late 1990s that has spread across much of the Northeast and Florida has set in motion a cost problem that might be considered under "unintended consequences."

The long hours, including Saturdays and Sundays, are consistent with normal retailing patterns and a banking change waiting to happen. Customers may be slow to make use of the extended hours, but they factor it into their choice of banks—and there is no going back. As early morning to early evening hours plus Saturday and Sunday banking hours becomes more available, customers will increasingly view it as both the norm *and* an entitlement; but it also comes with a tremendous overhead burden.

The expense of long hours coinciding with reduced branch need is already a threat to small, general-purpose banks and a competitive advantage for big banks, but a threat that is in its infancy. The benefits of scale economies have been slow in coming to banking, but are a major factor in this scenario. The cost of keeping a branch open more than seventy hours a week requires a branch with a large customer base that measured in deposits could be upward of $75 million in all but the most rural markets. This raises the survival barrier beyond what many banks can afford *and* makes the case for remote access banking all the more compelling.

There are lessons to be learned from the delivery of banking services in other countries as well. In Europe, for example, branch traffic is far less than in the United States because of a much greater use of direct payment, not because Europeans are more internet savvy, but because the largest recipients of checks—utilities, credit card companies and lenders—demand it. The higher degree of competition in United States may preclude a credit card company from telling a customer that the monthly payments *must* come automatically from a banking account, but in time, this practice should become the norm in the United States on a voluntary or involuntary basis.

Large Banks

The large banks, themselves, will have something to say about the direction of banking, and they, like all large stock organizations, must keep satisfying investors by increasing earnings per share at meaningful rates, and along with it, their stock prices. This requires some combination of selling more of the same to existing customers, taking customers from others, expanding the geographic base, broadening the product base and cutting costs. In doing this, the large banks will be thinking about what is best for them and their market value, not what keeps others competitive.

Success for the large banks will not be business as usual any more than for their smaller brethren. They will have to compete like retailers in other businesses. This means worrying about the cost of a delivery system, providing optimum convenience and being price competitive. What large banks bring that others may not is brand recognition, economies of scale accompanied by "deep pockets" and the advantages that flow from each.

The big banks also will be major beneficiaries of remote access banking by just being there. Remote access banking takes away the major advantage of small banks, personal service, and favors the banks that can deliver the broadest array of services, which are the large banks.

How the big banks use these advantages will determine who wins and loses among them, albeit losing is likely to be only a declining market share and lower stock price increases, not disappearing from the scene. The homegrown large banks also start well ahead of existing and potential foreign competitors.

Globalization

Not much attention has been paid to the impact of globalization on the domestic banking structure, but it also can have a big effect on who wins and who loses among the large banks and on the expansion of foreign banks, particularly European, in the American market. In United States, it is not until banks reach the size of Citigroup, Bank of America and JPMorgan that the desire and long-term need to go beyond their home country's borders becomes a priority. In smaller countries, which is just about everybody else, the lead bank(s) typically already has such high in-market coverage that it has to go beyond its home market if it hopes to show growth satisfactory to investors and avoid being dwarfed by banks from other countries.

In Europe and Japan, this is a particularly acute problem in that the projections of Gross Domestic Product, or GDP, by country suggest by 2025 their combined share of global GDP will have fallen from 46% to 32%—a one-third share decline. To maintain good investment value gains and maintain parity with American, and eventually Chinese, banks, they will have to either get a much larger share of their home market, which is difficult because of already large market shares, or expand into other countries. The most obvious expansion targets are China whose GDP is expected to grow from 4% to 15% of the world's GDP during this same period—and to 28% by 2050—and a United States that is expected to retain close to its present 28% share of world GDP.

World GDP by Country or Group—2004 to 2050

	Percent of Total		
	2050	2025	2004
China	28%	15%	4%
United States	26	27	28
India	17	5	2
European Union	15	25	34
Japan	4	7	12
Other	10	21	20
Total	100%	100%	100%

Source: Business Week, August 22, 2005.

Bank expansion into China will not directly impact banking structure in the United States, but the rush in the last couple of years to invest in the leading Chinese banks is an indication of which banks are most attuned to global expansion. Among the large banks, Bank of America has been one the most aggressive in moving into China, and HSBC and Royal Bank of Scotland are in there as well in a big way. Others, including Citigroup, are scrambling to catch-up.

Global spread will not be limited to these banks as national leaders like Barclays in England, Banco Santander and Banco Bilbao in Spain, BNP Paribas in France, Deutsche Bank in Germany, ING in the Netherlands, UBS and Credit Suisse in Switzerland and Mitusbishi UFJ in Japan also need to move well beyond their home countries to avoid being marginalized. BNP Paribas and Banco Bilbao's acquisitions in southern and western United States and the Banco Santander purchase of 25% of Pennsylvania-based Sovereign are indications of United States being part of the global plans of foreign banks other than HSBC and Royal Bank of Scotland.

Globalization, helped by the growing importance of remote access banking that can facilitate geographic expansion without the high cost of extensive branch networks, can impact the domestic banking structure in many ways. It adds to the size of the largest banks and, presumably, increases their overall market clout vis-a-vis everyone else. At least a couple of foreign banks, HSBC and Royal Bank of Scotland being the most likely, will be major factors in United States banking going forward, possibly even rising to the level of a Wachovia and Wells Fargo—and bringing with them lessons learned elsewhere.

Economic Recessions

History also has shown that nothing changes the banking structure and drives consolidation like bad times, and one does not have to go back to the Great Depression to see this phenomenon. A turbulent 1970s with huge budget deficits, oil shocks and inflation sent interest rates soaring and brought a thrift industry to its knees. In the 1980s, a speculative building boom financed by banks and thrifts ended in the most serious banking crisis since the 1930s and resulted in more than 2,000 bank and thrift failures in a six-year period. The first crisis greatly reduced the size of an entire industry, and the second eliminated most of the banking leaders in some very important states.

During the early 1990s recession, banks in Ohio, North Carolina and Minnesota, states that were relatively untouched by the economic problems from 1989 to 1992, had a clear path to national prominence while banks in New England, the Middle Atlantic states, California and Florida either disappeared or were badly hurt. Chase Manhattan, Manufacturers Hanover, Bank of New England, BankBoston, First Fidelity, C&S/Sovran, First Interstate and Security Pacific were among the most prominent victims.

It is unlikely United States has experienced its last severe economic recession, and when the next one comes, some banks will fare better than others, which will result in further consolidation. Even the mild downturn following the dotcom implosion and the resulting 2000 stock crash played a role in changing the bank structure. Without these negative economic events, Bank One and Fleet might still be part of the nation's banking elite.

Recession-driven problems that force a sale of a second-tier domestic bank, even if only because of investor pressure, will dictate that the buyer be one of the largest banks because of the size of the seller. This is how five dominant, domestic banking leaders can be reduced to just four and a diminishing handful of second-tier banks will increase the share of bank assets held by the largest banks.

Investor Activism

Investor activism also can cause a further restructuring of the banking leadership domestically and/or globally. In 2007, ABN AMRO, the largest Dutch bank, responded to the pressure of a hedge fund investor by agreeing to sell to an even larger British bank, Barclays, in conjunction with spinning off the American operation to Bank of America. This was followed by a hostile bid from a consortium led by Royal Bank of Scotland to acquire and split ABN AMRO between three European banks. No matter what the outcome, the European banking structure will not look quite the same in 2008. There also have been investor calls for Citigroup to break into its key components to maximize shareholder value.

Banks the size of Bank of America, Citigroup, HSBC and JPMorgan may be too big to be forced into a sale, particularly since the buyer has to be a bank and acceptable to numerous regulators, but ABM AMRO has shown that the next level down is vulnerable to investor activism if performance is not up to par. They are small enough to be bought in their entirety by larger banks, divided among a consortium of banks or enter into equal mergers with similar size banks without necessarily setting off bells of alarm among regulators. In United States, this could apply to Wells Fargo and Wachovia as well as smaller regional banks.

Looking Forward

So what will the structure of banking look like ten or twenty years from now? Looking at the past is always easier than projecting the future, but the expansion of remote access banking will accelerate the pace of change within the framework of natural evolution. There will be fewer bank branches, and a lot fewer that have a positive impact on a bank's earnings. There will be much greater use of remote means to access accounts and transfer funds. Much the same could have been said looking back ten years from 2007, but the game has changed, and those most capable of using remote access banking to the fullest are no longer busy trying to acquire to survive.

As mentioned earlier, it is also likely in the not-too-distant future that instead of talking about five banks having close to 50% of all domestic banking assets, the share will be 60%—throw in a couple of large foreign banks, and it could be 70% or even 75%. Ten years from now bank assets, though, should be at least $20 trillion, and 25% to 30% of that is $5 trillion to $6 trillion for everyone else assuming a modest 8% growth rate. Thus, even as bank consolidation and concentration marches on, what is left for others will be revenues that on their own constitute one of the nation's largest businesses.

What is not so certain is who that 25% to 30% will be and how much of it will be traditional banking. There will be domestic regional banks and foreign-based global giants in the mix, but the gap between the largest banks and others will be much greater than it is today. Mid-sized banks, the $3 billion to $50 billion banks in today's dollars, are likely to be far-and-few between as they already are, or almost are, in most states.

Despite this expanding position of the largest banks, there may be as many as 4,000 banks and 1,000 thrifts ten years from now. Many of these will be in outlying areas that do not justify a large bank presence as remote access will not take away totally the need for a physical presence. There also will be local urban banks that specialize in commercial lending—real estate and other—that does not interest the large banks—albeit remote access lines of credit will reduce the scope of even this market from what it is today. Small banks may have less than 8% of all bank assets in another decade. Even today, banks with assets of less than $1 billion have only 12% of bank assets—down from about 30% in 1990. Raising the bar to $3 billion assets only lifts the share to 17%.

Who will have the other 10% to 15%? It will be a conglomeration of insurance companies, investment banks, foreign banks and others using bank charters to hold funds. This will be almost exclusively remote access banking, if it is considered banking at all.

The end result will be further consolidation and a further reduction in the number of local banks, but it will be far less of a change than what has occurred since 1990. It will *not* be the five largest banks tripling their share of bank assets or 7,000 banks disappearing. What it will be is a continuation of the natural evolution of domestic banking as a vibrant financial services industry that continues to be America's biggest business, but with a more convenient and cost-efficient delivery of its services. Not insignificantly, banking will still be a vital activity in which the United States continues to be a dominant global force.

Acknowledgments

Much of this book is based on my personal recollections from the last 35 years refreshed by articles and reports I had written, the rereading of which was often painful, but occasionally gratifying. Over time, though, memory blurs, and often what seemed to be the case then no longer seems quite the same now. Sometimes the recollections were just wrong.

Fortunately, the books and articles listed in the bibliography filled many of the gaps and improved my recollections. Of particular assistance were two books of the FDIC available on the Internet—*History of the Eighties— Lessons for the Future* and *Managing the Crisis: The FDIC and RTC Experience*. They provided much needed details on what happened in the 1980s when the consolidation process was in its early stages and my memory was being sorely stretched. *The International Directory of Company Histories* also was invaluable in providing historical background on the banks that led the way in the consolidation process.

I also had the good fortune of having access to the SNL Financial data through Danielson Capital. This Charlottesville firm has been providing the firm with bank and thrift call report data and merger information for about 15 years. With a data base that goes back to 1990, it allowed me to write most of the latter part of the book on a combination of personal experience and its numbers and dates.

For older statistical information, there were standard data sources such as the *Federal Reserve Bulletins*, FDIC's *Historical Statistics on Banking, American Banker, Polk's Bank Directory* and *Moody's Financial Directory*. I had kept copies of the annual *Polk's Bank Directory* since 1971, *Federal Reserve Bulletins* since 1978 and tables from the *American Banker* from 1978 through the early 1990s. The FDIC data, like so much other good information, is readily available on the internet.

This book also could not have been written without the tireless editing and data gathering of others, most which was a company and family effort. My son, Dave Danielson and Jon Holtaway, who together now run Danielson Capital, provided proofing, and more importantly, critical analysis. John Putman, who understands the SNL data base so much better than I, did much of the statistical data gathering, and Carol Shin and Laura

Kozinski, also Danielson Capital employees, did the final internal page-by-page proofing. My daughter, Diane Danielson, who is publishing her second book, edited each of the chapters as they were written.

An important link between my writing and getting this book to press was Progressive Publishing Alternatives, an Emigsville, Pennsylvania firm. Heather Meledin, in particular was extremely helpful in getting the book ready for printing and taking charge of a final proofing and the compilation of a complicated index.

Last, but certainly not least, was my wife, Vivian. She read through the document more than once to correct the grammar and improve the flow. Most important, though, was her subtle, sometimes not so subtle, pressure to finish the book and get it printed. The book was a labor of love on my part, and once I had finished a first draft, I lost some of the urgency to have this book see the light of day. That was not acceptable to her.

Largest Banks or Bank Holding Companies, 1930 to 2006

			Assets (In millions)
	1930		
1.	Chase National Bank	New York	$2,697
2.	Guaranty Trust	New York	2,022
3.	National City Bank	New York	1,947
4.	Continental Illinois	Chicago	1,249
5.	Bank of America	San Francisco	1,162
6.	Irving Trust	New York	881
7.	Bankers Trust	New York	849
8.	Central Hanover	New York	835
9.	First National Bank	Boston	751
10.	Security First	Los Angeles	611
11.	First National Bank	New York	564
12.	Bank of Manhattan	New York	552
13.	First National Bank	Chicago	496
14.	Bank of America	New York	437
15.	Peoples Wayne County	Detroit	422
	1940		
1.	Chase National Bank	New York	$3,824
2.	National City Bank	New York	3,095
3.	Guaranty Trust	New York	2,718
4.	Bank of America	San Francisco	1,817
5.	Continental Illinois	Chicago	1,620
6.	Bankers Trust	New York	1,580
7.	Central Hanover	New York	1,368
8.	First National Bank	Chicago	1,238
9.	Manufacturers Trust	New York	1,050
10.	Chemical	New York	958
11.	First National Bank	Boston	940
12.	First National Bank	New York	935
13.	Irving Trust	New York	893
14.	Bank of Manhattan	New York	795
15.	J.P. Morgan	New York	773

(continued)

311

Largest Banks or Bank Holding Companies, (*continued*)

			Assets (In millions)
1950			
1.	Bank of America	San Francisco	$6,863
2.	National City Bank	New York	5,526
3.	Chase National Bank	New York	5,283
4.	Guaranty Trust	New York	2,940
5.	Manufacturers Trust	New York	2,773
6.	First National Bank	Chicago	2,598
7.	Continental Illinois	Chicago	2,591
8.	Bankers Trust	New York	1,837
9.	Security First	Los Angeles	1,824
10.	Central Hanover	New York	1,770
11.	Mellon	Pittsburgh	1,717
12.	Chemical	New York	1,714
13.	First National Bank	Boston	1,602
14.	National Bank of Detroit	Detroit	1,568
15.	Irving Trust	New York	1,360
1960			
1.	Bank of America	San Francisco	$11,942
2.	Chase Manhattan	New York	9,260
3.	First National City	New York	8,668
4.	Western Bancorporation	Los Angeles	5,112
5.	Chemical	New York	4,540
6.	Morgan Guaranty	New York	4,424
7.	Manufacturers Trust	New York	3,974
8.	Security First	Los Angeles	3,594
9.	Bankers Trust	New York	3,430
10.	First National Bank	Chicago	3,136
11.	Continental Illinois	Chicago	2,886
12.	Wells Fargo	San Francisco	2,700
13.	Mellon	Pittsburgh	2,226
14.	Hanover Bank	New York	2,192
15.	Irving Trust	New York	2,104

		Assets (In millions)	Banking Offices
	1970		
1.	Bank of America	San Francisco	$29,366	955
2.	Chase Manhattan	New York	24,474	150
3.	First National City	New York	25,219	182
4.	Manufacturers Hanover	New York	12,665	102
5.	Western Bancorporation	Los Angeles	11,409	654
6.	Morgan Guaranty	New York	11,153	5
7.	Chemical	New York	10,979	145
8.	Bankers Trust	New York	9,930	155
9.	Continental	Chicago	8,812	1
10.	Security Pacific	Los Angeles	8,038	398
11.	First National Bank	Chicago	8,028	1
12.	Marine Midland	Buffalo	7,638	261
13.	Charter	New York	6,309	82
14.	Wells Fargo	San Francisco	6,209	–
15.	Crocker-Citizens	San Francisco	5,917	280
	1980		
1.	Citicorp	New York	$114,920	426
2.	BankAmerica	San Francisco	111,617	1,207
3.	Chase Manhattan	New York	76,190	214
4.	Manufacturers Hanover	New York	55,552	NA
5.	J.P. Morgan	New York	51,991	21
6.	Continental Illinois	Chicago	42,089	–
7.	Chemical	New York	41,342	285
8.	Bankers Trust	New York	34,202	117
9.	First Interstate	Los Angeles	32,110	901
10.	First Chicago	Chicago	28,699	–
11.	Security Pacific	Los Angeles	27,794	607
12.	Wells Fargo	San Francisco	23,638	403
13.	Crocker National	San Francisco	19,074	382
14.	Irving Bank	New York	18,089	121
15.	Marine Midland	Buffalo	17,480	295

(continued)

313

Largest Banks or Bank Holding Companies, (*continued*)

		Assets (In millions)	Banking Offices
1990			
1. Citicorp	New York	$216,996	–
2. BankAmerica	San Francisco	110,728	1,200
3. Chase Manhattan	New York	98,064	342
4. J.P. Morgan	New York	93,103	20
5. Security Pacific	Los Angeles	84,731	550
6. Chemical	New York	73,019	425
7. NCNB	Charlotte	65,295	923
8. Bankers Trust	New York	63,596	4
9. Manufacturers Hanover	New York	61,530	221
10. Wells Fargo	San Francisco	56,199	547
11. First Interstate	Los Angeles	51,356	1,041
12. C&S/Sovran	Norfolk	51,237	1,012
13. First Chicago	Chicago	50,799	55
14. PNC	Pittsburgh	45,333	535
15. Bank of New York	New York	45,496	258
2000			
1. Citigroup	New York	$902,210	199
2. J.P. Morgan	New York	715,348	572
3. Bank of America	Charlotte	642,664	4,390
4. Wells Fargo	San Francisco	272,426	2,982
5. Bank One	Chicago	269,300	1,810
6. First Union	Charlotte	254,272	2,193
7. Fleet	Boston	179,519	1,220
8. SunTrust	Atlanta	103,660	1,174
9. National City	Cleveland	88,619	1,132
10. U.S. Bancorp	Minneapolis	87,336	1,179
11. Key Corp	Cleveland	87,270	940
12. Firstar	Milwaukee	77,585	1,166
13. Bank of New York	New York	77,114	359
14. Wachovia	Winston-Salem	74,032	668
15. PNC	Pittsburgh	69,921	717

			Assets (In millions)	Banking Offices
		2006		
1.	Citigroup	New York	$1,994,318	997
2.	Bank of America	Charlotte	1,459,737	5,752
3.	JPMorgan	New York	1,351,520	3,143
4.	Wachovia	Charlotte	707,121	3,445
5.	Wells Fargo	San Francisco	481,996	3,249
6.	U.S. Bancorp	Minneapolis	219,232	2,573
7.	SunTrust	Atlanta	182,162	1,789
8.	Capital One	Falls Church, Va.	149,739	705
9.	Regions	Birmingham	143,369	2,052
10.	National City	Cleveland	140,191	1,433
11.	BB&T	Winston-Salem	121,351	1,476
12.	State Street	Boston	107,353	1
13.	Bank of New York	New York	103,370	16
14.	PNC	Pittsburgh	101,820	1,115
15.	Fifth Third	Cincinnati	100,669	1,185

Source:1931 Moody's Financial Directory, New York; 1951, 1961 and 1971 Polk's Bank Directory; American Banker, April 20, 1982; and February 8, 1992; and SNL Financial, Charlottesville, Virginia.

List of Tables

Bibliography

Books

Adams, James Ring. *The Big Fix: Inside the S&L Scandal.* John Wiley & Sons, Inc., New York, 1990.

Brewster, Mike, and Stone, Amey. *King of Capital: Sandy Weill and the Making of Citigroup.* John Wiley & Sons, Inc., New York, 2002.

Chernow, Ron. *The House of Morgan: An American Banking Dynasty and the Rise of Modern Finance.* Atlantic Monthly Press, New York, 1990.

Covington, Howard E. Jr., and Ellis, Marion A. *The Story of NationsBank.* The University of North Carolina Press, Chapel Hill, North Carolina, 1993.

Golembe, Carter H., and Holland, David S. *Federal Regulation of Banking.* Golembe Associates, Inc., Washington, D.C., 1981 and 1983–84.

Hector, Gary. *Breaking the Bank: The Decline of BankAmerica.* Little, Brown and Company, New York, 1988.

Mayer, Martin. *The Greatest-Ever Bank Robbery: The Collapse of the Savings and Loan Industry.* Charles Scribner's & Sons, New York, 1990.

McCollom, James P. *The Continental Affair: The Rise and Fall of Continental Illinois Bank.* Dodd, Mead & Company, New York, 1987.

McFadyen, James, and Voesar, Detta. *Federal Deposit Insurance Corporation: The First Fifty Years.* Federal Deposit Insurance Corporation, Washington, D.C., 1984.

Sprague, Irvine H. *Bailout: An Insider's Account of Bank Failures and Rescues.* Beard Books, Washington, D.C., 1986.

Yockey, Ross. *McColl: The Man with America's Money.* Longstreet, Inc., Atlanta, 1999.

Zweig, Phillip L. *Wriston: Walter Wriston, Citibank and the Rise and Fall of American Financial Supremacy.* Crown Publishers, Inc., New York, 1995.

General Resource Data

History of the Eighties—Lessons for the Future. FDIC, Washington, D.C., 1997.

International Directory of Company Histories. St. James Press, Chicago and London.

Managing the Crisis: The FDIC and RTC Experience. FDIC, Washington, D.C., 2003.

Moody's Financial Directory. Moody's Corporation, New York.

Polk's Bank Directory. R. L. Polk, Nashville, Tennessee.

Articles

Amel, Dean F. *Trends in Banking Structure since the Mid-1970s. Federal Reserve Bulletin.* March 1989. Washington, D.C.

Golembe, Carter H. *Forces Affecting Bank Expansion in the 1980s. Bank Expansion Quarterly.* Fourth Quarter 1979. Golembe Associates. Washington, D.C.

Mahoney, Patrick I., and White, Alice P. *The Thrift Industry in Transition.* Federal Reserve Bulletin. March 1985. Washington, D.C.

Savage, Donald T. *Developments in Banking Structure, 1970–81.* Federal Reserve Bulletin. February 1982. Washington, D.C.

Notes and Sources

Chapter One—What Happened?

1. *American Banker,* July 10, 1991.
2. FDIC, Historical Statistics on Banking.
3. Background on Citigroup comes from *Wriston*, Phillip L. Zweig, Crown Publishers Inc., New York. *The House of Morgan,* Ron Chernow, Atlantic Monthly Press, New York, 1990, and the *International Directory of Company Histories,* St. James Press, Chicago and London, Volume 59, pp. 121–127.
4. Economist.com, October 29, 2004.
5. Background on Sandy Weill and the Citicorp-Travelers merger comes from *King of Capital*, Amey Stone and Mike Brewster, John Wiley & Sons, Inc., New York, 1990.
6. Economist.com, October 29, 2004.
7. Background on NCNB and NationsBank comes from *McColl*, Ross Yockey, Longstreet, Inc., Atlanta, 1999 and *The Story of NationsBank*, Howard E. Covington, Jr. and Marion A. Ellis, The University of North Carolina Press, Chapel Hill, North Carolina, 1993.
8. Background on JP Morgan comes from *International Directory of Company Histories*, St. James Press, Chicago and London, Volume 14, pp. 101–104.
9. Background on Wells Fargo comes from *International Directory of Company Histories*, St. James Press, Chicago and London, Volume 38, pp. 483–491.
10. Background on Wachovia comes from *International Directory of Company Histories*, St. James Press, Chicago and London, Volume 10, pp. 298–307.
11. *USBANKER*, "What Makes Fast Eddy Run?" September 1996, pp. 44 and 48.
12. *Business Week Online*, March 28, 1998.
13. Background on U.S. Bancorp comes from *International Directory of Company Histories*, St. James Press, Chicago and London, Volume 12, pp. 164–166.

Chapter Two—The Early Years

1. *From Revolution to Reconstruction*, "A Brief History of Central Banking in the United States," Edward Flaherty. March 6, 2003.
2. *All Bank Statistics 1896 to 1955*. "United States Summary," Federal Reserve Board, May 11, 2007, p. 59.

3. Ibid., p. 59.
4. "Depression-era Bank Failures: The Great Contagion or the Great Shakeout?" John R. Walter, *Federal Reserve Bank of Richmond Quarterly*, Winter 2005, p. 45.
5. Background on the original Bank of America comes from *Breaking the Bank*, Gary Hector, Little Brown and Company, New York, 1988.
6. FDIC, Historical Statistics on Banking.
7. Listing of largest banks at the end of a decade can be found in the tables at the end of the book.

Chapter Three—Uncharted Waters

1. "Forces Affecting Bank Expansion in the 1980s," Carter H. Golembe, report drawn from a paper delivered at a conference at the Virginia Commonwealth University, Richmond, Virginia, March 10, 1980.
2. Data on interest rates, stock market indexes and prime rates come from various editions of the *Federal Reserve Bulletins*.
3. *Federal Regulation of Banking—1981*, Carter H. Golembe and David S. Holland, Golembe Associates, Inc., Washington, D.C., p. 114.
4. *Wriston*, Phillip L. Zweig, Crown Publishers, Inc., New York, p. 256.
5. Ibid., p. 362.
6. *Managing the Crisis: The FDIC and RTC Experience*, "First Pennsylvania Bank, N.A.," FDIC, Washington, D.C., 2003, p. 518.

Chapter Four—Consolidation on Hold

1. Background on Bank of Commonwealth comes from *Bailout*, Irvine H. Sprague, Beard Books, Washington, D.C., 1986.
2. Ibid., p. 75.
3. *Long Island Business News*, "1974: Franklin National Bank goes under," Natalie Canavor, August 27–September 2, 2004.
4. *Federal Reserve Bulletin*, November, 1982, p. A.14.
5. The Nilson Report, Carpinteria, California, January, 1982.

Chapter Six—Thrift Crisis: Early Stages

1. *'81 Savings and Loan Sourcebook*, United Sates League of Savings Associations, Chicago, p. 38 and FDIC, Historical Statistics on Banking.

2. *History of the Eighties—Lessons for the Future*, "The Savings and Loan Crisis and Its Relationship to Banking." FDIC, Washington, D.C., 1997, p. 168.

3. *Business, Government and Society*, 8th Edition, 1997. "The Savings and Loan Debacle." (internet)

4. *History of the Eighties—Lessons for the Future*, "The Savings and Loan Crisis and Its Relationship to Banking," FDIC, Washington, D.C., p. 169.

5. FDIC, Historical Statistics on Banking.

6. *History of the Eighties—Lessons for the Future*, "The Savings and Loan Crisis and Its Relationship to Banking," FDIC, Washington, D.C., p. 168.

7. *History of the Eighties—Lessons for the Future*, "The Mutual Savings Bank Crisis," FDIC, Washington, D.C., p. 226.

8. Ibid., p. 226.

9. *Monthly Market Report*, SNL Financial, Charlottesville, Virginia, January 1991, p. 5.

10. Sheshunoff Information Services, Inc., Austin, Texas.

11. *History of the Eighties—Lessons for the Future*, "The Savings and Loan Crisis and Its Relationship to Banking," FDIC, Washington, D.C., p. 168.

12. Ibid., p. 181.

Chapter Seven—Trouble in the Oil Patch

1. *History of the Eighties—Lessons for the Future*, "Banking Problems in the Southwest," FDIC, Washington, D.C., 1997, p. 291.

2. Ibid., p. 292.

3. Ibid., p. 291.

4. Ibid., p. 291.

5. *The Handbook of Texas Online*, Texas State Historical Society, October 10, 2004.

6. *Managing the Crisis: The FDIC and RTC Experience*, "Penn Square Bank, N.A.," Washington, D.C., 2003, p. 528.

7. *Managing the Crisis: The FDIC and RTC Experience*, "Continental Illinois National Bank and Trust Company," FDIC, Washington, D.C., 2003, p. 546

8. *Bailout*, Irvine H. Sprague, Beard Books, Washington, D.C., 1986, p. 113.

9. *Managing the Crisis: The FDIC and RTC Experience*, "Continental Illinois National Bank and Trust Company," FDIC, Washington, D.C., 2003, p. 560.
10. *History of the Eighties—Lessons for the Future*, "Continental Illinois and 'Too Big to Fail'", FDIC, Washington, D.C., 1997, p. 237.
11. Ibid., p. 240.
12. Ibid., p. 242.
13. *Managing the Crisis: The FDIC and RTC Experience*, "Continental Illinois National Bank and Trust Company," FDIC, Washington, D.C., 2003, p. 560.
14. *History of the Eighties—Lessons for the Future*, "Banking Problems in the Southwest," FDIC, Washington, D.C., 1997, p. 299.
15. Ibid., p. 303.
16. Ibid., p. 323.
17. *Managing the Crisis: The FDIC and RTC Experience*, "First City Bancorporation of Texas, Inc.," FDIC, Washington, D.C., 2003, pp. 569–70.
18. Ibid., p. 570.
19. Ibid., p. 572.
20. Ibid., pp. 573 and 577–78.
21. Ibid., pp. 578–79.
22. Ibid., p. 582.
23. *Managing the Crisis: The FDIC and RTC Experience*, "First RepublicBank Corporation," FDIC, Washington D.C., 2003, p. 595.
24. Ibid., p. 600.
25. *The Story of Nationsbank*, Howard E. Covington, Jr., and Marion A. Ellis, The University of North Carolina Press, Chapel Hill, North Carolina, p. 214
26. *Managing the Crisis: The FDIC and RTC Experience*, "First RepublicBank Corporation," FDIC. Washington, D.C., 2003, p. 601.
27. *Managing the Crisis: The FDIC and RTC Experience*, "MCorp," FDIC, Washington, D.C., 2003, p. 619.
28. Ibid., p. 623.
29. Ibid., p. 628.

Chapter Eight—Interstate Banking Gathers Momentum

1. *McColl*, Ross Yockey, Longstreet, Inc., Atlanta, 1999, p. 171.
2. *The Story of NationsBank*, Howard E. Covington, Jr., and Marion A. Ellis, The University of North Carolina Press, Chapel Hill, North Carolina, p. 157.

3. Ibid., p. 173.
4. *McColl*, Ross Yockey, Longstreet, Inc., Atlanta, 1999, p. 247.
5. *History of the Eighties–Lessons for the Future*, "LDC Debt Crisis," FDIC, Washington, D.C., 1997, p. 191.

Chapter Nine—Thrift Crisis: Changing the Landscape

1. *Cincinnati Enquirer*, January 8, 2000 (internet).
2. *Ibid.*
3. *Big Fix: Inside the S&L Scandal*, James Ring Adams, John Wiley & Sons, New York, 1990, p. 176.
4. *Cincinnati Enquirer*, January 8, 2000 (internet).
5. *Big Fix: Inside the S&L Scandal*, James Ring Adams, John Wiley & Sons, New York, 1990, p. 176 and internet story.
6. *Ibid.*
7. *History of the Eighties—Lessons for the Future*, "The Savings and Loan Crisis and Its Relationship to Banking," FDIC, Washington, D.C., p. 183.
8. *The Greatest-Ever Bank Robbery*, Martin Mayer, Charles Scribner's and Sons, New York, 1990, p. 14.
9. *New York Magazine*, 1989 (internet).
10. *The Greatest-Ever Bank Robbery*, Martin Mayer, Charles Scribner's and Sons, New York, 1990, p. 14.
11. Ibid., p. 256.
12. *S&L Bailout Costs*, Franklin Mancuso, updated 1999 (internet.)
13. SNL Financial, Charlottesville, Virginia.
14. *History of the Eighties—Lessons for the Future*, "The Savings and Loan Crisis and Its Relationship to Banking," FDIC, Washington D.C., p. 187.

Chapter Eleven—New England "Miracle" Ends

1. *History of the Eighties—Lessons for the Future*, "Banking Problems in the Northeast," FDIC, Washington, D.C., p. 337.
2. *New England Banking Report*, Danielson Associates Inc., February 19, 1993, p. 2.
3. *New England Banking Report*, Danielson Associates Inc., November 15, 1990, p. 1.
4. *Wriston*, Phillip L. Zweig, Crown Publishers, Inc., New York, p. 868.
5. *Managing the Crisis: The FDIC and RTC Experience*, "Bank of New England Corporation," FDIC, Washington, D.C., p. 641 and 648.

6. *Managing the Crisis: The FDIC and RTC Experience,*" Seven Banks in New Hampshire," FDIC, Washington, D.C., 2003, pp. 672, 674 and 679.

Chapter Twelve—Charlotte's Web

1. *McColl*, Ross Yockey, Longstreet, Inc., Atlanta, 1999, p. 429.
2. *The Story of NationsBank*, Howard E. Covington, Jr., and Marion A. Ellis, The University of North Carolina Press, Chapel Hill, North Carolina, p. 281.
3. Ibid., p. 293.
4. Ibid., p. 295.
5. Ibid., p. 296.
6. Ibid., p. 306.
7. *Managing the Crisis: The FDIC and RTC Experience*, "Southeast Banking Corp.," FDIC, Washington, D.C., 2003, p. 657.
8. *The BCCI Affair* a Report to the Committee on Foreign Relation United States Senate by Senator John Kerry and Senator Hank Brown, December 1992, Executive Summary.
9. Ibid., Executive Summary.

Chapter Thirteen—California Dreaming

1. *Far West Banking Report*, Danielson Associates Inc., April 2, 1988, pp. 1, 3 and 4.
2. *Sheshunoff S&L Quarterly: December 1988 Ratings*, pp. 19 and 39.
3. *History of the Eighties—Lessons for the Future*, "Banking Problems in California," FDIC, Washington, D.C., 1997, pp. 382–84.
4. Ibid., p. 387–89.
5. Ibid., pp. 391 and 394.
6. Ibid., p. 394.
7. Background on Security Pacific comes from *International Directory of Company Histories*, St. James Press, Chicago and London, Volume II, pp. 349–350.
8. *Business Week Online*, August 19, 1991.
9. Ibid.
10. *History of the Eighties—Lessons for the Future*, "Banking Problems in California," FDIC, Washington, D.C., 1997, pp. 409–410.

Chapter Fourteen—New York Banking at a Crossroads

1. Background on Manufactures Hanover comes from *International Directory of Company Histories*, St. James Press, Chicago and London, Volume 11, pp. 312–314.
2. Background on Chase Manhattan comes from *International Directory of Company Histories*, St. James Press, Chicago and London, Volume 13, pp. 145–148.
3. Economist.com, October 29, 2004.
4. *Business Week Online*, "Mighty Morgan," December 23, 1991.
5. *International Directory of Company Histories*, St. James Press, Chicago and London, Volume 46, pp 59–63.

Chapter Fifteen—Midwest's Changing of the Guard

1. *International Directory of Company Histories*, St. James Press, Chicago and London.

Chapter Sixteen—Every Other Monday

1. *Business Week Online*, "Is 'Nice, Big Dull' Good Enough?" May 12, 1997.
2. *Business Week Online*, "First Interstate: Up for Grabs." September 18, 1995.
3. *Business Week Online*, "First Interstate Snubs Wells Again," December 4, 1995.
4. *Business Week Online*, "Why Wells Fargo is Circling the Wagons," June 9, 1997.

Chapter Seventeen—1998: The Superbanks Cometh

1. *Bank Investor*, SNL Financial, January 1996, 1997 and 1998.

Chapter Eighteen—Beyond Traditional Banking

1. TIME.com, "Bankers Trust Acquires Alex Brown," April 7, 1997.
2. *King of Capital—Sandy Weill*, Amey Stone and Mike Brewster, John Wiley & Sons, Inc., New York, 2002, pp. 44–119.
3. *Business Week*, "The Best Performers," March 24, 1997 and March 30, 1998.

4. *King of Capital—Sandy Weill*, Amey Stone and Mike Brewster, John Wiley & Sons, Inc., New York, 2002, pp. 224 and 225.
5. *Business Week*, "The Coca Cola of Personal Finance," April 20, 1998.
6. Ibid.
7. *International Herald Tribune*, June 5, 2007, p. 19.
8. *Barron's*, September 15, 2004, p. 24.
9. *American Banker*, October 16, 1991.
10. *National Mortgage News*, Annual data report for 2006.
11. Ibid.
12. Ibid.
13. Ibid.
14. Ibid.
15. *Business Insurance*, July 17, 2006 with Wells Fargo and BB&T numbers updated for 2006.
16. *Financial Services Fact Book*, Financial Services Roundtable, Washington, D.C., 2006, p. 49.

Chapter Nineteen—And Then There Were Five

1. CNNMoney, June 26, 2000 (internet).
2. Citigroup 2004 Annual Report, p. 31.

Chapter Twenty—Beyond the Big Five

1. FDIC, Historical Statistics on Banking.
2. Ibid.

Index